D1084511

The Handbook of Infant, Child, and Adolescent Psychotherapy

THE HANDBOOK OF INFANT, CHILD, AND ADOLESCENT PSYCHOTHERAPY

A Series of Books Edited By

Bonnie S. Mark, Ph.D.
and
James A. Incorvaia, Ph.D.

A Guide to Diagnosis and Treatment
Volume 1

New Directions in Integrative Treatment
Volume 2

The Handbook of Infant, Child, and Adolescent Psychotherapy

NEW DIRECTIONS IN INTEGRATIVE TREATMENT
REISS-DAVIS CHILD STUDY CENTER
VOLUME 2

edited by
Bonnie S. Mark, Ph.D.
and
James A. Incorvaia, Ph.D.

JASON ARONSON INC.
Northvale, New Jersey
London

The editors gratefully acknowledge permission to reprint excerpts from the following:

Studies on Hysteria, by Josef Breuer and Sigmund Freud. Published in the U.S. by Basic Books, Inc. by arrangement with The Hogarth Press, Ltd. Reprinted by permission of Basic Books, a division of HarperCollins Publishers, Inc., and The Hogarth Press, Ltd.

"Iphigenia in Aulis," by Euripides, in *Complete Greek Tragedies*, vol. 4, edited by D. Green and R. Lattimore. Copyright © 1958 by the University of Chicago Press.

Production Editor: Elaine Lindenblatt

This book was set in 10 pt. Garamond Book by Alpha Graphics of Pittsfield, NH, and printed and bound by Book-mart Press of North Bergen, NJ.

10 9 8 7 6 5 4 3 2 1

Library of Congress Cataloging-in-Publication Data

The handbook of infant, child, and adolescent psychotherapy / edited by Bonnie S. Mark and James Incorvaia.
p. cm.
Includes bibliographical references and index.
Partial Contents: v. 2. New directions in integrative treatment.
ISBN 0-7657-0044-1 (v. 2)
1. Child psychotherapy. 2. Infant psychotherapy. 3. Adolescent psychotherapy. I. Mark, Bonnie S. II. Incorvaia, James.
[DNLM: 1. Mental Disorders—in infancy & childhood. 2. Mental Disorders—in adolescence. 3. Disabled—psychology. 4. Psychotherapy—in infancy & childhood. 5. Psychotherapy—in adolescence. WS 350.2 H2356 1995]
RJ504.H3614 1995 1997
618.92'8914—dc20
DNLM/DLC
for Library of Congress 94-44248

Printed in the United States of America on acid-free paper. For information and catalog write to Jason Aronson Inc., 230 Livingston Street, Northvale, New Jersey 07647-1726. Or visit our website: http://www.aronson.com

Contents

Preface

This series of *The Handbook of Infant, Child, and Adolescent Psychotherapy* reflects the Reiss-Davis Child Study Center's commitment to offer mental health education to professionals across the country who are interested in working diagnostically and psychotherapeutically with children, adolescents, and their families. Volume II of the handbook, *New Directions in Integrative Treatment*, continues to offer professional writings of child, adolescent, and family specialists in the areas of psychiatry, psychology, clinical social work, education, and child development. The contributions in this second volume continue to span the globe as they include authors from Europe as well as across the United States. This book also spans the theoretical gamut of psychodynamic thinking from classical, object relations, and self psychology, to a more recent approach called integration psychotherapy. This latter approach, while using a psychodynamic underpinning, includes techniques from other schools such as cognitive behavioral, developmental, and family systems, as indicated in working with the patient.

As you read through the chapters that constitute this second volume, we hope you will be struck by the breadth and scope of ideas suggested for working with patients. We feel these ideas represent a change in the psychodynamic field from that of rigidly adhering to one school of thought while excluding all of the others, to a much more open acceptance of many schools, their approaches, and techniques, all in order to offer what is best for the treatment of the child or adolescent patient.

At a time when managed care is very much a model that practicing therapists across the country must deal with, there is a need for more flexible models of psychotherapy for children offered within a psychodynamic framework. Volume II of this handbook presents some of these models.

This very exciting second volume has been divided into four parts. Part I presents chapters from T. Berry Brazelton, Joseph Palombo and Anne Hatcher Berenberg, James A. Incorvaia, Esther and Sidney Fine, Carol A. Francis, and Robert J. Neborsky, each dealing with various aspects of innovative therapeutic work with young children. Part II includes chapters from Carol Gilligan, Bonnie S. Mark and Robert Anderson, Deborah Berger-Reiss, and Daniel J. Siegel, suggesting new ways to approach abuse, trauma, and neglect in working with children and adolescents. Part III offers chapters from Irving H. Berkovitz, Rita Lynn, Bonnie S. Mark, Shelley Alhanati, and Nancy VanDerHeide and Ronald A. Alexander, discussing new directions in working with adolescents. Part IV contains chapters from Bertrand Cramer, S. Robert Moradi, Paul and Anna Ornstein, Walter E. Brackelmanns, Irene Pierce Stiver, Barbara Zax and Stephan Poulter, and Carl F. Hoppe, focusing on the latest approaches in working with parents and families.

It is the hope of all of us at the Reiss-Davis Child Study Center that volume II of the handbook will present you with models that will not only be informative illustrations of new methods of working with children, adolescents, and their families, but also be an impetus for you to develop your own integrated psychodynamic methods of working with your young clients.

James A. Incorvaia, Ph.D.
Director
Reiss-Davis Child Study Center

Acknowledgments

This text was completed through the efforts of many wonderful people dedicated to improving the lives of children and their families. We wish to thank all the authors of the articles in Volume 2 for their contributions and willingness, without which the book could not have been compiled.

In addition to the authors, many others were integral to the success of this undertaking. We thank Marion Solomon, for her constant encouragement and wisdom as both a clinician and a writer and for inspiring us to create a collective text; Donald Tessmer, for reading and suggesting revisions; Jonathan Judaken, whose persistent search for clarity and editorial expertise were indispensable; Grayce Stratton, Angela Daley, and Maria Krusoff from Reiss-Davis, for their many hours of secretarial work; and Mary Elizabeth Rafferty, Allison Hoffman, Mayumi Hattori, Lynn Morgan, Velveth Dardon, and Jeff Blume for their assistance in research and revisions. A very special thank you to Ariel Mark, for continuing to be an inspiration to learn more and to understand.

We wish to acknowledge our debt to Lee Freehling, the Reiss-Davis librarian, for her encouragement and ongoing assistance. We thank, as well, Gerald Zaslaw, CEO of Vista del Mar Child and Family Services and its affiliate agencies, the Reiss-Davis Child Study Center, the Julia Ann Singer Center, and Home-SAFE, for his continued support of this project.

Thank you to everyone at Jason Aronson Inc. Publishers, including Michael Moskowitz, Norma Pomerantz, Elaine Lindenblatt, Nancy D'Arrigo, and most especially Jason Aronson, for the unflagging support and encouragement offered throughout the process of completing Volumes I and II of the *Handbook of Infant, Child, and Adolescent Psychotherapy.*

Finally, thank you to our patients, for granting us the rare privilege of intimate knowledge of their deepest thoughts and feelings. We have been inspired by their courage and have grown from their journeys.

Bonnie S. Mark, Ph.D.
James A. Incorvaia, Ph.D.

Contributors

Ronald A. Alexander, Ph.D., is a psychotherapist in family practice in Santa Monica, California, Chair of the Graduate Psychology Department and clinical core faculty member at Ryokan College, and adjunct faculty at UCLA extension.

Shelley Alhanati, Ph.D., is a consultant and supervisor at the Reiss-Davis Child Study Center, and a psychologist in private practice in Beverly Hills, California.

Robert Anderson, Ph.D., is a psychotherapist in private practice in Los Angeles, California.

Anne Hatcher Berenberg, Ph.D., is Director of Psychology at the Josselyn Center for Mental Health, Northfield, Illinois.

Deborah Berger-Reiss, M.A., is a psychotherapist in private practice in Los Angeles, California, and a nationally syndicated advice columnist.

Irving H. Berkovitz, M.D., is a psychotherapist in private practice in Los Angeles, California.

Walter E. Brackelmanns, M.D., is an adult and child psychiatrist and psychoanalyst. He is also an associate clinical professor of psychiatry at UCLA and a mental health consultant to the School Mental Health Center, Los Angeles Unified School District. Dr. Brackelmanns is a senior instructor UCLA extension.

T. Berry Brazelton, M.D., is Professor Emeritus, Pediatrics, at Harvard Medical School.

Bertrand Cramer, M.D., is a Vice President of the World Association for Infant Mental Health and a clinician and researcher in Geneva, Switzerland.

Esther Fine, L.C.S.W., is a child and adult psychotherapist in private practice and a clinical associate at the Los Angeles Psychoanalytic Institute. She is a consultant at the Reiss-Davis Child Study Center.

Sidney Fine, M.D. (died 6/28/95), was a training and supervising analyst at the Los Angeles Psychoanalytic Institute and an assistant clinical professor of psychiatry at the UCLA School of Medicine.

Carol A. Francis, Psy.D., is a clinical psychologist in private practice in Torrance, California.

Carol Gilligan, Ph.D., a professor at Harvard University, is co-artistic director of The Company of Women, a women and girls' theater project.

Carl F. Hoppe, Ph.D., is in private practice in Los Angeles, California. He is a clinical associate at the Los Angeles Institute and Society for Psychoanalytic Studies, a graduated postdoctoral fellow at Reiss-Davis, and consultant to the family court of Los Angeles.

James A. Incorvaia, Ph.D., is Director of the Reiss-Davis Child Study Center and a diagnostician and psychotherapist in private practice in Brentwood, California.

Rita Lynn, Psy.D., is a group analyst and supervisor in private practice in West Los Angeles, California.

Bonnie S. Mark, Ph.D., is an individual and group psychotherapist in private practice in Los Angeles, California, Project Coordinator of the book series for the Reiss-Davis Child Study Center, an instructor at UCLA extension, and a supervisor at the Maple Counselling Center.

S. Robert Moradi, M.D., is an assistant clinical professor of Psychiatry at the UCLA School of Medicine and teaches at the Reiss-Davis Child Study Center and at the Graduate Center for Child Development and Psychotherapy.

Robert J. Neborsky, M.D., is a member of the faculty of UCSD School of Medicine, is Co-founder of the San Diego Institute for Short Term Dynamic Psychotherapy, and is in private practice in Del Mar, California.

Anna Ornstein, M.D., is a training and supervising analyst at the Cincinnati Psychoanalytic Institute, Co-director of the International Center for the Study of Psychoanalytic Self Psychology, and Professor of Child Psychiatry Emeritus, University of Cincinnati College of Medicine, Department of Psychiatry.

Paul Ornstein, M.D., is Co-director of the International Center for the Study of Psychoanalytic Self Psychology, and Professor of Psychiatry and Psychoanalysis Emeritus, University of Cincinnati College of Medicine, Department of Psychiatry.

Joseph Palombo, L.C.S.W., is Founding Dean of the Institute for Clinical Social Work, Chicago Institute of Psychoanalysis and research associate, Department of Pediatrics, Rush-Presbyterian-St. Luke's Medical Center.

Stephan Poulter, Ph.D., is a clinical associate at the Sunset Psychotherapy Group, an instructor at UCLA extension, and in private practice in Los Angeles, California.

Daniel J. Siegel, M.D., is the Medical Director of the infant and preschool services at UCLA. He is a member of the Institute for Developmental and Clinical Neuroscience, and is in private practice in Los Angeles, California.

Irene Pierce Stiver, Ph.D., is a senior consultant in the Women's Treatment Program at McLean Hospital, Belmont, Massachusetts, and a lecturer on psychology, Department of Psychiatry at Harvard Medical School.

Nancy P. VanDerHeide, Psy.D., is a psychotherapist in private practice specializing in couples and families in Brentwood, California. She is an adjunct professor of clinical psychology at Ryokan College, Los Angeles, California.

Barbara Zax, Ph.D., is Clinical Director of the Sunset Psychotherapy Group, an instructor at UCLA extension, a supervisor at the Maple Counselling Center, and in private practice in Los Angeles, California.

PART I

Treatment Issues in Psychotherapy with Children

INTRODUCTION TO PART I

Working diagnostically and therapeutically with children has always been a major part of what we do at the Reiss-Davis Child Study Center. Over the years we have offered a variety of preventive and remedial therapeutic services that include mother–infant work, mother-as-therapist work, individual child work, and group therapy for children. These services have almost always been offered in conjunction with parent/family work (to be discussed in Part IV), so that the child isn't singled out as the "problem" in the family. Working with the child and parent(s) has also allowed the therapy to progress more quickly and hold more effectively once treatment has been completed. Our underlying theoretical orientation has integrated aspects from within a number of psychodynamic schools (e.g., classical, object relations, self psychology) as well as from outside (e.g., cognitive, behavioral, family systems, developmental, etc.). Thus, the Center has maintained its psychodynamic focus while broadening its approaches to treatment. The chapters in this section reflect that broadened scope.

Chapter 1, "Opportunities for Preventing Problems in the Parent-Child Relationship," by T. Berry Brazelton, addresses the issues of failures in childhood development through the fostering of a more positive attitude toward parenting as well as the guiding and supporting of parents, especially during stressful times. His chapter presents a model for forming successful relationships between parents and pediatricians or other professionals by creating a system of appointments that coincide with critical periods from pregnancy through early childhood. In this way the child's needs will be addressed early and allow for more fulfilling emotional and physical growth.

Chapter 2, "Psychotherapy for Children with Nonverbal Learning Disabilities," by Joseph Palombo and Anne Hatcher Berenberg, is a follow-up to Palombo's chapter in volume I of this handbook. It describes how children with nonverbal learning disabilities present a special challenge to therapists who attempt to provide treatment for them, and summarizes some of the characteristic symptomatic behaviors these children present along with explanatory dynamics for these behaviors and treatment approaches found to be effective with these children and their families.

Chapter 3, "Psychoeducational Psychotherapy," by James A. Incorvaia, provides an integrated psychological and educational services model that is primarily but not exclusively focused on helping reach the learning disabled and/or attention deficit disordered child who might not otherwise benefit from a more traditional psychotherapeutic intervention. Incorvaia explores the history of the concept and term *psychoeducational* and shows how this concept can be developed into a method that gives therapists the opportunity to offer younger learning disabled and attention deficit disordered patients with and without hyperactivity a more integrated and interactive approach to helping the whole child.

Chapter 4, "Three Theoretical Views of the Treatment of a Six-Year-Old," by Esther Fine and Sidney Fine, examines from three theoretical perspectives—classical, Kleinian, and self psychology—the treatment of a six-year-old boy who was labeled as a contrary and troublemaking child at home and school. The chapter illustrates the way in which each school of thought might understand and approach the boy's defenses, resistances, transferences, vulnerabilities, primitive impulses, and aggressive drives, and suggests that perhaps the differences in perspectives and their therapeutic effects are not merely illusory.

Chapter 5, "Tools of Play Therapy," by Carol A. Francis, illustrates that progress during play therapy does not happen by luck or good will as she demonstrates comprehensively how specific tools, acquired and cultivated by the therapist, facilitate a child's journey. The chapter focuses on understanding what a child is expressing by examining classifications that can guide the therapist as he/she explores the content and process manifested in a child's play. Armed with an understanding of what the child is trying to communicate, the chapter then offers various verbal and nonverbal forms of communication to help the therapist communicate with the child.

Chapter 6, "Sibling Rivalry: The Role of the Sibling in the Unconscious," by Robert J. Neborsky, presents a view of how preoedipal experiences and especially early childhood trauma can result in aggravated sibling rivalry and a lifelong history of self-sabotage. The chapter points out that sibling-induced trauma is an ordinary and common problem that does not necessarily lead to a neurosis, and notes that sibling relationships are potential hotbeds for neurotic conflict, especially when the child experiences preoedipal trauma in the mother–child dyad or when he/she participates in a triangle of rivalry.

1

Opportunities for Preventing Problems in the Parent-Child Relationship*

T. Berry Brazelton

The opportunity for pediatricians to play a role in the prevention of failures in child development is a vital one. The importance of their role in optimizing each stage of a child's developmental progress—motor, cognitive, and emotional—could be equal to the pediatrician's role in prevention of disease and physical disorders (Brazelton 1983). Support and guidance for families could play a critical role in mitigating the stresses within the family. We have found that when we emphasize the individuality of the infant, it enhances the capacity of

---

*Adapted from Brazelton, T. B. (1994). Touchpoints: Opportunities for Preventing Problems in the Parent-Child Relationship. *Acta Paediatrica Scandinavica Supplement* 394:35-39. Copyright © 1994 by The Scandinavian University Press, and used by permission.

the family to offer him[1] an optimally nurturing environment (Brazelton 1975). This becomes critical if one accepts that the optimal development of a child is dependent on the interaction between genetic endowment and environmental influences that are appropriate to his temperament. Work with high-risk infants has demonstrated that a vulnerable nervous system can easily be overloaded with stimuli that would be appropriate for an intact, mature central nervous system (Als et al. 1976). The cycle of learning to fail rather than learning to succeed is set in motion from which the nervous system must withdraw to protect itself. For an immature nervous system thrives on the stimulation it is offered, provided the baby is able to receive, utilize, and organize around the stimuli that are offered. The vital tasks of organizing motor and autonomic systems to receive and utilize information can be deeply affected when the threshold is too sensitive to stimuli that are inappropriate (e.g., too loud, too bright, too rapid, or too strong). The immature organism must either shut them out or become overwhelmed by them. Habituation to repeated noxious stimuli is a well-known but expensive process for a fragile baby (Als et al. 1979). This same mechanism must be operant for all babies and children. Hence, a stimulus that can be incorporated and responded to easily becomes a nurturant one. An overwhelming or inappropriate stimulus may cost the organism and may contribute to a deviant pattern of withdrawal or of distorted behavioral responses. Pediatricians are in an optimal position to recognize these patterns and to guide the parents toward an understanding of their baby's temperamental requirements.

In our own work with the Neonatal Behavioral Assessment Scale (NBAS), we have found that the earlier we can support the parent–infant relationship, the more powerful can be our effect on the child's development (Brazelton 1984a). Particularly in at-risk babies, early intervention can enhance the plasticity that is available after an insult to the immature central nervous system (St. James-Roberts 1979).

Malnutrition and intrauterine exposure to infection, toxemia, drugs, alcohol, and cigarettes can reduce cellular division (DNA) in organs

---

[1]For economy's sake, I shall use the masculine pronoun for the child, and the feminine pronoun for parents. This should not be assumed to represent a bias in the effectiveness of either.

such as the brain, the thyroid, and the adrenal glands at critical times in fetal development (Klein et al. 1971). The more chronic these influences, the more the developing brain will be affected. These adverse influences can reduce the potential of these brains to function effectively in such learning functions as activation, motivation, and prolonged attention—all necessary functions in a complex society. In other words, we can expect the children of women who expose their fetuses to such conditions to have the attributes ascribed to the "poor": laziness, lack of motivation, and feelings of helplessness and hopelessness in being able to change their futures. Our challenge as preventive physicians is to change this vicious cycle of poverty reproducing itself.

After a stress or an insult, the nervous system is liable to be either hyposensitive or hypersensitive. My concept is that an insult to the developing nervous system may create small areas of damage. Capillaries and neurons rush in to try to repair it. In the process, they create an area of hypersensitivity. This localized hypersensitivity spreads to the contingent areas. The baby becomes overly sensitive to sensory input. This sensitivity results in overreactivity of the motor system and/or a shutdown due to habituation. Hence, such a baby is likely to be hyperactive or hypoactive, easily overwhelmed, and difficult for an anxious parent to understand, unless the pediatrician is available to interpret this behavior and to guide the parent toward a model for interacting with him (Brazelton 1973, Brazelton et al. 1987).

Our responsibility to parents who are under stress is to reach them with adequate information about the importance of providing nurturing intrauterine conditions, and to support them as they attempt to maintain adequate nutrition and drug-free lives. Since our present medical systems are not likely to be set up for an outreach, preventive model in which at-risk parents feel welcomed and valued, we must change it if we are to reach the target population. We must change from the deficit, disease-oriented system in which we were so well trained as medical personnel to a positive model of valuing strengths in all patients. If we can emphasize the positive values—ethnic, religious, and lifestyle—that patients bring, they will feel valued. We need to enter the parent–infant system as a participant (Figure 1-1). This means that we greet prospective parents with a positive, encouraging approach. For example, a pregnant teenager could be treated as a failure, which will turn her away and foreclose

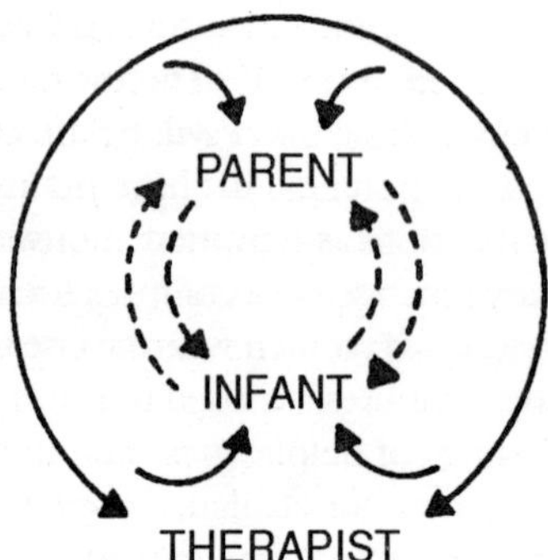

Figure 1–1. Family as a system. The therapist supports and points the family toward a goal.

our opportunity for successful participation with her. Or we could accept her pregnancy, point to the potential future opportunity for her baby, and offer her our support in optimizing that opportunity. In that way, we can play a role in the family system her pregnancy will create.

Systems theory presents an optimistic approach for all of us who are interested in prevention. First, each member of the system must react to every stress incurred by that system—such as to the birth and the adjustment to the new baby, as well as to each step in the baby's development. Since each member shares the reactions, our presence as a member of the system could soften the stress. Second, at each stress point, there is an opportunity for learning—learning to succeed or learning to fail. If we as supportive physicians can offer the necessary information and modeling for the parents to understand the baby's development and to enhance it, we can play a crucial role toward the success of the family system. With parents at risk for stress and/or failure in our complex societies, this can be a critical balance. Since all new parents are likely to be stressed parents, our role can be a critical one in the prevention of most of the familiar problems seen in our clinical practices. For this role, I have devised a map of *touchpoints*, the points at which a change in the system is brought about by the baby's spurt in development (Figure 1-2). No developmental line in the baby makes steady upward progress.

Motor, cognitive, and emotional development proceed in a jagged upward line. There are rapid spurts in development of any one of these lines. These spurts are costly to the organism himself but also to all those in the family around him. Learning to walk is an example of this. As a 1-year-old baby attempts to learn to walk, he is up and down all day, and all night. He screams at a parent when she turns her back on him, so eager is he to get going. He rouses every 3 to 4 hours at night, to stand at his cribside in rapid-eye-movement sleep, frustrated from his daytime attempts to learn to walk. His spurt toward walking costs a family a great deal of patience and sleeplessness. To understand this cost, a parent will need extra support. After the baby walks, he settles down in a plateau of contentment. In this plateau, he consolidates what he has just learned. The entire family can settle back—in homeostasis again (Brazelton 1992).

Just before each spurt in any line of development (motor, cognitive, or emotional), there is a short but predictable period of disorganization in the baby. The parents are likely to feel disorganized and to fear that the baby is regressing toward problem behavior. This

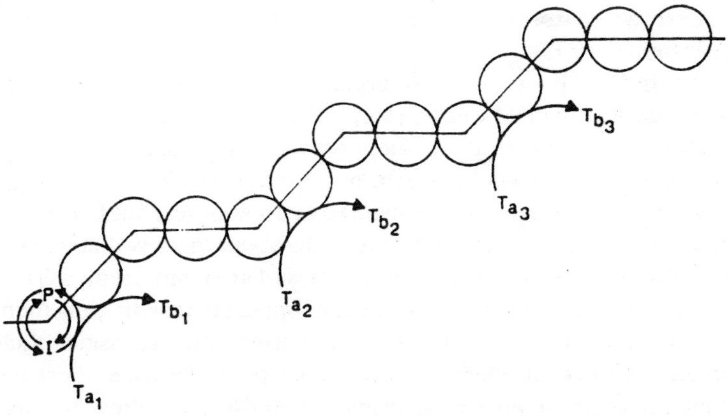

Figure 1–2. Touchpoints for intervention. (T_1 = prenatal, T_2 = perinatal, T_3 = 3 weeks)

period of disorganized, regressive behavior represents a period of reorganization, before the next spurt in development. Since these periods are predictable (one in pregnancy, seven in the first year, three in the second, and two in each subsequent year), they can be mapped out to fit the needs of each family with a developing infant. I have found in my own practice, and in outreach programs for families at risk, that I can predict and participate in these periods. By scheduling the routine pediatric visits for immunizations and checkups to coincide with these points of reorganization, I can offer parents the information necessary to understand these seven periods in the first year and predict the subsequent spurt in the child's development. Since these are the times when parents are likely to put more pressure on the infant or child, and they occur at a time when he needs less pressure, I can help them make the choices they need to make to feel successful when he reorganizes for the next developmental spurt. Thus the child's success in development is experienced as their success as parents and the family, as a system, feels fueled toward success. Additionally, we can prevent the failure patterns that might otherwise result in problems in the areas of sleep, feeding, toilet training, forming habit patterns, and so on. For example, there are four opportunities in the first year for the prevention of sleep difficulties, three in which feeding problems are likely to become fixed in the infant's first year; and four opportunities to prepare parents in the first two years for successful introduction of toilet training at age 2 (Brazelton 1992).

The first touchpoint is an important one for forming a relationship with parents-to-be. If I can meet and share concerns with parents in the seventh month of pregnancy, we will have created a trusting relationship between us before the new baby arrives (Brazelton 1981). This visit need not take more than 10 to 15 minutes, but because it occurs at a time when parents' concerns about the new baby are at a peak, our response to their questions is of great importance. They will see me as an understanding, caring support person helping them bond with the new baby. It is at this touchpoint that we discuss their choice for labor and delivery. "How does premedication affect the baby?" "Does an epidural anesthetic matter to the baby?" We also discuss the choices of breast-feeding and the comparative value to the infant of formula and breast milk. At this time, we gather information on family history of allergies and genetic problems, and on intrauterine exposures to agents that might affect the future baby. We discuss the parents' plans for caregiving and for future plans for working roles and caregivers of the baby.

But the two themes that will lead to the most important aspects of our work together will be as yet unstated. "How will I get to be the parent that I long to be?" We can offer to join them in this role of understanding the baby by learning to observe his language and his behavior. We can begin to help them to identify their own "ghosts from the nursery" (Fraiberg 1959), which can both aid and interfere with learning their roles as parents. They will feel we are allies. At this time, they are likely to tell us about their own experiences in being parented and we should agree to help them adjust to their untoward experiences should a conflict with the new baby arise.

The second theme arises from the fact that during pregnancy, all parents dream of two babies (Brazelton 1981). The first is the perfect, 3-month-old baby depicted in baby magazines. This baby is beautifully nourished and responsive with smiles and vocalizations. To balance this baby is always an impaired baby, who is damaged and similar to a baby from the parents' past experience. The dread of this baby, matched with the parents' concern about how they would ever nurture such a baby, raises a kind of alarm reaction or energy in the parents to face whatever baby they get. But their real concentration is on the fetus. The fetus's behavior is already a burning concern. They wonder whether he is "too active" or "too quiet." Can we tell by ultrasound whether he is well formed or not? Since we can visualize the fetus, we can add behavioral responses for the parents to view. If one uses a buzzer 18 inches from the abdomen, the first few buzzes create startle responses from the fetus. This response diminishes rapidly, and after four or five such stimuli the fetus stops responding, demonstrating a form of behavioral inhibition or habituation to the stimulus. Often the fetus puts its thumb in its mouth and turns away from the source of auditory stimulation. Then, if a rattle is used next to the uterus, the fetus takes his thumb away, opens his eyes, and turns in the direction of the new, more attractive auditory stimulus. Thus, he has demonstrated the ability to shut out a negative and attend to a positive stimulus. This ability to differentiate auditory stimuli can be repeated with visual stimuli. An intrusive bright light and a soft localized light can be presented through the abdomen, resulting in the same comparative behaviors—habituation to the bright light and an orienting response to the softer pinpoint light. At this time, parents-to-be are so struck with their baby "as a person already," that they will be willing to eliminate alcohol, cigarettes, drugs, or any toxins that might be affecting their fetus. We can share their dreams and fantasies for him. We can assure them that we will support them and participate with them toward optimizing the baby's development. We have established our relationships in this first touchpoint.

The second touchpoint is in the lying-in hospital or at home, soon after the birth of the baby. We can demonstrate to the parents the new baby's remarkable repertoire. Using the NBAS, we have demonstrated in numerous research studies that both mother and father can become significantly more sensitive to their new baby's behavior by sharing an assessment with them in the immediate neonatal period (Brazelton 1973, Brazelton et al. 1987). Both parents can profit by such an observation if they participate in this 10- to 20-minute assessment. During the examination, they become aware of our interest in their baby, in the fact that we see and understand the new baby as an individual. They begin to see his individuality and his remarkable capacity to respond to his world. If there are problems to be faced, we begin to share them as well. In this shared interval, we not only enhance their understanding of the new baby, but also ensure their return for the subsequent touchpoints. Using the baby as our language, we can now return to their questions about breast or formula feeding, and about their prospective handling of the baby's rhythms and responses. We are already speaking a shared language that includes the baby's temperament and his style of responses to his new world. We should remind them at this time that we would like to see the three of them at each subsequent touchpoint.

As the potential for early intervention increases, it becomes more and more important that we be able to evaluate at-risk infants as early as possible with an eye to more sophisticated preventive and therapeutic approaches. Early intervention may prevent a compounding of problems, which occurs all too easily when the environment cannot adjust appropriately to the infant at risk. Prematures and minimally brain-damaged infants seem to be less able to compensate in disorganized, depriving environments than do well-equipped neonates, and their problems of organization in development are compounded early (Greenberg 1971). Quiet, nondemanding infants do not elicit necessary mothering from already overstressed parents. Hyperkinetic, hypersensitive neonates may press a mother and father into a kind of desperation that produces child-rearing responses from them that reinforce the problems of the child so that he grows up in an overreactive, hostile environment (Heider 1966). Parents of children admitted to the wards of the Children's Hospital in Boston for clinical syndromes such as failure to thrive, child abuse, repeated accidents and ingestions, and infantile autism are often successful parents of other children. By history, they associate their failure with the one child to an inability to "understand" him from the neonatal period onward, and they claim a difference from the other children in his earliest reactions to them. If we are to improve the outcome for such children, assessment of the risk in early infancy could mobilize preventive efforts and programs for intervention before the neonate's problems are compounded by an environment that cannot understand him without such help.

The first evaluation of the neonate can provide an irreplaceable set of observations, which point to his interuterine experience and its effect on his fetal development. With the indications from animal research of the effects of intrauterine deprivation on the DNA content of the fetal brain and other vital organs, clinical assessment of depletion or underdevelopment in the neonate becomes of vital importance. The plasticity of the infant and his ability to recover from stress without external evidences of it make it more difficult to detect the signs in a viable neonate; there are not many ways that we can detect past injuries from which he has recovered. Neurological examination of reflex behavior may not detect minor damage to which he has made a functional adaptation in the uterus (Parmelee and Michaellis 1971). So, we must look for measures of intrauterine development that are sensitive to critical influences on his developing organs in the nine months of pregnancy.

Signs of prematurity out of proportion to the infant's gestational age may point to a chronically stressed circulation to the fetus and an underdeveloped organism as a result. Winick (1969) and Zamenhof and colleagues (1968) point to the significant decreases in cellular number (as reflected by DNA) and cellular content (as measured by

RNA) in the brain of neonatal animals whose mothers have had an inadequate protein intake during pregnancy. These quantitatively and qualitatively deficient brains are poorly adapted in normal development (as may be demonstrated by significant decreases in their ability to solve problems throughout their lives). They must be more susceptible to any insult, however mild, of hypoxia, maternal depressant drugs, and other paranatal events that are easily compensated for by normal fetuses. The Collaborative Study on Cerebral Palsy, Mental Retardation, and Other Sensory Disorders of Infancy and Childhood of the National Institutes of Health found that paranatal insults were easily withstood by normal neonates, but the incidence of damage from similar events was significantly correlated with babies who had demonstrated clinical evidence of intrauterine stresses of depletion or immaturity at birth (Drage et al. 1966).

Repeated evaluations in the neonatal nursery are necessary in order to record the depth and duration of effects. These include observations of alertness such as head turning to auditory and visual stimuli, the ability of the neonate to shut out interfering stimuli, as well as his ability to habituate to repeated pinprick, Moro's embrace reflex test, bright light, and loud noises. The baby's ability to be brought to a responsive "state" of consciousness is a further measure of his capacity to respond to his extrauterine environment and overcome the physiological demands of readjustment. By following infants for medication effects over the first 6 hours after delivery, we found a significant and reliable difference in observable effects of medication and anesthesia in this early period.

An early examination of the neonate should include a detailed assessment of any signs of dysmaturity such as dried or peeling skin (Warkany et al. 1961). A small-for-dates baby is more at risk than a well-nourished one. Evidences of extracellular depletion and speed of recovery may reflect the duration and depth of his deprivation in utero. Short-term signs such as skin texture and subcutaneous fat depletion may not be as significant as long-term effects such as decreased linear bony growth, decreased head circumference, or minor congenital developmental defects that may point to a chronic intrauterine depletion that affected the fetus at critical periods of development.

An estimate of the neonate's stage of maturity using such physical signs as size of breast nodule, palm and sole creases, scalp and body hair distribution, earlobe, testes, and scrotum, as recommended by Lubchenko and colleagues (1963), and behavioral signs that measure reflex behavior on the fetal continuum of Dubowitz (Escardo and de Coriat 1960) can be measured against a careful historical estimate of his gestational age from his mother's last menstrual period. When these do not coincide, the significance of relative immaturity becomes of predictive importance, suggesting long-term intrauterine deprivation that has affected cellular development in the fetus.

To record and evaluate some of the integrative processes evidenced in certain kinds of neonatal behavior, we have developed a behavioral evaluation scale that tests and documents the infant's use of state behavior (state of consciousness) and the response to various kinds of stimulation (Brazelton 1972).

Since the infant's reactions to all stimuli are dependent on his ongoing "state," any interpretation of them must be made with this in mind. His use of state to maintain control of his reactions to environmental and internal stimuli is an important mechanism and reflects his potential for organization. State no longer needs to be treated as an error variable but serves to set a dynamic pattern to allow for the full behavioral repertoire of the infant. Specifically, our examination tracks state changes over the course of the examination, and its lability and direction. The variability of state points to the infant's capacities for self-organization. His ability to quiet himself as well as his need for stimulation also measure this adequacy.

The behavior examination tests for neurological adequacy with 20 reflex measures and for 28 behavioral responses to environmental stimuli, including the kind of interpersonal stimuli that mothers use in their handling of the infant as they attempt to help him adapt to the new world. There is a graded series of procedures—talking, hand on belly, restraint, holding and rocking—designed to soothe and alert the infant. His responsiveness to animate stimuli (e.g., voice and face) and to inanimate stimuli (e.g., rattle, bell, red ball, white light, temperature change) are assessed. Estimates of vigor and attentional excitement are measured as well as assessment of motor activity and tone and autonomic responsiveness as he changes state. With this examination given on successive days, we have been able to outline (1) the initial period of alertness immediately after delivery—presumably the result of stimulation of labor and the new environmental stimuli after delivery; (2) the period of depression and disorganization that follows and lasts for 24 to 48 hours in infants with uncomplicated deliveries and no medication effects, and for longer periods of 3 to 4 days if they have been compromised from medication given their mothers during labor; and (3) the curve of recovery to "optimal" function after several days. This third period may be the best single predictor of individual potential function and it seems to correlate well with the neonate's retest ability at 30 days (Horowitz et al. 1971). The shape of the curve made by several examinations may be the most important assessment of the basic CNS intactness of the neonate's ability to integrate CNS and other physiological recovery mechanisms, and the strength of his compensatory capacities when there have been compromising insults to him during labor and delivery.

This neonatal behavioral examination has been used in cross-cultural studies to outline genetic differences (Brazelton et al. 1969, Freedman and Freedman 1969, Tronick et al. 1976) with prematures to predict their outcome successfully (Scarr and Williams 1971), to document behavioral correlates of intrauterine protein depletion (M. J. Sellers, personal communication), to determine the effects of uteri depleted by rapidly repeated pregnancies (Tronick et al. 1976), and to assess the influence of heavy medication given the mother during labor (Brazelton 1970).

We feel that the behavioral items are tapping in on more important evidence of cortical control and responsiveness, even in the neonatal period. The neonate's capacity to manage and overcome the physiological demands of this adjustment period in order to attend to, to differentiate, and to habituate to the complex stimuli of an examiner's maneuvers may be an important predictor of his future central nervous system organization. Certainly, the curve of recovery of these responses over the first neonatal week must be of more significance than the midbrain responses detectable in routine neurological examinations. Repeated behavioral examinations on any two or three days in the first ten days after delivery might be expected to be sensitive predictors of future cortical function.

Bowlby (1969) has stressed the importance of observing the earliest interactions between mother and infant as predictive of the kind of attachment a mother may form with the infant. He suggests that there is a kind of "imprinting" of responses from her that may be triggered by the neonate's behavior. Moss (1965) and S. Goldberg (personal communication) point to the trigger-like value in setting off mothering activities of the newborn's small size, helpless appearance, and distress cries. Klaus and Kennell (1970) have described the kinds of initial contacts that mothers make with their newborn infants and the distortions in this behavior when the mother is depressed by abnormalities in the baby, for example, prematurity, illness in the neonatal period, and so on. Eye-to-eye contact, touching, handling, and nursing behavior on the part of the mother may be assessed and judged for predicting her ability to relate to the new baby. Change in these behaviors over time is stressed as an indicator of recovery or nonrecovery of maternal capacity to attach to the baby by mothers who have been depressed and unable to function optimally because of having produced an infant at risk (Klaus et al. 1972).

The ability of the baby to precipitate and encourage her attachment and caregiving behavior must be taken into account. With an unresponsive neonate, the feedback mechanisms necessary to fuel mothering behavior are severely impaired. Since this is an observation of a rather gross level, interference in the interaction dissynchrony of more subtle "lack of fit" in the earliest mother–infant attachment interaction should be carefully watched for and observed over time. The possibility of creating or compounding the problems of infants at risk by a distortion of the environment's reactions to them is too important, and our tools for predicting this should be sharpened in the lying-in period. The opportunity for observing the pair together is never again as available, and surely we are missing valuable predictive information when we do not make regular, repeated observations of interactive situations, such as feeding periods, "play" periods after feeding, bathing, and documenting the maternal behavior and the infant's responses to it as well as the changes in each that occur over time in a supportive, protective situation such as the lying-in hospital. It is vital that we provide infants at risk with the best possible environment to foster their capacity for recovery and to integrate any intact mechanisms for development. Without an early assessment of this environment as it reacts to the baby, we may miss an invaluable opportunity to support the parents and improve the environment for an infant at risk.

The third touchpoint occurs optimally at 2 to 3 weeks. We should evaluate the new baby before the regular fussing that occurs in most infants (85 percent in the United States) at the end of each day between 3 and 12 weeks of age (Brazelton 1962). At this time we can see whether the mother is beginning to recover from the common postpartum exhaustion and depression. A checkup of mother and baby will be a major goal for the visit. In addition, we can help the parents toward organizing the baby for a predictable feeding and sleeping schedule. But, the most important subject for the visit will be the touchpoint—that of predicting the fussy period at the end of the day. If we consider as critical the irritable crying that occurs after the immature nervous system has handled environmental stimuli all day, we can help the parents plan for it in advance. In previous research, it was found that babies cycle through sleep–wake cycles all day (Brazelton 1962). In the process, they begin to overload their nervous systems until it seems inevitable for most active babies to fuss regularly for a period each evening. After the fussy period, they will eat and sleep better for the next 24 hours. This fussy period seems to be a necessary organizing period for them. Mothers who kept records reported that carrying or feeding their babies often reduced the crying period. But nothing they did was successful in eliminating it. If they worked too hard to try to soothe the baby, it resulted in overstimulation and more crying.

The first maneuver is for them to understand this as a developmental process and as a normal part of his day. When parents discuss this with me, we decide on a strategy that will mitigate their feelings of helplessness in eliminating his fussy crying and that can help them reduce the baby's upset. The routine I suggest is that parents do what they can to help him, that is, feed him, change him, burp him. But when nothing works, parents should turn to a reduced routine that will not add stimulation to an already vulnerable nervous system. Let him fuss for 5 to 10 minutes until he begins to be frantic, then pick him up to calm him. Soothe him, feed him water to bring up the bubble he may have gulped down. After burping him, put him down to fuss 5 to 10 more minutes. This routine will last for about an hour; the baby is likely to fall asleep thereafter. A more intense, active baby may cry for a longer period. If he begins to build up with more intense crying and this routine is not effective, parents should be instructed to seek a diagnosis. I have found that a routine approach helps me to triage any significant problem with them at a much earlier time than they might have consulted me otherwise. This fussy period seems to be an organizer for the 24-hour cycle. By predicting it and explaining its positive value to parents at this touchpoint, I have found that the 2- to 3-hour period can be reduced significantly. The baby is less frantic and the parents feel successful in dealing with this period calmly each day.

The next touchpoints become the focus for each subsequent visit. For example, at the 4-month visit, one can predict that there will soon be a burst in cognitive awareness of the environment. The baby will be difficult to feed. He will stop eating to look around and to listen to every stimulus in the environment. He will begin to awaken again at night, even though he may have been sleeping through before. Both feeding and sleeping patterns will be disrupted for a short period in this next few weeks. This is coincident with the rapid burst in his development. New awareness of his environment, of strangers, is accompanied by a burst in motor development. He starts to try to sit, he loves to be stood up, he reaches successfully with each hand and plays with objects more effectively. The period of disorganization has served its purpose. When parents understand this period as a natural precursor to the rapid development that will follow, they will not need to feel as if it represents failure. They will not need to press the baby to eat at each feeding. A short feeding followed by his looking around will serve the purpose during the day. Two feedings in a dark, quiet room will be sufficient to stimulate the breasts to produce milk and to preserve breast-feeding. A formula-fed baby will take a formula well in a nonstimulating environment. Pressure to feed is not necessary for this brief period (Brazelton 1984b).

Sleep issues can be predicted. This visit can be a time to discuss a preventive approach to sleeping problems. At this time, I ascertain whether the baby knows how to get himself to sleep when he is put in bed at night. If he is put to sleep in the parents' arms, he has not had the chance to learn to get himself to sleep. Then, when he comes up to light sleep every 3 to 4 hours during the night, he will fuss, cry out, and he will need the parents to intervene—to feed him, to pick him up, to try to get him back to sleep. If he has learned to comfort himself with an independent pattern of putting himself to sleep, e.g., thumbsucking or clinging to his blanket, he can put himself back down to sleep at each 4-hour rousing. At this time, we can help the parents to make decisions about co-sleeping, about whether to go to the baby at each rousing. We can help them understand the baby's sleeping behavior so that they make appropriate decisions about their responses to him. This is the first touchpoint to help to prevent sleep problems. This visit and the discussion of feeding disruptions can give parents insight into their feelings about feeding refusals. This visit, which may last 20 to 30 minutes, becomes a productive opportunity for parents to understand these issues from the standpoint of the baby's development and it offers us important insights into their issues. We can rely on this information to help them in the future, no matter what their decision will be about handling these issues.

There are three more touchpoints in the first year, each of which presents opportunities for discussing parenting issues which will arise, and for preventing the tensions between them, which could lead to failure. Each touchpoint precedes a developmental spurt in one or more areas (Table 1-1) (Brazelton 1973).

These are examples of the kinds of issues that can be addressed at each checkup. The parents will feel that the health care professional is concerned about the baby's psychological development as well as his physical progress. They will feel more confident in themselves and in their baby as a result of this support and interest.

These touchpoints can be useful and can be predicted as opportunities to support parents in understanding their child's development throughout childhood. The timing for them may be somewhat delayed for a premature or fragile infant, but they will be even more important as opportunities for supporting their anxious parents. Pediatricians and parents can join in optimizing the child's developmental progress.

Table 1–1. Three additional touchpoints in the first year

Age	*Developmental areas*	*Potential areas for conflict*
7-8 months	Crawling Sitting alone Handling food with a pincer grasp Stranger anxiety and sudden awareness of differences Object and person permanence	Feeding—wanting to participate with finger foods Sleeping-waking to rock in the crib Frustrated about not crawling Awareness of important strangers—grandparents, mother's sister, father's brother Awareness of new, strange situations Separation issues
10 months	Standing at side of crib Wanting to get cruising Beginning of causality Wanting to feed self	Waking up every 3 to 4 hours again Standing at cribside as if he can't get down Frustration at wanting to do everything for self Finger feeding, handling cup
12 months	Wanting to start walking New awareness of independence Beginning of negativism Testing for limits Refusing proffered food	Waking all over again Wanting to start walking Early temper tantrums Wanting to do all his own feeding

REFERENCES

Als, H., Tronick, E., Adamson, L., and Brazelton, T. B. (1976). The behavior of the full-term yet underweight newborn. *Developmental Medicine and Child Neurology* 18:590–603.

Als, H., Tronick, E., Lester, B. M., and Brazelton, T. B. (1979). The Brazelton Neonatal Assessment Scale (BNAS). In *Handbook of Infant Development*, ed. J. Osofsky, pp. 780–802. New York: Wiley.

Bowlby, J. (1969). *Attachment and Loss, vol. 1. Attachment.* New York: Basic Books.

Brazelton, T. B. (1962). Crying in infancy. *Pediatrics* 29:579–588.

——— (1970). Effect of prenatal drugs on the behavior of the neonate. *American Journal of Psychiatry* 126:95.

——— (1972). *Neonatal Behavioral Assessment Scale*. London: National Spastics Society Monographs.

——— (1973). Assessment of the infant at risk. *Clinical Obstetrics and Gynecology* 16:361–375.

——— (1975). The origins of reciprocity. In *Effect of the Infant on the Caretaker,* vol. 1, ed. M. Lewis and M. and L. Rosenblum, pp. 49–75. New York: Wiley.

——— (1981). *On Becoming a Family: The Growth of Attachment.* New York: Delacorte.

——— (1983). Developmental framework of infants and children: a future for pediatric responsibility. *Journal of Pediatrics* 102:967–972.

——— (1984a). *Neonatal Behavioral Assessment Scale,* 2nd ed. Spastics International Medical Publications. London: Blackwell; Philadelphia: Lippincott.

——— (1984b). *To Listen to a Child.* Reading, MA: Addison-Wesley.

——— (1992). *Touchpoints: Emotional and Behavioral Development*. Reading, MA: Addison-Wesley.

Brazelton, T. B., Nugent, J. K., and Lester, B. M. (1987). *Neonatal Behavioral Assessment,* 2nd ed., pp. 780–818. New York: Wiley.

Brazelton, T. B., Robey, J. S., and Collier, G. A. (1969). Infant development in the Zinacanteco Indians of Southern Mexico. *Pediatrics* 44:274.

Drage, J. S., Kennedy, C., Berendes, H., et al. (1966). The 5-minute Apgar scores and 4-year psychological performance. *Developmental Medicine and Child Neurology* 8:141.

Escardo, F., and de Coriat, L. F. (1960). Development of postural and tonic patterns in the newborn infant. *Pediatrics Clinics of North America* 7:511.

Fraiberg, S. (1959). *The Magic Years.* New York: Scribner's.

Freedman, D. G., and Freedman, N. (1969). Behavioral differences between Chinese-American and American newborns. *Nature* 224:227.

Goldberg, S. (Personal communication). Some stimulus properties of the human infant.

Greenberg, N. H. (1971). A comparison of infant-mother interactional behavior in infants with a typical behavior and normal infants. In *Exceptional Infants,* vol. 2, p. 390. New York: Brunner/Mazel.

Heider, G. M. (1966). Vulnerability in infants and young children. *Genetic Psychology Monograph* 73:1.

Horowitz, F. D., Self, P. A., and Paden, L. N., et al. (1971). *Newborn and four-week retest on a normative population using the Brazelton New-*

born Assessment procedure. Paper presented at the annual meeting of the Society of Research in Child Development, Minneapolis.

Klaus, M. H., Jerauld, R., and Krueger, N. C.(1972). Maternal attachment, importance of the first postpartum days. *New England Journal of Medicine* 286:460.

Klaus, M. H., and Kennell, J. H.(1970). Mothers separated from their newborn infants. *Pediatric Clinics of North America* 17:1015.

Klein, R. E., Habicht, J. P., and Yarbrough, C. (1971). Effect of protein calorie malnutrition on mental development. *Advances in Pediatrics* 1:571–582.

Lubchenko, L. O., Hansman, C., Dressler, M., and Boyd, E. (1963). Intrauterine growth estimated from liveborn, birthweight data at 24 to 42 weeks of gestation. *Pediatrics* 32:793.

Moss, H. A. (1965). Methodological issues in studying mother–infant interaction. *American Journal of Orthopsychiatry* 35:482.

Parmelee, A. H., and Michaellis, R. (1971). *Neurological Examination of the Newborn Exceptional Infant,* vol. 2. New York: Brunner/Mazel.

Scarr, S., and Williams, M. (1971). *The assessment of neonatal and later status in low-birthweight infants*. Paper presented at the annual meeting of the Society for Research in Child Development, Minneapolis, April.

Sellers, M. J. (Personal communication). Prediction of infants at risk for marasmus in Guatemalan babies. Incap study, Guatemala.

St. James-Roberts, I. (1979). Neurological plasticity. In *Advances in Child Development and Behavior,* ed. H. Reise and L. Lipsett, pp. 38–62. New York: Academic Press.

Tronick, E., Koslowski, B., and Brazelton, T. B.(1976). Study of neonatal behavior in Zambian and American babies. *Annual Progress in Child Psychiatry* 15:97–107.

Warkany, J., Monroe, B., and Sutherland, B. (1961). Intrauterine growth retardation. *American Journal of Diseases of Children* 102:127.

Winick, M. (1969). Malnutrition and brain development. *Journal of Pediatrics* 74:667.

Zamenhof, S., Van Marthens, E., and Margolis, F. L.(1968). DNA (cell number) and protein in neonatal brain. *Science* 160:322.

2

Psychotherapy for Children with Nonverbal Learning Disabilities

Joseph Palombo and
Anne Hatcher Berenberg

Learning disabilities are conditions presumed to be of neurological origin that occur in children or adults of at least average intelligence. These conditions are not the result of trauma or medically diagnosed neurological abnormalities. The conditions affect one or more of a broad range of cognitive functions. Nonverbal learning disabilities (NLD) are identified under a variety of labels including right-hemisphere deficits syndrome, right-hemisphere developmental learning disability, and social/emotional learning disability (Denkla 1983, Semrud-Clikeman and Hynd 1990, Voeller 1986, 1995, Weintraub and Mesulam 1983). These labels indicate the belief among researchers that the etiology of the deficits of children with nonverbal learning disabilities are found in the right hemisphere. A contrast is drawn between nonverbal learning disabilities and the dyslexias, which are presumed to represent left-hemisphere deficits (Rourke 1989, 1995). However, others challenge this assumption, expressing the belief that the etiology is more broadly distributed among a variety of brain systems (Pennington 1991).

In a previous publication, Palombo (1995) discussed the relational and psychodynamic problems that children with nonverbal learning disabilities encounter. This chapter focuses on the problems these children present to psychotherapists, and the treatment approaches found helpful in working with these children.

Nonverbal learning disabilities include the learning disabilities related to the processing of visual spatial information and problems in social competence. Also included are poor graphomotor skills, difficulties in adapting to novel situations, and poor fluid reasoning. These difficulties can occur along a continuum of severity ranging from mild to extreme. Some children are affected in one area, while others are affected in several areas. Because the areas affected are different from child to child, it is impossible to generalize about the psychological impact these difficulties have on children's psychological development or on the psychopathology that is likely to result. In most cases, the disabilities lead the child to experience the world differently from the way the world is experienced by other children of the same age. At times, the information available to the child is processed in a highly idiosyncratic way, resulting in responses by the child that are markedly different from those of most of the child's peers. Adults and caregivers in the environment are often puzzled by the child's responses or interpret those responses as hostile, negativistic, or intentionally confusing. A set of complex relational patterns emerge that are characteristically symptomatic of the child's efforts to deal with the deficits. In addition, a set of psychodynamics evolve that center around the child's feelings of being different from peers. These psychodynamics often lead to serious self-esteem problems.

If diagnosticians do not consider the learning disability as part of the etiology of the emotional problems, the child's problem will be misdiagnosed. Therapists who base their treatment of these children on faulty or incomplete understanding of the child's dynamics often face serious difficulties. Therapists cannot disregard the fact that children with nonverbal learning disabilities are endowed differently from their peers, that they often construe idiosyncratic personal meanings from their experiences, and that, therefore, the psychopathology they present reflects their inability to make sense of their experiences in the same way as others do. Furthermore, to be effective, the treatment plan must involve the child's total milieu. It must include parents, teachers, pediatric neurologists, as well as all other professionals involved in the treatment of the child or remediation of the child's deficits. Depending on the age of the child, the goal of treatment can range from complementing the child's deficits through support and tutoring, to dealing with their relationship problems and the psychodynamics that produce some of the symptomatic behaviors.

This chapter addresses the treatment approaches most useful to children of primary school age. Adolescents present even more complex problems; the discussion of their treatment is found in Part III of this book. We begin with a summary profile of the NLD syndrome and the types of psychopathology that result (Palombo 1995), then move to a discussion of treatment issues. When possible, we provide representative case vignettes.

PROFILE OF CHILDREN WITH NONVERBAL LEARNING DISABILITIES

From a developmental perspective, caregivers report that as infants and toddlers these children are passive, fail to engage in exploratory play, and do not respond as expected. Many children cannot use toddler toys or enjoy coloring or drawing. They are unable to put puzzles together and appear clumsy and ill coordinated. Their difficulties processing visual spatial information become evident. They are slow to learn from their caregivers' limits and instructions, and appear unable to understand causal relationships. Caregivers find themselves having to intervene frequently to prevent them from harming themselves or getting into trouble. In turn, the children respond to the parents with frustration and anger (Johnson 1987).

By the age of 3, the children go through an initial stage when their speech is difficult to understand because of articulation problems. These problems dissipate as they become adept at verbal communication. This channel becomes reinforced by caregivers, who then become overreliant on it to relate to their children. By the time the children reach kindergarten or first grade, other problems emerge.

They have difficulties with the classroom setting; some academic tasks are hard for them, and they are unable to form friendships or to sustain being with other children even for brief periods of time without eruptions ensuing.

By latency, children with NLD are generally referred for evaluation or treatment, boys usually because of behavioral problems, girls because of their social isolation. Both boys and girls often present with clinical signs of severe anxiety, depression, attentional problems, obsessional preoccupations, and self-esteem problems. They perform poorly in some academic areas, but not in all. As readers they are good decoders, although their comprehension of abstract contents seems impaired. Tasks involving writing or arithmetic are usually difficult for them. Neuropsychological testing reveals their cognitive deficits, while their histories and the clinical impressions from diagnostic interviews disclose their social and emotional distress.

What becomes evident is that, although the children may interact reasonably well with adults in social situations, they do not interact as well with peers. They are unable to decode social cues involved in "reading" other people; they appear socially inept, seldom make solid eye contact, cannot decode prosodic or vocal intonations, and have difficulty reading facial expressions and bodily gestures. It is as though they suffer from a "nonverbal dyslexia" (Badian 1986). Also, they do not use appropriate body gestures; they seem wooden and constricted or use overly dramatic gestures that are not concordant with the context. Their moods are difficult to read from their facial expressions or posture. When frustrated, they lose control and have temper tantrums. To adults, some children appear to have little compassion or empathy for others.

Finally, the children also exhibit a number of psychiatric symptoms. They generally suffer from one or more of the following: high levels of anxiety, severe self-esteem problems, depression, obsessive-compulsive symptoms, and attentional problems. Often they are diagnosed as having attention deficit disorder (ADD), which they may display, but the nonverbal deficits are not taken into consideration. Sometimes they are mistaken for children who suffer from Asperger's syndrome (*DSM-IV* p. 75) or mild autism.

RELATIONAL AND PSYCHODYNAMIC PROBLEMS OF NONVERBAL LEARNING DISABILITIES

Relational Problems

Two types of sequelae emerge in these children's relationships to others; one is related to the child's perceptions of the world being different from that of others, the other to the tangled dependence they develop on others.

Since these children's experiences are filtered through their neurocognitive deficits, the information they obtain about their interactions with others and of the world around them is incomplete. The conclusions they draw about the events they encounter are different from those most children would draw under the same circumstances. Their inability to integrate into their understanding the meanings of other people's facial expressions, vocal intonations, gestures, and other nonverbal communications causes them to miss the significance of many of the affective messages these channels convey. It is not that they "distort" what they perceive so much as that they do not fully grasp or observe many of the cues that people convey. Consequently, their responses are based on erroneous or incomplete information. At the same time, they carry a conviction that their perceptions are correct and that they are justified in their responses. For them, negotiating interactions with others becomes as difficult as running an obstacle course at night with a flashlight. What is perceived is negotiable or avoidable; it is what is not observed that trips up the runner, leading to bewilderment and frustration. NLD children are unaware that these failures are due to their deficits and not to obstacles placed in their path by others.

As a result, their experiences acquire personal rather than shared meanings, meanings that do not include elements of the communications with others that are highly significant. They develop patterns of interaction that are dysfunctional. These patterns are incorporated into themes or motifs that become organizing features of their self-narrative. When these motifs are concordant with others' responses, the child's view of reality appears similar to that of others. When they are not, the child's construction of reality gives rise to relational problems. Since the child is convinced that his or her self-narrative is coherent, there is little awareness of the dissynchrony that exists between his or her view and that of others (Bruner 1990).

Relational difficulties also can result when children develop a reliance on others to complement their deficits. Complementarity, in this context, consists in the use of others to help achieve a goal. A complementary function is a function performed by another person who fills in an affective, cognitive, social, or functional deficit. The person performing the function augments the competencies of the person requiring the function (Palombo 1991). If a caregiver devotes herself or himself to complementing a child's deficits, a complex relationship evolves that presents the child and the caregiver with difficult dilemmas. On the one hand, the child may become extremely dependent on the caregiver, making it impossible for the caregiver to distinguish between what the child can and cannot do. This dependence is further complicated by the anxiety and uncertainty the caregiver feels about how to proceed. On the other hand, if the caregiver is unable to complement the function or refrains from responding, the child either fails or his or her coping capacities are taxed maximally. The child develops serious behavioral problems and withdraws, or simply fragments, feeling defeated by the environment. The caregivers are then experienced as unempathic, negligent, or uncaring (Fairchild and Keith 1981).

Psychodynamics

The psychodynamics of children with NLD are difficult to ascertain, not only because the data are often unavailable, but also because of the complexity of sorting out what is primary and what is secondary in these dynamics. Among the factors that lead to defenses and symptomatic behaviors are the children's anxieties, which can sometimes be pervasive, the injuries they suffer from others' responses to them, and their inability to modulate their affect states.

As we have seen, the children's clinical presentation is complex and difficult to characterize. We can infer from the transferences they form that, although the parents may be willing and able to provide the emotional experiences that would lead the child to perceive these parental functions as selfobject functions, serious selfobject deficits develop because the children cannot experience the mirroring, soothing, and comforting that are essential to a healthy, cohesive sense of self. Rather, they interpret their transactions with caregivers as having different meanings than those intended by the caregivers. Their cognitive and affective deficits seem to interfere with the use of the selfobject functions caregivers are ready to provide. They experience the interchanges as failures in empathy. The resulting selfobject deficits impose severe limits on the range and depth of connection between child and caregiver.

Similar difficulties lie in the path to the acquisition of idealizing and alter ego functions. Since most selfobject functions are performed nonverbally, they occur in a domain that is difficult for these children to decode. Along the line of idealizing selfobject functions, experiences such as those of being held safely by a protective caregiver, of being reassured by the modulating influence of a caregiver's regulatory interventions, or of being admired by a caregiver, have a different meaning for these children than such interactions would have for other children. They either cannot perceive or they misread the affects the caregivers convey. For example, if gestures are misinterpreted, the personal meanings the child draws at best only partially reflect what occurred. As a result, the child may, in fact, experience the caregiver as unempathic or cruel. Children then do not acquire the psychological structures associated with the internalization of the idealizing selfobject functions. They will feel unsafe and unprotected in ordinary life situations, have difficulties regulating and modulating affects, or may become contemptuous and disdainful of authority figures, unable to take pride in their own achievements.

These children suffer most from the absence of the alter ego experiences that provide a linkage with others whose humanity they share. Although aware that they are different from other children, they cannot understand why others respond by avoiding or rejecting them. They feel injured and dehumanized, as though they are aliens in this world. This sense of alienation leads them at times either to play up their differences, rather than hiding them from others, or to exaggerate the means through which to communicate, much like a person who, speaking to someone who does not understand his or her language, turns up the volume and speaks louder, thus hoping to be understood. These children then display oppositional behaviors that make it difficult for them to get along with others. At times, they feel a deep sense of shame, fearing that their deficits will be exposed. They then retreat from social contacts and appear uninterested in people.

Mitigating the effects of some of these deficits are the compensatory functions children sometimes develop. Some children learn to compensate through the verbal mediation of nonverbal tasks. They achieve the goal of completing a task by talking their way through the nonverbal steps. Some learn to structure their environment to minimize the reliance on visual cues. Others, with help, learn to rehearse verbally what is to occur in anticipation of an encounter with a new situation.

Since the deficits are found across a spectrum of severity, the extent of symptomatic behaviors varies with each child. It is incorrect, however, to expect a direct correlation between the severity of the deficit and the extent of symptomatic behaviors. The influence of complementarity and the ability to compensate will, at times, mitigate the effects of the deficits and diminish the symptoms a child will display.

If the deficits are extensive and are not complemented or compensated, such children will present with borderline pathology. Their responses are chaotic and reflect the absence of an internal sense of cohesion. Often it is difficult to sort out whether the level of pathology is related to the severity of the deficits, to the unresponsiveness of the environment, or to a combination of both (Christman 1984, Palombo 1991, 1992, 1993a,b, Palombo and Feigon 1984).

TREATMENT OF THE NLD CHILD

Before instituting any treatment plan, it is essential that a clear diagnosis be made through psychoeducational and/or neuropsychological testing. While it is possible to arrive at a clinical diagnosis from neurological or behavioral observations, these alone do not establish a definitive diagnosis. In addition, it is most helpful for therapists to have a clear idea of the specific areas of the child's strength or deficits, which such testing can provide. If available, projective testing can be very helpful, provided the tester appreciates that the child's visual spatial problems will affect the child's perceptions and consequently his or her responses to visually presented projective materials such as Rorschach and Thematic Apperception Test (TAT) cards. If these problems are not taken into consideration, the protocols will often be interpreted as presenting a much more pathological picture than might actually be the case.

Generally, the principles of child therapy apply to this group of children, although there are differences in specific techniques. We begin with a discussion of work with parents and other professionals, then turn to issues related to the individual treatment of the child.

First and foremost, the success of any treatment of children with NLD is dependent on the establishment of a sound alliance with the parents. The parents are entitled to the best explanation available of their child's problem. To the extent possible, it is desirable to give the parents general advice on the management of the child and on ways to provide the child with positive experiences (Garber 1988, Rourke 1995, Vigilante 1983). When parents are given an understanding of the nature of the child's deficits and the ways in which these deficits impact the child's life, they often experience considerable relief at finally having answers to their questions. They begin to make connections between situations and the child's deficits. Often they will seek to educate themselves about the disorder. If they feel comfortable in joining a group of parents of children with the same problems, they may find support in learning that they are not alone in their struggles with this kind of child. Sharing their experiences and learning from others can alleviate their anxieties and dispel their confusions. It can also help them learn different strategies for dealing with some of the child's difficult behaviors.

Parents cannot avoid the problems of complementarity described earlier. They often will either provide functions for the child or get into power struggles by insisting the child perform tasks, not realizing that the child is often unable to perform those tasks. At times, the parents will vacillate between two extremes. Understanding the dynamics that drive these interactions is essential to avoid these dilemmas. A caregiver who is exquisitely sensitive and responsive to the child's distress may find that the child has become totally dependent on him or her. The caregiver intuitively reads the child's messages and soon finds him- or herself being the only one able to communicate effectively with the child. A symbiotic tie may then evolve. As placement in day care or preschool becomes necessary, the child will display severe separation anxiety. Parents may then be accused of fostering the child's dependence or not permitting the child to become autonomous. Their motives in responding to the child as they do are brought into question, and their confidence in their parenting is shaken. It is important to recognize that the caregivers' responses often are motivated by the child's survival needs and not necessarily by their unconscious needs to maintain the child's helpless state.

On the other hand, caregivers who fear the consequences of the child's dependence and insist that the child be more self-sufficient discover that the child will respond to this approach with constant distress and increased helplessness. In many instances, caregivers are frustrated by what they experience as the child's negativism; they feel placed in the position of constantly having to correct, limit, or punish the child, who in turn responds with fury at what he or she experiences as unfair treatment. The family often feels controlled by the child in all its activities. Caregivers then end up feeling guilty, blaming themselves for their failure to parent properly. This frustration initiates a cycle in which the caregivers either reject or feel rejected by the child. They then distance themselves emotionally, leaving the child to feel isolated and helpless.

One way out of these dilemmas is to have a good understanding of the nature of the child's deficits at the earliest possible stages of development. Since that is not possible before the ages of 3 or 4, clinical judgment must be exercised as to how best to proceed in those early years. Our clinical experience leads us to recommend that the better alternative for young children is to allow the symbiosis between parent and child to form, reserving attempts to resolve the dependence for a later time when the nature of the deficits are clearly identified and the child has matured sufficiently to cope with the challenges the environment presents.

At times, caregivers contribute to the complexity of the interaction because of their own personality difficulties. Some caregivers themselves have nonverbal learning disabilities, in which case the confusion is compounded. The household then appears more like a family in which each member speaks a different language. While a measure of communication occurs, there are vast areas that are fraught with misunderstandings. Some spouses become aware that their mates suffer from a disorder similar to that of the child and that they have complemented their spouse's deficits from the earliest days of their relationship. The shock of that realization may bring on a period of sadness or depression that is resolved when the spouse can make an adjustment to this new understanding of his or her mate's problems. Tactful handling by therapists of this discovery can help relieve tensions between the couple and lead to greater empathy for the child's distress.

Parents will often raise concerns for their child's future. They will want to know whether the condition will handicap their child permanently. Except in cases of extreme deficits, the answers to these questions should be framed in the most optimistic light. Children's capacities for adaptation, for compensation, and for maturation must be emphasized. The younger the child at the point of diagnosis, the more aggressive the interventions, and the more optimistic the outcome.

Second, close attention should be given to collaborative efforts with school personnel and others who are in a position to help the child. While schools vary in their capacities to commit resources for special services to these children, collaboration with the school can be extremely productive. The behavior of the child is usually quite puzzling to the school staff. Many teachers have not heard of NLD. The therapist then has an opportunity to share information about the syndrome in general and the child in particular. Those who work with the child usually welcome an explanation for the inconsistent academic performance, social difficulties, and seeming unresponsiveness to aspects of the classroom routine. Teachers can be helped to analyze their classroom for nonverbal signals, ranging from such signals as when a teacher holds up his or her hand to request the class to be silent, to the frown he or she displays as a sign of disapproval. If teachers can remember to pair nonverbal signals with explicit verbal cues, the children are more apt to grasp the meanings the teacher is attempting to convey. When teachers can identify these nonverbal modes of communication, they can become aware of areas of potential miscommunication between them and the NLD child and expand the use of strategies to make sure the child understands the messages being sent. They can then avoid many pitfalls to which these children are prone (Badian 1992).

Direct instruction regarding nonverbal cues in the classroom can be of great benefit to children with NLD. It can provide them with an opportunity to learn essential real-life skills. If a special-education teacher is present in the classroom, he or she can point out the nonverbal signals to the child. Some teachers are able to review instances of miscommunication with peers as these are happening; they may then be in a position to help the child become more aware of his or her contribution to social interactions. If the child leaves the classroom for pull-out services, he or she can be taught how to figure out what is going on in the classroom by systematically noting the position of the teacher, the groupings of other children, the level of noise in the room, and so forth. Teachers' creative interventions can be the product of teamwork between the therapist and the educators who meet regularly to discuss the needs and capabilities of the child. No less important for teachers is an understanding of the effects of the disabilities on the child's personality. Insight into the erosive effects these disabilities have on the child's relationships can help the teacher to minimize the negative responses to the child.

Close contact, therefore, should be maintained with the school and with other specialists such as tutors, occupational therapists, and physical therapists. Consultation with a pediatric neurologist or child psychiatrist can clarify the extent to which medication is indicated or helpful in symptom relief particularly if, in addition, the child suffers from depression, severe anxiety, or attention deficit hyperactivity disorder (ADHD). Intervention in small therapeutic groups can demonstrate to the child some of the interactional problems between the child and peers as these emerge directly in the group. This type of data, which is unavailable to a therapist seeing the child individually, can be of great help in the development of strategies that can result in the modification of the child's behavior.

The popular approach of social skills training in groups may be a useful intervention when available. Such groups focus on inappropriate behaviors, helping children by modeling different social skills. Our limited experience with such groups indicates that it may not be as effective in the remediation of the children's NLD as would other modes of intervention, although they may be useful adjuncts to individual therapy. The reason appears to be that for children with NLD, learning to read nonverbal communications is much like learning a different language. It requires an approach that focuses on the child's communicative competencies, both receptive and expressive, as well as on the capacity to process the meanings of such communications (Nowicki and Duke 1992).

A critical part of any treatment plan is the careful review of the child's areas of strength, and the exploitation of those strengths to enhance the child's self-esteem and feelings of competence. For example, since children with NLD are often poorly coordinated, their athletic successes are usually limited. Some children may become competent in activities such as swimming, track, or karate, which require little team interaction and highlight one of the child's strengths. However, their strength in the verbal areas usually make them excellent candidates for other activities such as children's theater groups. In such settings, once the child overcomes his or her initial anxiety about the novel situation, the child can begin to enjoy recognition, or find momentary episodes of mirth and applause. Children who have musical talents can benefit from learning to play an instrument, to dance, or to sing. Other children with excellent memories can develop expertise in areas in which they can take pride. Real successes produce greater results in shorter periods of time than long-term psychotherapeutic interventions. The recognition of the child's accomplishments that comes from peers and adults can go much further in building a child's self-esteem than praise given by parents, which the child often discounts because it is considered as coming from a biased source. The inclusion of such activities within a broad treatment plan is essential to a final positive outcome.

It should be kept in mind that these children tend not to do well in structured or semistructured group activities. Scouting, competitive sports or games, and summer camping are usually not good avenues for them unless the programs are designed with special sensitivity to such a child's needs. These activities require levels of social skills these children do not possess. Involvement in them often leads to frustration and failure.

Indications for Individual Psychotherapy

Because this discussion centers on the population of children between ages 6 and 12, the issue of recommending individual psychotherapy is complex. The primary consideration is the usefulness of such an approach to children with these types of difficulties. Most of these children are in a good deal of pain. However, they feel that it is the world around them that needs modifying and not themselves. This view is not motivated by resistance to acknowledging the existence of problems. It reflects an inability to make the transition from their point of view to that of others. Often the children feel an unmovable conviction as to the correctness of their perspective; it may be impossible to win them over to a different perspective. These considerations aside, the real question is whether a therapeutic relationship can effect any change that will lead to the alleviation of the child's symptoms. Ultimately the decision to recommend individual psychotherapy must be made on the basis of the clinical judgment that the child can form an alliance with the therapist and that the process can help the child achieve some of the following goals:

1. manage the anxiety and depression he or she experiences;
2. attain a cognitive understanding of his or her neurocognitive deficits and their impact;
3. learn to decode social situations by observing some of the different ways he or she experiences others and the ways others experience him or her;
4. break out of the patterns of withdrawal and isolation by establishing a dialogue of shared meanings with the therapist;
5. deal with some of the repetitive narcissistic injuries that result from miscommunications with others.

Unless some of these goals are attainable, individual psychotherapy is not indicated. In addition, there are circumstances under which it would be wise to either defer or forgo making a recommendation for individual therapy. Among these circumstances are the following:

1. If the child is functioning adequately because the parents are currently providing the child with sufficient complementarity,

and if he or she is receiving and making use of a variety of interventions, such as tutoring, occupational therapy, and other supports, then it is advisable to schedule periodic reevaluation to determine whether the child is doing well or is in need of intervention.

2. If, following diagnosis, the child needs to experience some successes in academic areas prior to beginning to deal with the injuries and pain caused by his or her deficits, then a period of psychoeducational intervention is indicated prior to instituting treatment.
3. If the child is currently receiving support from several resources and many professionals are involved, the addition of still another person in the child's life may be experienced either as a burden or as someone who is indistinguishable from others. Treatment should then be deferred to a more propitious time. Under these circumstances, providing guidance to the parents may have a greater overall impact than seeing the child individually.
4. If the child's defenses are well integrated into the child's character structure so that the child is functioning reasonably well within the narrow confines of the domain he or she has chosen, then, although it would appear that the child has arrived at a premature closure to his or her development, it may be best to leave well enough alone and postpone intervening.
5. If the family's dynamics or circumstances are such that the child's involvement in treatment may threaten a tenuous balance within the family, either a different modality or a postponement of treatment ought to be recommended.
6. If the therapist feels shut out by the child, so that no matter how hard the therapist tries to enter the child's world, no access seems available, the wisdom of psychotherapeutic intervention at that moment ought to be evaluated carefully. Alternatives such as educational therapy, art therapy, dance therapy, children's theater, or other interventions need to be considered. After the child has had some successes and positive experiences in other contexts, he or she may be ready for the task of examining what he or she does that contributes to derailing dialogues.

The Child's Experience

Therapists obtain an understanding of the child's self-narrative through the behaviors, fantasies, and play the child displays in the therapeutic setting. Once individual treatment is initiated, it is imperative that the therapist enter into the child's world to experience what the child experiences. With a clear understanding of the child's specific deficits, the therapist can begin to form a picture of the way in which the child's world is structured and the means through which the child tries to cope with the deficits. Through this understanding the therapist will become immersed in the themes and motifs that organize the child's narrative. The following is a composite, based on our experience with some of these children, of how a child with NLD would experience the world. We will assume these to be the experiences of an 8-year-old boy:

1. From the earliest days, the child had no reason to doubt that his perceptions were correct reflections of the world around him. Yet experiences did not validate his perceptions. Physical objects around him did not respond in a predictable manner. He found himself bumping into things he thought he was avoiding. He spilled his milk trying to reach for it, he misjudged heights when jumping from steps, he could not hold his crayons to draw, and could not put puzzles together. These failures led him to distrust himself in situations that involved manual dexterity or physical agility.
2. His confusion was compounded by the criticism he received from caregivers. He found it hard to understand why they were being so hard on him. Children avoided or stigmatized him. He felt he was always being treated unfairly. In response he often fought back, protesting that they were picking on him. Eventually he found himself in so much trouble that it seemed easier to withdraw into solitary play or watching television.
3. As he got older the world became a place where satisfactions were difficult to obtain. The world was unrewarding, unpredictable, and unintelligible. He tried to memorize rules that would explain how people were supposed to behave, but then

was mystified about when they applied and when they did not. Yet part of him very much longed for contact with others. He occasionally made forays to befriend someone, hoping for different responses from those he had received in the past. For a while things would go smoothly, but then, inexplicably, relationships would fall apart, and he once more would be thrown into his former isolation.

4. Given this unpredictability, he felt that he must exercise great caution in negotiating situations. His anxieties escalated. Soon he became fearful of many situations and unfamiliar places. He could not organize his perceptual world to be sure of where he was or how to find his way back from where he came. Since he could never quite get his bearing and could not follow directions, he started refusing to go to neighbors' homes or to stay on overnights at friends' homes. Even going upstairs in his own home to get ready to go to bed became fraught with pitfalls. He also developed night fears, and fears of going down into the basements or of going to rooms in different floors of the house. He began to require someone to accompany him and to stay with him at bedtime until he fell asleep. He insisted that his parents not leave him with babysitters, fearing that the parents would get into serious accidents or die. He would then be bereft of their help.
5. His parents became increasingly impatient with these fears. Not only did they not understand them, but they also began to force him into the very dangers he wished to avoid. He developed a terrible sense of uncertainty as to the responses he was likely to receive from them. He feared he would be punished or criticized. The only defense left was to fight back or to withdraw from all activity. If he withdrew, he became more passive and more unmotivated, losing interest or curiosity in any activities. Television became the focus of his life. The world of fantasy was more inviting than reality. If he fought back because he felt that his life depended on opposing the tasks imposed on him, he was punished. His parents could not understand how endangered he felt. He resorted to violent tantrums or assaultive behavior to make his point. But these responses only led to more severe counterresponses.

6. His school performance was below his own expectations, bringing disappointment to him and his parents. While he was convinced that he was smarter than many of the kids in his class, he felt that he was never given the chance to demonstrate his capabilities. Alternatively, he concluded that he was "dumb," incapable of doing the work or of succeeding in school. Feeling unrewarded, he became school-avoidant, since that setting represented a world filled with painful and unmanageable situations.
7. At times one of the parents, usually his mother, provided some solace. She was able to make things comprehensible for him. She verbally translated situations so that they no longer appeared as unintelligible or dangerous. It then became imperative that she be his constant companion. Without her intercessions, chaos ensued; only she could restore the good feelings necessary to regain a sense of security.
8. In totally familiar situations, things were not as bad as when he was exposed to new settings or routines. New settings evoked a feeling of estrangement and disorientation. It was like entering a Halloween haunted house. He could not gain a footing as to where he was or the significance of what surrounded him. He tried to pick up clues through other than visual means to guide him. Yet these were not enough. Consequently, powerful anxieties were stirred up and the wish to escape from them overwhelmed him.
9. Experiences with people and situations often made no logical sense. The attempt to process occurrences were defeated by his inability to find connections between discrete happenings. Causal relationships eluded him. He experienced adults and peers as unreasonable, as acting entirely arbitrarily. At other times he found adults to be more receptive to listening to him than were his peers. He therefore got into the habit of approaching adults he met with the expectation that he could befriend them. He experienced no stranger anxiety; to the contrary, the conversations with adults willing to listen were very gratifying.
10. He understood the world of feelings only intellectually, because people talked about feelings. But to him it was like a

foreign language. Only when feelings reach a threshold of intensity that led to an eruption could he find himself having a feeling. Most often those feelings were rage, frustration, and terror. Otherwise, he lived in a gray world, lacking the colors associated with modulated emotional states.

Case Illustration: Matt

Matt was a 9½-year-old boy at the time of referral. His parents asked for help because of a long history of problems in school. Their concerns were that at this time they were having an increasingly difficult time managing his behavior. The school was complaining that he was a serious behavior problem. They stated that everything revolves around him, everything has to be on his terms; that he is rigid, will not bend on any aspect of his behavior; that he has no respect for authority, so teachers avoid confrontations because he "loses it" when caught in minor infractions of the rules, and then no amount of reasoning works when he is so upset. Academically, teachers were complaining that he seems inattentive, but usually knows the answers, his handwriting is almost illegible, reading is a problem, and in gym he has trouble because his eye-hand coordination is so poor. In addition, he does not do well with peers, and when teased doesn't understand.

Matt had his first evaluation by a neurologist at 4 years of age. The neurologist found that he had fine and gross motor delays, low muscle tone, low confidence level, fear of climbing, had difficulty with rapid alternating movements, mild choreoathetoses, a movement disorder, and mild dystonia. In addition his attention was poor, he "stared off," was overactive and exuberant. He also was found to have a café-au-lait spot. The diagnosis given at the time was attention deficit disorder. Occupational therapy was recommended. Multiple evaluations followed; all came to similar conclusions. Trials of medicating with Ritalin produced no improvement. The occupational therapy, which lasted for three years, led to improved motor control in some areas.

At age 10 the latest psychoeducational testing revealed a 38-point discrepancy between his Verbal and Performance IQ on the WISC

III. His Verbal IQ was 120, while his Performance IQ was 82. In the nonverbal areas he was found to have poor spatial relation, poor visual-motor integration, poor visual figure/ground discrimination, poor visual closure, and poor spatial construction. He was given a diagnosis of a nonverbal learning disability.

In the initial diagnostic sessions Matt presented as a likable, verbal child who sat and talked the entire session. His eyes wandered all over the room while he talked and he made little eye contact. When asked a question he appeared not to be listening, but then would go on to answer it. His responses, however, had the quality of a monologue rather than a dialogue. As he talked he revealed the following as his experience of the world. Kids at school pick on him constantly. But he is used to it, so he tries to outsmart them to avoid their insults. He gets back at them by tripping them up when they walk by him in class. The teachers are unfair. They always punish him, but they overlook what other kids do to him. Sometimes he gets so mad that he will get into fights with kids. He doesn't like to do that because he gets blamed for the fighting. The teachers don't notice that the other kids started it all. He has only one friend who sides with him and protects him from other kids' attacks. Otherwise, he likes school because he does well in reading and math. The problem is that his handwriting is bad, so he ends up not doing well in his best subject—English.

He gets mad at his parents because they are always limiting what he wants to do. He ends up screaming at them that they're not fair. But they don't listen. "They don't know the word 'Yes!' All they know is 'No, No, No!!'" They punish him by sending him up to his room and he ends up there for hours. When asked whether the punishments were really that severe, he acknowledged that they seemed so to him. Mostly, he argues with them about watching TV. He loves basketball and wants to watch every game. They don't understand that. So when they send him to bed before the game is over, he ends up furious at them.

Asked about some good experiences, he recalled going to Space Camp with his father. He loved the experience. He learned the names of every space mission, the names of the rockets, the astronauts that manned them, and the dates they were launched. He had an overwhelming amount of information on the subject, which he eagerly shared. In fact it was difficult to get him to discuss anything else once he got going on this topic.

Once-a-week therapy was recommended to interrupt the cycle of negative responses and help him gain a better understanding of the nature of his learning disabilities. Part of the treatment plan included an initial school conference with everyone involved with Matt, meetings with the mother every other week as well as being available to her on the phone whenever management problems occurred, a recommendation for an updating of the psychoeducational testing, and referral to a tutor who specializes in the educational problems of children with nonverbal learning disabilities.

NATURE OF TRANSFERENCE

A confounding factor for therapists who treat children with learning disabilities is the distinction between a child's responses based on transference and those based on the child's search for complementarity. While sharp differentiations cannot be made, some distinctions are possible that would help therapists in making interventions. The child suffers from two types of deficits that often cannot be distinguished: selfobject deficits and cognitive deficits. Each has its own history and its own associated set of symptoms. Each leads the child to look to others to fill these in. Cognitive deficits do not result from disruption in relationships but from the child's endowment or innate givens. Selfobject deficits arise from the complex interplay between what the child brings to the relationship and the responses of significant others to what they experience the child as expressing. The child, through his or her innate givens, contributes significantly to the shape of the relationship with caregivers. For their part, caregivers who are unaware of the child's deficits respond to what they believe the child to be requesting. The failure in the dialogue results in the child's experience of the parents as unempathic. The therapist must be attuned to the subtle or not so subtle miscommunications that inevitably arise in the transference.

Yet the two sets of deficits, the cognitive and selfobject deficits, are inextricably entwined in their emergence in the therapeutic setting. The problem therapists face is how to distinguish between the two and what are appropriate responses and interventions to each (Palombo 1987). The following is a clear example of a child's cognitive problem with fluid reasoning in which the therapist chose to deal with the cognitive issues.

Case Illustration: Paula

Paula, age 8, came in one day complaining bitterly to her therapist that her brother was calling her names. When asked what he had said, she replied that he had greeted her with "Hey, girl!" As a result they got into a big fight. In talking about the incident, Paula and her therapist reconstructed how Paula felt and what she thought. Her explanation was that since her brother knows who she is and knows her name, the only reason he would not use her name was that he was being mean or was mad at her.

Rather than deal with the transference meanings in this recital, the therapist addressed the cognitive confusion. He asked her if she had heard anybody else being called "Hey, girl!" She answered that she had, a few times, and it had always confused her, but since it didn't have anything to do with her directly, she didn't think about it. Had her brother called anyone else "Hey, girl!"? She answered that he had done that to her cousins. When asked if he liked his cousins, she replied that he did. But she still didn't connect with the idea that he might not be mad at her or at them when he says that.

In the next session, Paula's therapist took a different tack, realizing that what she wasn't getting was the idea that something could stand for something else. He asked if she knew about nicknames. He walked her through several nicknames until they found one that wasn't a real name. Although Paula softened in her stand, she still wanted to know how "Girl" could be a nickname for an individual person, since it could stand for lots of people. The therapist talked with Paula about a 2-year-old she knew who was just learning to talk and who might say "Paula-girl" or "Jenny-girl." Paula could accept that possibility, but wondered why her 10-year-old brother, who knew how to talk, would still say "Girl." But by this time, Paula had exercised enough options that her thinking was no longer so rigid and automatic. Going through the process made it harder for her to stick with her initial interpretation as the only possibility.

The issue of the relative weight to give the caregivers' responses versus brain dysfunction in the emergence of the symptoms is at the heart of the distinction between deficits related to responses experienced as unempathic and those related to neurocognitive dysfunctions. This is true not only for children with NLD but for all children who have complex developmental timetables. Since, as therapists, our focus is always on the transference, the question can be posed as follows: Can we as therapists distinguish between behaviors that are "brain driven" (hence, unmotivated) from behaviors that are motivated by conscious or unconscious factors and hence will manifest as transference reactions? If we could answer this question, we would be well on our way to defining appropriate interventions and gaining a better understanding of these children.

An analogy can be drawn between the behaviors these children present and the behaviors of a person who has suffered a stroke or closed head injury. We do not attribute a motive to an aphasic who either cannot express his/her thoughts or understand verbal communications and would not look for transference meanings to these responses in a treatment relationship. We simply recognize that the symptoms are directly related to the brain injury the person suffered. However, all people with such injuries continue to have motives that impel their behaviors; for example, they continue to desire closeness to others or defend against such wishes. These motives may also be entwined with unconscious desires that they themselves do not recognize. These will manifest themselves within the transference. In such instances, it may difficult to sort out what is motivated from what is unmotivated. For children with NLD, the situation is as complex, if not more so, because of their developmental problems. Testing does help make some differentiations, but primarily at the level of the elements that enter into the processing of information, that is, visual-spatial difficulties or difficulties with the reception, expression, and processing of nonverbal social cues. These findings do not help us penetrate further below the surface to the other factors that may indeed be motivated, although carefully interpreted projectives can be helpful. Compensations and complementarities only confound the picture further.

Since the child has little or no awareness of his or her own deficits, the burden falls upon the therapist to make the distinction and to respond differentially. Problems arise less at the extremes than in the middle ground. When a child clearly transposes onto the therapist attitudes that were not invoked by the therapist and manifests patterns of interaction that occurred with significant others, such episodes bear the clear imprint of transference. But when a child asks the therapist to accompany him or her to the bathroom because the series of corridors the child has to negotiate to get to the destination are totally disorienting, it is an injustice to the child to attribute such a request to regressive motives or transference. The request does have meanings to the child based on past interactions, however. But in most situations these meanings are not clear-cut, so considerable overlap exists between them. The therapist's focus and the context must help determine the proper intervention. Ultimately, a differentiation may be made by observing the results of interpretations of such behaviors. An interpretation may attenuate the effects of selfobject deficits. But no interpretation modifies the cognitive deficits; only compensations or new skills can do that.

The Therapeutic Process

There are a number of features that distinguish the therapeutic process with children with NLD from that with other children. First, since most children with nonverbal learning disabilities tend to miss subtle social cues, verbal mediation takes on an important role in conveying the therapist's meaning. The therapist must pay close attention to all nonverbal channels to make sure that the child understands the meanings the therapist intends to convey. Gestures often need to be made with broader strokes than usual. It may be necessary to tactfully ask the child to make eye contact so as not to miss facial expressions. Since the child has difficulty reading between the lines, making inferences, and understanding humor and the double meaning of expressions, these must be clarified with specific examples from the child's experience. Sometimes the therapist will need to verbally explain his or her nonverbal communications to the child. This is an opportunity for the very impaired child to learn this new language. Similarly, many children benefit from having their own nonverbal signals labeled verbally so that they know what their faces and bodies are communicating to others. Sometimes a child will express surprise at the disparity between the message he or she meant to give and what the therapist understood him or her to be conveying.

Second, the child with NLD is an unreliable informant as to what transpires in his or her life. While it is most important to convey to the child the sense that the therapist believes what the child experiences, it is often the case that the child has missed so much of the interaction with others that it can be impossible to get a clear picture of what occurred from the account he or she gives. When reporting an event, the child's account is likely to be disconnected, fragmentary, and confused, and the recital may be devoid of feeling. Alternatively, the child's expressions of feeling are likely to be exaggerated or unmodulated, leaving the impression of a dissynchrony between the feelings and the content. Often the child cannot pick out the main points from the supporting details, the relevant from the irrelevant, or organize a coherent narrative. He or she may grasp one aspect of the total picture and miss the broader gestalt. This presents a difficult technical problem to therapist who must rely on the child's communication to learn about day-to-day events. The experience of those who work with these children is that it is wise to remain in constant contact with the caregivers, and to bring them into the sessions as often as necessary to have them clarify significant events if they can.

Nonetheless, some children with strong verbal skills and severe nonverbal disabilities may be able to relate the verbal aspects of their social interchanges with considerable accuracy, but simply fail to take note of the relevant nonverbal cues—an omission that probably led them astray in the original interaction. The therapist can replay the scene using different tones of voice, facial expressions, gestures, and interpersonal distance to help the child fill in the picture. The therapist can also uncover the set of overly rigid rules the child may have acquired to cope with his or her confusion about the world. Often the child feels injured when he or she uses these rules and finds them unhelpful. The therapist can create an atmosphere in which these are jointly examined and playfully modified so as to enhance the child's communicative skills and fluid reasoning.

Third, while play occupies a central position in the therapeutic process with most latency-age children, this is not generally true of children with NLD. There are multiple reasons for these children's lack of interest in play or inability to play. Some cannot play because of the rigidity or concreteness of their approach to situations, or they may not be able to engage in unstructured imaginative interactions that are nonverbal in content. Other children prefer to use their strengths in verbalization to relate to the therapist. The therapy can take on an adult-like character that may lead the therapist to overestimate the child's capacity to work through his or her problems verbally. Keeping in mind that this is the child's preferred mode of communication, the therapist must beware of the dangers of intellectualization at the expense of dealing with the child's feelings. On the one hand, the therapist can, through verbal interchanges, reframe issues so as to introduce some flexibility in the child's way of thinking. Since most children with NLD are not used to considering that there are several options for understanding their experiences, learning to do so in the safety of the relationship with the therapist can produce significant shifts in the way they approach the world. On the other hand, since they are unable to deal with feelings at the verbal level the introduction of imaginative play or fantasy may help give them a channel for their expression. An indication of progress would then be their ability to participate in imaginative play. However, some children go through the whole course of successful treatment without taking this step.

Fourth, therapy with children with NLD—like that with most children with learning deficits—usually must include helping the child come to some useful understanding of his or her disabilities. This understanding occurs through a gradual process of working through. While simple didactic explanations may be helpful for some children, they are often not sufficient. The issue must be revisited at different stages in the treatment with different goals for each step.

Most children enter therapy having had numerous experiences of being frustrated because of their learning disabilities. If they had received no explanations as to why they have had so much trouble or why they were receiving special help in school, they are in the dark as to the source of their difficulties. Even if they had been told about their learning disabilities, they often come away feeling that they have been told that something is wrong with them; they do not have a clear cognitive grasp of the nature of their difficulties. In part, this is because the explanations themselves may have constituted injuries to which they responded by "not hearing" what was being said. In larger part, it is because the words alone are difficult for the child to translate into an integrated understanding of the deficits. With the assistance of the test results and the direct experience with the child, the therapist is able to "educate" the child about the nature of his or difficulties. Such explanations occur in the context of the therapeutic relationship. The most powerful explanations come when the therapist can concretely demonstrate to the child how the deficits impede what is happening in the clinical setting, whether it be the construction of a project, the child's recital of an event at school, or a failed communication between the therapist and child.

Conversely, demonstrations of the child's strengths and affirmations of the child's capacities are essential to the child's self-esteem. When the child reports instances of frustration or failure in school or social settings, the therapist can help the child understand those in terms of his or her learning difficulties and assets. The child may need similar help in understanding successful instances, too. For many children, the goal is to provide them with a clear enough understanding and acceptance that they can become self-advocates, helping to structure the learning situations in a manner they feel is suitable to them. As self-confident children who are clear about their learning styles, they can become active participants in planning their own educational and social interventions.

Case Illustration: Robert

Robert, age 9, came into therapy convinced he was stupid. He struggled in school, particularly in math and writing. He compared himself to other kids in his class and found himself severely wanting. Other kids noticed his embarrassment and found him to be a good target for teasing. He had a vague idea that he'd been labeled, but did not understand what "learning disability" meant, nor how to identify his own disabilities. Once an alliance was established, the therapist approached the subject of his disability. Robert listened with growing interest when his therapist told him that he had many strengths, such as a good vocabulary and a good ability to remember what he had heard. Robert was then able to give examples of instances when he had used those strengths. He listened with considerable discomfort but also considerable recognition when his therapist talked about the things that were hard for him, such as making sense of what he saw or making his hand move a pencil the way he wanted when writing. The therapist talked with Robert about ways in which he had used verbal explanations to make sense of visual experiences and reminded him, "When you said the numbers out loud, you remembered them better than when you just saw them on paper." While it was clear that this didactic explanation only touched the surface, Robert showed a measure of relief at gaining that understanding.

Whenever an opportunity arose, the therapist helped Robert work on both the receptive and the expressive aspects of nonverbal communication that interfered with Robert's being understood and understanding other people. For example, when his gestures and facial expression in the therapy room did not match what he was saying, she gently and tactfully pointed that out to him, gradually raising his level of consciousness about these nonverbal indicators. The explanation was given that these were harder for him to observe and he had to think about them more explicitly if he wanted to be sure people understood him. The discussion could then move on to talking about his puzzlement when he felt the teacher's facial expressions did not match her words.

Over the next year, as he talked about his school experiences the discussions focused on how his disabilities specifically fit into the ways he learned from school materials. When he spoke of his struggles with handwriting, the therapist could convey easy acceptance, stating that task would of course be harder for him than he would wish, but the question was how to help him find ways to manage the task. They worked at separating out his experience of frustration over the process of writing from his experience of having good ideas he wished to communicate. The therapist helped him think about compensations, such as use of the computer. She followed up these discussions with contacts with teachers and parents to make sure that the suggestions were implemented successfully. She legitimized his feelings that math speed tests were painful as they did not provide a good measure of his competency. Since his math teacher required all students to take such tests weekly, Robert was helped to develop a defensive stance that allowed him to survive those tests without feeling that it was his fault that he could not demonstrate how well he could do. Eventually, his parents provided him with a math tutor to help shore up his skills. When Robert was ready to enter middle school, he was given a voice in deciding which math class he would take. He chose a slower-paced class in which the teacher used a step-by-step approach that was more suitable for him.

By the end of the second year of therapy, when he found himself disciplined by a teacher for an infraction he did not understand, Robert discussed the problem with his therapist, concluding "I'd do better if the teacher would give me a warning first, telling me what I'm doing wrong!" The therapist agreed to call the teacher to lay the groundwork for Robert to talk to her. This became an opportunity for the therapist to discuss NLD with her and to point out the importance of verbal cues in communicating with Robert. The teacher and Robert then talked, agreeing that the teacher would give Robert verbal signals when he was doing something wrong and when he was doing something right. Robert felt greatly empowered by this negotiation, feeling that it provided him with an avenue for problem solving that was not available to him previously.

When treatment is instituted, one goal is to produce a shift in the themes or motifs—the patterns that guide the child's conduct—that provide the motives for much of the child's behavior and are part of the plot of the child's narrative. For some children a theme or motif might be, "Everybody hates me!" or "I can't do it, it's too hard!" or "I'm scared, don't leave me!" or "Everybody thinks I'm dumb. I can't do anything right!" By replacing such motifs with other motifs, the child can begin to dialogue with others, to experience a greater sense of self cohesion, and to achieve a more integrated self-narrative. Only through such a shift may we be assured of the permanence of changes in motives. The means through which this modification is achieved are educational, corrective, and/or interpretive.

The younger the child, the less likely it is that he or she would be able to obtain insights into his or her psychodynamics or relationship patterns or even gain cognitive understanding of the neurocognitive deficits. In that case, the goals are to alleviate the child's symptoms of overwhelming anxiety, negatively toned interactions with others, and poor self-esteem. This is possible through the help the child receives to develop compensatory strategies, the enhancement of complementarity with others, medication, or other means. These goals may be carried out simultaneously.

MOMENTS

It is wise not to conceptualize the trajectory of the therapy with these children as having a beginning, middle, and end, as one would ordinarily expect in insight-oriented child therapy. In part this is because the child's problems are not simply the result of regression or fixation but part of the child's psychic makeup; in part it is because the therapeutic tasks must be conceptualized differently. The therapeutic process can be conceptualized as including three types of "moments" (Pine 1985): the concordant moments, the complementary moments, and the disjunctive moments (Palombo 1985b, Racker 1968). We use the term *moments* to describe nodal aspects of the process that occur during sessions at any phase of treatment. These moments consist of specific interactions in the dialogue between therapist and child. They do not necessarily occur sequentially but arise episodically, at which times they become organizing events that capture for the therapist the essence of the issues with which the child is struggling. As such, they present opportunities for the therapist to intervene through supportive statements, interpretations, or other interventions.

Concordant Moments

These are the moments when maintaining empathic contact with the child's experience is in the foreground of the process. During such moments, the therapist becomes attuned to the child's experience and its meaning. The therapist can then catch a glimpse of the ways the child experiences and organizes his or her perceptions. In such moments the therapist may be able to see how the child's learning disabilities filter the messages the child receives and how he or she processes information. The world as the child experiences it emerges. Valuable insight is gained into the personal and idiosyncratic meanings the child draws from those experiences, meanings that were integrated into patterns that are motifs or organizing features of the child's self narrative. During such moments, the therapist may focus on maintaining a "holding environment" to help the child feel safe in dealing with his or her feelings and thoughts, however idiosyncratic they may be. The therapist may struggle to be a "container" for the child's anxiety or rage. Often in these moments, the only interventions necessary are the quiet understanding the therapist conveys by listening to the child or some soothing comments that mirror the child's experience.

By establishing an empathic connection with the child's experience and creating a holding environment, the therapist's concordant responses have the effect of allaying the child's anxiety. For example, the therapist's verbal description of the sense of abandonment the child experiences on the playground when other kids avoid him or her can enhance concordant moments. The therapist verbally mediates on the one hand and concretely expresses in action on the other by being available to the child. As a result of such shared experiences, the child's most crippling anxiety symptoms can improve quite dramatically over a short period of time. The child can cease feeling all alone in his or her distress and can use the therapist as a container for the anxiety. The rage and frustration at not being understood are modulated, and the child can make a better integration of new experiences than had been possible previously.

During these concordant moments the therapist provides a corrective emotional experience to the child. The therapist becomes someone who contains the child's anxiety, who does not get angry at the child's confusion, and who does not abandon the child in the face of difficulties. The therapist is always guided by an awareness of the child's neurocognitive weaknesses and their impact as well as by an appreciation of the ways interactions with others evolved.

Case Illustration: Patrick

Treatment with 7-year-old Patrick began with the therapist wondering what it felt like to be this child, whose neurocognitive deficits led him to process the world in the way he did. In many ways, Patrick made this first step easy, because he wanted to play school. Patrick became the teacher while the therapist was the child. First came math class. As Patrick wrote out the math problems with numbers out of alignment, signs unclear, and problems virtually on top of each other, the therapist was completely confused. She played out experiencing what it must be like for him to be confronted with such a task. She dramatized how inept and incompetent she felt, how befuddled she was. Patrick and the therapist repeated the school game trying to draw maps, with Patrick as the teacher chastising the therapist for not remembering which way was east and which way was west, a hopeless task given that the instructor changed directions with each map. The therapist played out how desolate she felt being a child with these kinds of difficulties, trying her best to please the teacher. Patrick's relief in feeling that someone could connect with this kind of world was palpable. He was reassured that he was not totally isolated; someone finally knew what it feels like to be in that place. The therapist was becoming a container for his anxiety and could dramatize his feelings by playing out these experiences. For the therapist, however, the experiences did not lead to her disintegration the way they did when Patrick attempted the tasks. He could then begin to look at himself. By observing the therapist and directing her, he could indirectly become aware of some of his own patterns. Her difficulties mirrored his experiences.

Complementary Moments

These are moments when positive or negative transference issues gain ascendancy. The child attempts to establish or restore a sense of cohesion by having the therapist complement both selfobject and neurocognitive deficits. In these moments, sorting the patterns that drive the transference from those that simply reflect the neurocognitive deficits is very difficult. Depending on the child and the stage in treatment, a variety of interventions are appropriate during such moments, ranging from support to clarification to interpretation.

To address the problems in the areas of visual-spatial relationships and visual orientation, the first steps are helping the child become aware of his or her confusion when encountering tasks that require those functions and assisting the child in the management of his or her anxiety when confronting perplexing situations. Once aware of that confusion, the child may be able to use alternative means to compensate for the deficits. At times, greater attention to visual cues can lead to compensations. For example, some learning can take place by habituating the child to associate some other source of stimulation, such as a mole on one hand or watch on the left wrist, with his right hand or his left hand, thus allowing the child to make the necessary adjustments when needing to follow directions. The child can also learn to consciously verbalize the steps necessary for nonverbal activities and to verbally anticipate changes that are about to take place. These strategies, in concert with the help the child receives in school through academic remediation, can be very constructive in ameliorating the child's symptoms. Only the creativity of the therapist and the learning disability specialist limits the variety of compensations to which the child can be exposed. Some children, however, are much more adept at finding ways in which to compensate than are other children. It is not clear why this might be so; it is an area that requires further exploration.

Areas other than those of visual spatial relationships may become the focus of discussion. We discussed previously the children's problems with fluid reasoning and their misinterpretations of situations because of their rigid, often concrete thinking. In the example of Paula, given above, her problem stemmed from the rigid application of a rule to all context indiscriminately. Her inability to contextualize the remark led to her misinterpretation. The therapist was able to help her realize that there were other possible interpretations of her brother's remark.

Often therapists will feel a strong urge to fill in the child's deficits. The therapist can recognize that these feelings reflect the child's frustrations with his or her areas of dysfunction and longings for a response that would bring some relief. When the positive transference is in the foreground, the therapist may be moved to complement the child's social and cognitive deficits by providing the child with missing functions related to the learning disability. This activates the child's hope that someone is there who understands. At other times, the therapist may wish to demonstrate to the child that the therapist is not like others in the child's milieu who get angry, set impossible expectations, or punish for nonconformity. The therapist then provides a corrective experience to the child.

On the other hand, when the organizing motifs in the child's narrative emerge, the child brings to the therapy a set of expectations about the world based on previous experience. The child expects the therapist's anxiety to be aroused by his or her anxiety and helplessness. When a firm alliance with the child exists, it is possible to help the child begin to look at his or her own contribution to the derailed dialogue. By taking examples from the treatment relationship, the therapist can illustrate for the child how cues were missed and how information was distorted within a shared experience. Depending on the age of the child and on the child's cognitive capacities, such interpretations may be taken in by the child and may begin to help the child understand some of the reasons for his or her confusion.

There are times, particularly early in the treatment, when the negative transference dominates the interaction. During such moments, the therapist must keep in mind that the child is experiencing the therapist as the child had experienced others in his or her context. The child attempts to create a complementarity between his expectations and the therapist's responses based on the child's experiences with others in the past. Only if the therapist is driven to actually replicate past experiences with the child will the child's despair be mobilized. If that occurs, the stage is set for a rupture in the relationship, a derailment of the dialogue, or a disjunction in the treatment. Otherwise, these moments provide an opportunity for the therapist to deliberately alter the patterns in which he or she has been caught by responding to the child in a different fashion. The child is then in a position to develop compensatory strategies to deal with the deficits that caused the problems.

Alternatively, the child may expect the therapist to take over, but then, no matter how the therapist responds, experiences the therapist as not being helpful. In either case, the ultimate expectation is abandonment. The child enacts in treatment situations that re-create this scene. When the therapist responds differently to this negative transference, there emerges a powerful opportunity to alter the child's story. The opportunity presents itself to shift the motif from the child feeling helpless to that of becoming a proactive explorer and experimenter in a world that is exciting and potentially gratifying. This shift may be made through the metaphor of the play themes that the child enacts in the sessions. Through these activities the therapist not only models for the child the ways in which to approach problem solving, but also presents alternative experiences that could help the child conceive of himself or herself as experimenting rather than fumbling and as exploring rather than being disoriented. All these issues are worked through when the child re-creates moments in his or her life that are reminiscent of the motifs that organized his or her sense of helplessness.

Case Illustration: Mary

Mary, age 7½, and her therapist made fortune tellers and paper airplanes, activities that were popular with her peer group and hence very important to Mary. The fortune tellers were complicated and particularly difficult for Mary. She could not follow the numerous steps involved in making them. The task was challenging to both the therapist and to Mary, who became confused when the therapist had trouble remembering how to make them. The therapist remained calm, again serving as a container for her own anxiety. The therapist modeled a problem-solving approach, reframing the task as one in which both were experimenters trying to solve a problem. The therapist hoped to thus undo Mary's expectation that the only alternatives were for immediate success or no hope for success whatsoever. Once they figured out how to make the fortune tellers, the therapist accompanied the task with a running verbal commentary while Mary tried to make them herself. The intent was to provide her with a compensatory strategy that she could subsequently use herself. When in the next session the therapist asked Mary to show her again how to make the fortune tellers, the therapist verbalized once more each step as she performed the task. At times the therapist had to provide verbal instruction prior to a step Mary had forgotten. The therapist felt she was consciously reinforcing the image of Mary as someone who could perform the task while also reinforcing the strategy of verbal mediation. As they turned to making and flying the paper airplanes, that activity gave the therapist another chance to provide Mary with a metaphor that she could carry with her in working on other challenges. She interpreted the activity as one in which Mary and she were experimenters who tried things out to see which approaches work.

Disjunctive Moments

Disjunctions occur when the dialogue between the child and the therapist becomes derailed. The therapist must distinguish these disjunctions from negative transference reactions. Negative transference reactions occur as a result of the child experiencing the present as re-creating the past, while disjunctions occur because of a different set of dynamics. The primary dynamic that creates disjunctions is the experience of being injured by something the therapist did or said or the absence of a wished for response from the therapist. For the patient such incidents represent failures in empathy. If the therapist is unable to fill in the selfobject function required by the patient, for whatever reason, the patient will experience that incapacity as an intentional assault. In a sense, the therapist's motives are irrelevant; only the effect on the patient is relevant. Such disjunctions become crises in the treatment that require repair to make further work possible. For example, there are moments when the frustration and rage that has accumulated in the child from years of feeling isolated and misunderstood may surface in the relationship with the therapist. The therapist in turn responds with impatience, anger, puzzlement, or distancing. Such moments inevitably occur, and need not be interpreted as therapeutic failures. Rather they represent opportunities for the child and therapist to work through an important interaction. The child's rage at others must be distinguished from the frustration and rage the child may feel toward the therapist. While both are understandable, the therapist must be able to look at and acknowledge any contribution he or she has made to provoking the child's response. That piece of reality must first be addressed before the transference dimensions can be dealt with.

A different type of disjunctive moment occurs when the therapist tells the child that he or she wants to meet with the child's teacher. If a child has managed to keep the appointments with the therapist a secret from everyone except the immediate family, the child may experience the therapist's request as a serious threat to his or her privacy. Some children can meet the suggestion that the therapist talk to his teacher with a full-scale tantrum, alternatively sobbing and yelling, begging that the therapist not do this. Reassurance and close coordination with the parents and the teacher can eventually pull the therapist and the child through the crisis. Such an event can become the beginning of a long, gradual process culminating in the child's ability to talk in a rather objective fashion about learning problems and styles as well as the teaching styles that work best and the ones that do not.

Case Illustration: John

A major disjunction occurred early in John's treatment when his therapist referred him for psychological testing. Despite the experienced testing psychologist's best efforts, John, age 9, found the process to be an assaultive experience. He felt betrayed by the therapist for having imposed this task on him. John's therapist received his fury with calmness and respect. She allowed him to play the role of the merciless examiner who repeatedly asked her to do impossible test-like tasks. When she passed his test of being able to tolerate experiencing what he experienced, it then became possible to reconnect with him. The therapist could then verbalize the affective and cognitive contents of his experience. Much later they were able to discuss the test findings and demonstrate to him its usefulness to his teachers, his parents, and himself.

We see then, that as the therapist responds differently from the way others have, a new set of experiences is generated for the child.

This new set of experiences lays the groundwork for what is to be curative in the process. The child's incomplete or faulty processing of others' responses leads to responses that others in turn cannot understand. Others respond to the child's faulty responses. Finally, the child responds to others' responses with what seem to be totally inappropriate responses. A vicious circle is established in which it is impossible to conduct a dialogue. In treatment, the child experiences patterns that are different from those he or she resorted to in the past, and gains an understanding of the old patterns through the therapist's interpretations. The child is then in a position to compensate for his or her deficits. The child not only creates a new theme or motif in his or her narrative, but also looks upon the narrative in a different light. The new patterns include the meanings of past experiences and the new meanings gained through the relationship with the therapist. The understanding the child acquires through this set of shared experiences with the therapist serves to break through the child's former isolation. Patterns and motifs that were central in the configuration of the narrative are reshaped. New motifs come into play and the child's expectations are modified. These new motifs give the child greater hope for success than he or she had in the past.

The evidence for the greater integration of the child's experiences is found in the greater coherence of the child's self-narrative. Themes that formerly reflected the construe of personal meanings now encompass a set of shared meanings that grew out of the child's maturation and experiences in therapy. It is difficult to point to specific events or interventions that produce this greater sense of coherence; it usually results from the cumulative effects of the implementation of the broad treatment plan. The child's rehabilitation and restoration to better function can be credited to the combination of greater parental understanding, appropriate school programming, improved social functioning, and the therapist's educative, corrective, and interpretive efforts.

COUNTERTRANSFERENCE

It is useful to review some of the kinds of countertransference problems children with nonverbal learning disabilities present. Therapists at times experience extreme frustration at what they perceive to be a child's resistance to treatment. They may then resort to power struggles or to punitive measures in an attempt to involve the child. What therapists must keep in mind is that, from the perspective of the child, the environment has felt so hostile that the child cannot allow the therapist to experience the world as the child experiences it (Palombo 1985a).

Another possible source of countertransference can be the therapist's theoretical orientation. Some therapists do not believe that learning disabilities are neurologically based conditions that have a heritable or constitutional basis. In the treatment of these children, such therapists cannot fully understand the child's view of the world and often inadvertently re-create disjunctions similar to the ones the child has experienced already, the consequence being that the treatment is stalemated. We believe that if some improvement does not occur from individual treatment with nine months to a year of once- or twice-a-week therapy, the therapist must take responsibility for the lack of progress. It is not enough to say that the child's problems are severe or the parents are sabotaging the treatment or the environment is not conducive to change. The therapist must consider that diagnostically some important aspect is missing. It may be that individual therapy is not indicated or that the match between the child and therapist is not optimal or that the deficits have not been accurately identified. The stalemate must be brought to a resolution or the therapy interrupted. Referral for interventions through other modalities, such as educational therapy or tutoring, may be indicated.

CONCLUSION

Children with nonverbal learning disabilities present along a wide spectrum of disabilities, which ranges from mild to severe. Children who function in the moderately to severely impaired range are unable to carry out the normal routines of children their ages. Work with these children involves several strategies. First, it is essential to work with parents on a regular basis, making them active partners in the therapeutic process. Although the focus with them is primarily educational, the process parallels the three moments that are described as taking place in the child's treatment. In the concordant moments, when the therapist makes empathic connection with the parents and resonates with their experiences, they feel relieved, and their anxiety and rage are better contained. In the complementary moments, when they are helped to go back over interactions that had gone awry, identifying the patterns and figuring out new ways of handling situations based on what is known about the child, positive transference with them is dominant and they usually leave these sessions feeling calmer and empowered. At other times, however, there are disjunctions when their helplessness overwhelms them and when they feel the therapist was not sufficiently available to them or could not concretely help them with specific interventions they could use with the child. However, if these disjunctions are managed, the parents feel positive and pleased with the successes the child encounters.

Second, visits to the school and telephone contacts with teachers and other professionals are essential to create a context in which the child can begin to perceive himself or herself differently, to act differently, and to make efforts in areas where he or she had given up previously. The direct work on skills that is done through the teachers, such as the pairing of verbal cues with nonverbal signals, helps to diminish the child's confusion and frustration. The child's self-esteem is also assisted when his teacher stops telling him or her to "be more careful" and begins to give specific, repeated guidelines, such as how to align the work on the paper, as well as encouraging the child to ask for help when becoming confused.

A primary goal of therapy is to help the child modify the themes that organize the child's self-narrative. Two major factors influence the modification of the motifs in the child's narrative: the corrective aspects of the relationship with the therapist, and the understanding the child gains about the influence of those themes on his conduct and relationships. The themes that emerge in therapy are interpreted as metaphors for—expressions of—the motifs that have organized his or her narrative. As changes occur in the relationship to the therapist, shifts in the metaphor occur. The therapist may also actively introduce shifts in the metaphor that reframe for the child his or her view of the world. The child may then be able to view himself or herself differently, as an adventurous experimenter rather than as an ineffectual bumbler. While this may be a primary goal in the treatment of any child, what is specific to the treatment of the NLD child is the way the process is conceptualized. Viewing the process as a series of moments in which the therapist addresses issues as they arise avoids framing the process as one in which the sole aim is to resolve a set of transference reenactments. The aim is also to help the child develop compensation for his or her cognitive deficits.

In this chapter we have attempted to illustrate a treatment approach to children with nonverbal learning disabilities that specifically addresses some of the emotional problems resulting from such neurocognitive deficits. We have emphasized that for such children the neurocognitive deficits shape their experience of the world and their responses to the world. Every child lives within a context and each child's responses to the context is based on his or her own experiences. In addition, the response of the context to the child cannot be minimized. Thus, the family setting, the school setting, and peer relationships all contribute to the child's ultimate integration of experiences.

Treatment is an encounter between a child who brings in a personal narrative that organizes his or her responses to the world and a therapist who attempts to understand and modify the child's narrative. This goal is achievable only through a process in which the child can experience being understood and can have his or her perceptions validated. Once a set of shared experiences occurs, it becomes possible for the child to experience the differences between the therapist's responses and those of others. A set of shared meanings is created that can lead to helping the child reframe his or her understanding of the problems.

ACKNOWLEDGMENTS

We would like to acknowledge the considerable assistance we received from our colleagues in thinking through many aspects of this chapter, particularly the members of the Nonverbal Disabilities Study Group, which includes Meryl Lipton, Pearl Rieger, Karen Pierce, and Warren Rosen. We are grateful to Steven Vogelstein for the case illustration of Paula.

REFERENCES

Badian, N. A. (1986). Nonverbal disorders of learning: The reverse of dyslexia? *Annals of Dyslexia* 36:253–269.

———(1992). Nonverbal learning disability, school behavior and dyslexia. *Annals of Dyslexia* 42:159–178.

Bruner, J. S. (1990). *Acts of Meaning.* Cambridge, MA: Harvard University Press.

Christman, D. M. (1984). Notes on learning disabilities and the borderline personality. *Clinical Social Work Journal* 12(1):18–30.

Denkla, M. B. (1983). The neuropsychology of social-emotional learning disabilities. *Archives of Neurology* 40:461–462.

Diagnostic and Statistical Manual of Mental Disorders, Fourth Edition. (1994). Washington, DC: American Psychiatric Association.

Fairchild, M., and Keith, C. (1981). Issues of autonomy in the psychotherapy of children with learning problems. *Clinical Social Work Journal* 9(2): 134–142.

Garber, B. (1988). The emotional implications of learning disabilities: a theoretical integration. In *The Annual of Psychoanalysis,* vol. 16, pp. 111–128. Madison, CT: International Universities Press.

Johnson, D. J. (1987). Nonverbal learning disabilities. *Pediatric Annals* 16(2):133–141.

Nowicki, S., and Duke, M. P. (1992). *Helping the Child Who Doesn't Fit In: Deciphering the Hidden Dimensions of Social Rejection.* Atlanta: Peachtree.

Palombo, J. (1985a). Self psychology and countertransference in the treatment of children. *Child and Adolescent Social Work Journal* (2)1:36–48.

——— (1985b). The treatment of borderline neurocognitively impaired children: a perspective from self psychology. *Clinical Social Work Journal* 13(2):117–128.

———(1987). Selfobject transferences in the treatment of borderline neurocognitively impaired children. In *The Borderline Patient: Emerging Concepts in Diagnosis, Psychodynamics and Treatment,* ed. J. S. Grotstein, M. Solomon, and J. A. Lang, vol. 1, pp. 317–346. Hillsdale, NJ: Analytic Press.

———(1991). Neurocognitive differences, self cohesion, and incoherent self narratives. *Child and Adolescent Social Work Journal* 8(6):449–472.

——— (1992). Narratives, self-cohesion and patients' search for meaning. *Clinical Social Work Journal* 20(3):249–270.

———(1993a). Neurocognitive differences, developmental distortions, and incoherent narratives. *Psychoanalytic Inquiry* 3(1):63–84.

——— (1993b). Learning disabilities in children: developmental, diagnostic and treatment considerations. *Proceedings of the National Academies of Practice, Fourth National Health Policy Forum, Healthy Children 2000: Obstacles and Opportunities,* April 24–25, 1992.

——— (1995). Psychodynamic and relational problems of children with nonverbal learning disabilities. In *The Handbook of Infant, Child and Adolescent Psychotherapy: A Guide to Diagnosis and Treatment,* vol. 1, ed. B. S. Mark and J. A. Incorvaia, pp. 147–178. Northvale, NJ: Jason Aronson.

Palombo, J., and Feigon, J. (1984). Borderline personality in childhood and its relationship to neurocognitive deficits. *Child and Adolescent Social Work Journal* 1(1):18–33.

Pennington, B. F. (1991). *Diagnosing Learning Disorders: A neuropsychological framework.* New York: Guilford.

Pine, F. (1985). *Developmental Theory and Clinical Process.* New Haven: Yale University Press.

Racker, H. (1968). *Transference and Counter-transference.* New York: International Universities Press.

Rourke, B. P. (1989). *Nonverbal Learning Disabilities: The Syndrome And The Model.* New York: Guilford.

——— (1995). Appendix: Treatment program for the child with NLD. In *Syndrome of Nonverbal Learning Disabilities: Neurodevelopmental Manifestations,* ed. B P. Rourke, pp. 497–508. New York: Guilford.

Semrud-Clikeman, M., and Hynd, G. W. (1990). Right hemisphere dysfunction in nonverbal learning disabilities: social, academic and adaptive functioning in adults and children. *Psychological Bulletin* 107(2):196–209.

——— (1991). Specific nonverbal and social-skills deficits in children with learning disabilities. In *Neuropsychological Foundations of Learning Disabilities: A Handbook of Issues, Methods and Practices,* ed. J. E. Obrzut and G. W. Hyde, pp. 603–629. San Diego: Academic Press.

Vigilante, F. W. (1983). *Working with Families of Learning Disabled Children.* Washington, DC: Child Welfare League of America.

Voeller, K. K. S. (1986). Right-hemisphere deficit syndrome in children. *American Journal of Psychiatry* 148(8):1004–1009.

——— (1995). Clinical neurologic aspects of the right-hemisphere deficit syndrome. *Journal of Child Neurology* 10(1):16–22.

Weintraub, S., and Mesulam, M. M. (1983). Developmental learning disabilities of the right hemisphere: emotional, interpersonal, and cognitive components. *Archives of Neurology* 40:463–468.

3

Psychoeducational Psychotherapy: An Alternative Form of Therapy for the Learning Disabled Child/Adolescent

James A. Incorvaia

DO LEARNING DISABLED STUDENTS ALSO HAVE EMOTIONAL PROBLEMS?

In over thirty years of working in the field, I have never met a learning disabled child who did not also suffer from some form of emotional problems either due to or concomitant with the learning disability. Although this issue has for some time been an area of contention among those who work with learning disabled students, more recently the literature seems to support this personal observation. For example, Ruth Ochroch (1981) reports that learning disabled children "are more vulnerable to emotional disturbance" (p. 26). Jonathan Cohen (1985) reports, "There are virtually no learning disabled children or adolescents who do not evidence significant psychological conflict and concerns" (p. 177). Cohen further comments,

"Over time it becomes more and more difficult to distinguish the neuropsychological from the psychological and the reactive aspects of the person from the characterological" (p. 178). He goes on to note, from a study he did, that learning disabled adolescents show two particular configurations of problems with work and learning: (1) problems owing to the cognitive disability itself, and (2) problems owing to the psychological factors that are directly or indirectly related to the learning disability. His study also found that all learning disabled children had two major affective configurations: (1) an unusually high propensity to experience stress or anxiety, and (2) a low level of chronic depression.

J. D. McKinney and his colleagues (1989) have studied the behavioral and emotional problems of learning disabled children by both observing their classroom behavior and obtaining teacher ratings. In general, they found that 65 percent of learning disabled children exhibited maladaptive behavior that could interfere with classroom learning. They also noted that academic progress with learning disabled students declined relative to normal peers as the years went by, especially by three years later, and that social and emotional problems became more evident when learning disabled children were older.

Rourke (1988) identified a particular subtype of learning disabled children at particular risk for developing internalizing problems, which he labeled as nonverbal learning disabled (NLD). These NLD students were characterized by psychomotor clumsiness, tactile insensitivity, visual/spatial/organizational deficits, difficulties dealing with novelty, and weakness in intermodal integration. He also found these students to have cognitive deficits including poor achievement in mechanical things, in arithmetic, and in nonverbal problem solving, but with better achievement in reading and in general verbosity of a repetitive/rote nature. These problems were usually found in those learning disabled young people with severe right-hemisphere injuries, hydrocephalics, and those with leukemia who were treated by large doses of x-rays. These NLD students were unable to appreciate and process the social context of novel situations, which led to internalizing problems. Instead of accommodating to changing life demands, NLDs were found to rely on "verbal prescriptions" and to a display of inappropriate social behavior, leading to chronic social failure, frequent rejection, and the possibility of social withdrawal, isolation, anxiety, depression, or suicidal behavior.

Achenbach and McConough (1992) present research that further supports the finding that learning disabled students have emotional problems, as they discuss the profile patterns of learning disabled children with behavioral and emotional problems. They indicate that although much of the research on learning disabilities focuses on identification of cognitive and neuropsychological defects, a number of behavioral and emotional problems have also been identified in learning disabled children, including "feelings of insecurity, low self-esteem, poor adaptability, and inflexibility and social maladjustment" (pp. 37–38). They then conclude, "In summary, a growing body of research has shown that many learning disabled children establish behavior and emotional problems" (p. 39).

DOES THE LEARNING DISABLED STUDENT UTILIZE TRADITIONAL PSYCHOTHERAPY WELL?

Although it can be concluded that most, if not all, learning disabled young people have emotional problems, learning disabled children and adolescents, even more than other child and adolescent patients, usually do not feel they need or want psychotherapy and often do not understand why they must undergo it.

On the other hand, learning disabled children and adolescents know that they need help with their disability and usually understand why they must get help in that area. Thus, they are motivated from the start to work on those academic issues that they can readily see they need to work on in order to "get better."

Learning disabled children and adolescents, while often not motivated to go for psychotherapy, and, when made to go, often unwilling or unable to communicate easily, appear to be able and willing to work on educational problems they may have. Therefore, it seems easier for them to deal with their educational problems than to deal with the emotional problems that either result from or are concomitant with their learning difficulties.

To deal with this issue, we at Reiss-Davis have developed an approach that utilizes the motivation of learning disabled children to accept educational help for their disability while allowing, within that context, for emotional problems to be dealt with psychotherapeutically. We call this approach *psychoeducational psychotherapy*.

HOW DID THIS APPROACH FOR HELPING LEARNING DISABLED STUDENTS DEVELOP?

The idea for psychoeducational psychotherapy first came in the early 1970s when I was both the part-time clinical director at the Marianne Frostig Center for Learning Disabilities and the Director of Psychological Services at the Reiss-Davis Child Study Center. At the Frostig Center I was seeing a number of learning disabled children and adolescents in psychotherapy, and I knew of many more who were receiving educational therapy but did not also have concomitant psychotherapy. One particular educational therapist, who had very good rapport with his students, would from time to time suggest that a particular student he was seeing would benefit from receiving psychotherapy along with his educational therapy. In one such case he referred for psychotherapy, where the boy had formed a very good relationship with this educational therapist, I suggested that because of the close relationship they had established, rather than also assigning the boy to a psychotherapist, he and I might rather work in a consultative/supervisory manner while he did the "psychoeducational work." Although reluctant at first, with some instructional help and support he agreed and began to work on both psychotherapeutic and educational remediation. The boy, trusting him, opened up to him about many issues that the educational therapist was able to deal with through our consultation-supervision meetings, leading to his making a dramatic impact on both the academic and emotional growth of this child. With the success of this first case, other cases that seemed appropriate for this treatment approach followed, all under close consultation-supervision, with equally good results.

Although the process of this form of treatment, which allows for shifts in treatment based not on the theoretical orientation of the therapist or the therapeutic techniques of the theory but rather on the needs and situations of the learning disabled child, was developed many years ago, and, although I used it many times in my own work with learning disabled children and adolescents, it would take many more years before I would call it psychoeducational psychotherapy.

WHAT DOES THE TERM *PSYCHOEDUCATIONAL* MEAN?

I have searched the literature for any mention of the term *psychoeducational psychotherapy* and have found none. The descriptor *psychoeducational* can, however, be found in the mental health and educational literature, but it is used in many different ways, some of which are discussed below.

The editor of the *Menninger Bulletin* reports that Hagod Akishol (1991) "summarizes his research effects to establish the clinical legitimacy of a chronic depression and suggests that supportive psychotherapeutic and *psychoeducational approaches* can enhance the therapeutic gains achieved through pharmacotherapy"(p. 156). The term *psychoeducational* seems to refer here to vocational-educational work along with therapy to help depressed people.

Furst and colleagues (1993) use the term to suggest that "the Boys Town educational treatment medium is a structured psychosocially oriented approach." They further describe how the staff uses techniques from this model "around-the-clock to teach the patients social skills, reinforce adaptive behaviors, and solve problems. The social skills training addresses the aspects of behavior most affected by the patient's diagnosis. Corrective teaching is also used to identify and respond to problematic behavior and to teach patients adaptive behavior, specifically linked to treatment plans" (p. 864). They add, "It is a more concrete structure for guiding interaction with patients" (p. 867). The term refers here to a particular psychoeducational model that utilizes a therapeutic milieu approach within a therapeutic community. Pollak (1985) uses the term to refer to "an in-depth comprehensive evaluation" including cognitive and emotional assessment.

In the learning disabilities literature, *psychoeducational*, when referring to evaluation, seems to indicate cognitive and achievement testing along with psychosocial assessment, as, for example, it is used by Perlman (1975). Baldauf (1975) defines the term as "a psychological and educational assessment for a child demonstrating learning problems that measures his intelligence, school achievement, as well as critical processes of perception, language development, speech, and emotional factors" (p. 186).

Roth-Smith (1983) reports, "Assessment data in psychoeducational planning is collected to assist educational personnel in planning programs for learning disabled students that enhance their psychological adjustment and educational achievement" (p. 314).

Tessmer and Ciriello (1995) not only use the term but also define how it can apply to therapy: "Psychoeducational treatment requires that every patient be given an approach uniquely designed for that particular patient and his or her specific needs" (p. 180). This article reflects the work done at Reiss-Davis in psychoeducational psychotherapy by an educational-school psychologist who is trained in both educational and psychological remediation and who has been able to use this method with a long-term treatment case. However, not enough people are trained in these areas.

Wohl (1980) best describes the term *psychoeducational*:

> In recent years there has been little reason to differentiate the term "psychological and psychoeducational" when applied to children with minimal brain dysfunction. The latter has come to convey a broad spectrum of interrelated approaches, strategies utilized in a diagnostic conceptualization and in pragmatic remediation and therapy. As already noted, the term itself is a dynamic appellation applied to the whole child. It follows that those professionals implementing psychoeducational approaches are more likely to consider a wide variety of contributory data and to be more flexible in modifying remedial goals and techniques in view of the child's needs. [p. 362]

WHO SHOULD DO THE THERAPEUTIC WORK WITH LEARNING DISABLED STUDENTS?

There is little literature on training professionals in psychotherapy who are already trained in special education with learning disabled children, or on training professionals who are already trained in psychotherapy in educational remediation of learning disabilities. Some writers in the psychoanalytic literature suggest that educators can be therapists. For example, Anna Freud (1931) states, "You are in a most advantageous position . . . because you have to act as educators a long time before you can utilize psychoanalytic theory in the actual practice of teaching" (pp. 10–11).

Ekstein (1969) discusses the struggle that existed in Europe in the 1930s on the role of educators in psychoanalysis and psychotherapy:

> Before 1938, teachers and clinicians trained together in the Vienna Psychoanalytic Institute. We were all studying together to see whether psychoanalysis had something to offer the educator. During this training, there was no clear boundary between psychoanalysis, therapy and psychoanalytically oriented education. . . . There should be clearer boundaries between education and psychotherapy. It is not in terms of understanding the child but rather in terms of differentiation of functioning of purpose and purpose geared techniques. . . . It is the task of the therapist through psychoanalytic intervention to restore the lost functions. It is the task of the teacher and the educator *not* to restore function, but to develop functions by helping the child to acquire skills, knowledge and correct attitude. . . . Despite attempts to differentiate between the function of psychotherapist and the functions of the teacher frequently overlapping does occur. . . . Psychoanalysts have always felt . . . that the therapeutic function makes social sense only when psychoanalysis can be applied to the educational process and it is not utilized for therapeutic purposes alone. [pp. 157, 159]

Bettelheim (1969), too, seems to feel that educators are in a special position in terms of helping children both academically and emotionally: "This is why some of the best educators have become interested in psychoanalysis, stopped teaching and become psychotherapists. . . . [Education] must reach the child not only where he is but as the person he is—in order to guide him to where he is not." He feels it absolutely necessary that teachers have knowledge about their pupils—"a full understanding, including how he functions in terms of his personality" (p. 237).

Peller (1969) notes that "the child's intellectual and emotional development are clearly interdependent. Attempts to factor the one without caring for the other are self-defeating" (p. 265). Others, too, seem to support the idea that educators and those in an educational setting can and should be dealing with mental health issues (Alpert 1941, Pearson 1954, Seabrook 1980).

Highet (1958) suggests that a tutor (educational therapist/special educator) may be the best trained to know and work with the "whole child. The qualities of a good teacher include (a) knowing what he teaches, (b) liking the subject, (c) liking his pupils. . . . Togetherness, working and understanding each other [is the essence of teaching]." He asks, "Is it essential for (a teacher) to know the pupil?" He concludes, "Except for the tutorial system, it is generally sufficient that the teacher gets to know the type of students rather than each student as an individual" (p. 57). Thus, he suggests that a tutor or educational remediator must know the child emotionally as well as educationally.

Harris (1970) states, "Good remedial teaching has some of the characteristics of good psychotherapy" (p. 294). Rappaport (1964) advises educators to progress beyond their traditional areas of responsibility to consider the ego factors of the minimal brain dysfunction (MBD) and learning disabled children they work with. Hewitt (1968) gives high priority to the understanding of psychological causal factors and the development of a positive trusting relationship between adult and child in formal educational training.

Thus, there appears to be strong support for educators/"tutors" who must remediate to also be able to deal with the emotional life of the learning disabled child. But can this be done by all educators or do we need to develop a special type of specialist to do the work of psychoeducational psychotherapy? And can a psychotherapist, psychiatrist, psychologist, or social worker trained in psychotherapy with children and adolescents also play this role?

Kubie (1969) comes closest to suggesting the need to develop a hybrid form of educator-therapist: "We cannot hope to improve the educational process until we develop clinically sophisticated 'pathologists' of the learning process. . . . This is why the psychiatrist must come to understand education and why the educator must come to understand psychopathology. . . . The future will have to see close integration of these two disciplines" (p. 258). He goes on to suggest that education will need to produce a subtechnique of educational psychopathology where experienced teachers will withdraw from education and with postgraduate work will study educational failures.

This investigation of educational pathology would need to also study the influences of neurotic processes on learning. This process also necessitates the study of motivation of the educators and the need for self-evaluation as a discipline. They would not be flushed out, but studied to see how the school "failed" the child. Kubie summarizes, "The old reluctance to accept the unity of psychotherapy in education will have to be replaced by an open-minded, joint exploration of how to integrate them" (p. 258).

Connolly (1971) states:

> The traditional psychiatric framework is believed to be inadequate for learning disabilities; furthermore, the model can produce harmful effects in some cases . . . and the results of therapy in which there is little relationship between disorder and treatment methods are well known. The majority of disabled children could benefit from exposures to certain select psychotherapeutic methods . . . but relatively few require traditional psychiatric effort. . . . The only feasible solution seems to be that school personnel . . . must take on part of the role of counselor, psychotherapist. . . .What is psychotherapy? It is developing a relationship where a client is able to grow and change—a place where the client is accepted and not afraid to make mistakes. . . . Psychotherapy is a learning process in which a therapist serves as guide, tutor, model and primary source of reward. If the . . . remedial specialist (can do these therapeutic tasks), she has formed a therapeutic relationship. [pp. 156, 176, 177]

On the other hand, there are those who suggest that educators cannot hope to understand the child as well as mental health professionals do. For example, Rivlin (1954) states, "No teacher can ever hope to understand an individual child as fully as a psychiatrist does, even if the teacher has the necessary training and background" (p. 779).

But Pollak (1985) notes that due to such influences and psychoanalytic thought (the psychodynamic factor), "psychotherapy was often recommended for the child and sometimes for the family with considerably less emphasis on modifying the educational program or the strategies used to teach the child because the problems seem as psychogenic in origin" (p. 479).

Stein (1969) tells of a psychiatrist's struggle with learning disabled adolescents in his work and how he felt "quite inadequate to the task of understanding these phenomena. . . . The analytic framework . . . seemed too general and not readily applicable to the specific phenomena I was witnessing" (p. 460).

SHOULD THE EDUCATIONAL AND PSYCHOLOGICAL REMEDIATION OF THE LEARNING DISABLED CHILD BE OFFERED BY SEPARATE EDUCATIONAL AND PSYCHOLOGICAL THERAPISTS?

Some suggest that what is needed in helping the learning disabled child is a "two-pronged approach" as noted by Osman (1979), who suggests that some with learning disabilities need psychotherapy for social problems, emotional factors that interfere, and negative feelings about the self. But she also suggests that at times others need to see "if therapy or educational intervention or a 'two-pronged' treatment approach—educational and therapeutic—can help a child improve more quickly and more effectively than one form of treatment alone" (pp. 135–136).

McConville and Cote (1983) report that it is not easy to find a multidisciplinary facility and program.

> A directed multidisciplinary approach for a variety of behavioral and learning disorders, along with intensive remediation, seems to offer the best hope for a very large number of children who have both learning and behavioral difficulties. Unfortunately there are few facilities that offer such multidisciplinary services. If it is not possible to establish such facilities, then a reasonable alternative is to put together a strong multidisciplinary special education group which will be available to the schools for planning and evaluating complex interventions for children and adolescents with learning and behavioral disorders. [p. 81]

Hersch (1970) reports that it is evident that several disciplines usually are and should be involved in the treatment of any child with learning disabilities. He suggests that every learning disabled child would probably need clinical services in addition to the educational work. "But we must not forget that clinical therapy does not free a child from his learning problems. Educational remediation of special teachers, or special techniques must accompany the clinical services" (p. 180). He describes the services as a wheel: "If we have these many spokes helping, who should be at the hub?" He looks at a number of possibilities and suggests that the coordinator would best be an educator. "The job calls for an educator or educational psychologist because in the final analysis the problem is one of education. Any child who has a learning disability requires special education" (p. 181). If that is not available then he suggests an interdisciplinary clinical decision-making team approach.

Kessler (1966) suggests:

> Like the diagnostic process, the treatment program for learning disabled children usually entails the cooperation of educator parent, counselor and child therapist. Rarely can one person carry out all of these functions. Whatever the specific means it is imperative that the therapy and the education of the child with learning disabilities be closely related. [p. 223]

WHY DO TRADITIONALLY TRAINED PSYCHOTHERAPISTS OFTEN FIND THEIR WORK WITH THE TOTAL LEARNING DISABLED CHILD DIFFICULT?

Speaking specifically about psychotherapy of learning disabled children, Crastenopol (1992) notes,

> Excluded from consideration here is the adolescent diagnosed as learning disabled. Such youngsters who comprise 10–20% of the population have a presumed perceptual/neurological deficit that can be diagnosed by a neurological assessment. Problems of this nature require highly specialized psychoeducational techniques. [p. 233]

In describing how the patient should be encouraged to have tutoring she notes: "Or could it enable the student to understand that the problem as a psychoeducational difficulty and not an inborn deficit—is eminently open to change?" (p. 242). . . . "The psychotherapist doing long-term intensive work usually does not have the luxury of focusing solely on the patient's academic performance" (p. 243).

Rie and Rie (1980) speak of MBD in the same way that one can discuss learning disabilities:

> The school and educational personnel have a long-term relationship with this group of children during critical periods of the children's greatest need. This relationship has the potential to be of great value in serving the minimal brain dysfunction population. However, in current practice it is unusual for people in the educational system to capitalize on this potential. Their skills can be helpful in remediating some of the most serious consequences of the minimal brain dysfunction problem. A child who receives effective educational remediation is more likely to succeed in managing the manifestations of minimal brain dysfunction and entering more fully into general society. [p. 660]

Sapier (1980) suggests a clinical diagnostic treatment model using the Bank Street College of Education model, "which believes the children grow and function as beings with emotional, social, physical, and intellectual dimensions interacting with each other as well as that person's physical and psychological environments which surround the children" (p. 578). She suggests the need to relate the knowledge of normal children's development to learning disabled children.

Weil (1977) speaking about one form of learning disability and its relationship to psychotherapy, says, "Such neurotic-like disturbances represent direct consequences of dysfunctions and are not the end-result of unconscious elaboration like the truly neurotic symptoms, although they may amalgamate with the latter" (p. 60). O'Brien (1992) concurs, as he writes of learning disabled and attention deficit disordered children: "These children's basic problem is not neurosis and the techniques of psychotherapeutic intervention is not at all like the techniques used in neurotic children" (p. 120). He goes on to suggest to therapists that if they work with these type of children they must consider:

> (1) Don't deal with neurotic issues first; (2) don't foster regression; (3) insight is often not derived from interpretation; (4) use concrete

examples and concrete accomplishments; (5) don't use an open playroom technique; (6) you can't play a passive role; engage and be supportive; (7) focus; get something accomplished in each session; (8) put emphasis on the positive and not the negative; (9) organize and channel feelings; (10) motoric expression will precede verbal expression. . . .

Once this has occurred, this process is related to the school experience in a manner that compares what the child has accomplished in treatment along with what he or she has done at school. In treatment children must come to terms with their deficiencies and must try to change them if possible. . . .

Obviously the therapist must be more structuring, more active and more supportive at the beginning of treatment and probably for a long time. There also is a more didactic component in the treatment of ADHD [attention deficit hyperactivity disorder] (and LD [learning disabled]) children than there is in the treatment of neurotic children. Mastery in the session should be accomplished and then transferred to outside situations. [pp. 121–123]

IS A NEW SPECIALIST NEEDED FOR WORKING WITH MANY LEARNING DISABLED CHILDREN WITH EMOTIONAL PROBLEMS?

Myklebust (1964) suggests that we consider that learning disabilities are psychoneurological and as such necessitate specialized treatment or remedial training. "The therapy must be based specifically on the altered psychological functioning that characterizes a given child" (p. 358).

Kurlander and Coladny (1969) suggest what they feel is necessary for the remediation of the learning disabled child:

> By comparison, we thought [learning disabled children] suffered mainly from neurological malfunction and their awareness of it as well as their secondarily disturbed family relationships. They expressed their primary biological anxiety and their secondary interpersonal anxiety in symptoms which were superficially much like those of other children. We thought they needed a really different kind of help instead of permissive insight therapy; we prescribed for them exter-

> nal guidance, medicine, and tutoring . . . rather than actual psychotherapy. . . . One need not spend years waiting for the patients or his parents to stumble on the truths in a prolonged, undirected psychotherapeutic experience. . . . Treatment must await a diagnostic conclusion. We find no eventfulness in the practice of drifting into open-ended psychotherapy and waiting for a diagnosis to become apparent. . . . A remedial class or a good tutor . . . is often worth a trial. With respect to performance secondary symptoms sometimes subside without further treatment. Psychotherapy is a last and expensive resort. . . . One fact is clear: if he [learning disabled child] cannot learn in school, no amount of talk will restore his pride till he is helped to learn. If his is organically driven behavior, this too is out of the province of the "talking cure." Tutoring, medicine, training and understanding are the treatments of choice. [pp. 133, 139–141]

This different approach to remediation is necessary, they feel. "Because his disability so often includes a tendency to think too concretely for his age, we must teach him in a most literal fashion how to stay out of trouble, how to acknowledge his limitations and how to allow and engage others to treat him better. This is unlike our old techniques which focused on changing motives" (p. 142). They conclude, "If the handicapped can be approached first by the least expensive, most practical and available measures, the more costly, time-consuming psychotherapy can be reserved for those who can respond to nothing else" (p. 151).

Prentiss and Sperry (1965) describe programs needed for children with psychogenic learning inhibitions and learning disabilities as they note three remedial approaches:

> 1) Brief tutorial interventions in psychotherapy for the purpose of illuminating the dynamics of a learning inhibition, 2) simultaneous tutoring therapy where the tutor and the therapist each nonetheless function separately with different techniques and in different areas, and 3) therapeutic tutoring alone, which combines aspects of both a therapeutic and educational function but retaining as the primary emphasis the teaching approach. [p. 522]

It is this last suggested approach that best describes psychoeducational psychotherapy.

WHAT IS THE PSYCHOEDUCATIONAL PSYCHOTHERAPY APPROACH?

In the psychoeducational psychotherapeutic approach, it is believed that starting with educational issues and helping children with educational problems builds a therapeutic alliance in learning disabled children, who are usually suspicious of adults who feel that the children have problems and are fearful that these adults will only be critical of their deficiencies as others have been before. Dealing with a different type of "therapist"—a helpful adult figure who wants to aid them in overcoming their disabilities, in doing better in school, and in keeping up in their classes and on tests—puts the "therapist" in a role of someone different from the other adults in their lives, someone whom they can trust to help them with other aspects of their lives, including emotional concerns. In this approach the therapist is able to break through the more concrete defenses erected early by learning disabled children as the therapist helps the children to deal with two very important parts of life—learning (the work of childhood) and emotional/social development.

The approach that is recommended is to help the children to understand that they and the therapist will be working together on both educational issues that they know are problematic and on feelings and other psychological issues that seem to go along with having learning problems. They should be told that the shift in focus of the sessions will be determined by what seems most pressing or salient in their life that hour. If, for example, there is to be a test at school and they need help to pass it, or if they have a report to write and are not sure how to begin it, then the therapist will focus on that area and only secondarily on emotional or interpersonal problems. On the other hand, if there are clear indications of intrapsychic or interpersonal conflicts, and these seem to be problematic, that session should center on these and only secondarily on school issues. The consideration for where to put the focus in any given session, although based on the observation and clinical acumen of the therapist, should lead to a decision that is mutually agreed on or explained in such a way that the children can see that their own material led to the decision. In this way they will come to understand the structure of the therapeutic work in psychoeducational psychotherapy and will feel totally involved in the process, rather than feel that the process is occurring merely at the whim of the therapist.

WHAT ARE THE REQUIREMENTS FOR BECOMING A PSYCHOEDUCATIONAL PSYCHOTHERAPIST?

The credentials for doing this form of therapy should include experience in psychotherapy with children/adolescents as well as experience in educational/special educational work with children/adolescents. Although it seems easier, I feel, to train a psychotherapist to do the educational work with the child than it is to train an educator to do psychotherapy, that doesn't mean that the latter cannot become adept at this approach. There can be a danger in both approaches. In the former situation, the psychotherapist may not be able to relinquish the psychotherapeutic role in order to help the child with purely educational remediation. In the latter situation, the educational specialist who is studying psychotherapy may want to do more and more psychotherapy and less educational intervention.

WHAT ARE THE BENEFITS OF THIS APPROACH?

By utilizing only one therapist the psychoeducational psychotherapeutic approach also prevents the splitting in therapeutic work that occurs when two different specialists are each seen as helping only one area of the child's functioning. This avoidance of splitting is especially important in the case of the borderline child who is also learning disabled.

The use of one therapist is also more cost-effective when a family cannot afford both educational remediation and psychotherapy but the child is in need of both.

Parents, too, may find it easier to accept that their child has a learning problem than an emotional one. This approach focuses on the learning problem but does not stop there. It also is able to address emotional concerns as they arise in the course of the child's school and home life, as well as dealing with those earlier traumas and experiences that have not been properly worked through and integrated into the child's life. Just as play therapy helps the therapist to see how the child deals with issues in life, the educational arena can also illustrate those approaches that generalize to more than just specific learning situations. If the child is avoidant in learning, he will usually demonstrate this defense in other areas, too. In fact the defensive structure of the child/adolescent can be explored very nicely by working with him on academic tasks. Self-esteem, self-confidence, and issues of self-image and self-value are all reflected in the child's learning difficulties and how he deals with them. Developing learning and compensating strategies in the areas of learning difficulties will carry over to other areas of life, as the child realizes that things can change and he has the power to change them. When "I can't" changes to "I can," it can create that attitudinal change in more than just school issues.

With the advent of managed care programs that do not usually pay for educational work with the learning disabled child, this approach offers what is needed—educational as well as psychological intervention. Because the work is more efficient and cost effective, and because it is more focused and less prone to resistance than traditional child psychotherapy, the therapy may also be shorter term, another appealing characteristic for managed care companies.

WHEN IS IT APPROPRIATE TO REFER FOR PSYCHOEDUCATIONAL PSYCHOTHERAPY?

1. When the child/adolescent with learning and emotional problems and/or the parent is resistant to or afraid of psychotherapy.
2. When the child with learning and emotional problems has not made much progress or has been unsuccessful in working within a more traditional psychotherapeutic intervention program.
3. When the child with learning and emotional problems is too concrete to use a more traditional psychotherapeutic program and needs something on which he/she can more easily focus.
4. When the educational therapist and/or psychotherapist notices that there is splitting going on in a child with learning and emotional problems who is being seen by both the psychotherapist because of emotional problems and an educational

therapist because of learning problems, and that the spitting is creating problems in helping the child in either or both intervention programs.

5. When the child with learning and emotional problems needs both interventions, but the family cannot afford to pay for both.
6. When a child with learning and more severe emotional problems has a distrust of "doctors" and needs an opportunity to develop trust, so that the child can later be persuaded to go into psychotherapy.

SOME FINAL THOUGHTS ON THE PSYCHOEDUCATIONAL PSYCHOTHERAPY APPROACH

Since the concern for outcomes is essential in today's world of mental health and learning disabilities, it is believed that the results of the psychoeducational psychotherapy approach will mirror what was found in outcomes research, which suggested that with the proper comprehensive intervention program learning disabled students can improve in all areas. Silver and Hagan (1985) report, "The prognosis for academic achievement and acceptable adjustment in children and adolescents with learning disabilities who have the benefit of appropriate and sufficient educational intervention and receive optimal and necessary environmental support (including psychotherapy when needed) is favorable" (p. 211).

REFERENCES

Achenbach, T. T., and McConough, S. (1992). Taxonomy of internalizing disorders of childhood and adolescence. In *Internalizing Disorders in Children and Adolescents*, ed. W. Reynolds, pp. 19–60. New York: Wiley.

Akishol, H. (1991). Chronic depression. *Bulletin of the Menninger Clinic* 55(2):156–171.

Alpert, A. (1941). Education as therapy. *Psychoanalytic Quarterly* 10:3–24.

Baldauf, R. (1975). Parental intervention. In *Progress in Learning Disabilities*, vol. 3, ed. H. Mykelbust, pp. 179–199. New York: Grune & Stratton.

Bettelheim, B. (1969). Education of emotionally and culturally deprived children. In *Learning to Love to Love of Learning*, ed. R. Ekstein and R. Motto. New York: Brunner/Mazel.

Cohen, J. (1985). Learning disabilities and adolescents: developmental considerations. In *Adolescent Psychiatry*, vol. 12, ed. J. Cohen and S.Finestein, pp. 177–196. Chicago: The University of Chicago Press.

Connolly, C. (1971). Social and emotional factors in learning disabilities. In *Progress in Learning Disabilities*, vol. 2, ed. H. Myklebust, pp. 151–178. New York: Grune & Stratton.

Crastenopol, M. (1992). Older adolescents with academic achievement problems. In *Psychotherapies with Children and Adolescents*, ed. J. O'Brien, D. Pelowsky, and O. Lewis, pp. 231–252. Washington, DC: American Psychiatric Press.

Ekstein, R. (1969). Boundary lines between education and psychotherapy. In *Learning to Love to Love of Learning*, ed. R. Ekstein and R. Motto, pp. 157–163. New York: Brunner/Mazel.

Freud, A. (1931). *Introduction to Psychoanalysis For Teachers.* London: Alan and Levinson.

Furst, D., Boener, W., Cohen, J., et al. (1993). Implications of the Boys Town psychoeducational treatment model in a children's psychiatric hospital. *Journal of Hospital and Community Psychiatry* 44(9):863–868.

Harris, A. (1970). *How to Increase Reading Ability*, 5th ed. New York: McKay.

Hersch, M. (1970). The multi-disciplinary approach. In *Interdisciplinary Approaches to Learning Disorders*, ed. D. Carter, pp. 180–183. Philadelphia: Chilton.

Hewitt, L. E. (1968). *The Emotionally Disturbed Child in the Classroom*. Boston: Allyn and Bacon.

Highet, G. (1958). *The Art of Teaching*. New York: Vintage.

Kessler, J. (1966). *Psychopathology of Childhood*. Englewood Cliffs, NJ: Prentice-Hall.

Kubie, L. (1969). How can the educational process become a behavioral science? In *From Learning to Love to Love of Learning,* ed. R. Ekstein and R. Motto, pp. 245–260. New York: Brunner/Mazel.

Kurlander, L. F., and Coladny, D. (1969). Psychiatric disability and learning problems. In *Learning Disabilities*, ed. L. Tarnopol, pp. 131–151. Springfield, IL: Charles C Thomas.

McConville, B. J., and Cote, J. (1983). Emotionally disturbed children and adolescents and their learning disorders. In *Advances in Research and Services for Children with Special Needs*, ed. G. Schwartz, pp. 76–82. Vancouver, BC: University of British Columbia.

McKinney, J. D. (1989). Longitudinal research on the behavioral characteristics of children with learning disabilities. *Journal of Learning Disabilities* 22:141-150.

Myklebust, H. (1964). Learning disorders of psychoneurological disturbances in childhood. *Remediation Literature* 25:354-360.

O'Brien, J. (1992). Children with attention deficit hyperactivity disorder and their parents. In *Psychotherapies with Children and Adolescents*, ed. J. O'Brien and L. Polowsky, pp. 109-124. Washington, DC: American Psychiatric Press.

Ochroch, R. (1981). Learning disabled children are more vulnerable to emotional disturbance. In *Review of Minimal Brain Dysfunction Syndrome—Diagnosis and Treatment of Minimal Brain Dysfunction in Children*, pp. 23-29. New York: Human Sciences Press.

Osman, B. (1979). *Learning Disabilities*. New York: Random House.

Pearson, G. (1954). *Psychoanalysis and the Education of the Child*. New York: Norton.

Peller, L. (1969). Psychoanalysis and education. In *From Learning to Love to Love of Learning*, ed. R. Ekstein and R. Motto, pp. 261-268. New York: Brunner/Mazel.

Perlman, S. M. (1975). Intervention through psychological and educational evaluation. In *Progress in Learning Disabilities*, ed. H. Mykelbust, vol. 3, pp. 67-83. New York: Grune & Stratton.

Pollak, G. (1985). Pitfalls in the psychoeducational assessment of adolescents with learning and school adjustment problems. In *Adolescence*, vol. 20, no. 78, pp. 479-493.

Prentiss, N. H., and Sperry, B. (1965). Therapeutically oriented tutoring of children with primary and neurotic learning inhibitions. *American Journal of Orthopsychiatry* 35:521-531.

Rappaport, S. (1964). *Childhood Aphasia and Brain Damage*. Narbeth, PA: Livingston.

Rie, H., and Rie, E., eds. (1980). *The Handbook of Minimal Brain Dysfunction.* New York: Wiley.

Rivlin, H. (1954). Roundtable: contemporary concepts of learning. *American Journal of Orthopsychiatry* 24:776-781.

Roth-Smith, C. (1983). *Learning Disabilities.* Boston: Little, Brown.

Rourke, B. P. (1988). The syndrome of non-verbal learning disabilities and developmental manifestations in neurological disease, disorders and dysfunctions. *Clinical Neuropsychologist* 2:293-330.

Sapier, S. (1980). Educational interventions. *Handbook of Minimal Brain Dysfunction,* ed. H. Rie and E. J. Rie, pp. 569-589. New York: Wiley.

Seabrook, J. (1980). Specific learning disability demands remedial teaching.

In *Approaches to Learning*, vol. 1, ed. W. Cruickshank. Syracuse, NY: Syracuse University Press.

Silver, A., and Hagan, R. (1985). Outcomes of learning disabilities. In *Adolescent Psychiatry*, vol. 12, ed. S. Finestein, Chicago: University of Chicago Press.

Stein, S. (1969). The child psychiatrist revisited: innovations and training in treatment of learning disabilities. In *Selected Papers on Learning Disabilities, Fifth Annual International Conference of the ACLD, California*, ed. J. Arena, pp. 458–461. San Rafael: Academic Therapy Publications.

Tessmer, D., and Ciriello, J. (1995). The game ain't over till it's over—a long-term psychoeducational parent and child treatment case. In *Handbook of Infant, Child, and Adolescent Psychotherapy,* ed. B. Mark and J. Incorvaia, pp. 179–197. Northvale, NJ: Jason Aronson.

Weil, A. (1977). Learning disturbances with special consideration of dyslexia. *Issues in Child Mental Health* 5:52–66.

Wohl, T. H. (1980). Psychological and psychoeducational assessment techniques. In *Handbook of Minimal Brain Dysfunction*, ed. H. Rie and E. Rie, pp. 362–387. New York: Wiley.

4

Three Theoretical Views of the Treatment of a Six-Year-Old

Esther Fine and Sydney Fine

The loosely woven theoretical framework of psychoanalysis has led to many different ways of understanding psychic phenomena; some have been out of kilter with others, and some have provided linkages and building blocks for more systematic theory construction. We have selected for concentrated study three different analytic groups: classical, self-psychological, and Kleinian. Using material from the treatment of a 6-year-old, we will try to understand the nature of the differences among these groups, focusing on the interpretive interventions characteristic of them.

In a previous study we used clinical data drawn from the psychoanalysis of an adult to examine the divergence in treatment approach among four analytic schools; analysts utilizing Otto Kernberg's theoretical constructs in their work made up the fourth group (Fine and Fine 1989). In this research project, we were able to determine at a highly significant statistical level that analysts could be distinguished as belonging to one of these four groups on the basis of the kind of interpretations they gave to a detailed written account of an analytic hour. We examined six variables derived from a consensus of raters, who identified these factors as making it possible for them to make correct identifications. These six factors dealt with (1) the manner in which defense and resistance were interpreted, (2) the way in which the transference was interpreted, (3) the focus on the patient's vulnerability, (4) the focus on the patient's primitive impulses, (5) the focus on the patient's hostile aggressiveness, and (6) the use of special catchwords or phraseology.

We conjectured that one could also detect theoretical differences in the psychotherapeutic treatment of a child. To test this hypothesis, we presented a written summary of a case of a 6-year-old boy to six child analysts; two identified themselves as classical in orientation, two as self-psychological, two as Kleinian. We eliminated the Kernbergian perspective in this current study primarily because we had no immediate access to Kernbergian child analysts. The case presentation included a brief history of the family and the child and a summary of the treatment, with a sharper focus on a few sessions that were likely to provide a window through which to view the different interpretive approaches of our participants as a function of their theoretical school. We note that this case presentation was submitted prior to the publication of our research project on the adult case, so that these participants were not privy to the findings of that study.

Each of the three theoretical schools under study has evolved its own schema and timetable for child development along with explanations for normality and pathology. We believe that these differences in theoretical formulations influence interpretive interventions. To illustrate this contention, we put forth our understanding of these three theories, in highly abbreviated form, particularly as they pertain to child development.

As Calvin Settlage (1980) has pointed out, there have been essentially three periods of theory building in the classical analytic frame. The first period primarily proposed the libido theory and the role of sexual and aggressive instinctual drives. In the libido theory it was postulated that the sources of sexual instinct stem from somatic processes, biological in nature, that in turn pressure the psychic apparatus. It was also hypothesized that child development followed a sequence of libidinal stages: oral, anal, phallic, oedipal, latency, puberty, adolescence, and the mature genital phase. The concepts of regression and fixation are essential ones in this phase-centered psychology.

In the second period of classical theory construction, the era of ego psychology, theorists turned their attention to how the mind responded to the demands thrust upon it by the libido. The psychic apparatus was divided into three agencies—the id, ego, and superego. The ego stands for the executive branch of the psyche, engaged in its task of regulating the id, superego, and the adaptation to external reality. It is the seat of perception, memory, affect, and thought. It was postulated that a struggle occurred among the three agencies of the mind, and indeed within the ego itself, which could pose a threat to the harmonious functioning of the total mental system; for example, a conflict might ensue if the ego attempts to participate with the id, then finds that this union is opposed by feelings of guilt (Sandler and A. Freud 1980). Now classical psychoanalysis, in this second stage of theory building, not only considered development in terms of its hypothesized psychosexual stages and attendant characteristic defenses, but it also attempted to understand the emergence of defense mechanisms in terms of ego development (A. Freud 1936). It was thought that a child had to achieve a distinction between ego and id before it utilized repression as a mechanism. By the same token, projection and introjection required a certain differentiation of the self from the environment. As sublimation was dependent on the existence of certain superego values, it did not emerge until later in development.

The third, most recent period of theory building focused on object relations as a central theme. The importance of the earliest object relationships was now stressed. The term *object* was introduced very early in psychoanalytic theory to stand for the loved person. The initial term Freud used to examine the sexual drive was in fact *sexual object*, the person to whom the individual felt sexually attracted. *Object* came to be the word to designate the significant other in a person's life. Object constancy became a central concept in classical developmental theory and referred to the individual's capacity to distinguish between objects and to maintain a relationship to one specific object, regardless of whether his needs were being satisfied or not. When object constancy has been achieved, the child is capable of maintaining a positive image of the absent mother, crucial for individuation and separation from the mother.

The classical theorists have proposed that at the outset of life the ego and id are not separated. This has been termed an undifferentiated phase. The infant is in a phase of primary narcissism and in this period the infant feels himself to be the source of all satisfaction. Such a concept precludes an object relation. This conceptualization is important to keep in mind when distinguishing it from the Kleinian view, for the Kleinians propose that object relations exist from birth. Mahler (1968) conceptualized this first period as a normal autistic phase in which there is no distinction between inner and outer reality. According to Mahler, it extends to about 8 weeks of life. The second phase, termed by Mahler the normal symbiotic phase, begins about the second month. In this period, the infant recognizes the identity of the mother as a need-satisfying object and reacts to her absence. The third stage, Mahler's milestone contribution, is the separation-individuation phase.

Anna Freud (1965) also came to recognize the importance of the earliest object relationships in the formation of early structure. It was realized that when there is an inadequate resolution of the dyadic-stage issues, there will be interference with the resolution of oedipal problems. It was also recognized that the most severe pathology stems from the early failure in the preoedipal period. Moreover, with the advent of ego psychology, defense was no longer viewed as necessarily pathogenic, but as serving adaptive, protective functions as well.

As attention became focused on the preoedipal period, there were attempts to relate the new knowledge about phase-derived developmental pathology to the therapeutic means by which it could be undone. Proponents of the developmental point of view, a subgroup of the classical school, looked at the possibility that the analyst might gratify or supply the patient with what was missing in his development (Settlage 1980). They considered that a therapeutic psychoanalysis might revive and repeat the original developmental process now in a way that could be helpful. However, there were those who claimed that such an approach tended to sidestep the importance of analyzing archaic conflicts, defense, and ego states. A cautionary note was sounded by Anna Freud and others when they noted the adaptive functions of some defense mechanisms; some defenses should not be disturbed by analytic intervention.

In any consideration of Klein's developmental timetable, it is important to understand that the ego exists from birth and employs defenses of a primitive nature from the very beginning of life. The Kleinians claim that the infant has fantasies that attempt to fulfill instinctual drives and that these fantasies provide a defense against the external reality of deprivation, and a defense against internal reality as well, for example, his own hunger and anger (Klein et al. 1955, Klein 1957). In normal development, the first phase of life is "the paranoid-schizoid position, . . . characterized by a split between the good and bad objects and the loving and hating ego, a split in which good experiences predominate over bad ones" (Segal 1964, p. 42), facilitating movement into the next phase, the depressive position. In the depressive position the infant becomes aware of whole objects. Once the infant perceives his mother as a whole object, he discovers that she has a life of her own that is separate from his. This fact underscores his feeling of helplessness and maternal dependence. Her absences are experienced like a death, primarily because he is afraid that he has destroyed the object with his own destructive impulses. It is his ambivalence toward the object and the resultant depression that leads to his wish to repair and restore the fantasied destroyed object.

It is also important to note that the Kleinian theorists have telescoped the Freudian psychosexual stages and relegated them to early infancy. The fact that the Kleinian timetable for its developmental stages is condensed into a very early period of infant development accounts for the use of more primitive defenses in dealing with anxieties related to both preoedipal and oedipal levels. The defenses of splitting, idealization, denial, omnipotence, projection, introjection, and projective identification have all come into operation by the age of 3 months during the Kleinian paranoid-schizoid position. Klein views the infant at a very early stage ejecting his terrifying superego, initially introjected in the oral sadistic stage of his development. The mechanisms of projection and expulsion are very closely tied up with superego formation.

Klein stresses that when the infant identifies himself with the good object, a basis is provided for the feeling that one possesses goodness of one's own. The failure of the infant to identify himself with the good object leads to the development of pathological defenses, in order to avert experiencing himself as bad, evil, greedy, and destructive. Excessive projective identification occurs, according to Kleinian theory, when parts of the self are projected into the object and there ensues a strong confusion between self and object.

The Kleinian view of the well-integrated personality places great emphasis on mature object relations, especially as they involve the respect for people as separate, differentiated individuals. According to the Kleinians the recognition of the separateness of self and object lays the foundation for good reality testing, creativity, sublimation, symbol formation, and the higher thought processes, such as linking and abstraction. Moreover, it forms the basis for the capacity to mourn, to love, to assume responsibility for the expression for one's instinctual impulses, as well as lessening the need to project hostility onto others and making it possible to tolerate one's own aggression.

Treatment goals from the Kleinian point of view are succinctly stated in this passage from Hanna Segal's (1964) book on the work of Melanie Klein:

> The fact that structure is intimately related to unconscious fantasy is extremely important: it is this which makes it possible to influence the structure of the ego and the supergo through analysis. It is by analyzing the ego's relations with objects, internal and external, and altering the fantasies about these objects, that we can materially affect the ego's more permanent structure. [p. 9]

The Kleinians have also stressed that the interpretation of defenses is not effective unless they are interpreted in the context of what the patient feels and does to the analyst in the transference and contact is made with maximum unconscious anxiety.

Self-psychology expounds a different view of child development. Unlike the other schools described above, it does not accept aggressiveness in man as a primary instinctual drive. What Kleinians and classical analysts consider uncontrollable rage in the infant is perceived by self-psychologists as healthy assertiveness. "Aggression is initially absent in the baby if, from the beginning, he is responded to with empathy" (Kohut 1977, p. 119). Only when the infant's security is undermined by unempathic parents does he react with rage; this rage, according to Kohut, is a "disintegration product."

It is important to underscore self-psychology's focus on the deficits and flaws in the child's developmental experience. This emphasis contrasts sharply with the classical view, which focuses on the conflicts that the child must resolve at each developmental stage. The obvious example is contained in the self psychologist's view of the oedipal period. According to Kohut's (1984) theory, oedipal conflict is the result of an earlier developmental failure, or deficit; in the classical view, the oedipal conflict is an important phase in development leading to the formation of the mature superego. Self psychologists have equated conflict with pathology, rather than a growth-producing experience, as conceptualized in the classical view, although self psychologists do view optimal frustration based on empathic failures of a nontraumatic nature as having a positive effect on psychic development. We believe that this latter conception is simply a restatement in self-psychological language of a classical premise, namely, manageable frustration promotes psychic growth.

Self-psychological theory with its emphasis on the crucial importance of parental empathy and on the development of the self, takes little stock in any predetermined unfolding, stage-dominated timetable, and restricts its interest in the development of defensive structures to those that guard the well-being and cohesiveness of the self. The development of psychic structure is both affected and effected by the primary defects acquired in early childhood; these defects are experienced as feelings of emptiness, loneliness, and worthlessness, resulting from inadequate parental mirroring and empathy and resulting in a lack of self cohesion and the formation of defensive structures. Whereas the classical analyst might look for a conflict between instinctual drives and the superego and/or ego demands, the self psychologist will seek out the patient's fear of being reexposed to the humiliating narcissistic injuries of his childhood. This psychopathology "is defined by the fact that the self has not been solidly established, that its cohesion and firmness depend on the presence of a selfobject and that it responds to the loss of the selfobject with simple enfeeblement, various regressions, and fragmentation" (Kohut 1977, p. 137).

Self psychologists minimize the role of insight as a curative factor. Kohut (1977) stressed instead the importance of the selfobject transference and transmuting internalizations in healing the defects in the self structure. A selfobject has been defined as an object experienced as part of the self—an external object that services certain self-preservation needs. We suggest that some form of internalization and possibly projective identification are the processes utilized in the formation of the selfobject. Transmuting internalization occurs when there is optimal frustration that allows for external support to become internal structure, i.e., the conversion of selfobject transferences into self structure (Kohut 1971). Perhaps there is a parallel between transmuting internalization and the classical concepts of identification and identification with the aggressor.

In summary, our review has exposed some sharp theoretical differences among the three schools regarding the development of the human psyche. Some of the differences, however, can be reduced to a question of semantics: closer examination reveals genotypic similarity in certain concepts disguised by language to appear distinctively different on the surface. Each theory contains a psychogenetic view of personality. They all believe that the individual's past has an influence on current functioning. They differ, however, as to which aspects of the individual's past are most significant and when they first originated. The classical school emphasizes oedipal and preoedipal traumas and includes as well traumas that occur at later phases of the life cycle: any of these sources can possibly lead to psychopathology. The Kleinian school, on the other hand, sees these traumas occurring in the first few months of life and tends to underplay the significance of experience. The self psychologists hold that the major difficulties arise in childhood as a result of unempathic mothering, especially in the preoedipal phase. This in turn leads to a derailment of the normal development in the child. In an empathic environment, however, the preoedipal phase is satisfactorily traversed and no oedipal complex develops.

Case Study

We turn now to the case study that was presented to the child analysts from the classical, self-psychological, and Kleinian schools.

It is followed by a discussion of the clinical material as viewed from the three theoretical perspectives. The therapist was Esther Fine.

Jay was referred for therapy at 6 years of age, primarily because he presented a behavioral problem at home and in school. His mother stressed that he was contrary; she described how he resisted cleaning up his room. It was quite clear that the mother was very annoyed with her only child; she said that he was a liar, although from her examples, his lies appeared to be wish-fulfillment fantasies. His teacher reported that he was a troublemaker in the classroom; she claimed that he was very provocative with her and the other children. He was a white child in an almost all-black school, and he would often call black children "niggers," inviting them to attack him. His teacher felt that he should be placed in a special class for disruptive children. She also informed the mother that he showed signs of having serious learning difficulties: he had a very short attention span and failed to complete tasks.

I saw Jay in psychotherapy twice weekly for almost three years. I also saw his mother in counseling sessions every other week; in addition, she was in individual therapy with someone else. During this period the mother moved from a very hostile, rejecting attitude toward her child to one in which she came to view him with great pride and pleasure.

Jay and his mother came to California from an eastern state when Jay was 5. At that time the mother had just left Jay's father and was now living with a new boyfriend. In short order the father appeared on the scene. He began to see Jay on a regular basis while the mother filed for divorce. Jay seemed to care a great deal about his father. He expressed a wish that his parents get back together again. However, Jay also told me that the father called him names: "jerk," "stupid," and "son of a bitch."

The father was a movie buff and very often took Jay to movies or watched films on late-night TV with him; however, many of them were R- and even possibly X-rated ones, filled with violence and explicit sexual scenes. Although the father was apparently a bright man, he led a rather marginal life; he chose to work as little as possible, occasionally making minimum wages at menial work. The mother, for her part, made a fairly good income as a registered nurse.

Jay described his father as a house-husband and indeed until the parents separated, the father stayed home and took care of the child.

He had wanted his wife to abort this child, but she very much wanted him and went ahead with the pregnancy despite her husband's disapproval. According to the mother, the father did not want to take on the responsibilities involved and in addition was very jealous of Jay in his early years; the father claimed that she paid too much attention to Jay and not enough to him.

The mother breast-fed the child for the first 7 months, at which time she claimed he weaned himself. She was working full time during this period, and would pump her breasts so that someone could give him her milk. He had early feeding problems; he had difficulty in shifting from pureed food to solid food, which would infuriate the father, who would insist that he eat. He was toilet trained very early because, the mother explained, he wanted to imitate his father. In later counseling sessions, the mother admitted that both she and the father were extremely impatient with Jay during this early period. Toilet training was accomplished by 13 months, although Jay continued to wet his bed almost up until the last months of therapy, when it was finally resolved in treatment. When Jay was 15 months of age, the father began to spank him. The father seemed to have very high expectations for his child, who always seemed to disappoint him in whatever effort he was making.

When Jay was 3½ years of age, the parents went on vacation and left him with one of his grandmothers. While he was there he developed otitis media, and the grandmother had him hospitalized. The parents did not return at this time and the child reacted intensely to their absence. The mother believed that Jay's personality changed dramatically after the hospitalization. Whereas he had been very cooperative prior to the hospitalization, he now became stubborn and oppositional. There were complaints even at the preschool level that he was a problem child. He became accident prone, too.

From the outset, Jay seemed to feel very positive about "counseling," as he called the therapeutic process. Throughout the treatment, Jay used the metaphor of play to explore and to understand his conflicts and express his feelings of deprivation. His fantasies seemed to provide the proper distance that made it possible for him to examine his problems. Nevertheless, there were those times when Jay would discuss his feelings regarding the separation and divorce of his parents, or his feelings about school, friends, his teachers, his enuresis, his resentment toward his mother and her new boyfriend, and his anger toward his father, but more likely his conflicts and feelings of parental neglect or inadequacy would be expressed in fantasy.

I found Jay to be a very bright, attractive-looking, imaginative 6-year-old, with a certain appealing cocky attitude that sometimes became a petulant and disgruntled one. In the early phases of therapy, I too observed his short attention span. He would flit from one thing to another, abruptly interrupting one activity to go on to another. Usually his fantasies included some conflict between good and evil. I was usually relegated to playing the bad guy, whom he would overpower. Some of the themes focused on his resentment toward a neglectful mother figure. He delighted in playing parents who rejected their children, and who had contempt for their children's neediness. He very often depicted parents having sexual intercourse. He reveled in showing how knowledgeable he was about sexuality, at the same time revealing his confusion about it.

In the initial stage of the therapy, Jay was very open and eager to let me know how much he liked coming to see me. As the therapy proceeded and he became more involved with me, he developed a coolness and toughness, an "I don't care" attitude. It was a thin cover for how much the therapy meant to him; for, if he missed a few minutes at the beginning of a session, he became irritable and demanded that it be made up at the end of the session. The struggle between good and evil took the form of cops and robbers, Nazis against Americans, Indians versus cowboys, and spacemen versus the aliens or the anthropoids, Sitting Bull versus Wild Bill Hickok, Mexicans versus Texans, Americans versus the Japanese or Russians. In countless ways, I felt that Jay expressed his attempt to control his hostile, destructive impulses, which he externalized in the various fantasied battles and wars that we fought on the same or opposing sides. Those battles became the most persistent fantasy that he introduced into the therapy, and they continued up until the very last session.

Another recurrent theme in the therapy was maternal neglect. In the fourth month of therapy, he had the following fantasy about a family of two sons and one daughter: The parents, apparently in an attempt to get away from the children, decided to sleep in the meadow. When I inquired as to what they were doing there, Jay told me, "They were probably humping." The children had been left in the forest and, during the night, were attacked by a robber. The daughter found the parents and reported to them that the son was unconscious. The mother responded, "It's nothing serious. I am a nurse, I know best." In actuality, Jay's mother tended to minimize illnesses and very often would send Jay to school when he complained of feeling ill.

There were many sequences in which Jay used the Ken and Barbie dolls for his fantasy play. Sometimes he would cover them with Kleenex so they could have privacy, Jay explained. During this phase, he was rather seductive with me, and he would attempt to exhibit himself. One time, he was in the bathroom and called to me to join him. I told him that here, people have privacy in the bathroom. "Esther, I have something very interesting to tell you," he said. I told him I could hear him from where I was. Once he realized that I was not going to join him in the bathroom, he called out to me. "I'm only 6 years old and I wear a size 10 underwear." When I rejoined that he was very big for his age, he was very pleased to agree with me.

It was typical for Jay to deprecate me and call me names and to attempt to make me feel stupid and inadequate. Both his parents related to him in this way. Once, while we were playing cavalry (he was the commander-in-chief and I the sergeant), he claimed everything I did was inept. I was called stupid at every turn until finally I complained about this abusive behavior. I told him that when I was a little boy (for in the play I was instructed to be a man), my father called me names like "stupid" and "jerk," especially when I did not get things right the first time. I complained that everyone should be able to make mistakes while they are learning something. I added: "When you call me 'dumbbell,' it reminds me of my father." He looked rather thoughtful and somewhat saddened, and finally he said, "Maybe you should hang around more with your mom." However, on another occasion when there was similar play and similar deprecatory treatment, I complained that he was a perfectionist, not allowing anyone to make any mistakes. He countered, "Better to be a perfectionist than dumb."

Jay brought in material related to the traumatic effects of his hospitalization in a most interesting manner. One day he was looking at the books in my office and inquired about *The Wolfman*. He paged through the book and wanted to know why they called this man "the wolfman." He certainly looked normal enough, Jay commented. I said that it was because he had a dream about wolves, a nightmare. "I have a nightmare," he told me. "They're the only kind of dreams I have. I have had a nightmare for three years since I was 4 years of age. [My mother's friends] are in it. They are good friends who live in [the East]. I'm with them and my mother. I get separated from them. The aliens come and take me away. They cover me with oil and put me in a covered pot. They're going to set the pot on fire. Instead it makes me stronger and stronger like Superman. Finally I break out of the pot and I can fly. I fly away from the alien ship." I asked him if this meant that there was a happy ending. "No," he said. "Because I never find my mother again."

I inquired if he had ever been separated from his mother, as far as he knew. "I've never left her," he told me. "She always leaves me. She's always going off to work." I wondered if he were sometimes scared that she would not come back, but Jay had dealt long enough with this dream and wanted to play out the fantasy of the Mohawk Indians in combat with the cavalry.

In the next session I told him that I had thought a lot about his dream, because it was so interesting, because dreams usually contain a wish, and sometimes they tell us what we are afraid of and how we try to get rid of the fear. He repeated the dream and this time he told me that when the aliens put him in the heater and he fell into the oil, he exploded, after which he had the strength of a thousand men. This made it possible for him to fly away. I told him that I thought his wish was that he would not feel small and helpless and at the mercy of the aliens, people he did not know. I told him that he wished he could be strong as a thousand men and get away from them and back to mother. I pointed out that he mentioned that his mother left him to go to work, but I wondered if there was a time when he might have been away from his mother in a scary place like a hospital with people he did not know who might have done tests on him. "No," he protested. "My mother never left me. She is a nurse. If I went to the hospital, she was with me." His mother told me in our next interview that as soon as she had picked him up after this session, he asked if he had been hospitalized and his mother confirmed that he had an ear infection while he was staying with his grandmother, who felt that he should be in the hospital. The mother stressed that she did not know about it or she would have been there.

It was a few weeks before the subject of the dream surfaced again. Jay told me that he had watched a friend of his mother nurse her baby, that he remembered nursing at his mother's breast. I marveled at such an early memory and he went on to tell me that he remembered being in diapers, too. I told him I knew he had a good memory because of how he remembered his nightmare. He made no comment to my reference to his dream, and instead became frightened of a noise he thought he heard outside my office. He became increasingly fearful and he felt I could not protect him if something were out there. "I'm stronger than you are," he told me. That evening he called me on the telephone to inquire whether I was all right and, with a sigh of relief, said he feared that the Martians might be coming.

In the next session I thanked him for calling me to see if I was safe. I told him that this had happened once before to another boy, who had also worried about me and called me to find out if I was all right. Jay wanted to know who that boy was. I told him that the boy was older than he was—8 years old. "I'm 7," he rejoined. I told him that this boy was concerned for different reasons. Jay wanted to know what those reasons were. I explained that this boy thought that it was the noises that he had heard that were scary, but really he was scared about what he was talking about. When he heard noises, he thought he was afraid of the noises. "What was he talking about?" Jay wanted to know. I told him that he was talking about a time when he was alone, by himself, without his parents. "How long was he by himself?" I told him it was a couple of days, because he was in a hospital. "Why wasn't his mother with him?" Jay demanded to know. I told him that the mother had left him with a babysitter and did not tell her where she was going, so the babysitter could not call her. He had developed tonsilitis and the babysitter had to take him to the hospital. "That couldn't happen to me," he said, "because my mother tells the babysitter where she is. That reminds me," he added, "only *once* my mother wasn't with me in the hospital." I asked him how old he was, and he told me that he was 3 at the time. I suggested that might be why he had the same nightmare for four years.

I learned from the mother that following this session, Jay asked if he could have his tonsils out. A few sessions later, when he was looking at the shelves in my office, I asked him if I could get some advice from him. I reminded him of the boy who had his tonsils out in the hospital at a time when his mother had left him with a babysitter. I explained that I wanted to ask his advice about the fact that the boy now wanted to have his appendix out, even though there was nothing wrong with his appendix. "Why would he want to have his appendix out?" I asked. After some reflection he replied, "His mother is going to go with him, isn't she? Because he told her about it!" "Are you telling me," I asked, "that he would want to make sure his mother came with him this time?" "Yes, that's the $64,000 answer!" he told me.

In a later session Jay chatted at length about different skits on "Saturday Night Live" and about which performers he preferred. He told me that he liked the actors better in the old "Saturday Night Live"; he missed them. I commented that a person gets attached to people and misses them when they are no longer around. He agreed, and he began to reminisce about his friends he had left behind in the East and how he missed them. He described how his mother had come out to California before him; later he flew on an airplane to be with her. He was only 5, he told me. I suggested that it might have been a little scary to come out by himself. At first he denied it, but then acknowledged that he had been scared.

In the fantasy that followed this discussion, he said that we were in a spaceship designed for landing on the Moon. It was a moonmobile and we were to be those people in the spaceship. He explained that we were equipped with ray guns and bombs because we might meet up with aliens. We had a robot by the name of Snickers. Jay fought the aliens who attacked us time and again. He dropped bombs on them. At one point, however, he said that he had been away from Earth twelve years; he wanted to return; he had a message from his wife that she was having a baby. I expressed surprise that he had been away for twelve years and she was now having a baby. Without missing a beat, he immediately responded, "That's right, and it only takes nine months to have a baby. That means my wife is having a baby with another man." He decided to blow up Earth, but after he did, he discovered that his wife and her boyfriend had already fled. He had killed the Earth people for nothing.

The play just described continued the following session. We continued to fight the aliens from our spaceship; but, in addition, we had to catch the mother ship, and he had to murder the two of them for having a baby together. Jay said that he wanted to handle the murder himself, and so he embarked on the mother ship alone. He returned to tell me that the boyfriend was dead; however, he had spared his wife. I asked what happened to the boyfriend. He told me he had poisoned his food, and that he was dead, but nobody knew that *he* had murdered him. I said that I was really surprised he was able to get along so well with his wife; I knew how furious he was with her for going off with her lover. "What's the matter with you?" he asked. "Don't you know about 'forgive and forget'?" I told him how much I admired his being able to forgive his wife, to see her faults and still care for her. Jay looked very proud of himself.

I wanted to understand how the specifics of this fantasy might be rooted in the realities of Jay's life; however, when I questioned his mother about this period of time, she was reluctant at first to discuss it. Finally, she confessed to me that she had become pregnant by a lover and had had an abortion shortly before coming to California. It was likely that Jay knew about it, as she had confided in Jay's babysitter while he was present. Jay's fantasy seemed to suggest that he was now ready to forgive what he had obviously not forgotten. Following this play sequence, his separation anxiety lessened considerably as he continued to work through problems related to it.

Discussion

Here are selected highlights from some of the classical, self-psychological, and Kleinian analysts' reactions to this case study. We focus on features that distinguish the differences in their respective treatment approaches.

The classical analytic camp detailed characteristic, expectable guidelines for a positive therapeutic outcome in accordance with accepted classical ideas about the therapeutic process. It was stated that the purpose of classical psychoanalysis is change via interpretations of unconscious conflicts by pointing to its manifestations in three arenas—the past, the present, and the transference with the aim of widening the scope of the ego over the inner life of the child. It was also clear that preoedipal and oedipal issues framed the classical analyst's thinking about this case. Another emphasis was on the analysis of defenses, also an important hallmark of classical psychoanalysis. A distinction was drawn between adult analysis and that of a child. In the latter it was crucial to have ongoing contact with parents in order to develop a therapeutic alliance with them and help them understand their child better, and in order for the therapist to have a better grasp of the child's reality. Clinical examples from the case material were used to exemplify these points. These will be described.

Indication of change via interpretation was cited as evidence in the session that Jay boasted of flying to California by himself and in this way denied his anxiety. Jay followed this claim by a fantasy in which he was in a moonmobile for twelve years. The results of the interpretations offered in this session were twofold: (1) there was a burst of insight expressed on a higher level, not within the play, which was reflected in Jay's comment, "Don't you know about 'forgive and forget'?" and (2) there was a lessening of his separation anxiety following a typical oedipal interpretation of "kill the father and spare the mother." It was also pointed out that the therapist represented the wished-for dyadic preoedipal mother who would spend twelve years exclusively with him and not the actual mother who divided her time between career, social life, and parenting.

Transferential issues were discussed from the classical point of view. It was noted that the therapist was relegated to playing the bad guy in most cases. It was Jay's parents who were impatient with him during the toilet training period, but in the therapy the child did describe actively, via a projection, what he experienced passively at the hands of both parents. *He* was the bad preoedipal child who wet his bed, but in the play he became the good person and the therapist the bad. His severe superego and his poor self-esteem were reflected in his battles between good and evil, those games when the therapist was called stupid, and in his comment, "Better to be a perfectionist than dumb!" In this fashion the child revealed his identification with his father, the perfectionist—his identification with the aggressor. Two aspects of the transference were revealed in this session: (1) the preoedipal and oedipal father transference and (2) the splitting of objects into good and bad.

The sexualization of the transference was mentioned as predictable because the child was the only son of a mother who obtained a divorce during the child's oedipal phase. In addition, he had a father who took him to R-rated movies instead of standing between the child and the child's oedipal wishes. Moreover, the child witnessed sexual relations on and probably off the screen; and these overstimulations were bound to come back in the transference. The bathroom scene in which the therapist was invited to join the child in the bathroom was cited as an example. In this case, the classical analyst would be concerned with the child's drive and especially his ego development and, therefore, he would follow the rule of abstinence and verbalization rather than enactment. Rather than joining the child in the bathroom and participating like the parents in the overstimulation of the child—or viewed from the child's inner life, participating in his voyeurism and phallic narcissistic exhibitionism—it is important to encourage the child to talk. The fact that the therapist elected not to make an interpretation about Jay's boast of size 10 underwear, and instead reassured him, might have slowed down the rate of the child's uncovering his inner life—in this analyst's view. He also suggested that the therapist's reassuring comment may have been indicative of a countertransference reaction. He conjectured what he might have interpreted to the child in this situation. He speculated that if the child had gone to the movies with his father just prior to this session, he might have been more anxious than usual. The analyst would then tell him a story about another boy who had also asked him to come into the bathroom. His reason for inviting him was that he had seen something in the movie with his father that had upset him very much; namely, he saw a man with a very big wienie and the boy was worried that his wienie would never be that big. Such an interpretation would be an attempt to deal with the anxiety provoked by these R- and X-rated movies. However, if the analyst sensed that the child was being seductive with him, he would have had the impression that the child was enacting a sexual masturbatory fantasy. He then would have offered a different story. He would have said that the boy in the bathroom thought that if he had a wienie as big as his mother's new boyfriend's, then his mother or the analyst would love him so much that they would want to hump with him and make babies with him.

This classical analyst also stressed the importance of the therapist as a developmental object in the real relationship with the patient. This emphasis coincides with the self-psychological view that the crucial therapeutic element in treatment is the therapist as a selfobject.

As mentioned earlier, the analysis of defenses is a crucial component of any classical analytic process. The classical analyst pointed out that Jay externalized his hostile bad self, not only in calling black children "niggers" but also in the many battles of good versus evil in the therapy. The identification with the aggressor was apparent in his punitive hostile stance with the therapist when he played out being her commander. The child also used the mechanism of denial in connection with a long solo airplane flight.

Another important element of any classical approach in therapy is reconstruction. Reconstruction was used in this case in analyzing the dream material the child presented. It seemed to help him integrate the memory of his traumatic hospitalization and lessen its deleterious effects, especially as it related to his separation anxiety. While such reconstruction was deemed appropriate from the classical point of view, as will be noted next, the self psychologists considered it injurious to the child's sense of self cohesion.

The self psychologists were highly critical of the therapeutic approach used in the case presented. They claimed it was based on two faulty assumptions: (1) the cure lies in the child's acceptance of objective reality, and (2) the child has a need to understand his hostile and destructive impulses. It was pointed out that, from the self-psychological view, Jay's problems were rooted in chronic repetitive interactions with vital selfobjects and did not originate from specific events, or hostile, aggressive feelings.

The self psychologists took issue with the interpretations of the battles between various factions. According to the self-psychological view, these were not battles of good versus evil, reflecting an attempt to control hostile, destructive impulses. Rather, they reflected the child's feelings about maternal neglect, which forced him to rely only on himself. The reason the child had to be a perfectionist, according to the self psychologists, is that the child felt that he had to take care of himself if he made a mistake; therefore, if he made a *fatal* error, there would be no one to whom he could turn. The reason Jay wanted his therapist to be a perfectionist, again according to the self psychologists, was because the therapist had become part of the child's expanded self.

The self psychologists claimed that the reported dream was a "self-state dream" in which the manifest content was most important and the transference was in the background. The dream was interpreted as expressing the danger in being separated from the mother. The task of reestablishing the tie to the mother was everything to him. The self psychologists agreed with each other that a rupture occurred when the dream was interpreted. In general they held the opinion that it was a mistake to focus on the hospitalization, because it forced Jay to defend his mother as a vital, idealized, structural part of himself, and it forced him to regress to grandiosity, reflected in his comment that he was stronger than his therapist; this suggested that she was no longer a safe haven for him.

The moonmobile fantasy was also interpreted incorrectly, from the self psychologists' point of view. Interpreting the defense of denial was too narrow, and the child's comment about forgive and forget was not a sign of improvement but an indication of submission to the therapist's wish that he be considerate and forgiving.

The self psychologists believed that the therapist traumatized the child in not appreciating his structural needs and his vulnerability. Although very critical of the therapist's understanding of the case and her interventions, they felt the need to explain the improvement that had occurred in the therapy, as well as the positive outcome of the treatment process. It was attributed to the internalization of the calming, equilibrating functions of the therapist; it was stated that the child loved the therapist, and therefore the treatment was successful.

One of the Kleinian analysts provided the following analysis of this case, highlighting a characteristic Kleinian approach. He stated that the task of therapy is to change a moral outlook to a scientific one: that is to say, the infant may see the breast as being powerful and, therefore, persecutory when not present, whereas the mother sees the breast as being cooperative and helpful. The parents' view is a scientific, cooperative point of view that contrasts strikingly with the moral point of view of the child. The scientific view contains the idea that there is an evaluation of reality as being true or false. In the moral point of view, reality is perceived as good or bad, driven by guilt or fear or the escape from these emotions.

In Jay's case, it is clear that his fantasies are dominated by the moral position, which is, in Kleinian terminology, the paranoid-schizoid position. The primary mechanisms that are used are splitting and projection—splitting self and object into good and bad parts with an attack upon the bad parts so that they are broken into little fragments and projected. The good remaining is idealized. The bad parts are projected with the result that the patient feels persecuted by many bad objects. The Kleinian points out that this is seen to be the case in a very profound way with this patient.

The preservation of the good object or the good mother, in this case the idealization of the therapist, is important in the therapeutic process; Jay perceived the therapist from the very beginning as someone who was a container of goodness, a portent of a positive treatment outcome.

According to Kleinian theorists, the whole object is recognized in the depressive position. The important defense against the depressive position is manic omnipotence, and it is used very commonly in learning disorders. Jay displayed many manic defenses. The child had experienced abandonment, depreciation, and neglect, and he had learned not to allow himself to feel helpless. In addition, his parents wanted him to act grown-up and, therefore, blocked his experiencing feelings of dependency. Jay's manic defenses were expressed in his stubbornness, his oppositional behavior, his "I don't care" attitude. There was evidence of splitting, projection, and feelings of persecution.

Continuing with the problem of learning disorders, it was stated that learning involves the capacity to bear the unknown. Paranoid-schizoid mechanisms caused terror and the need to control the unknown. Moralists do not learn because they already know what is right and wrong, what is good and what is bad. Splitting, a characteristic mechanism in the paranoid-schizoid position, attacks linking and interferes with the ability to understand connections.

The therapy, in the Kleinian's view, provided the needed person who contained, that is, who offered understanding, and "took all the splitting and projections and manic behavior and contained them, not by retaliating but by interpreting; therefore, he was able to identify with a containing, thoughtful, cooperative parent instead of a powerful, omnipotent one."

In contrast to the self-psychological point of view, this Kleinian analyst concluded that the proffered interpretations were ameliorative. He claimed that Jay showed slow evolution by introjecting the containing therapist with her interpretive insights. The changes that occurred were reflected in the fact that the child dealt more and more with his mother as a whole object, one who had a life of her own and had relationships with other people. As the child recognized his dependency on his mother and the therapist, he no longer could easily split and project. In Kleinian language, he shifted from projective identifications to introjective identifications of a good object and, therefore, the beginning formation of trust. No longer could he attack the internalized object by splitting, projecting it, and destroying it, because to destroy the bad object would destroy the good object, now one and the same. Therefore, the child needed to preserve and repair the relationship with the mother. The sadistic attacks on the mother had been clearly connected with feelings of loss and abandonment.

The Kleinian analyst's impression of the case can be summarized as follows: Jay began therapy dominated by mechanisms of the paranoid-schizoid position. He struggled against the recognition of the mother as a whole object, frequently through the use of manic defenses. He then entered the depressive position and, at the end, made reparative acts through his fantasies and, although tinged with manic traces, clearly indicated a concern and need for the mother and an experience of her as a whole object. Therefore, the issue of separation anxiety began to be dealt with in a more reasonable and manageable way.

The authors found the variation in the theoretical conceptualization and technical approach to the treatment of this 6-year-old boy a striking commentary on the extent to which theory governs perception, understanding, and intervention in a given clinical case. It raises considerable doubt about Wallerstein's (1988) idea that the actual differences among the analytic schools are more illusory than real. Indeed, we are increasingly doubtful that there could be a unitary theory that would incorporate these disparate conceptualizations, and that is not to say that one cannot borrow theoretical and technical ideas compatible with one's therapeutic modus operandi.

In her work with this child the therapist most closely followed the classical analytic model. However, as the classical analyst noted, she deviated from strict adherence; for example, she was reassuring instead of interpretive when Jay wanted her to be impressed by the size of his underwear. The divergence was greatest in the self-psychological view of this case. One could express the self-psychological perspective as follows: Jay, feeling there was no direction from either parent, had to make himself impervious to any criticism; he must be perfect, in order to steer a safe ship by himself in shark infested waters. Even from the self-psychological point of view, the authors see it differently. We believe that Jay was attempting to merge with an omnipotent, critical, perfectionistic parent, an idealized parent imago, in Kohutian terms, in order to maintain his self-esteem and self cohesion. However, from the classical view, the therapist was not only pointing out the child's defensive identification with his parents, she was speaking for the battered Jay, in an attempt to get him to be more tolerant of himself and, perhaps, to feel a little angry with his parents' intolerance of his imperfections.

It was also puzzling that a self psychologist would conclude that the therapist was making moralizing comments to Jay, forcing him to accept her view. It was the child who said, "What's the matter, don't you know about 'forgive and forget'?" By confirming his view, it would seem that she was helping him to deal with his strongly ambivalent feelings toward his mother. In self-psychological terms, it might be stated that she was mirroring him. In Kleinian terms, one might say that he was moving into the depressive position. After two years in which he either killed off the mother figure or at least sentenced her to death, it would seem that this was a generosity of spirit reflective of an advance in psychic development.

It is interesting to note that a Kleinian stresses the importance of dwelling on Jay's jealous and angry feelings, and accepts the idea that Jay has an internalized conflict between good and evil, whereas a self psychologist objects to such a view. This is consistent with each one's theoretical stance. The self psychologist does not acknowledge or interpret hostility directly; the Kleinian not only interprets it, he focuses on it.

The self psychologist stated that the therapist erred by making the assumption that the key to cure lay in ascertaining the true facts; then, Jay would be able to control his hostile impulses. Here, we believe that we see an important split between the classical and the self-psychological points of view. If one subscribes to the conflict theory of opposing forces, if one believes in the power of the unconscious and of repression to produce disturbing symptoms and behaviors, then the therapeutic focus is on bringing to light and liberating the repressed rage and hurt of the patient. Let us relate this to the case: Jay repressed his thoughts and feelings about being abandoned, not only in the hospital but when his mother left him for business or for a lover or for California. He had to repress memories connected with those thoughts and feelings, because they were too disturbing. However, they came back to him in the form of nightmares, separation anxiety, and disruptive behavior in school, with hostility aimed at his teacher and peers rather than his mother. His efforts, sometimes painful, at recalling and accepting the memory of his hospitalization led at first to increased fearfulness, but this was followed by a greater tolerance of his ambivalence as he allowed memories to surface and to become integrated.

The self psychologist's characterization of the dream interpretation as traumatizing again highlights the effect of viewing clinical data through a different theoretical lens. The Kleinians and self psychologists, each in their respective way, tend to minimize the effect of specific traumatic incidents on development, the Kleinians because of their focus on the primitive, instinctually derived internal fantasy world of the patient, and the self psychologists with their emphasis on the degree of overall empathic parenting. The classical school is more likely to acknowledge the effect of specific traumatic incidents on psychological development, especially when they are reflective of an ongoing theme in other events in the child's life. It is, therefore, not surprising that self psychologists and Kleinians might object to a focus on the effect of Jay's hospitalization on his formative years. It is also not surprising that the self psychologists would regard Jay's increased anxiety in dealing with the dream material as indicative of rupture in the patient–therapist relationship.

On the other hand, the classical view holds that as the patient approaches the unconscious conflict, his anxiety does increase. Indeed, Jay became more anxious as he came close to facing the painful memory of his hospitalization, which reinforced his fears of abandonment. He defended against the surfacing of this memory by projecting the danger onto the noises outside the therapy office.

However, he *did* struggle with and face these dangers, and he *did* place them in perspective, and his separation anxiety *did* diminish. His response to the dream interpretation marked the turning point in the treatment. It was followed in short order by the moonmobile fantasy where Jay touched base with another disturbing memory—his mother's pregnancy and infidelity—and this play was followed by a request from Jay that we work on his enuresis. We cannot accept the idea that Jay's improvement related only to the therapist's being kindly and caring. It is our view that love is not enough. We are convinced that the interpretive work was indeed the therapeutic agent that fueled his improvement. No doubt Jay's sense of helplessness was mastered in part by means of hope combined with his attachment to an understanding companion (i.e., the therapist), but it is also our contention that Jay required help in assessing how his mind worked and how his mind scared him "out of his mind." Our readers, of course, may well conclude that we, too, are prisoners of our theoretical perspective.

ACKNOWLEDGMENT

The authors are very grateful to Drs. Heiman van Dam, Elliot Tressan, and Lionel Margolin for their excellent analyses of the case study.

REFERENCES

Fine, S., and Fine, E. (1989). Four psychoanalytic perspectives: a study of differences in interpretive interventions. *Journal of the American Psychoanalytic Association* 38:1017–1047.

Freud, A. (1936). *The Ego and the Mechanisms of Defence.* New York: International Universities Press.

——— (1965). *Normality and Pathology in Childhood.* New York: International Universities Press.

Klein, M. (1957). *Envy and Gratitude*. New York: Basic Books.

Klein, M., Heimann, P., Money-Kyrle, R., et al. (1955). On identification. In *New Directions in Psychoanalysis*, pp. 309–345. New York: Basic Books.

Kohut, H. (1971). *The Analysis of the Self.* New York: International Universities Press.

———(1977). *The Restoration of the Self.* New York: International Universities Press.

———(1984). *How Does Analysis Cure?* Chicago: University of Chicago Press.

Mahler, M. S. (1968). *On Human Symbiosis and the Vicissitudes of Individuation.* Madison, CT: International Universities Press.

Sandler, J., and Freud, A. (1980). Discussions on the Hampstead Index: 1. Ego as the seat of observation. *Bulletin of the Hampstead Clinic* 3(4):199–212.

Segal, H. (1964). *Introduction to the Work of Melanie Klein.* New York: Basic Books.

Settlage, C. (1980). Psychoanalytic developmental thinking in current and historical perspective. *Psychoanalysis and Contemporary Thought* 3(2):139–170.

Wallerstein, R. S. (1988). One psychoanalysis or many. *International Journal of Psycho-Analysis* 69:5–21.

5

Tools of Play Therapy

Carol A. Francis

Play therapy is effective because a therapist travels beyond the typical understanding of a child's play activities and decodes the metaphors, symbols, and processes that occur in playing. Thereafter, the therapist utilizes the decoded information to enhance the child's ability to observe and understand himself or herself. In other words, the unconscious messages revealed in play activities become usable to the child because the therapist translates the play activities into significant conscious messages. This translation produces changes in the child; the more conscious the internal psychological world of the child becomes, the less negative impact internal conflicts, fears, and confusions will exert over the child.

In the following three sections, different aspects of play therapy that facilitate the therapist's journey with any child are detailed. In the first section, seven ways that children use play to express psychological issues are discussed (Table 5-1), to help therapists organize what the child is expressing into significant categories. Organizing the child's words and actions into one or more of these seven categories enables therapists to observe better and to analyze a child's messages. These categories, however, are not intended to be used as a rigid classification of a child's behaviors.

The second section discusses six verbal tools that a therapist can use to relate with the child during play therapy. Whenever a therapist needs to communicate something to or interact with the child, one or more of these verbal tools might be employed.

Table 5–1. Seven Categories of Expression during Play Therapy

Category	*Definition*
Sensations	Play that expresses sensations of touch, taste, hearing, seeing, smelling, or maneuvering may be associated with developmental issues or with aspects of past experiences.
Discharge	Aggression, anxiety, desires, or drives to live, die, or learn may become central to sessions as the child demonstrates the need to respond to such basic internal states.
Defenses	Defensive responses against insights, anxieties, memories, or change can include many playful or nonplayful forms of distractions, repression, or disguises.
Mastery	Age-appropriate tasks and skills are explored in the play and talk during play therapy. They are associated with developmental progression predominantly as well as with the experiences of praise, personal success, and self-esteem.
Problem solving	Issues, events, or complications may be played out in the therapy as a means of exploring and experimenting with various ways to solve the problems facing the child.
Establishing relationships	When difficulty with family members, friends, teachers, or neighbors confronts a child or when a child cannot seem to effectively establish friendships or get along with a particular individual, the therapy becomes an arena in which the child practices many ways to understand, cope with, and interact with a person.
Inner world	Expression of internal fantasies and processes can be directly expressed and explored by the child during every aspect of therapy.

The third section discusses four nonverbal tools a therapist can use to relate with the child. When talking is distracting, impinging, or meaningless, nonverbal therapeutic interventions can speak effectively to a child.

SEVEN CATEGORIES OF EXPRESSION IN PLAY THERAPY

Children use words, activities, and objects in the therapy room to express psychological experiences that involve sensations, discharge, defenses or resistances, mastery of skills, problem solving, relationships, and internal fantasies or processes. These seven categories of expression are described and illustrated below. While observing a child's activities, the therapist can contemplate which categories are being depicted. The therapist will then be able to tailor responses that will further enable the child to explore that area of concern.

Sensations

Children may use play therapy as a means of focusing on the *sensations* that are symbolized or created by the objects or activities used in the play. The therapist needs to note what sensations are being symbolized or created, and thereafter to ascertain why such a sensation is significant for the child. There are many reasons why sensual experiences become central aspects to a child's play.

Infants first experience people, objects, and events sensually. Through proprioceptive processes (Spitz 1965, Sullivan 1953) infants perceive, interact, and organize the outside world based on bodily sensations. Thus, a child's focus on sensual aspects of play activities and objects could be associated with these early developmental proprioceptive memories. Children may attempt to resolve or share painful proprioceptive memories by replicating the sensations of that past experience. They may also attempt to recapture lost or desired proprioceptive experiences by regressing to that developmental level of awareness.

> Sarah, age 7, would wrap her body inside a large one-inch-thick foam pad in the therapy room. She would squeal delightedly as she calmly rested or gently wrestled within the pad. Apparently, being wrapped in the foam pad replicated early memories of being held in her mother's lap or perhaps in mother's womb. Sarah longed to recapture that safe and cozy sensation that was lost prematurely due to her mother's depressive withdrawal.

In terms of diagnostic considerations, therapists need to note that certain preoccupations with sensual aspects of objects or activities are typical of autistic states (Tustin 1981, 1990).

> During an evaluation with Randy, age 13, this sensual use of objects was demonstrated. He held the rubber ball against his face and leaned his head against it as if to feel the softness and buoyancy. Soon he began to rub the ball on his cheek, reddening his face as a consequence. Throughout the remainder of the session, he would hold the ball and alternatingly squeeze it and rub various parts of his body with it. These types of behaviors were characteristic of his daily activities at home and at school. He was diagnosed as having a pervasive developmental disorder, that is, autism.

Discharge

Discharging energy or urges is another feature of children's play during therapy. Unwanted or painful urges, impulses, drives, or tensions might be symbolically eliminated through various actions.

> Eddie, age 10, feverishly flung his toys and papers out of his closet, simultaneously expressing pent-up tension and his urge to explode.

Urges that are more pleasant when they are being discharged might also be represented in play activities.

> Four-year-old Lindy pretended to be ravenously hungry and began searching the office for hidden "food." After she discovered

the "food" underneath her therapist's chair, she insisted that the therapist hold it. She then licked and chewed the "food" out of her therapist's hands. Many psychological issues were represented in this play scenario, but the primary theme experienced by Lindy was her urge to eat and her drive to become satiated.

Different discharge themes that children manifest in therapy include the following: Anxieties or fantasies that have become attached primitively to biological urge, such as sucking, urinating, and defecating, may be portrayed. Aggression and attachment as drives, not as more complex states of emotion, may be expressed through play activities resulting in either pleasure or pain. Survival and death instincts, sexual drives, and epistemophiliac impulses (that is, the urge to explore and the ecstasy of discovery) also can be observed as predominant reasons for a child's play activities (Klein 1961, 1975).

Four-year-old Pedro mounted up on the desk as one would mount a horse and then jumped off, landing on the floor with a shoulder roll and a wild animal-like grunt of pleasure. This process was repeated for the entirety of five consecutive sessions with slight modifications as interpretations were offered. During the sixth session, Pedro dropped a male doll on a female doll with similar energy and sounds. The mounting, dropping, and grunting began to organize into a series of sexual acts between the male and female doll. Sexual and aggressive urges were being discharged, producing pleasure for Pedro during these sessions. While the play could also be considered a representation of other material, the predominant experience for Pedro was release and satisfaction of sexual and aggressive drives.

Defense or Resistance

As in adult therapy, defenses against anxieties, conflicts, or insights are prevalent in child play therapy. Toys, actions, dramas, games, questions, or dialogues can function primarily as disguises, distractions, or repressions. All defenses, such as projection, splitting, idealization, denial, repression, sublimation, and intellectualization are evident at one point or another in a child's play (A. Freud 1965).

Once the child's use of defenses is identified, the therapist might choose to discuss the nature of the child's defenses or discuss what the defenses are shielding against.

> When 9-year-old Sarah begins hiding drawings of her brother, the therapist can comment on the defense being used, such as hiding, by stating, "You're hiding pictures of your brother in the hopes that you will be able to forget he exists." The therapist could also comment on why Sarah is using repression or denial (hiding). "You wish you could forget your brother existed so you wouldn't have to feel so jealous about the attention he is getting from your mother. So, you are hiding his pictures as if you could be rid of him and have your mother's full attention again."

If play therapy appears stuck or nonproductive, consider the possibility of needing to interpret the activity of the session as defensive or resistant in nature. Failure to deal with the defenses manifested in play therapy causes the work to become stale, meaningless, or stagnant. When therapists feel most frustrated and incapable of making a difference for and with the child, the defenses may be the formidable opponent.

Change can be as threatening to a child as it is to an adult. Interventions in therapy that might produce change may be considered by the child to be destructive to self, parents, or the family structure. As a consequence, a child may view resistances or defenses in therapy as vitally important to survival. The child will not automatically view the therapist as a benevolent person with the ability to ease pains or conflicts. Therefore, the child may depend on defenses to protect against the therapist's capacity to reveal unwelcome information or produce unwanted changes.

> Mick, age 11, performed magic tricks with coins, strings, and other pocket-sized materials. While at first such play seemed indicative of his developmentally appropriate attempt to master a task, such interpretations of the magic failed to produce movement in the sessions. When the magic was interpreted as a defense against becoming aware of feeling powerless at home, movement occurred. The

magic symbolically represented manic defenses such as denial, idealization, and omnipotence (Klein 1940, 1946). These defenses were being employed to ward off feelings and conflicts that seemed too painful to face. As long as these defenses and the reason for the defenses were ignored, the therapy remained ineffective and Mick retained an artificial security by remaining unchanged.

Mastery

At every age, children are confronted with skills that they need to master. These developmental skills are discussed by many researchers and theoreticians. Piaget's (1962) cognitive skills, Erikson's (1950/1963) psychosocial skills, and Mahler's (1979) separation-individuation phases are a few of many developmental schemata worthy of study.

Familiarity with the broad range of information regarding child development is essential in order to appreciate and recognize the skills, tasks, or developmental processes a child's behavior reflects during play therapy. If the child is expressing behaviors that seem age-appropriate, therapeutic interventions might be mainly supportive. If the child's behaviors are immature, therapy may be dealing with regression, fixation, or developmentally delayed issues.

Through trial and error, experimentation, dramas with dolls and toys, question-and-answer sessions, and many other avenues, children demonstrate their awareness and concerns about mastering skills and tasks. They also react to their successful and unsuccessful attempts to master those tasks in therapy.

Nicole, age 6, methodically maneuvered the putty into long snake-like shapes and chopped the snake into carefully measured, equal parts. Slowly, she began to position the equal parts into the shape of the capital letters of the alphabet. Through trial and error, she ultimately succeeded at recalling and reproducing the alphabet as she had recently learned in school. She was thus expressing her mastery of an age-appropriate task to the therapist. In addition, she clearly received little recognition at home for her accomplishments and was hungry for such acknowledgment.

Problem Solving

When children recognize that a problem exists and when children feel or think the solution to the problem is their responsibility, therapy may be selected as the arena for attempting to solve problems. The problems to be solved vary depending on the development and environment of the child.

Darren, age 13, erroneously blamed himself for his father's depression. To solve his father's depression, Darren unconsciously devised plans for removing himself from his father's home, thus relieving his father of the depressing burden of raising his son. Darren realized that his father would feel too guilty about returning Darren to his mother's turbulent home. However, Darren felt that he should live with his mother in order to rescue his father from the depression that might lead to another suicide attempt.

Darren's plans, therefore, needed to include ways of "forcing" his father to return him to the mother so that his father would be free of guilt or responsibility. Darren began manipulating the clinic, his therapist, his father's therapist, his father's girlfriend, his school, and his father by a number of clever but disturbing maneuvers. When interpretations began to address this motivation for his misbehavior, Darren insightfully and purposefully began to change. He developed friendships with boys and girls who were his age, and he reduced the behaviors that were intended to anger and alienate his father. He had believed that he was responsible for reducing his father's depression, and, as a consequence, therapy as well as the therapeutic setting became the arena in which he attempted to solve this perceived problem.

Nine-year-old Jane was the youngest and most sensitive individual in her family. Her parents were unhappily married. Jane was distracted and disruptive at school to such a degree that she was diagnosed as a provisionally schizophrenic by the school psychologist. Extensive testing did not reveal this disturbance but suggested, among other things, a low self-esteem and high verbal skills. However, the behavior was severe enough to force her parents to seek therapy for her. The obvious distress in the family was the parents' marital power struggles and emotional blackmail. After ten months of marital therapy, Jane's parents were happier. During these ten months, Jane's misbehavior stopped and academic progress was noteworthy. In essence, Jane's behaviors mobilized her parents to resolve their problems.

Coping with and working through reactions to traumatic events is another set of problems children attempt to resolve in therapy. Traumatic events include death of a significant person, divorce, abuse, natural or man-made disasters, and sudden and disruptive changes. Play activities typically symbolize the child's perception of both the nature and the impact of these traumatic events. When the defenses against reenacting or reexperiencing the trauma are lessened, children traverse through painful recollections, fantasies, guilt, confusion, or anger as they repetitively reproduce slices of different reactions to the trauma.

Raphaela's father died in an accident from which his body could not be recovered. She felt (1) angry at her mother for not protecting her father, (2) jealous of other children who had their fathers, (3) condemned to miss her father and be forever depressed in order to keep his memory alive, and (4) conflicted by urges to be happy despite her father's tragic ending. Defenses of denial, isolation, and projection kept Raphaela from working through her reactions. Once such defenses were lowered, extremely angry and painful play sessions occurred that eventually led to catharsis, modification of perception, and reduction of conflicts regarding her father's death.

Practicing to Establish Relationships

Improving relationships with other people and with one's self is often the objective of patients and therapists throughout therapy. However, sometimes in play therapy, a child is predominantly manifesting behaviors and emotions that are associated with the issues of relating with others.

Anna, age 9, her parents, and two therapists discussed Anna's "problem behaviors" in a small play-therapy office. After asking for and receiving permission, Anna began playing with the toys in the room. At first, she played in a solitary manner and only interacted when her parents stated something she felt needed a comment. By these comments, Anna demonstrated that she was closely attending to what was being discussed. During this time, her parents explained how they appreciated her ability to entertain herself at home.

Anna's father then began to complain in an irritated manner that as soon as he arrived home, Anna wanted his attention, asking him to walk to the park, play ball, or read to her. He felt these behaviors were too demanding, insensitive, and inappropriate. Her mother added her observations about these "misbehaviors" and agreed with the father's objections. Anna, at this point, quietly began to "make" a "cupcake" out of a sponge ball and a cup. She pretended to eat it. Then she offered it to her therapist who took the cupcake and pretended to eat, too. Anna next offered the cupcake to her father. He took the object and held it as if intending to keep Anna from disrupting the session. He soon thereafter told Anna to stop distracting him. Her play activities clearly indicated her unsuccessful attempts to connect with her parents, her father in particular.

Steve, an immature 14-year-old, had never liked girls. His mother's rejections had initiated this dislike. Much teasing from girls during elementary and junior high school about his weight problem and his glasses reinforced this reaction. But when a cute, female schoolmate befriended Steve, he wanted to reciprocate. However, his dislike of girls had become too ingrained and interfered with his ability to return this girl's interest without becoming critical or cruel toward her. He used therapy as a means of addressing his dislike of females and his associated lowered self-esteem. Transference with his female therapist, rehearsal of different conversations he might wish to have with this girl, modeling of different clothing styles, and spontaneous role-playing games (in a play-therapeutic, nondirective manner) were employed by Steve to increase his ability to relate to this girl without animosity or awkwardness. This first relationship with a girl grew into a simple, warm, and sincere friendship.

Expressions of the Child's Inner World

Internal fantasies and internal processes are expressed during play therapy. Self-expression of fantasies may include symbolic, metaphoric, or literal representations of beliefs, feelings, thoughts, perceptions, or values that the child has adopted. In addition, children manifest conflicts and concerns about who they are or what they perceive themselves to be experiencing personally. They will also share their own opinions and reactions to other people or circumstances. The relationship between internalized objects and between internalized aspects of the self may also be evident.

Children may need to use the therapy as a place for exploring internal fantasies. For example, attention and recognition are often unavailable to a child in the home or at school. By utilizing the therapist as a means of addressing the need for attention and recognition, the child may be expressing the need to be valued, affirmed, observed, or noticed. Children can also use therapy to learn more effective means of attaining the type of attention they desire.

Recognition of the internal world is not the only reason for such expression, however. Self-definition or identity formation is often attained in therapy by way of self-exploratory processes. The self-exploration can be in terms of expressing reactions to external people and events, or reactions to internal feelings and thoughts. The therapist at these moments serves the purpose of reflecting and describing the information. In addition, the therapist can offer statements of clarification and questions that allow for further self-examination.

Resolution of internal conflicts frequently motivates children to reveal themselves to a therapist. Opposing feelings of love and hate for a mother, need for one's own identity, fear and need of an abusive adult, oedipal issues, or guilt about death or divorce are a few examples of internal conflicts confronting children.

If these reasons for expression of internal processes are not addressed as the intimate private concerns of the child, the purpose of the expression may be lost for the child. These types of issues may have nothing to do with external events or relationships. Rather, the child may use therapy as a place where one can be occupied with the self, one's identity, or one's internal core without external distractions.

Jenny, age 10, suffered diagnosable separation anxiety and overeating that were accompanied by feelings of persecution, isolation, and anger. Her parents' recent divorce was hostile and sudden. Her well-meaning but depressed mother attempted to comfort Jenny's reactions to the divorce and other complications by giving advice and by minimizing statements such as, "You need to play with the neighbor's kids more. You aren't too upset to do that." Her father was too involved in the excitement and guilt about his girlfriend, the former mistress, to realize Jenny's troubles.

Jenny discovered that therapy was the one place she could talk about internal concerns without being dismissed, minimized, or ignored. Drawings, stories, role-playing games, and reality-oriented discussions were play-therapy tools that Jenny used to explore and expose herself. At the end of one year, she had assembled a book of pictures, stories, skill-games, and letters that described her fears, hopes, hates, skills, and goals. She utilized this book as a symbol of assembling herself into an unfinished but defined individual. She had developed enough of her own identity so that she did not feel the separations in her life were a threat to her existence. Her eating was reduced, her exercising was increased, and her enjoyment of playing and being with friends were developing. Her internal thoughts, feelings, and reactions had been heard and sorted out without excessive or undue attention being given to the external factors impacting her life. As a consequence, Jenny could develop her personal world and face the disjointed aspects of the external world with herself better intact.

Tanya, age 7, cried constantly and quietly during her sessions. She spoke no more than two sentences during each session. Her body gestures appeared relaxed but withdrawn. However, when her mother entered the room, Tanya would tensely smile, chatter, and giggle, which appeared to relieve her mother. Apparently, Tanya had developed a separation between her happy and sad "selves." She had learned that she was not to show her unhappy self to her mother, but at school, in therapy, and with her father she would be disruptive and tearful.

Summary

Seven categories of expression that are manifested during play therapy have been discussed and exemplified. After a play therapist learns to observe, recognize, and differentiate these categories of expression, the significance of each play activity is easier to determine.

VERBAL TOOLS USED TO COMMUNICATE WITH THE CHILD DURING THERAPY

Communication with the child during play therapy requires the use of many verbal tools. Many books contain valuable instructions regarding these tools in play therapy. Violet Oaklander (1988) examines various active and playful techniques. Joyce Mills and Richard Crowley (1986) discuss how metaphoric language and stories can be utilized during play therapy. Rudolf Ekstein (1966) and Ekstein and Ekstein (1995) illustrate how stories imaginatively told by therapist and child can facilitate a child's therapy. Anne Jernberg (1979) provides information regarding the structure of play in the therapeutic setting. D. W. Winnicott (1971a,b, 1975, 1978), Anna Freud (1965), and Melanie Klein (1975) illustrate in detail the use of verbal, analytically oriented interpretations with children. Moustakas (1975) provides examples of play therapy interactions from a humanistic-existential perspective.

The six verbal tools discussed here can help the therapist facilitate the child's self-expression and self-clarification (Table 5-2). In addition to a sound and attuned therapeutic relationship, a patient's expressions and clarifications are significant means by which growth, resolution, and reconstruction occur in therapy for adults and children. These verbal tools could also be used to moralize or to manipulate the child's thoughts and behaviors. However, moralizing or manipulating a child is not considered to be as helpful to the child as the effects of increasing insightfulness during therapy. Using these tools to moralize or manipulate may prove to be temporarily helpful at best. Usually, however, the therapeutic process is jeopardized, derailed, or even eliminated when the following tools are used for purposes other than to assist expression and clarification.

Table 5–2. Verbal Tools Used for Communication during Play Therapy

Tools	*Definition*
Description	Describing what a child is doing, saying, or playing is the simplest verbal interaction with children and is helpful when a therapist wants a child to know that clues are being collected or the play is being watched carefully.
Narration	When story lines are being played by a child while the therapist watches or participates, the therapist can verbally narrate the events, plot line, and characters' behaviors or words. Children become self-observant, corrective of the therapist's perceptions, and aware that a story is being told in the play.
Casual chats	While something else is being done or while the therapist and child are sitting comfortably, the child and therapist can casually discuss difficult, personal, or insignificant information. Some children feel more at ease revealing information when the environment feels casual and relaxed.
Questions	Questions can be misused, resulting in a child feeling bombarded and quizzed.
Story telling	Imaginative but strategic telling of stories about other children, about make-believe characters, or about events can be constructed to illustrate the child's conflicts, issues, concerns, or solutions.
Interpretation	Statements that reveal the various purposes, meanings, causes, or connections of the child's play with the child's psychological world are interpretations.

Description

Description is the most basic verbal tool available to therapists. While the child engages in activities, the therapist simply describes what is occurring.

As 7-year-old Bret glues Popsicle sticks together in a bunch, the therapist observes, "You are gluing one stick to the three sticks you glued together earlier."

Verbally describing what is being observed can be therapeutic in four ways. First and most simply, if a child's psychological need at the moment is to have attention, verbal description informs the child that attention is available and is actively being provided. Second, children become unaware of what they are doing or saying. At these instances, the therapist can function as a substitute observer until the child can resume self-observation.

> Bret did not realize that he had poured glue all over the table until the therapist neutrally described his actions. He was startled and puzzled by his actions and began to watch himself more carefully. The therapist did not use observation as a tool to create shame over the spilled glue but rather, through nonmoralizing description, had been able to increase Bret's self-awareness temporarily.

Third, describing is a helpful tool when the meaning of an activity is not understood. The therapist can use description as a verbal means of collecting clues. Once children recognize that the therapist is collecting clues like a detective, they often begin assisting in the detective work by repeating actions until the therapist notices the clues or by correcting the therapist's verbalized observations.

> Bret continued to glue more and more Popsicle sticks together as the therapist described the process. Bret realized that the therapist did not understand the meaning of his actions but recognized that she was collecting clues. Finally, he held one Popsicle stick up to the therapist's face and said, "See, this is just one. These are many." This was offered as an additional clue that later could be interpreted as, "That Popsicle stick is alone but wants to belong to a group or family of Popsicle sticks. You also feel left out and wish you could be joined to a group of friends or to your family."

Fourth, the tool of description can enhance the child's recognition that therapy is a unique process. As a therapist details a child's behaviors verbally, a child starts to appreciate that in therapy each behavior is considered significant. The child becomes able to differentiate play activities that occur with teachers, friends, parents, or babysitters where play is predominantly for fun from the play that is mainly therapeutically meaningful. The child recognizes that play within the therapy room is considered meaningful and purposeful and he or she will begin to play with the intent of communicating instead of only having fun.

Narration

Narrating the story being revealed by a child's play activities is another tool available to therapists. In contrast to the tool of description, narration requires some insight into the meaning suggested by each activity and into the meaningful connections between each activity. As the child develops the story line or scenario through play activities, either the child, the therapist, or both can narrate the story's setting, character, development, unfolding plot line, climax, and resolution. Typically, a story is revealed by the child one activity at a time. The therapist narrates each event when it is uncovered and waits until the next scene is created by the child.

Often, after hearing the narration, the child modifies the story by adding to or altering what the therapist stated. These additions or alterations may provide pertinent information about what the child views as significant. These changes might also prove to be defenses erected to obscure what is being revealed by the story.

> Sherry, a precocious 7-year-old, selected a male and a female doll to play with. She explained that the female, named Christine, lived in luxurious surroundings and had limitless funds available to support extravagant activities. Craig, the male doll, was in love with Christine but was poor. Christine snubbed Craig's repeated attempts to be friends with her. Each of these attempts was played out between the dolls and the therapist and Sherry narrated these scenes as the story unfolded. When Sherry took the dolls and enacted an argument, the therapist narrated the activities. "Christine just became very angry at Craig and began to yell at him, telling him to go away and stop bothering her. This saddens Craig since he only wishes to be a kind friend to Christine. He doesn't seem to understand why Christine is so rejecting."

After this narration, Sherry directed the Christine doll to explain to Craig that he was too poor for her to befriend. The Craig doll was made to fall down at this point. The therapist narrated, "Craig is so upset with what Christine said that he falls over. He's feeling kicked or hurt and is in a lot of pain." Over several sessions, this play scenario was narrated as Sherry provided many clues about her difficulty with forming friendships. Eventually, these clues formed a clear and cohesive profile of Sherry's dilemma. When timely interpretations were made about this material, Sherry began to recognize how she was alienating friends by a superior attitude and rejecting gestures.

Often the tools of description and narration are used interchangeably depending on the level of understanding the therapist possesses at a given moment. The following example illustrates how descriptions are used until the therapist gains an understanding of the child's play that allows for the tool of narration to be utilized.

While Pedro mounted the table, jumped off, and rolled onto the floor, the therapist described his behavior at first simply and then more complexly. For example, "Pedro, now you are climbing on the table, jumping off, and landing on the floor with great excitement." "Pedro, again you are climbing the table, jumping off, and then rolling on the floor. It seems to make you feel powerful." Pedro announced at this point that he was Batman. "Now you are Batman who is climbing the table, flying off, and landing with a scream of power." When he landed, he began to stomp his feet and swing his hands as if fighting something and someone. "Pedro, now you are a powerful Batman who is fighting someone who you think needs to be fought." He mounted the table in the same manner and the therapist described the process. Shortly thereafter, the therapist begins a narration, "Batman, who is you, climbs the table and looks down on a monster and now decides to jump on the monster in order to destroy the monster. When you land on the floor, you fight the monster trying to defeat it." Many times thereafter, this last narration is stated as the actions are repeated. Eventually, the actions change slightly and those changes are at first described and then attached to some apparent meaning or feelings that Pedro seems to be conveying. When the therapist described or narrated inaccurately, Pedro would shout, "No!" but would continue the actions until the correct labels, descriptions, and narrations were applied.

Casual Chats

Seemingly relaxed, chatty conversations (with defensive or older children) while other play activities take place can be used to address issues, collect information, or explore ideas that are deep, painful, or complex. The same active therapeutic work can sometimes be done more effectively when the therapist adopts a language, inflection, and attitude that is genuinely casual.

Four-year-old Zinnie needed an evaluation for potential sexual abuse since sexual exploration and masturbation had become evident to friends of the family. Clearly, if the sexual play was within the normal developmental range, the evaluator did not want to alarm or to shame Zinnie about her sexual interests. Information gathered from her parents provided the background needed for the therapist to casually talk about trips, visits, games, birthday parties, Power-Ranger characters, and relatives. During the two sessions, Zinnie played with dolls, sand-tray figurines, and Legos, but mostly actively talked with the therapist about anything that came to mind. The therapist parallel-played and casually chatted about whatever came to Zinnie's mind. In total, about 20 minutes scattered throughout the two sessions addressed the issues concerning her sexual curiosities, sexual play, and exposures to others. Zinnie began to feel shameful, as if needing to hide her curiosities (and hide toys under the sand simultaneously), but as she progressively experienced the casual chatting atmosphere, she openly asked and answered questions. In this situation, Zinnie's sexual concerns were addressed explicitly and sufficiently by the end of the two sessions.

Questions

Therapists often resort too quickly to using questioning as a means of collecting information or exploration. This can jeopardize play therapy. Questions used to clarify clues or collect information may ineffectively force a child to discuss information that is not yet ready to be shared or acknowledged by the child. The child may retreat from therapy and stop working cooperatively with the therapist.

Also, children fabricate irrelevant answers merely to appease or please the therapist. Fabricated responses derail therapy and obscure the messages. Questions inappropriately used or timed can also reveal to the child that the therapist is impatient or unwilling to allow the child to express messages in his or her own time and manner. Moreover, if it is important for a child to feel understood by the therapist, questioning may reveal too harshly that the therapist failed to comprehend. Also, asking questions puts the responsibility on the child to understand and explain information that he or she may be ill-equipped or unable to grasp. Often, children come to therapy to learn what they do not know.

In contrast, questioning used sparingly and wisely serves as a tool to assist discovery and clarification. If questions are posed when the child is on the threshold of an insight, they help the child discover information. Questions that are asked before a child has begun to explore or understand an issue typically distract, confuse, or rush the child.

When a therapist is confused or unclear about an explanation or statement a child makes, honest questions aimed at understanding that one issue are essential and helpful. This is nonintrusive questioning and demonstrates an interest in the child's attempt to explain something already felt to be pertinent and already understood by the child. However, some children may experience such questioning as a wound because of the wish and need to be automatically understood. In such cases, children can become quiet, angry, and withdrawn, and a therapist will feel that the questioning has somehow hurt the child.

Some children respond poorly to direct description, narration, or interpretation, and prefer being asked questions at times during therapy. For these children, inquiry feels less intrusive, less controlling, and less authoritative. In such situations, questions serve the function of description, narration, and interpretive explanation but are worded and inflected differently. For example, an interpretive explanation of a situation that has been described or narrated might be: "You're feeling sad about not having a father who can watch you play softball like the other girls have. That's why you are sitting in the corner with your back turned to me and your head down, with the ball and bat thrown across the room." In contrast, such a statement might be phrased as a question for children who respond better to questions, such as: "Do you have your back turned to me and did you throw the bat and ball across the room because you feel sad about not having a father to watch you play like the other girls?" Such questioning can serve as an invitation for certain children to accept, confirm, clarify, reject, or modify.

Story-Telling

Children who cannot directly face issues may listen to stories about people facing similar issues. Sometimes the therapist constructs a story as a means of describing feelings, behaviors, and thoughts that seem to pertain to the child's personal reactions. The stories provide the child with an opportunity to look from a safe distance at a mirror image and become able to personalize and apply the story's revelations.

If play therapy is based on exploration, self-revelation, and personal processes, the therapist utilizes the tool of story-telling to reveal to the child what the child is ready to understand. Therapies that aim to teach, solve, moralize, or correct use stories as a means of altering behavior by examples set or resolutions provided in the story. New perspectives or corrective suggestions are embedded in the story-telling process.

> Carrie initially made up stories about her therapist, revealing transferences related to envy, deprivation, and idealization. During the middle period of therapy, Carrie told graphic stories of monsters as well as chase and kill scenes directed toward parents. She instructed the therapist to tell stories about parents being monstrously murdered too. Toward the end of therapy, Carrie wrote stories about a girl's successes with friends, school, and at home. Story-telling throughout this treatment was the primary tool used by both the patient and therapist to convey feelings of inferiority, envy, and anger with parents, and to promote the development of self-worth.

Interpretive Explanations

After the therapist has decoded the various components of the child's verbal and nonverbal messages and understood the psychological processes being expressed, the tool of interpretive explanations can be used. Interpretive explanations reveal to the child the purposes, meanings, causes, or connections of his or her psychological process.

Three brief case examples of interpretive explanations have been given above. Mick's therapist interpreted his use of magic tricks as a defense against feelings of powerlessness. Darren's antagonistic behaviors were explained interpretively as aimed at alienating a depressed father so that the father would relinquish the burden of raising Darren. Bret's gluing of Popsicle sticks was explained as a revelation of his wish to belong to a group of friends and family. In the discussion on questions, above, a contrast between an interpretive explanation and a question used for the sake of interpretation was provided regarding a girl and her absent father.

Interpretive explanations are offered when the child is ready to understand the messages and endure the consequences or impact the interpretations might have. Children's readiness to understand interpretive explanations or to endure the emotional impact of pertinent and potentially penetrating interpretive explanations can be assessed by four indicators.

First, when the play is clearly and easily understood and, second, when the child demonstrates verbally or nonverbally a grasp of the material the therapist is about to explain, an interpretive explanation is warranted. Bret, for instance, understood the meaning of his Popsicle gluing before the therapist had decoded and verbally interpreted the meaning of his actions. Third, if the child appears to have a positive working alliance with the therapist, interpretive explanations are easier to present and explore. Fourth, if the child proves responsive to tentative, partial, or preliminary interpretive explanations about an issue, the interpretive explanation likely will be received.

Sherry's play with the Christine and Craig dolls, as described earlier, revealed how Sherry rejected others and how she felt rejected. When her play activities clearly revealed this and when Sherry seemed emotionally available to hear the interpretive explanation, her therapist said, "Sherry, Christine is the part of you that sometimes feels good about pushing others away because it makes you feel better than others. This is how you felt when you called that boy in your class 'stupid' today. Craig is the part of you that feels awful and hurt when you are rejected by people like the twins down the road who refused to let you join their game."

Interpretive explanations cannot always be offered at the ideal time, however. Because of the child's negative transference reactions (viewing the therapist as mean, cruel, unkind), unrelinquishing defenses (denial, repression, or dissociation), or difficult, negative, and painful issues (death, abuse, abandonment), timely interpretive explanations may result in strong protests and resistances. In such situations, interpretive explanations need to be offered tentatively, partially, and carefully. Such statements are given when there is plenty of time in the session to follow up as well as to support the child emotionally. If a strong statement proves necessary, the therapist must be prepared to handle strong reactions both during and after the session. Parental support and understanding will also need to be employed.

If interpretive explanations are needed to deal with the negative transference, defenses, or painful issues, it is not helpful to avoid offering the explanations merely to preclude the child's negative reactions. Avoiding pertinent material merely because the situation may become uncomfortable can (1) aggravate problems in the long and short term, resulting in a stalemate in therapy and ineffective treatment; (2) prolong unconscious pain and irresolution; and (3) cause further interference with the normal developmental processes disrupted by the issues at hand.

Raphaela, whose father died, as described earlier, would not directly address her father's absence or death for many months of stalemated therapy. Her defenses erected against this issue were formidable and hid a tremendous amount of pain, anger, and desire to retaliate. Her therapist decided to begin to directly and pointedly explain interpretively Raphaela's slightest symbolic play regarding her father. Each interpretive explanation was received with intense negative reactions toward the therapist, including hitting the therapist on her head with the intent of hurting her even though the objects were soft. It became clear through a number of incidents that Raphaela felt that the therapist was purposefully hurting her by mentioning her dad. When she felt hurt, she wanted to hurt in retaliation. Feelings of retaliation were also directed toward her mother whom she felt was responsible for not protecting her father from dying. Assaultive language and actions were endured during this portion of therapy. This reaction was inevitable because the nature of her pain and the feelings of blame and hurt were intrinsic to the issues surrounding her dead father. The therapist's empathy with her pain and wish to be silent helped her endure information about her father and move forward.

Further study and clinical training regarding the art and application of formulating interpretive explanations are necessary for the serious child therapist and can be found in works by Langs (1973), Levy (1984), and Schafer (1976). Case studies written by M. Klein (1975), D. W. Winnicott (1971a,b, 1975, 1978), A. Freud (1965), Axline (1947), and McDougall and Lebovici (1969) provide invaluable exposure to the art of formulating and utilizing interpretive explanations with children. Interpreting child's transference in play therapy is discussed by Francis (1995).

NONVERBAL TOOLS USED TO COMMUNICATE WITH THE CHILD DURING THERAPY

Some children rage any time the therapist speaks because of a defense against or anger with the therapist's message or presence. Other children hear behavioral messages clearer than verbiage. And all children use silent play, quiet concentration, or calm, restful activity in daily activity. It becomes imperative, therefore, for the therapist to use nonverbal means of communication or participation throughout the therapy (Table 5-3).

Table 5–3. Nonverbal Tools Used to Communicate during Therapy

Tools	*Definition*
Active watching	Active and quiet observation by the therapist is experienced by the child as either a background or foreground person who is participating by watching and processing silently.
Parallel play	Therapist and child play actively but as two separate individuals who neither exchange words nor share activities but, nonetheless, are in each other's presence. Not only is this a developmentally specific level of play, it is also a way of being involved but maintaining individuality, being distant but present for defensive reasons, or transition between togetherness and aloneness.
Symbolic play	Therapists can orchestrate play activities that symbolize the child's issues without having to put them into words. This helps when words are experienced as intrusive, damaging, or confrontational.
Participatory play	The child and therapist both become characters within a story line that is directed by the child or therapist actively. Plots, roles, and conversations become fictional representations of the child's issues that both the child and therapist play out.

Active Watching

Therapeutic watching is parallel to therapeutic listening. While the child plays, active and quiet observation and processing are essential. As a watcher of the child's play, the therapist may be representative of a background object (Grotstein 1981). The background object in a child's world is always felt, always needed, and, when absent, is always sought after. For a child, the background object contains the child's feelings and thoughts while also assuring safety. Insecurity, bewilderment, or extreme anxiety is observed in children when they become aware that their background object has left or is not watching.

As a foreground object (Grotstein 1981) who is actively watching, the watchful therapist provides the child with an audience. When such attention is symbolic of involvement or caring, this silent and involved audience is perceived as an active participant who is absorbing the messages the child conveys and a caring person who is eager to understand and know what the child is communicating. The calm, patient nature of the active watcher also provides the child with a sensation of space, availability, and expanded time. The child is in charge of the pacing, knowing that an active but quiet partner watches. Children with busy or anxious parents rarely experience such room to be themselves. Winnicott's (1968) concept of the child's object use and object creation is associated to both aspects of the watchful therapist.

Watchfulness does not give license to passiveness or noninvolvement on the part of the therapist. If anything, done well, watchfulness requires mental and emotional alertness and active internal dialogues. Moreover, during the silence, many messages are being transmitted either symbolically through play or through the fantasies of the child who aggressively projects into the background/foreground object of the watchful therapist. (For further discussion of symbolically transmitted material between child and adult, see Francis 1997.)

> The playroom that Michael and I used was large and filled with balloon characters he would hit, kick, and hug. I was silently instructed to stand in the corner and watch him interact with these balloons. If I narrated, described, or interpreted, he would glare at me hoping to silence my intrusions. If I participated in the play through parallel play or symbolic play, he would stop his activities and direct me to the corner. Clearly, I was to observe, silently recording and understanding the emotions intrinsic to his activities.
>
> After a month of such sessions, I could move into the play activity, having gained a strong sense of Michael's play rhythm, style, and content. I could play as if I were he because I had studied carefully who he was. He would allow my participation as long as I mirrored his play style, but as soon as I introduced an alternate or deviant gesture, I was to watch and learn again, sometimes standing in the corner and sometimes sitting beside him. It was verified later that the mirroring he received from his mother was greatly lacking. She apparently would not tolerate any independent gestures

from Michael and paid no attention to his personality as he attempted to differentiate, other than to punish or ignore him, similarly to what he had done with me in the playroom. Simultaneously, Michael was attempting to show me how he had been treated and was attempting to attain some needed mirroring that exactly reflected who he was.

Parallel Play

Young children play side by side with other children and adults. With little or no interaction or exchange, children imitate, move about, and select play activities. The presence of the playmate, however, proves important often as a source of companionship or as a reference point (Brazelton 1992, Leach 1992).

In similar manner, a therapist sometimes is a quiet playmate who is instructed by the child to parallel play. If the therapist begins to play at any activity while the child is in the same or a different activity, the child may experience the pleasure of having company or the power of having an active and playful background object that at any moment can be summoned into an active playing. The significance of this type of play may be associated with the toddler developmental process or phase that the child needs to visit, rework, or experience (Francis 1995). Such developmental issues may be associated with Mahler's (1979) differentiation or practicing subphases, as well as to Winnicott's (1951, 1968) developmental object relations issues described as Object-Presenting, Object-Use, and the transitional arena.

Technically, whether the patient or therapist decides to initiate parallel play, the therapist can always use such times to watch the patient and gather clues within the symbolic play or utilize verbal interventions lightly peppered throughout the parallel play that addresses the child's therapeutic work. Occasionally, the therapist's playing becomes the focus of the child's attention out of curiosity or need for connection. At these times the parallel play activities the therapist uses can be transformed into symbolic play (discussed below).

Both Renee and I were playing with Play-Doh. She was modeling her family sitting in the living room during a typical evening. I was creating a family playing in the yard. It did not matter to

Renee at this moment what I was doing for she was quite absorbed in her work. She, however, was less self-conscious and less pressured if she felt that I was occupied elsewhere. Occasionally, I would break the silence, and while I continued to form my Play-Doh figures I would briefly narrate or interpret what Renee was demonstrating in her modeling. She would form her next scenario based on what I had said either to clarify, affirm, or disagree with what I had verbally offered. This type of parallel play, combined with occasional verbal interventions, became the primary pattern of the play therapy with Renee.

Symbolic Play

When verbal interventions are ineffective, too intrusive, or need to be supplemented, therapists can design play activities that convey interpretation or empathic responses. These activities can be either participatory or parallel in nature. For example, if a child is playing a certain pretend game that becomes interpretable, the therapist can begin to play with the same objects (participatory play) or with another set of toys (parallel play) in a way that represents the message the therapist wishes to convey.

Symbolic play provides another avenue for communication between the therapist and patient other than talking, but can be used simultaneously with narration or description as the symbolic play occurs. If the message to be conveyed needs to be tested first, needs to be subtle (as if speaking to the unconscious), or will only make sense to the child through playing, symbolic play can be quite effective alone. Symbolic play is illustrated in the case vignettes in the next section.

Participatory Play

Often children direct the play activity, assigning roles, lines of conversation, and scripting plots. Children expect the therapist to participate in a lively way that is congruent with the developing story line. Much is learned about the child's perspective on people, social rules, actual events, and relationships. Sometimes children will require that the therapist script all or a portion of the play activity. At such times, the therapist becomes the director and the child the participant. Symbolic play can be employed at these moments, or the therapist can develop a story line that will help the child explore issues that the child is reluctant to examine.

> Troy, age 4, piled sheets on top of me and declared that I had been killed by him and sent to heaven. Then, because I was safe in heaven, I could be hit vigorously by Troy without being harmed. Of course, this was symbolic play on Troy's part but, since he could not endure the impact of any verbal interpretations, I confined myself to narration and participatory play. I was directed by Troy when to die, when to groan, when to come back to life, and how to react to being hit. He scripted my role and then responded out of his character.
>
> During another session, he arrived with no idea what to do. I piled the soldiers and household toy furniture onto the floor and created a story about wars, enemies, and battles that took place in a home environment. He soon began to participate and then directed who was to die, how they were to be killed, and who was to be victorious. I narrated the play and what was being thought and felt by the different dolls. I scripted the dolls' words that addressed the meaning of the play and the feelings of the characters. I also moved the toys based on Troy's directions and initiated some activities of my own.
>
> My goals were (1) to allow some discharge for Troy's angry, destructive impulses; (2) to enable Troy to direct such impulses toward imaginative play that was safe and not directed toward humans (in the form of hitting or biting); and (3) to practice functioning within a relationship in which another person had imput without feeling violated, misunderstood, or overridden. All this had to be performed in terms of strategic verbal responses and nonverbal actions within the various play scenarios.

OVERVIEW AND SUMMARY

Having been exposed to these aspects of play therapy, the therapist may feel the need to see how these ingredients intertwine into a therapy session. This case example illustrates how the seven categories of expression, six verbal tools, and four nonverbal tools can be combined to effectively help a child observe, gain insight, and work through relevant issues.

Troy, discussed above, started therapy a few months before age 4. He could not reason, explore, or gain insight into his behavior. He was action-driven and his impulses were channeled destructively. His play would be symbolic but he could not digest any *verbal explanations* or *interpretations* during his first year-and-a-half of therapy. He broke toys, painted the room with anger, hit and bit me, and vigorously scattered toys everywhere as a form of tantrum.

The psychological experiences Troy was expressing at home, at preschool, and in sessions revolved around discharge, defenses against sadness and self-denigration, and confusion about how to interpersonally interact. He was viewed as lacking age-appropriate impulse controls and possessing large amounts of anger and aggression toward himself and others. He was socially unskilled and developmentally behind other children his age. Other children did not enjoy Troy because of his aggressive, bad-tempered outbursts.

Verbal tools that worked best with Troy were *description*, *narration*, and *casual chats*. *Questions* were too intrusive and appeared to make Troy both defensive and hurt. *Story-telling* began to work toward the end of the second year only after the therapist could carefully tailor scenarios that would not result in defensive and injured responses. *Interpretations* were also felt to be invasive; he would feel as if I were physically hitting him if I provided insight into his feelings or behaviors, even if mildly stated.

Nonverbal tools were more useful because I could form actions and scenarios that channeled his impulses for constructive *discharging*. I could design playful responses to his play and direction that symbolically addressed issues pertaining to interpersonal processes such as empathy and respect without becoming preachy, scolding, or directive. Also, I could respond to or mirror his anger, sadness, and self-denigration playfully and avoid any confrontations that would have triggered his defenses.

One example of *participatory play* has already been discussed regarding Troy's therapy. *Symbolic play* occurred frequently as well; I would draw pictures of tearful reactions to being hit, or draw angry wolves whom others feared as he told his symbolic, personal version of the Three Little Pigs.

Active watching was the most useful nonverbal tool when Troy needed to feel admired and appreciated. If someone spoke, the spell of being admired was broken—he would not trust verbal praise. But nonverbal watching felt like praise and caring to Troy.

Parallel play was less frequently used than the other nonverbal tools but would occasionally be employed when he seemed to wish to experience a comraderie or team-spirited interpersonal process. Parallel play increased as Troy developed better internalized object representations (people could like him) and better self-representations (he could like himself), as well as a sense of empathy for and from others around him.

Participatory play was the predominant tool used as he urgently needed to interact with others and figure out how to be himself and to manage his impulses while doing activities with others. This was his biggest struggle and his biggest wish: how to manage being angry and learn to be liked by others.

During each moment of play therapy, a therapist can first think carefully about which of the seven categories of expression a child's play may reveal. Thereafter, the child therapist can select a combination of verbal and nonverbal interventions that will facilitate expression and clarification. Through these means, a therapist with almost any theoretical orientation can provide sophisticated and constructive play-therapy treatment.

REFERENCES

Axline, V. (1947). *Play Therapy*. New York: Ballantine, 1969.

Brazelton, T. B. (1992). *Touchpoints: The Essential Reference*. New York: Addison-Wesley.

Ekstein, R. (1966). *Child of Time and Space, of Action and Impulse*. New York: Appleton-Century-Crofts.

Ekstein, R., and Ekstein, J. (1995). Children's and adolescents' own fairy tales and their treatment implications. In *The Handbook of Infant, Child and Adolescent Psychotherapy: A Guide to Diagnosis and Treatment*, ed. B. S. Mark and J. Incorvaia, pp. 401–418. Northvale, NJ: Jason Aronson.

Erikson, E. (1950/1963). *Childhood and Society*. New York: Norton.

Francis, C. A. (1995). The therapeutic issues of transference and countertransference in the play therapy world. In *The Handbook of Infant, Child and Adolescent Psychotherapy: A Guide to Diagnosis and Treatment*, ed. B. S. Mark and J. Incorvaia, pp. 305–341. Northvale, NJ: Jason Aronson.

——— (1997). Every parent's nightmare: parental horrific imaginings. In *Primitive Mental States*, vol. 1, ed. S. Alhanati and K. Kostoulas, pp. 221–244. Northvale, NJ: Jason Aronson.

Freud, A. (1965). *Writings of Anna Freud. Volume VI: Normality and Pathology in Childhood: Assessments of Development*. Madison, CT: International Universities Press.

Grotstein, J. (1981). *Splitting and Projective Identification*. New York: Jason Aronson.

Jernberg, A. (1979). *Therapy: A New Treatment Using Structural Play for Problem Children and Their Families*. San Francisco: Jossey-Bass.

Klein, M. (1940). Mourning and its relation to manic-depressive states. In *Love, Guilt and Reparation and Other Works, 1921–1945*, ed. R. Money-Kyrle, B. Joseph, E. O'Shaughnessy, and H. Segal, pp. 344–369. New York: Free Press, 1975.

——— (1946). Notes of some schizoid mechanisms. In *Envy and Gratitude*, ed. R. Money-Kyrle, B. Joseph, E. O'Shaughnessy, and H. Segal, pp. 1–24. New York: Dell, 1977.

——— (1961). *Narrative of a Child Analysis*, ed. R. Money-Kyrle, B. Joseph, E. O'Shaughnessy, and H. Segal. New York: Free Press.

——— (1975). *The Psycho-Analysis of Children*, ed. R. Money-Kyrle, B. Joseph, E. O'Shaughnessy, and H. Segal. New York: Free Press.

Langs, R. (1973). *The Technique of Psychoanalytic Psychotherapy, volumes I & II*. New York: Jason Aronson.

Leach, P. (1992). *Your Baby and Child: From Birth to Age Five*. New York: Knopf.

Levy, S. (1984). *Principles of Interpretation*. New York: Jason Aronson.

Mahler, M. S. (1979). *The Selected Papers of Margaret S. Mahler, M.D., Volume II: Separation-Individuation*. New York: Jason Aronson.

McDougall, J., and Lebovici, S. (1969). *Dialogue with Sammy: A Psychoanalytical Contribution to the Understanding of Child Psychosis*. London: Hogarth.

Mills, J. C., and Crowley, R. J. (1986). *Therapeutic Metaphors for Children and the Child Within*. New York: Brunner/Mazel.

Moustakas, C. (1975). *Who Will Listen? Children and Parents in Therapy*. New York: Ballantine.

Oaklander, V. (1988). *Windows to Our Children*. Highland, NY: Center for Gestalt Development.

Piaget, J. (1962). *Play, Dreams and Imitation in Childhood*. New York: Norton.

Schafer, R. (1976). *A New Language for Psychoanalysis*. New Haven: Yale University Press.

Spitz, R. A. (1965). *The First Year of Life*. New York: International Universities Press.

Sullivan, H. S. (1953). *The Interpersonal Theory of Psychiatry*. New York: Norton.

Tustin, F. (1981). *Autistic States in Children*. London: Routledge and Kegan Paul.

——— (1990). *The Protective Shell in Children and Adults*. London: Karnac.

Winnicott, D. W. (1951/1975). Transitional objects and transitional phenomena. *Through Paediatrics to Psycho-Analysis*, pp. 174–193. New York: Basic Books.

——— (1968). The use of an object and relating through identifications. In *Playing and Reality*, pp. 86-94. New York: Tavistock.

——— (1971a). *Playing and Reality*. London: Tavistock.

——— (1971b). *The Piggle*. New York: International Universities Press.

——— (1975). *Through Paediatrics to Psycho-Analysis*. New York: Basic Books.

——— (1978). *Therapeutic Consultations in Child Psychiatry*. New York: Basic Books.

6

Sibling Rivalry: The Role of the Sibling in the Unconscious

Robert J. Neborsky

Sibling rivalry is frequently a major issue in healthy as well as dysfunctional families. As a parent, it is a perennial challenge to face the dilemmas our sibling children throw our way. Who has not heard the tearful, plaintiff wail, "It's not FAIR!" echoing through the house? Just this evening I found myself separating two of my children who nearly came to blows over a dispute as to who arrived at the car first. They both delighted at who was going to get to their mother earliest to tell their story and further irritate the other if Mother aligned with one or the other.

Yesterday I was waiting for the elevator. As the doors opened a 5-year-old boy leaped over his older sister and, like a panther, pounced over her back in order to be the first to press the elevator button. She, about 7, burst into tears at the injustice, crying, "It's my turn." The poor mother, somewhat chagrined, looked at me and shrugged.

I commented that she shouldn't feel bad, that I've been in the same boat in at least a hundred elevator rides. I could elaborate on more examples, but by now you have the idea.

These examples are the more benign forms of sibling rivalry. We can look to the Bible for more extreme examples of sibling misconduct. After Adam and Eve were kicked out of the Garden of Eden, they had to work for a living. Adam became a farmer and Eve a housewife. After a time, Eve gave birth to the first baby in the world, Cain. Before long a second came along and he was named Abel. Despite being the firstborn, it seemed that Cain was not everyone's favorite. He had a bad disposition and angered easily. He was also quite miserly, and he was even resentful of having to sacrifice to God, and he angered God. Cain even got angry that God was angry at him! We can see that Cain had traits that could be explained if Eve were a depressed mother who was unable to supply the holding environment Cain needed. Perhaps she was depressed by her banishment from the Garden of Eden. Clearly, she recovered from her depression when she bore Abel. It seems Abel was a free-spirited sort and sacrificed willingly and with joy. His preoedipal experience truly sufficed. Abel's cheery disposition brought much praise from God and Adam. This made matters worse for Cain as he saw Abel getting all this approval and favor. Attitude, it seems, counted for a lot in God's eyes. Cain stewed and stewed, and couldn't take it any more. He let go of his rage and committed the first murder in recorded history, that of his younger brother. When God inquired as to Abel's whereabouts, Cain uttered the famous line, "Am I my brother's keeper?" God knew that Cain was lying. He said, "The blood of your brother cries out to me from the ground. Because of that, the earth that drinks the blood shed by your hand shall forever curse you. When you till the soil it will not yield its crops for you: from this day you will be a wanderer and fugitive throughout the land." Cain protests and asks for leniency. God is unimpressed, but does spare him from the death sentence by putting a mark on him. "You will be known wherever you go as a man to whom no harm shall come."

Here, so soon after the creation of man, we have a seriously heinous crime—fratricide. This Bible story highlights for us the importance of sibling rivalry in the universality of human experience. The thread of sibling rivalry continues through the Bible in an amazing way. Abraham's son Jacob steals his father's last blessing from his older brother Esau, and thus must leave home. Many years later, Jacob's youngest son, Joseph, lies at the bottom of a well because his older brothers were jealous of his special favoritism from Jacob. Only through good luck did he survive and get sold into the Pharaoh's slavery instead of starving to death. Jacob was told that Joseph was dead.

If we treat these biblical stories as myths, then we have our first entrée into our understanding of the unconscious. Primitive societies struggled with aggression. Human sacrifice of children by parents was a common Canaanite practice. Clearly, sibling competition for paternal favor was a major family tension in a rural society where survival depended on ownership of land and water rights. Murder of favored siblings by other siblings needed to be controlled. How better than by developing a superego countercathexis against the murder of a blood relative.

I practice intensive short-term dynamic psychotherapy. This therapy gives me a unique opportunity to examine sibling relationships in the unconscious of adult neurotic patients. This therapy is an accelerated analytic therapy in which ego and superego resistance are exhausted in the first few hours of treatment, and a unique phenomenon referred to as the *unconscious therapeutic alliance* occurs. In this state of mind, the unconscious repressed sadistic impulses and feelings emerge and give the clinician a crystal-clear picture of the core patricidal, matricidal, and fratricidal emotions from the patient's dynamic past.

Traditionally, neurotic psychopathology is traced back to the Oedipus complex. Discussing the male as an example, the child experiences the father as a rival for the primary nurturant/sexual object (mother), and the child thus feels excluded from the mother–child dyad. This results in traumatic rage for the child, experienced as murderous impulses toward the rival and a subsequent sense of guilt for the psychological murder of the father. In the best of circumstances, when there is an adequate nurturant paternal bond combined with good maternal boundaries, the child represses the oedipal attraction for mother and develops a strong positive sense of masculine self based on identification with the father. Latency gives a quiescence to the intensity of oedipal passion, and an opportunity presents itself for father and son to further consolidate their identification through schoolwork, games, play, and family life in general.

With the onset of adolescence and the resultant upsurge of the libido from the hormonal surge, sexuality again presents itself. In normal adolescent males the sexual instinctual urges are now directed away from incestual objects toward girlfriends, movie stars, teachers, or the nudes in men's magazines. In neurotic patients, I frequently find the recall of masturbation fantasies involving the primary nurturant object as well as the female siblings. Frequently, these fantasies are commingled with disguised competitive themes as well. For example, one neurotic patient reported the repetitive masturbation fantasy of him approaching his nude mother from behind as she offered herself to him for his sexual satisfaction. The important aspect of this fantasy was that she was submitting herself to him. His unconscious revealed this to be a retaliatory fantasy against both his mother and his stepfather. The patient was competing with his stepfather for both the power role and the favored role within the family system. Mother's fantasized act of sexual submission was designed to bolster and repair his weak sense of his masculine self. The patient's identification with his own biologic father was that of a weak, castrated, banished victim.

In normal adolescent male development, the pursuit of a nonincestual nuturant/sexual relationship begins. Different subcultures within our society define how and when this unfolds, but the developmental task is the same: to separate from the primary nuturant/sexual objects and to replace her or them with a nonincestual selection. At this time the father's role changes from that of first a rival and second a buddy to a role model whom the son either further identifies with or rebels against to consolidate an identity. The peer group takes on an importance that cannot be overemphasized. Social grouping takes place; complex issues related to competition and cooperation are worked through successfully, or they create in and of themselves traumatic points of fixation. In some ways, this is the cauldron of sibling rivalry that all youngsters must master as they find their social rank within the peer group and deal with the painful issues of popularity/unpopularity, achievement/failure, selfishness/sharing.

Following adolescence the final stage of separation occurs in which the young adult either successfully establishes himself as an independent self-sufficient person with a role in a social system, or underlying neurotic and characterologic unconscious instincts begin to create reenactments in adult life. These reenactments are referred to as *repetition compulsions*. In this chapter I discuss how early childhood trauma results in aggravated sibling trauma rivalry in three patients' lifelong histories of self-sabotage.

Preoedipal experience clearly plays a factor in the development of neurotic psychopathology. In my practice I find the greater the preoedipal trauma, the harsher the superego and the more severe the masochistic needs of the patient. Our work confirms that the foundation of the superego is formed in the preoedipal stages of life. The appearance of a sibling in a compromised mother–child dyad forms early triangulation trauma that can prestage the relatively less toxic oedipal triangulation. What occurs is a severely sadistic unconscious organization of a particularly virulent nature. These patients frequently have markedly fragile ego organizations. They also have a proclivity for self-destructive acting out involving alcohol, drugs, and self-mutilating behavior. The degree of self-destructive behavior directly correlates with the degree of unconscious sadism, which directly correlates with the depth of the trauma to the developing ego in the child.

Instinctual endowment plays a role, but it is hard to quantify. Suffice it to say that overendowment of aggressive or libidinal instinct causes trauma as the child tries to work out its equilibrium with the environment. We now refer to this child as the difficult child, who presents challenges to even the most talented, sophisticated, and empathetic parents. In this cluster lie children with neuropsychologic deficits who have either short attention spans, impulse control difficulties, or hyperactive motor problems. Each one of these are potential contributory factors to create neurotogenic traumatic developmental situations.

PREOEDIPAL SIBLING DISTURBANCE

The role of grandparents in either the development or prevention of neurotic trauma is severely underemphasized in the traditional psychoanalytic literature. It is our finding that the infantile and childhood attachments to grandmothers and grandfathers are critical cathexes in the unconscious. Frequently, grandparents are the prime nurturant figures, and the mother is experienced as the rival in preoedipal triangulation trauma.

I am currently treating a woman with a severe fragile ego organization whose grandfather was her primary nurturer, and, in fact, he slept in the same bed with her during her first four years of life. She attached to him as both mother and father. She also experienced traumatic sexual overstimulation from him. It is unclear whether there was direct sexual contact between the two. Her mother developed the belief that he sexually molested the girl and blamed the daughter for the event. The mother relentlessly punished and insulted her, calling her evil. She also flew into rages and would beat her for the mother's impression that she was having sexual impulses. The father was a passive and ineffectual man who was wrapped around the mother's finger. In the patient's adolescence he became the enforcer of the mother's sadistic need to punish the daughter for her perceived sexual transgressions and passive rebellious behavior or attitudes. He would take the adolescent daughter to their bedroom with the mother as witness/chaperon and pull her dress up and her panties down and spank her with a belt until her buttocks were sore.

Needless to say, this patient is quite fragile, with a proclivity for psychotic depressive reactions. What is important for this discussion is the manifestation of the repetition compulsion in this patient's history. On leaving home as an adolescent, she joined the military. She was not yet sexually active as an adolescent. At a party one evening she drank too much and vaguely remembers a gang rape that was later confirmed. On leaving the service, she became a call girl. In her thirties she became involved with a television star with whom she fell in love. She became pregnant and married him, even though she was forced to sign a restrictive prenuptial agreement. He was much older and is a highly controlling man. He required her to follow a strict budget and supply him with receipts for all family and personal expenditures. If she spent too much, which she frequently did, he shamed her relentlessly. She could have no independent life of her own. Initially before and early in the marriage, they had an active sexual life, until he began to age. He also began to cross-dress for his arousal, and he also wanted sadomasochistic foreplay. She gradually withdrew from him and became completely frozen in all sexual activity. However, she lived some rich secret sexual fantasy life involving masturbation. In these fantasies, she was a passive victim of a sexually exciting man to whom she willingly submitted, and in so doing felt tremendous excitement and satisfaction. The accompanying masturbation included sucking a dildo as well as penetrating herself anally and vaginally. Frequently, before a climax she would transform into a male hero who would retaliate against the forces of international oppression with tremendous ferocity. He would sadistically cut, chew, bite, punch, shoot, bomb, or nuke the powerful enemy threat.

The patient also abuses alcohol and self-mutilates her skin for "pleasure from pain."

Herein, we see a reenactment of the core neurotic structure. On a superego level her life is a pure repetition of her childhood experience. She is a "kept" woman-child who is owned by her husband-mother with no rights and no autonomy. He rules her with the same iron hand as her mother ruled her as a child. She expresses her hostility toward the husband-mother passively, but she also leaves enough evidence to be caught by him. He then punishes her with shame each time she transgresses by defying his authority. This is also a reenactment of the way her mother had her father punish her by the humiliating beatings in the parents' bedroom. Moreover, the core repetition compulsion is the cycle between sexual pleasure/satisfaction and maternal/superego punishment. The masturbation fantasy demonstrates the memory of the pleasure she felt in the symbiotic closeness with her grandfather-mother with oral, anal, and genital excitation; however, her female receptive pleasure is so contaminated by the punishment from the mother that the unconscious sadistic impulses against the mother for her punishment organizes itself into the grandiose fantasy of a male destroying the destructive force of the mother. (This also encapsulates her hope that her father would regain his power and moderate the rage in the mother. The obvious transference implications and the technique of dealing with them will not be explored here.)

The relationship with the husband is a particularly threatening one. Originally, he provided her with a sense of stability and structure, and he was not part of the neurosis. As he aged, he began to stimulate her unconscious with memories of her excitement of her grandfather-mother. The unconscious link was further catalyzed when he began to cross-dress for purposes of enhanced sexual excitement. To my patient's unconscious, the identification with her grandfather-mother was complete and she could allow herself no further libidinal access to her husband for fear of encountering her mother's abuse. This did not succeed, as the "abuse" occurred in the form of a massive clinical depression that ultimately brought her to treatment. The patient experiences painful sadness and depression following the masturbation as well.

It is clear then that preoedipal triangulation pathology existed in this family system. What, we should ask, was the effect of this on sibling relations? This was a large family. The patient was the firstborn. Her next sister is three years her junior. She remembers initial delight at the sister's birth, and there is little reactive unconscious sadism toward her. The patient was isolated from the other siblings by the mother's scapegoating of her. She developed the sense of herself as an outsider from the family and lived a depressed life with retreat from the pain into fantasy. She developed self-image disturbances, believing herself to be ugly. This lasted until she entered the military where her peers found her attractive. She subsequently entered and won beauty contests. After her military service, upon returning home from college to visit her family, she was criticized by her mother. Later on that visit she went into a fugue state and sexually molested one of her younger teenage sisters (who willingly participated). This sister was beautiful and was particularly favored by the mother. The reenactment of her own "molestation" by her grandfather is now complete. The molestation of the sister was a preoedipal bonding, looking for her grandfather-mother by becoming him. The sister was her good self before being victimized by the mother's anger. The sadomasochistic needs of the unconscious were met when the mother discovered the event, and my patient was summarily banished from the family. Mother's prophecy of the evil acting out of sexuality was fulfilled. Currently the patient reports feeling on the outside of society, despite an outwardly lavish social life.

This is a somewhat extreme example of the effect of preoedipal traumatic triangulation and its interactive effects on the sibling relationships. I will now describe another case from my clinical practice that illustrates a more common form of sibling rivalry.

MIXED PREOEDIPAL AND OEDIPAL SIBLING DISTURBANCE

Phillip, 49, sought treatment for an acute anxiety condition caused by the disappearance of his 18-year-old male lover, Jamie. He believed Jamie was kidnapped and locked away by his parents in an involuntary drug treatment facility. He was frantic. He hired a private investigator in a desperate attempt to rescue Jamie from involuntary confinement. He was flooded with anxiety. He had nightmares. He was also morbidly obese, and his eating was out of control. He was so fat that his oxygen supply to his brain was impaired (pickwickian syndrome), and he would nod off to sleep at inopportune times.

We began the unlocking process. Phillip's defenses were staunch and the superego masochism was severe, but what unfolded was equally interesting. Phillip loved Jamie but it was a narcissistic love. Why was Phillip's unconscious so severely activated by Jamie's disappearance? The focus of the entire therapy became family loss and parental betrayal, which answered the above questions.

The initial unlocking revealed severe sadism toward his now-deceased father, Ralph, who was a successful real estate attorney/developer. He married Hanna, Phillip's mother, primarily as a way of raising investment capital. On the other hand, Hanna married Ralph to escape her dependency on a cruel and vindictive first husband. She had two children by that marriage: David and Leah. Phillip was the oldest of three full sibs, Phillip, Zack, and Andrew. Ralph was a dominating, grandiose father who controlled everyone with whom he came in contact. Ralph decided that Phillip needed to attend Wellington House, an English boarding school that catered to nobility. Wellington House was supposed to prepare Phillip to be one of the leaders of his generation. Phillip repressed the sadistic rage he harbored toward Ralph. This rage was all-pervasive. His life was organized around seeking revenge against Ralph for separating him from his brothers, sister, grandmother, and mother by sending him to the austere English "prison." The weapon of his revenge against Ralph was himself. Everything that Ralph wanted for Phillip was destroyed by Phillip, even if Phillip wanted the same thing for himself.

So the link between himself and Jamie became clear. Jamie was a reenactment figure—a lost child, found and rescued by Phillip, taken in and given a home and the love he was unable to receive from his family. Phillip was thus different from the father he had experienced. The homosexuality was reactive as well. Ralph was a lusty man who reveled in heterosexuality. Phillip, too, was primarily heterosexual in interest and fantasy life, but in his sadistic rebellion against Ralph's control he rejected his primary sexual object choice. He also rejected women in order to protect them from his rage.

Phillip's primary maternal figures were his grandmother Rose and his sister Leah. The attachment with Leah was flooded with sexual feeling, and she was the archetype of sexuality in his unconscious. Phillip, it turned out, was the designated heir to the real-estate empire that Ralph spent a lifetime building. This was why he sent Phillip to Wellington House. After two years, Phillip returned home and refused at age 8 to return to the school. To his recollection, the family was never the same. The closeness he remembered with his brothers was gone. Unaware, the cycle of revenge with the self as victim had begun. He began acting out in his new school and got himself removed. He now began a life as an underachiever and a background figure, never allowing himself to achieve recognition. He withheld from Ralph that which Ralph desired the most—a successful son. He became a computer hacker instead, working in the shadows of society.

After many infidelities, Ralph and Hanna eventually divorced and Phillip lived primarily with Hanna. On a vacation to Greece, Phillip was seduced at age 16 by Hanna's lover. He felt massive shamefulness and did not bathe for a month. He developed seething anger toward gays and would harass and bash them over computer bulletin boards. Eventually one of the gays asked him to meet him and address why he was so hostile to gays. Phillip became a practicing homosexual from his early twenties until the time he saw me for therapy over the Jamie "kidnapping."

His prior heterosexual experiences were fraught with anxiety. He avoided sexual relationships with women and rationalized that they were only relationships that were mired in a cesspool of dependency and exploitation. He had totally isolated himself from women with a wall of fat and homosexual relationships. After unlocking the unconscious, what appeared was quite amazing. Phillip continued in an unconscious libidinal bonding with his sister Leah. He was in massive sibling rivalry with his younger brothers for her attention, love, and sexual favoritism. However, there was a sadistic element. His rage over his exile to England commingled with his sexual feelings, so the bond to the sister was both erotic and sadistic. Each female who came too close risked violent rape and torture to death. Thus, he experienced intense anxiety whenever around a female to whom he was attracted. After the unlocking of the sadism toward Leah, the murderous and sadistic cathexis to his brothers Zack and Andrew was released. He was enraged with them because the preoedipal closeness he experienced with them was gone and could not be recaptured when he returned home in latency.

This left their sibling relationship in tatters. When the brothers were adults, Ralph died suddenly of a cardiac arrest. All of the estate was left in overlapping pieces, keeping the brothers in business together and fighting at the same time over who had to pay what expense. Phillip was seething with conscious and unconscious anger at his brothers and his neurosis was further aggravated by Ralph's death. Time and time again he allowed his brothers to take advantage of him and thus was victimized by them.

During his treatment, he lost 200 pounds; he has reasserted himself as the senior brother and has demanded and received the money owed to him by Zack and Andrew. He has sold the part of Ralph's empire he inherited and is now managing his own business as well as his money. For the first time in adulthood, he has established an identity free of masochistic revenge against Ralph. He is no longer exclusively homosexual and is dating a woman in whom he is interested.

What points does this case illustrate about sibling rivalry and the unconscious? Again this family was clearly troubled from the beginning. Ralph was obsessed with power and dynasty building and his children were victims of that obsession. He sculpted the family to become a group of aristocratic barons whose assigned task was to till the fertile soil he acquired during his life. Like so many power-obsessed individuals, he found it impossible to respect the free will of his children, and he created intricate webs in which his children become entrapped and thus are forced to follow Dad's will. To Phillip, Dad's will was a toxic acid that burned him badly when he was sent to Wellington House. Therefore, Dad's will had to be resisted because of its power to harm. Phillip's rage at this violation colored his perception of the family when he returned home from England. The closeness and intimacy he enjoyed didn't exist anymore. He didn't realize that what had changed was him. His psyche had been changed from prolonged abandonment trauma. His future ability to relate to men and women was now also disturbed.

His longing for a close and intimate relationship with Ralph led him to homosexuality. In his homosexual relationships he sought and frequently received the nurturance that he could not receive from Ralph without a network of conditions. Soon the neurosis unfolded, and, as he aged Phillip began acting out the repetition compulsion. Because of his unconscious murder of his father and of his brothers, and the rape/murder of his sister, it was his destiny to live the unfulfilled life of a morbidly obese outcast. His lifeboat to the outside world was his connection to Jamie. Jamie was his own abandoned 6-year-old child whom Phillip rescued from an isolated existence. Although now heterosexual, Phillip still reports a strong compulsive attraction to young male drug addicts, wanting to "rescue" them.

His unconscious rage and guilt toward his brothers led him to avoid intimacy with his brothers and to encourage them to treat him like a doormat in their financial lives. Healthy love and competition were replaced by resentment and manipulation. This is only half the picture of the intrapsychic puzzle. Hanna is the keystone to this achieving understanding. Phillip's preverbal experience of her and her mother Rose was quite good. Once Phillip could discriminate for himself, he realized there was something wrong with Hanna. She was a contradictory mixture of a martyr and a narcissist. She seemed willing to sacrifice for her children, but in the here and now of everyday life she was incapable of delivering a consistent maternal connection. Phillip recalled several important events in his life that Hanna would forget. He would be left waiting for rides home from the movie theater and country club. Phillip left the maternal dyad with unfulfilled dependency needs and an incomplete sense of his own uniqueness. His rage at Hanna was created by the fact that she was too narcissistic to perceive him as a unique individual. Thus, through generalization and displacement, women are viewed as takers, not givers. Hanna acquiesced to Ralph's plan that Phillip go to Wellington House. In Phillip's view she betrayed her basic covenant to him: to be the center of his universe and to nurture him and his brothers as long as he needed her. Hanna married Ralph to be taken care of, bore Phillip to ensnare Ralph, and conspired with Ralph to send Phillip to England to be heir to the estate, and thus take care of Hanna. He was used, not loved for himself.

His reactive, retaliatory rage at her is nearly limitless. She and her surrogates in his unconscious are raped (used) and then killed. Phillip felt used by Hanna to consolidate her marriage toward Ralph. The main source of positive connection was Leah. Phillip felt loved, nurtured, and advocated for by Leah. He also found her to be incredibly sexually exciting. The problem was that each of the brothers felt the same way toward her and she to them. Leah, who was also deprived by Hanna, loved the attention and adoration she received from the boys. This aggravated an already inflammatory family situation by producing rivalry for Leah because of her seductiveness. Phillip's finely tuned unconscious sensed this dynamic, and thus Leah compounded the trauma to Phillip by using him for her own narcissistic and dependent needs. The second most important nuturant figure in his life also exploited him. She used him selfishly to create a court of admirers. She was narcissistic like her mother, only in a more subtle way. To this day Leah finds ways to get the brothers to compete for most-favored status. Leah's hysteria was preordained by her difficulties with Hanna's narcissism. Phillip recalled feeling devastated when

Leah, who became a teacher, had a love affair with one of her high school students. This, to him, confirmed what he expected all along: it was not him that she loved uniquely; he was only a role player in her life.

In summary, Phillip appeared in treatment for an acute anxiety state caused by a current life situation (loss of Jamie) that reactivated his dormant neurosis. The neurosis originated when he was sent to an English boarding school at age 6 at the initiation of his father's dynasty dream in which Phillip was designated as the heir apparent to the empire. His mother did not intervene to stop this plan and her passivity, combined with the father's grandiosity and controlling qualities, resulted in a severe actual trauma to Phillip. The separation anxiety became commingled with reactive sadism in Phillip's unconscious. On return to his family he experienced the family as different, when in fact it was his perception that changed. He began to experience more isolation trauma and became angrier. He is placed in unconscious rivalry for his mother/sister by her need to be adored. Unconsciously, he is now the murderer of Hanna-Ralph. He is the rapist-murderer of his sister/surrogate mother and the murderer of his brothers Zack and Andrew. Feeling unconsciously that he is a serial killer, the masochism dynamic is activated, and Phillip began to retaliate against his perpetrators by acting out and failing (success neurosis). He then began to slowly execute himself by overeating and by inactivity, resulting in morbid obesity. His coming to see me represented the last attempt to save himself from the fate scripted by the superego.

OEDIPAL SIBLING DISTURBANCE

Josh is a 45-year-old emergency room physician. He sought treatment for episodic depression and a severe marital disturbance. He had seen other therapists but had not improved. He was an excellent candidate for intensive short-term treatment. He was high functioning and low resistance. He complained that his wife would enrage him near the threshold of violence. He was aware of a relationship between the rage and the depression that would soon follow. He also complained of a distant, uninvolved way of relating to his wife, colleagues, and patients. He had two daughters whom he loved deeply. His father, a psychiatrist, was dead, probably by an assisted suicide. Before his father's death, Josh was estranged from his father, who was cold, distant, and exploitative of Josh and his wife. His father disinherited Josh and gave his money to an endowed chair at a university's department of anthropology in order to memorialize himself. Josh's mother as well is extremely self-centered and ferociously competitive with his wife. On their wedding day, she vowed to destroy their marriage because she would not allow any woman to come between her and her son. Josh's younger brother David suffered from severe schizophrenia and lived on the East Coast in a board and care facility. When Josh's father retired he turned to Josh and told him that he would do nothing for David any longer, that David was now Josh's total moral and financial responsibility. He was, indeed, to be his brother's keeper. Josh's mother and father divorced soon after Josh left home for medical school. David developed schizophrenia at the same time while in college. David was four years Josh's junior.

David was an incredibly gifted child. He had a talent for language, music, mathematics, and the dramatic arts. He was a prodigy. In contrast, Josh was a studious, shy, reserved, and socially awkward child.

The unlocking first revealed pathologic bereavement for his father. The father was the steadier of the two parents and served as a positive role model for Josh. He spent many hours teaching his sons the history of the world. He loved philosophy, religion, and psychology and shared this with his sons. The father was a Hungarian refugee who came to the United States before World War II. There was a sadistic cathexis to the father for his passivity in shirking his responsibility to Josh and David to intervene with their mother. Josh was bonded to his mother in an unconscious marriage. His mother adored Josh and elevated him as a child-hero above his father. In her eyes, Josh was the child genius, the apple of her eye, until David came along; then she dropped Josh like a hot potato. He recalled a visit in which she replayed the same dynamic with his two children. He observed her drop all the attention from the older child and idealize the younger. The older grandchild was devastated and became reactively depressed.

Josh was seething with unconscious hatred for David, who had supplanted him from the throne of his mother's excessive adoration. As the unlocking gathered steam, plot after plot emerged from the unconscious about David's death, and Josh's restoration to pre-David glory. Mixed with this anger was profound survivor guilt. Josh unconsciously blamed himself for David's schizophrenia. He felt if it wasn't his fault that David's personality was destroyed, it was his mother's fault for her seductiveness and volatility. If not her fault, then it was his father's distant obsessive rigidity that caused David's emotional deterioration. Josh felt tortured.

Josh was emotionally unavailable to his wife. He realized that he was in constant sibling rivalry with her. They would bicker endlessly over who was right and who was wrong in family disputes, what was fair and what was unfair. This interminable marital stalemate was a twofold superego punishment: One, the destruction of closeness from his wife was the punishment for his fratricide. (Remember, Cain could not till fertile soil as punishment for the murder of Abel.) Two, the distance created by the bickering sustained his unconscious loyalty (incestuous attachment) to his mother. Josh, it seems, could not be married to two women. As therapy progressed Josh remembered more and more instances in which his mother aggravated the rivalry between him and David. Also, David's gifted nature made it even more difficult for Josh to gain his fair share of the maternal attention. Further complicating the neurosis, his mother demanded complete submission to her authority and her will in the home. Any demonstration of unauthorized self-initiative was punished cruelly and without mercy. Josh's sense of self was quite damaged by this triangulation between his mother, David, and him. He married late in life and would have remained a bachelor if not pursued by his wife. At the wedding, his mother established a triangle between herself, Josh, and his wife. After the marriage, his wife, observing the behavior of her in-laws, in a very healthy way disengaged from Josh's family and suggested to him that he seek therapy.

In therapy, Josh rapidly mourned his father's death and overcame his rage at him. Josh forgave himself for his jealous rage at his now severely impaired brother, and flew East to meet with his mother face to face to tell her how much he loved his wife and family. He offered her a place in his life as his mother and grandmother to their children. He stressed the importance of not hurting the relationship between his two children by lavishing attention on the younger to the detriment of the older child.

Clearly, the mother was the victim of a dysfunctional childhood, as Josh came to understand. Her father was a marginal psychopathic individual who was a compulsive womanizer. Her mother was a passive and depressed woman who could not control her husband's acting out. The mother's depression caused Josh's mother's emotional needs to go unfulfilled. Her older brother received all of the attention from both her father and mother. Josh was the victim of his mother's repetition of her own childhood experience. The older child was the perpetrator of her narcissistic wound. She punished Josh as she would have liked to have punished her older brother. She repaired her narcissistic trauma by doting on the younger child (herself). Her husband was the depressed unavailable mother, and she the hurtful narcissistic father who rejected her. Josh terminated treatment with a remarkable outcome. He no longer suffers from depression, his marriage is rich and intimate, and he is respected and loved by the other physicians in the emergency room.

SUMMARY

These are three complicated clinical examples of how sibling conflicts become embedded in the unconscious life of neurotic individuals. What is essential to recognize is that sibling-induced trauma is an ordinary and common problem that we all deal with in the human condition. It does not necessarily become part of a neurosis. I treat numerous patients who have warm and caring relationships with their siblings, many of whom were cruel to one another during their childhood. The competition, sadism, and hatred is balanced by companionship, playfulness, and love. Sibling relationships teach social cooperativeness and teamwork in healthy family systems. Many times siblings balance out the deficiencies of either parent and are life- and psyche-saving for the child. However, sibling relationships are potential hotbeds of neurotic conflict. A sibling rivalry gets pulled into the vortex of a developing neurosis when the child is heir to a pre-oedipal trauma in the mother–child dyad or becomes a participant in a triangle where the natural rivalry is aggravated because of unconscious needs of one of the parents or parent surrogates in the oedipal phase.

The suffering that then ensues in the lives of these patients can be devastating. The biblical stories of Cain and Abel, Jacob and Esau, and Reuben and Joseph attest to the centrality of sibling rivalry to the human unconscious. As it turns out, we *are* our brother's keeper. The superego would not have it any other way.

SUGGESTED READING

Agger, E M. (1988). Psychoanalytic perspectives on sibling relationships. *Psychoanalytic Inquiry* 8:3–30.

Bank, S. P., and Kahn, M. D. (1980–81). Freudian siblings. *Psychoanalytic Review* 67:493–504.

——— (1982). *The Sibling Bond.* New York: Basic Books.

Bernays, A. (1940). My brother, Sigmund Freud. *American Mercury*, November, pp. 334–340.

Boer, F., and Dunne, J., eds. (1992). *Children's Sibling Relationships.* Hillsdale, NJ: Erlbaum.

Colonna, A. B., and Newman, L. (1983). Psychoanalytic literature on siblings. *Psychoanalytic Study of the Child* 38:285–310. New Haven, CT: Yale University Press.

Davanloo, H. (1990). *Unlocking the Unconscious.* Chichester, England: Wiley.

Leichtman, M. (1985). Influence of an older sibling on the separation-individuation process. *Psychoanalytic Study of the Child* 40:111–162. New Haven, CT: Yale University Press.

Parens, H. (1988). Siblings in early childhood: some direct observational findings. *Psychoanalytic Inquiry* 8:31–50.

Sharpe, S., and Rosenblatt, A. (1994). Oedipal sibling triangles. *Journal of the American Psychoanalytic Association* 42(2):491–523.

PART II

Treatment Issues in Working with Abuse, Trauma, and Neglect

INTRODUCTION TO PART II

Because the words *abuse*, *trauma*, and *neglect* have been of concern in the mental health field, the Reiss-Davis Child Study Center offers comprehensive intervention that includes a concentrated look at the children and adolescents who have been abused, traumatized, and/or neglected. It is not surprising, therefore, that we are always interested in finding new ways to better understand and remediate in these areas. The chapters in this section suggest new ways to work with and to work through abuse, trauma, and neglect.

Chapter 7, "Remembering Iphigenia: Voice, Resonance, and a Talking Cure," by Carol Gilligan, describes the unconnected inner and outer worlds of women who throughout their developmental years have sacrificed their free will and have internalized their painful wounds and angry voices in order to maintain stability within a patriarchal world.

Chapter 8, "A Multimodal Approach for Working Through a Therapeutic Impasse in the Case of Childhood Sexual Abuse," by Bonnie S. Mark and Robert Anderson, addresses family collusion in abuse and presents a multimodal team treatment approach to healing the wounds of long-standing abuse. This chapter discusses the treatment of an adolescent girl and illustrates the role of hypnosis as an adjunct to traditional psychotherapy in helping expedite the patient's knowledge of the past. The authors follow the patient through her exploration of her childhood early adolescent experiences, including molestation by her brother, her relationship with parents, the physical and psychological effects of chronic eczema, and other significant issues pivotal to her development.

Chapter 9, "Generations after the Holocaust: Multigenerational Transmission of Trauma," by Deborah Berger-Reiss, looks at the relatively new phenomenon of third generation trauma, going beyond studies that have shown that the Holocaust has scarred a generation with psychic trauma, and describing the ongoing wounds of trauma in descendants some fifty years later. The chapter follows three generations in one family, all of which were affected by the Holocaust, although only the oldest generation had any direct experience of the event. The author discusses her work with a second-generation survivor who suffered from severe panic attacks that enabled the patient to uncover the roots of his attacks, which were connected with his experiences as a child of a survivor of the Holocaust, and the significant impact of the trauma on his offspring, a third generation of the family.

Chapter 10, "Memory, Trauma, and Psychotherapy," by Daniel J. Siegel, provides a concise overview of the basic processes of the mind and how they may become impacted by, and used to adapt to, trauma. Issues such as posttraumatic stress disorder, disturbances of amnesia, intrusive recollections, and flashback phenomena are addressed in this review, and tools for evaluation as well as treatment implications are suggested. A central focus of the chapter is on amnesiac reactions around the abuse, which are part of the defense that makes the abuse an ongoing problem that persists for years.

7

Remembering Iphigenia: Voice, Resonance, and a Talking Cure*

Carol Gilligan

It behooves you to go by another way . . .
If you would escape from this wild place.

Dante, *The Inferno*

VOICE AND RESONANCE: THE INNER WORLD IN THE OUTER WORLD

Eleven-year-old Nina tells me that she is writing a story about "someone during the Civil War" and making it "a little bit sad," because when the father goes to war, the girl in the story is "really upset." She says,

---

*Originally published in Shapiro, E. R., ed. (1996). *The Inner World and the Outer World*. New Haven, CT: Yale University Press. Copyright © 1996 by Yale University Press, and used by permission.

> He talks to her before he goes, about how he feels about leaving and that he is just as worried as she is, or more worried and more scared. . . . And, you know, she feels like he's never going to come back, which is possible, but, you know, it's not a fact yet. So she has a very, um, a very strange feeling sometimes.

I ask Nina about this strange feeling, and she explains,

> Before he left, she realized that he was not, um, totally powerful, but she didn't, um, feel angry at him for that, but she felt very, um, very sorry, sort of very sorry for him, and very shocked or surprised, mainly, and still upset that he was leaving. And, um, he was trying to comfort her when he told her about, um, about his own fears of going, but really she was just mainly surprised, and she hadn't realized that he could feel like this, too.

I have known Nina for almost a year at the time of this interview conversation. A gifted writer of Latina and Jewish background, she is taking part in a study of girls' development and a prevention project designed to strengthen girls' voices and their courage (see Gilligan and Rogers 1993, Gilligan et al. 1992). I ask Nina why the girl in the story didn't know that "her father could feel like this too," and she continues her layered and psychologically nuanced description of the girl, the father, and the flow of realizations and feelings between them:

> He had always been there for her, you know. She had been, um, she'd been hurt . . . and she had been humiliated because she was a girl. And he always understood her, and she was very close to him. Her siblings thought it was really brave of him to [enlist] right away, but she knew that he was, he just, if he waited any longer he wouldn't be able to do it, he wouldn't have enough courage to do it.
>
> [How did she know that?]
>
> She knew because of the way he talked to her, that he was feeling really scared and upset, and he didn't want her to make it any harder or anything. After that, she didn't get so upset, or she didn't show it.

By listening to her father's voice and "the way he talked to her," the girl picks up his fear and his upset feelings, as well as his need to cover these feelings in order to enlist in the army. Sensing his vulnerability and his wish that she not make it any harder for him, she also covers her feelings and begins not to feel so upset or not to show how upset she is feeling.

The following year when Nina is 12 and we resume our interview conversation, she tells me again of the stories she is writing, stories that are now winning prizes in local story-writing contests. But now the inner world of the Civil War story is nowhere in evidence. In contrast to the intimate and direct, naturalistic rendering of the human world, Nina now writes about how "things would feel," if they "were able to see, like a pen with its cap off." In one story, a girl

> is trying to, well, she falls in love with this boy . . . and they have these adventures. It starts when they're at a dance, and then when she has to leave, his car gets stolen, and then they go to the gang. . . . This group has stolen it . . . and he has to fight one of the guys, and then they set off in the car, and there's a storm and the car stalls.

Nina says, "It's a really good story. I can tell. It's a lot better than the ones I wrote a couple of years ago, anyway." In another story, a queen who is "really a bad queen" is assassinated on the anniversary of her coronation. Three generations later, she becomes "a beautiful, wonderful queen." Sensing with me that something is missing—some understanding or even interest in the process of this transformation—Nina observes by way of explanation, "It's just the way memory covers up the bad things." Attributing the cover-up to "it"—to memory—Nina signals the onset of dissociation.

An inner world has been sequestered, perhaps as the Civil War story suggests, because the voicing of that world set off disturbing resonances and emotional vibrations in other people, making it harder for them to live in the outer world. Nina has become aware of the difficulties and dangers of being able to feel and to see, or of recording what she is seeing and feeling. She also feels the stirrings of new desires: to fall in love, to go on romantic adventures, to win prizes in story contests, to be good and beautiful rather than bad. As the outer world of civilization dims the inner psychological world, casting a shadow over its illumination, Nina for the moment sees this eclipse as the good covering over the bad.

In a short story called "An Unwritten Novel," Virginia Woolf addresses a buried self. The speaker asks, "When the self speaks to the self, who is speaking?" And answers,

> the entombed soul, the spirit driven in, in, in to the central catacomb; the self that took the veil and left the world—a coward perhaps, yet somehow beautiful as it flits with its lantern restlessly up and down the dark corridors. [Woolf 1921, p. 24]

Like Nina at 12, the speaker of Woolf's "unwritten novel," is keeping her light under cover.

In Edith Wharton's short story "The Fullness of Life," the narrator muses:

> I have sometimes thought that a woman's nature is like a great house, full of rooms. There is the hall through which everyone passes going in and out. The drawing room where one receives more formal visits, the sitting room where members of the family come and go as they list; but beyond that, far beyond, are other rooms the handles of whose doors are never turned; no one knows the way to them, no one knows whither they lead, and in the innermost room, the holy of holies, the soul sits alone and waits for a footstep that never comes. [Wharton 1968, p. 14]

This startling, piercing rendition of what the narrator refers to as "a woman's nature" is shocking in part because through the extended simile comparing a woman's nature to a great house, Wharton has so seamlessly joined nature and culture, women and civilization. It is within the great house of civilization that a woman seeks sanctuary within her own house, within her own nature, because the absence of her soul from both formal and familial relationships goes unnoticed and arouses no interest or curiosity. While the soul sits alone in its inner sanctuary listening, nobody comes, no one has followed her.

Wharton finds the voice of this early story troubling. Writing to her editor, she explains her wish not to include it in her first published collection:

> As to the old stories of which you speak so kindly, I regard them as the excesses of youth. They were all written "at the top of my

> voice," . . . I may not write any better, but at least I hope that I write in a lower key, and I fear that the voice of those early tales will drown all the others. It is for that reason that I prefer not to publish them. [Wharton, quoted in C. G. Wolff 1995, p. 59]

"The Fullness of Life," she says, "is one long shriek" (p. 63).

REMEMBERING IPHIGENIA

When Agamemnon's ships are becalmed at Aulis, he is under internal and external pressure to sacrifice his daughter, Iphigenia, to the goddess Artemis in order to gain the winds that will carry his army to Troy. He writes to Clytemnestra, his wife, telling her to bring Iphigenia to Aulis, ostensibly for marriage to Achilles. When Iphigenia discovers her father's purpose, her first response is that he is mad. He has forgotten their relationship, their closeness, the words they have said to one another, their love. It is as if he has forgotten himself. Wishing that she had the voice of Orpheus so that she could "charm with song the stones to leap and follow me," or words that could beguile others and work magic, she says, "O my father," appealing to their relationship and reminding him that,

> I was the first to call you father,
> You to call me child. And of your children
> First to sit upon your knees. We kissed
> Each other in our love. "O Child,"
> You said, "surely one day I shall see you
> Happy in your husband's home. And like
> A flower blooming for me and in my honor."
> Then as I clung to you and wove my fingers
> In your beard, I answered, "Father, you,
> Old and reverent then, with love I shall
> Receive into my home, and so repay you
> For the years of trouble and your fostering
> Care of me." I have in memory all these words
> Of yours and mine. But you, forgetting,
> Have willed it in your heart to kill me.
> . . . Let me win life
> From you. I must. To look upon the world

Of light is for all men their greatest joy—
The shadow world below is nothing.
Men are mad, I say, who pray for death;
It is better that we live ever so
Miserably than die in glory.

[Euripides 405 B.C.E., pp. 359-361]

Agamemnon, caught in a tragic conflict ("Terrible it is to me, my wife, to dare/This thing. Terrible not to dare it"), feels compelled to sacrifice Iphigenia. "My compulsion [is] absolute," Agamemnon explains, it is "beyond all will/of mine" (p. 361).

When Iphigenia takes in the hopelessness of her situation, she chooses to die nobly rather than ignobly, to align herself with her father's purpose, to separate herself from her mother's grief and anger, to "fix her mind." She pleads then with Clytemnestra not to make it any harder for her, but instead to "listen to my words," to "hear me now," to "follow my words and tell me if I speak well," to take in how her death can become not a cause for anger but a good and right thing:

Mother, now listen to my words. I see
Your soul in anger against your husband.
This is a foolish and an evil rage.
Oh, I know when we stand before a helpless
Doom how hard it is to bear.
But hear me now.
. . . And now hear me, Mother,
What thing has seized me and I have conceived
In my heart.
I shall die—I am resolved—
And having fixed my mind I want to die
Well and gloriously, putting away/
From me whatever is weak and ignoble.
Come close to me, Mother, follow my words
And tell me if I speak well. All Greece turns
Her eyes to me, to me only, great Greece
In her might—for through me is the sailing
Of the fleet, through me the sack and overthrow
Of Troy. Because of me, never more will
Barbarians wrong and ravish Greek women,

Drag them from happiness and their homes
In Hellas [Greece]. The penalty will be paid
Fully for the shame and seizure of Helen.
And all
These things, all of them, my death will achieve
And accomplish. I, savior of Greece,
Will win honor and my name shall be blessed.
It is wrong for me to love life too deeply. . . .
To Greece I give this body of mine.
Slay it in sacrifice and conquer Troy.
These things coming to pass, Mother, will be
My children, my marriage; through the years
My good name and my glory. It is
A right thing that Greeks rule barbarians,
Not barbarians Greeks. [pp. 369–371]

The chorus, composed of women from Chalcis, praise Iphigenia's ability to weave what have now become corrupt words (love, marriage, conception, children—now linked not with life but with death) into a speech of great dignity:

Child, you play your part with nobleness.
The fault is with the goddess and with fate. [p. 371]

Locating the fault with Artemis and with fate, the women of the chorus echo Iphigenia's feelings of helplessness and powerlessness. Initially, these women from Chalcis had doubled the voice of Clytemnestra, amplifying her plea as the plea of "all women": "Oh, what a power is motherhood, possessing/ A potent spell. All women alike/ Fight fiercely for a child" (p. 346). They urged Agamemnon to "yield to her!" and "save the child," saying "It is good/ That you together save the child. No man/Can rightly speak against this word of mine" (p. 359).

The chorus's turn then signifies their internalization of the shame ethic of the culture of honor that both the men and the women are now enforcing. The desire for life and for love has become shameful, and pride has become the overriding motivation. Iphigenia makes this change explicit when she says, "My good name and my glory" will be "my children, my marriage." And following Iphigenia, the chorus now names her choice of death over a culturally defined dishonor not as madness but nobility (see J. Gilligan 1996).

The inner and outer worlds are incompatible, and Iphigenia's turn is radical. Her two speeches—the first, an appeal to relationship that proves ineffective, and the second, a wish to go down in history, to be her father's sacrifice and to realize his purpose as her own—define a pattern that young women continue to articulate across the millennia, carrying the powerful suggestion that the father's sacrifice of his adolescent daughter is woven into the fabric of civilization.

In a startling production called *Les Atrides*, Ariane Mnouchkine, the creator of the Theatre du Soleil in Paris, prefaces Aeschylus' *Oresteia* trilogy with Euripides' play, *Iphigenia in Aulis*, and by doing so, radically reframes both the story of the house of Atreus and the birth of Athenian civilization. The *Oresteia*, or story of Orestes, begins with Clytemnestra's murder of Agamemnon as he returns triumphantly from Troy. Orestes, their son, then avenges the murder of his father by killing his mother, and he in turn is pursued by the Furies, until Athena comes and organizes a trial. Bringing the family feud into the public space of the city, she replaces private vengeance with the rule of law and the principle of justice. The *Oresteia*, in dramatizing the long working through of the tensions between the claims of the city and the ties of the household, has long been regarded as the foundational drama of Western civilization. As such, it links the birth of the legal system, the establishment of government or the state, and the origin or hegemony of patriarchy to the freeing of Orestes from the Furies. He is released when Athena casts the deciding vote in his favor at the trial.

By insisting that we remember Iphigenia and hear her story before we listen to the saga of Orestes, by beginning with Agamemnon's sacrifice of his daughter rather than with Clytemnestra's killing of her husband, Mnouchkine's production raises a question that otherwise tends not to be voiced or even formulated: Why is Orestes, and even more pointedly Electra—the other daughter of Clytemnestra and Agamemnon—so bent on avenging the murder of the father who has sacrificed their sister? In this light, the final play of Aeschylus' trilogy takes on new meaning. The long drawn-out struggle between Athena and the Furies becomes riveting in its implication that the working through of conflicts among women may hold a key to replacing violence with speaking, bringing private feuds into public places, and healing wounds that otherwise fester from generation to generation—in short, to establishing democracy and civilization.

Let me be more specific. The Furies, played as a group of old women who unleash a seemingly boundless and high-spirited energy, will not let go their anger at what has happened to Clytemnestra and, by implication, Iphigenia as well. Athena, the goddess born from the head of Zeus, the young woman whose mother was swallowed by her father, is, as she says, "wholly of the father" (the patriarchy), and unequivocally committed to realizing his (its) projects. As Athena arrives again and again to work through her struggle with the old women, to tame their wild energy and bring them into the city as the Eumenides or the good spirits, the visual impact of her repeated returning conveys the difficulty and the urgency of this reconciliation.

In *Civilization and Its Discontents*, Freud (1929–30) asks the question: Why have men created a culture in which they live with such discomfort? The corollary question is why have women supported, defended, and reproduced this culture? How can women maintain a coherent inner world within an outer world that is patriarchal, or can they? How can women breathe psychologically within this civilization, or do they?

REPEATING, REMEMBERING, AND WORKING THROUGH

At the end of ten years' research into women's psychological development, I remembered the hysterical women of the late nineteenth century, the women whom Freud called his "teachers" (Appignanesi and Forrester 1992). I reread Breuer's description of Anna O.:

> She was markedly intelligent, with an astonishingly quick grasp of things and penetrating intuition. She possessed a powerful intellect. . . . She had great poetic and imaginative gifts, which were under the control of a sharp and critical common sense. Owing to this latter quality she was *completely unsuggestible*; she was only influenced by arguments, never by mere assertions. Her willpower was energetic, tenacious, and persistent; sometimes it reached the pitch of an obsti-

> nacy which only gave way out of kindness and regard for other people. One of her essential traits was sympathetic kindness. . . . The element of sexuality was astonishingly undeveloped in her. [Breuer and Freud 1895, p. 21, emphasis in original]

When Anna fell ill at the age of 21, she was not able to speak, losing words, losing language, not able to see or to hear, not able to move, suffering from severe hallucinations and suicidal impulses, and alternating between two states of consciousness that were entirely separate from one another: a melancholy and anxious state in which she was present and seemed normal, and a state of "absence" where she lost time and could not remember. In her states of absence, Anna was "not herself," but wild, naughty, abusive, throwing cushions at people, pulling buttons off her bedclothes and linens, hallucinating, seemingly crazy.

Breuer notes,

> She would complain of having "lost" some time and would remark upon the gap in her train of conscious thoughts. . . . At moments when her mind was quite clear she would complain of the profound darkness in her head, of not being able to think, of becoming blind and deaf, of having two selves, a real one and an evil one which forced her to behave badly, and so on.
>
> In the afternoons, she would fall into a somnolent state which lasted till about an hour after sunset. She would then wake up and complain that something was tormenting her—or rather, she would keep repeating in the impersonal form "tormenting, tormenting." For alongside of the development of the contractures there appeared a deep-going functional disorganization of her speech. . . . In the process of time she became almost completely deprived of words. [pp. 24–25]

Breuer, observing that Anna had felt very much offended by something but had determined not to speak about it, encouraged her to speak and offered a resonant presence. And when in this resonant space, Anna had discovered that she could enter her absences and speak and see and hear for herself, she discovered what she called "a talking cure." Given that voice depends on resonance, that speaking depends on listening and being heard, loss of voice was a symptom of loss of relationship. It was a relationship that enabled Anna to regain her voice, and it was the recovery of her voice that set her free.

Freud observed that loss of voice was the most common symptom of hysteria, and given this observation, hysteria itself becomes a sign of a relational impasse or crisis. But the resonances set off by the voices of the hysterical women when they began to speak were deeply compelling to the men who treated them. Describing the character of his patient Fraulein Elisabeth von R., Freud notes "the features which one meets with so frequently in hysterical people," citing as typical:

> her giftedness, her ambition, her moral sensibility, her excessive demand for love which, to begin with, found satisfaction in her family, and the independence of her nature which went beyond the feminine ideal and found expression in a considerable amount of obstinacy, pugnacity and reserve. [Breuer and Freud 1895, p. 161]

When these intelligent, sensitive, stubborn, and mute young women began speaking of incestuous relationships with their fathers, Freud wrote to Fliess that he had arrived at Caput Nili—the head of the Nile; he had traced the origins of hysteria to childhood sexual trauma and linked neurosis with the structure of relationships between men and women and children in patriarchy. The difficulty that the hysterical women experienced in keeping inner and outer worlds connected, however, now began to affect their physicians as well. It was not possible to take in the inner worlds of these women and continue to live and function in the same way in the outer world of civilization. Psychoanalysis, as it developed in relationship with women who were teaching Freud about the close connection between body and psyche, between inner and outer worlds, was a radical inquiry. The talking cure was deceptively simple, given its ability to heal dissociation.

In 1896, the year following the publication of *Studies on Hysteria*, Freud's father died, and on the night after the funeral, he had a dream. In the dream, he is in a barbershop and a sign on the wall says: "You are requested to close the eyes" (Freud 1887–1904, p. 202). Freud writes to Fliess that "the old man's death has affected me deeply," and shortly thereafter he begins his self-analysis.

The following year, in the letter to Fliess in which Freud (1887-1904) explains that he no longer believes in his neurotica (theory of the neuroses), he expresses his "surprise that in all cases, the *father*, not excluding my own, had to be accused of being perverse," adding that "the realization of the unexpected frequency of hysteria, with precisely the same conditions prevailing in each, whereas surely such widespread perversions against children are not very probable" (p. 264, emphasis in original). His "certain insight" was "that there are no indications of reality in the unconscious, so that one cannot distinguish between truth and fiction that has been cathected with affect" (p. 264). The sexual trauma that had seemed a reality, might more probably be regarded as a sexual fantasy.

Psychoanalysis would predict that once Freud has said that he will no longer talk about incest, in an effort, perhaps, to close off this widespread accusation of fathers, he will be able to talk about nothing else. And in fact, in the first of the major theoretical works of psychoanalysis—"The Interpretation of Dreams"—Freud places the Oedipus story, an incest story, as the cornerstone of his new science. But the Oedipus story signifies a radical shift in voice and perspective. In place of the young woman speaking from experience about an incestuous relationship with her father, it is now the young boy who has fantasies of having an incestuous relationship with his mother—the young boy who will grow up to be Oedipus Rex, the son/husband/father/king of the Oedipus tragedy. The shift in Freud's emphasis from reality to fantasy, from outer world to inner, follows this shift in narration. The young woman hysteric has been eclipsed by the little boy who will in time grow up to become Oedipus Rex—the incestuous father.

The Dora case—"A Fragment of an Analysis of a Case of Hysteria"—becomes so tumultuous in part because it marks the return of the repressed. Dora comes for analysis in the year that Freud published "The Interpretation of Dreams," at a time when he was seeking confirmation for his theory of dreams. And Dora, beside herself at the thought that her father did not believe her or take her seriously, speaks to Freud through two dreams.

In the first dream, the house is on fire and Dora's father is standing by her bed and wakes her up. She wants to save her mother's jewel case, but her father insists that they leave the house at once, saying that he cares only for the safety of his children. They hurry downstairs and as soon as she is outside of the house, Dora wakes up. Freud maintains a deaf ear to what seems a thinly encoded incest narrative, or rather insists that this incestuous drama represents Dora's wish, Dora's fantasy.

In response, Dora dreams that her father is dead. She receives a letter from her mother telling her of the death, and begins an arduous journey home, arriving after everyone has left for the cemetery. Then, climbing the stairs, she "went calmly to her room, and began reading a big book that lay on her writing table" (Freud 1900, p. 140). Initially, Dora forgets this final dream segment, and while Freud focuses on the encyclopedia as signifying Dora's secret pursuit of sexual knowledge, the detail of the writing table suggests that Dora may now have come to the realization that the encyclopedia does not contain her story and that if she wants her story, her sexual experience, to become knowledge, she may have to write it herself. Shortly after this dream, Dora leaves the analysis.

In "Three Essays on the Theory of Sexuality," published in 1905—the same year that Freud releases the Dora case for publication—Freud writes that men's "erotic life alone has become accessible to research. That of women . . . partly owing to the stunting effect of civilized conditions and partly owing to their conventional secretiveness and insincerity . . . is still veiled in an impenetrable obscurity" (Freud 1905b, p. 151). Freud has left his hysterical women patients, the women whose voices he had encouraged, up to a point. Freud's "teachers" now would become "Freud's women," as the seeing and speaking hysterical young women became screened or hidden by images of the Madonna and (male) child—the iconography in Western culture of female devotion and compliance. Until the end of twentieth century, images of the preoedipal couple—the silent and unseeing mother and infant—were taken as fixed and central to the psychology of human development.

Discussing the case of Fraulein Elisabeth von R., Freud (1905b) observed that "the group of ideas relating to her love had already been separated from her knowledge" (p. 157). This dissociation had entered psychoanalysis. The love of their women patients that is evident in Breuer and Freud's early case histories was connected with momentous discovery, including the psychological causes of physical symptoms, the method of free association, and the power of the talking cure to heal dissociation. But this knowledge depended on relationship. Writing about his treatment of Elisabeth von R., Freud reveals the wellsprings of empathy, his willingness to enter into her feelings: "If we put greater misfortune to one side and enter into a girl's feelings, we cannot refrain from deep human sympathy with Fraulein Elisabeth" (p. 212). It may be that the sexual implications or overtones of such entry overwhelmed the knowledge gained through such connection with women, or perhaps the knowledge was so forbidden that it led to the reimposition of domination through sexual conquest. In Dora's case, Freud struggles between entering into a girl's feelings and drawing a girl and her feelings into the framework of history—the framework of the Oedipus story. Dora's brief analysis plays out the struggle of a young woman's initiation into a patriarchal culture, and Freud, in publishing his fragmentary case history, records the ambivalence and in the end the compulsion of the father in her sacrifice.

But predictably, the repressed returns. The late nineteenth century drama between women and psychoanalysis with its central struggle over the question of truth and reality has been reenacted at the end of the twentieth century. Again, women were encouraged to speak and in resonant relationship, the power of the talking cure once again became apparent. Again, women's voices revealed a problem of relationship—a break in connection between fathers and daughters that appeared so widespread as to seem improbable. And again a radical skepticism has set in. The discovery of a profound and troubling connection between inner and outer worlds has again been followed by the claim that Freud makes in the case of Dora—the claim that he knows her inner world better than she does.

A TALKING CURE

The issue is explicit: the cure for not speaking is relationship. Because voice depends on resonance, speaking depends on relationship. The breach between inner and outer worlds or the dissociation from parts of the inner world can be healed through a talking cure.

Normi Noel, a voice teacher who trained with Kristin Linklater, joined the Strengthening Healthy Resistance and Courage in Girls project to observe what happens to girls' voices at the edge of adolescence (Gilligan et al. 1992). Drawing on Linklater's *Freeing the Natural Voice* (1976), Noel (1995) makes the following observations:

> Linklater defines vibrations as needing surfaces to resound or amplify the initial impulse to speak. The body creates its own resonators. We build theaters to amplify the truth of the human voice. Musical instruments require surfaces and enclosed spaces to create more vibration. . . . Linklater's mantra for all young actors studying voice is that "tension murders vibration," while "vibrations thrive on attention"; with attention, the voice grows in power and range to reveal the truth.

In the course of the three-year project with girls, Noel picked up and followed the psychological dynamics that lead the impulse of the voice to go off sound. She named a series of steps leading from full speaking voice, to half-voice, to breathiness, and into silence. In the silence, Noel picked up the almost imperceptible vibration of the impulse to speak, which remained alive, vibrating in what she called an inner "cello world or resonating chamber." Keeping a journal to record her observations, Noel writes about resonance:

> Just as the acoustics for the strengthening of sound require certain physical properties, so too do the voices of the girls depend on a sympathetic "sounding board" or environment. Gilligan warns of the risk to girls around 11 or 12 who enter a patriarchal culture. It is filled with a dissonance that separates intellect from feeling. When there is no longer a "place" or "room" to strengthen their truth or practice speaking directly what they know, the girls then leave the vibrations of their speaking voice and move from breathiness to silence. In this silence, an inner cello world or resonating chamber keeps alive the energy of initial thought/feelings, preserving an integrity that risks everything if taken back onto the speaking voice in a culture still unable to provide a resonance for such clarity, subtlety, and power.

Noel concludes that by keeping alive the initial impulse to speak in an inner "cello world" or "resonating chamber," girls at adolescence create an inner sanctuary for a voice that holds a truth that others do not want to hear—a speaking voice that finds no resonance in the outer world. In this way, girls becoming women find a way "to hold their truth by *not* speaking," and their speaking voice becomes a cover for and at the same time gives off soundings of a "hidden world [that] women have rooted themselves in and survived" the dampening effects of a patriarchal language and culture (Noel 1995).

Iris, age 17, is a senior at the Laurel School in Cleveland. She has come to Harvard with two classmates to interview Lyn Mikel Brown and me about our research on women's psychology and girls' development. We have been interviewing girls and going on retreats with women at the school for the past five years, and now that our project is ending, they want to know about the book we are writing, and also about our methods and our findings (see Brown and Gilligan 1992). As we settle into a formal interview rhythm, with the girls asking us questions and we responding, I notice that there is no evidence of a very different conversation about the research that took place in the course of a day-long retreat with their entire class the previous June. Listening to their questions, I find that I have an odd sensation—it is as if the intense and impassioned conversation of that day had never taken place.

Iris's questions were about standards—What standards did we use to measure women's psychological health and girls' development? I look at her questioningly, curious as to why she is interested in standards, and she explains that she finds standards comforting, that she likes to know where she stands. And by the commonly used measures of psychological health and development, Iris is doing very well. She has been accepted by the competitive college that is her first choice and chosen by her classmates to speak at their graduation. She describes her family as loving and supportive of her aspirations. Lively, articulate, engaging, and responsive, Iris seems to be flourishing.

At the end of the session, after the girls have turned off their tape recorder, we continue to sit around the table and talk as the light lengthens at the end of the afternoon. The conversation returns to the young girls in the study, and we tell the stories illustrating their outspokenness, their courage in relationships, their willingness to speak their minds and their hearts. Iris suddenly leans forward and says, "If I were to say what I was feeling and thinking, no one would want to be with me—my voice would be too loud." And then, flustered by what she is saying, she adds, by way of explanation, "But you have to have relationships."

I ask Iris, "If you are not saying what you are feeling and thinking, then where are *you* in these relationships?" Immediately it is clear that she also sees the paradox in what she is saying; she has given up relationship for the sake of having "relationships," muting her voice so that "she" can be with other people. The words *self* and *relationship* lose their meaning and the feeling of impasse becomes palpable as Iris, her face momentarily shadowed, looks into a relational impasse, a psychological blind alley.

Jean Baker Miller (1988) has formulated this paradoxical sacrifice of relationship in a struggle to make and maintain relationships as the core dynamic of what has been called *psychopathology*—a confusing term because while the suffering is psychological, the pathology is relational, stemming from a disconnection that seemingly has to be maintained between inner and outer worlds. I came to a similar formulation of this paradox in the course of studying girls' development, seeing it as signaling a developmental impasse—a fork in the psychological road. Listening to Iris and other girls her age describe this paradox with stunning clarity, I realized that these girls are facing and bringing to conscious awareness a relational quandary with serious psychological and political ramifications. Witnessing girls' resistance to muting their voices and their courage in fighting for relationship, often taking considerable risks in the process, my colleagues and I came to a new understanding of why adolescence is an especially turbulent time in girls' development and also why girls at this time are under such pressure. As we observed girls' resistance, their resilience, and their courage, we also recorded the onset of dissociative processes and came to see various forms of psychological splitting as brilliant although costly solutions to seemingly insoluble relational problems. By splitting off parts of themselves, girls and women often managed to keep a vital sense of self and the hope of relationship alive but hidden, while at the same time struggling to maintain relationships in the world. Our research on women's psychology and girls' development led us to examine the necessity and also the costs of such strategies, and to learn from girls and women who maintain their resilience the conditions that support psychological health (Brown and Gilligan 1992, Gilligan 1990a,b, 1991, 1996, Gilligan and Rogers 1993, Gilligan et al. 1992, Rogers 1993, Rogers et al. 1994, Taylor et al. 1995).

Anne Frank (1942–1944), in what turns out to be her final diary entry, says that she has gained the reputation of being a "little bundle of contradiction." She writes that it fits her, but then asks, "What does contradiction mean?" observing that, "like so many words, contradiction can mean two things, contradiction from without and contradiction from within." Giving words to her experience, Anne distinguishes between two forms of relational impasse: one coming from an experience of confrontation and leading her to become known as unpleasant, and one coming from an experience of inner confusion and conflict.

Contradiction from without is difficult but familiar; it is "the ordinary not giving in easily, always knowing best, getting in the last word, *enfin*, all the unpleasant qualities for which I am renowned." But contradiction from within is shameful and hidden: "Nobody knows about it; that's my own secret. . . . I have, as it were, a dual personality" (p. 697). Anne describes the two Annes. One is exuberant, cheerful, sensual and insouciant: she "does not mind a kiss, an embrace, a dirty joke" (p. 697). This is the Anne whom she calls "bad." The other Anne is "better, deeper, purer"; she is the "nice Anne," the "quiet Anne," the "serious Anne," and also the Anne who is silent and frozen. She never appears or speaks in public, because

> They'll laugh at me, think I'm ridiculous, sentimental, not take me in earnest. I'm used to not being taken seriously but it's only the lighthearted Anne that's used to it and can bear it; the deeper Anne is too frail for it. [p. 698]

In contrast to the vital but seemingly superficial and bad Anne, Anne characterizes the deeper, silent, and frozen Anne as good.

Like Nina's rejection of her vibrant Civil War story in favor of the more conventional and pallid romantic adventure or the clever story about the pen, like Edith Wharton's dismissal of her early short stories as "quite dreadful," like Iphigenia's abandonment of her appeal for relationship in the realization that it has become hopeless and shameful, Anne Frank is struggling against a vital part of herself, and the question of standards or judgment, like the question of relationship, becomes intensely confusing.

Melanie Klein and the object relations theorists would trace the origins of this splitting into a good and bad self to the preoedipal period of infancy and early childhood—a time seemingly outside civilization. And they would consider the splitting or what Erikson has called the "totalism" of adolescence—the adolescent's penchant for either/or, all-or-nothing formulations—as a recapitulation of an earlier developmental process, a revisiting of early conflicts around sexuality and relationships and an opportunity to work them through differently. In the case of young women, however, beginning with the hysterics, adolescence seems to witness the onset of a problem of relationship or to bring a problem of relationship to crisis—a crisis that cannot be worked through on an intrapsychic level. The splitting or dissociation, rather than being a naturally occurring developmental phenomenon, appears instead to be a costly although necessary psychological adaptation to a deeply confusing split in reality—the division between inner and outer worlds, and also within the inner world, which is essential to the perpetuation of patriarchy.

From somewhere outside the division within herself that Anne Frank describes, someone speaks in the direct first person. Her subjects are voice, honesty, and the seeming impossibility of becoming herself in relationship.

> I never utter my real feelings about anything. If I'm to be quite honest, I must admit that it does hurt me—that I try terribly hard to change myself but that I'm always fighting against a more powerful enemy. A voice sobs within me: "There you are, that's what's become of you, you're uncharitable, you look supercilious and peevish, people you meet dislike you and all because you won't listen to the advice given you by your own better half." Oh, I would like to listen, but it doesn't work. . . . I can't keep that up, if I'm watched to that extent I start by getting snappy, then unhappy, and finally I twist my heart round so that the bad is on the outside and the good is on the inside and keep on trying to find a way of becoming what I would so like to be and what I could be, if—there weren't any other people living in the world. [p. 699]

As she records her efforts to bring her inner world into the outer world, Anne describes herself as embattled from without and from within.

When I taught with Erik Erikson at Harvard in the late 1960s, he was writing *Gandhi's Truth* and actively exploring the relationship between *satyagraha*—the force of truth that is at the heart of nonviolent resistance—and the power of truth that is at the center of psychoanalytic healing (Erikson 1969). Erikson's belief that one cannot understand a life outside of history, that life history and history are two sides of a coin, led him to search for the creative edge, the place where life history and life-history join. In *Young Man Luther*, Erikson (1958) focuses on the psychological and historical energy released when the young Martin Luther, unable to face his own father whose use of authority was corrupt, turns to face God the father and speak out against the corruption of his authority in the late Holy Roman Empire. Taking on for his age the problem that he could not solve for himself, Luther initiated the Reformation, driven by an intense desire for relationship: the desire to meet his father face to face.

For over a century now, women who have suffered corrupt relationships within the family have taken on the corruption of relationships on an historical scale. Like the corruption of authority in Luther's time, this corruption of relationship is part of a social fabric that is rotten. The Women's Movement, in linking psychological and political health with the reformation of a patriarchal social order, also finds its wellsprings in a desire for relationship: a desire to speak for oneself and have a voice in the world. This powerful convergence of voice and relationship has set in motion profound social change. But at the point where relationship comes into tension with relationships, women's voices begin to sound too loud.

A THEORETICAL FRAME

Freud conceptualized the tension between civilization and psychological health and development as forcing a "compromise formation"—some accommodation between inner and outer worlds. This compromise formation marked the resolution of the Oedipus complex, the relational crisis of boys' early childhood, and it left a psychological wound or scar that was a seedbed for neurosis. The wound, although it is generally not conceptualized in these terms, came from giving up relationship; it marked the tearing away from or walling off of the most vulnerable parts of the inner world, in a self-defeating and often inchoate attempt to protect the capacity to love.

The evidence that girls are psychologically stronger and more resilient than boys throughout the childhood years and the fact that vibrant and psychologically vital girls are at risk in adolescence provide the grounds for shifting the theoretical frame. More specifically, what is at risk are girls' abilities to maintain both voice and relationship, their efforts to connect inner and outer worlds. Rather than continuing to speak of psychological development as a more or less uniform process with infancy, childhood, and adolescence following after one another like the cars of a train, we can now retell the narrative of development in light of the realization that our theories and assumptions about human psychology have been historically and culturally framed within the civilization of the *Oresteia* and the Oedipus tragedy.

Within this cultural framework, a separation of inner from outer world occurs typically for boys in early childhood (between, roughly, the ages of 3 and 5) and constitutes a cultural initiation. It is tied in with male identity and the establishment of manhood, and seems essential to the young boy's claim to his manhood or his integrity as a male—his "symbolic castration," which signifies his willingness to sacrifice his physical and psychological integrity within a patriarchal civilization. In short, the separation of inner from outer world in young boys is a culturally mandated separation that becomes psychologically necessary if boys are to be able to make and maintain relationships in the world, at the same time that it creates the most powerful obstacle to their capacity for relationship and intimacy. Symbolically, this separation of boys from their mothers is represented by the freeing of Orestes. Psychologically, this separation or walling off of the innermost parts of the inner world makes it possible for a boy to be hurt without feeling hurt, to leave without feeling sadness or loss.

Boys' early childhood separation constitutes a process of initiation that is essential to the structuring and maintenance of a patriarchal social order, and it ensures the continuation of that order generation after generation. A boy's resistance to this separation in patriarchal cultures leads men, women, and the boy himself to question and doubt his masculinity, making him an object of shame. Men live with discomfort in the civilization they have created because of this disconnection from the inner world. The dissociation of self from relationship leaves, as Freud describes in *Civilization and Its Discontents* and as Klein (1975) and Kohut (1971) and other object relations theorists and self psychologists have noted, an unsatisfied and unsatisfiable yearning for connection, an inner emptiness, a longing for relationship that developmental psychologists have now discovered is grounded in the infant's experience of relationship, but which, following infancy, seems illusory or culturally proscribed as shameful.

Girls' extraordinary love and knowledge of the human world throughout childhood can only be explained in terms of a continuing connection between inner and outer worlds. Otherwise, it is hard to understand how girls know what they know or can sustain their openness and vulnerability. Girls' full initiation into a patriarchal "not knowing" and "invulnerability" tends not to occur until puberty and adolescence, when girls are under intense pressure from without and within to separate the inner world and take in an outer world that changes what they will feel and think and know. The contrast between Iphigenia's two speeches, or Nina's early and later stories, or the two conversations with Iris and her classmates captures this turn—this fixing of one's heart and mind.

Girls show greater psychological strength and resilience than boys up until the time of adolescence. Beginning in early childhood, boys are more at risk than girls for depression, suicide attempts, accidents and injuries, bed-wetting, learning disorders, and various other forms of "out of touch" and "out of control" behavior, all of which suggest a rift between inner and outer worlds. Among girls, there is a sudden high incidence of depression, suicide attempts, eating disorders, learning problems, and dissociative phenomena at the time of adolescence (J. Gilligan 1996). In adolescence, girls appeal for relationship, and following a pattern that repeats through the millennia, when this appeal finds no resonance or is rendered hopeless and ineffective, young women feel under pressure from without and within to sacrifice or to sequester themselves—to hide what they most want and value. Girls at this time often protect an inner world that seemingly cannot be in the outer world, saying, as Anne Frank says, that the innermost part of themselves cannot survive the experience of not being listened to, not being taken seriously, or of being ridiculed, sentimentalized, overwhelmed with feelings of shame, or defeated by other people.

Beginning then with the voice of Iphigenia, as Euripides heard or imagined her, a search for resonance—for relationship—has been vital for women coming of age in a patriarchal culture. In the absence of resonance or the possibility of relationship, women begin to lose their voices, often becoming hysterical in the process. A talking cure then becomes at once deceptively simple and profoundly radical, because it exposes the roots of civilization. Generation after generation, girls becoming young women counterpose their experience of relationship to the patriarchal construction of relationships, and in the working through of the ensuing crisis lies the potential for love and the fate of civilization.

ACKNOWLEDGMENTS

I wish to thank Dr. Edward R. Shapiro, whose invitation to participate in the 75th Anniversary conference at Austen Riggs in October, 1994 led to the writing of this chapter, first published in his book *The Inner World in the Outer World: A Psychodynamic Perspective*. I also want to thank the Spencer Foundation for the generous support and encouragement of a Senior Research Scholar Award; the Lilly Endowment for supporting the Strengthening Healthy Resistance and Courage in Girls Project; my colleagues on that project, Dr. Annie G. Rogers and Normi Noel; and the University of Cambridge for inviting me to spend two years in England as visiting Pitt Professor and then as a member of the faculty. I am indebted to my colleagues at Cambridge—Terri Apter, Mary Beard, Gillian Beer, John Forrester, Simon Goldhill, Mary Hamer, Mary Jacobus and Elizabeth Wright—for spirited and inspiring conversations on aspects of this work. To Kristin Linklater, Normi Noel, and Tina Packer, my gratitude for the understanding of voice and resonance that I have taken from their brilliant work in the theater. I am grateful also to Dineka Stam and other staff members at the Anne Frank Institute in Amsterdam, for their courtesy to me during my visit in the Spring of 1993.

REFERENCES

Aeschylus (458 B.C.E.). *The Oresteia*. In *The Complete Greek Tragedies*, vol. 1, ed. D. Green and R. Lattimore. Chicago: University of Chicago Press, 1956.

Appignanesi, L., and Forrester, J. (1992). *Freud's Women*. New York: Basic Books.

Breuer, J., and Freud, S. (1895). Studies on hysteria. *Standard Edition* 2:21-183.

Brown, L. M., and Gilligan, C. (1992). *Meeting at the Crossroads: Women's Psychology and Girls' Development*. New York: Ballantine.

Erikson, E. (1958). *Young Man Luther*. New York: Norton.

——— (1969). *Gandhi's Truth*. New York: Norton.

Euripides (406–405 B.C.E.). Iphigenia in Aulis. In *Complete Greek Tragedies*, vol. 4, ed. D. Green and R. Lattimore. Chicago: University of Chicago Press, 1958.

Frank, A. (1942-44). *Diary*. The Critical Edition. New York: Doubleday, 1989.

Freud, S. (1887-1904). *The Complete Letters of Sigmund Freud to Wilhelm Fliess*, transl. and ed. J. M. Masson. Cambridge, MA: Harvard University Press, 1985.

——— (1900). The interpretation of dreams. *Standard Edition* 4/5:1-626.

——— (1905a). *Case Histories I: "Dora" and "Little Hans,"* transl. J. and A. Strachey. London: Penguin, 1977.

——— (1905b). Three essays on the theory of sexuality. *Standard Edition* 7:3-122.

——— (1929-30). Civilization and its discontents. *Standard Edition* 21:64-149.

Gilligan, C. (1990a). Teaching Shakespeare's sister: notes from the underground of female adolescence. In *Making Connections*, ed.C. Gilligan, N. Lyons, and T. Hanmer, pp. 1-30. Cambridge, MA: Harvard University Press.

——— (1990b). Joining the resistance: psychology, politics, girls and women. *Michigan Quarterly Review* 29(4):501-536.

——— (1991). Women's psychological development: implications for psychotherapy. In *Women, Girls and Psychotherapy: Reframing Resistance*, ed. C. Gilligan, A. Rogers, and D. Tolman, pp. 5-33. Binghamton, NY: Haworth.

——— (1996). The centrality of relationship in human development: a puzzle, some evidence, and a theory. In *Development and Vulnerability in Close Relationships*, ed. Noam and K. Fischer, pp. 237-261. Hillsdale, NJ: Erlbaum.

Gilligan, C., Brown, L. M., and Rogers, A. (1990). Psyche embedded: a place for body, relationships and culture in personality theory. In *Studying Persons and Lives*, ed. A. Rabin et al., pp. 86–127. New York: Springer.

Gilligan, C., and Rogers, A. G. (1993). Strengthening healthy resistance and courage in girls: a prevention project and a developmental study. In *Working Papers*. Cambridge, MA: Harvard Project on Women's Psychology and Girls' Development.

Gilligan, C., Rogers, A. G., and Noel, N. (1992). Cartography of a lost time: women, girls and relationships. Paper presented at the Cambridge Hospital/Stone Center conference "Learning from Women," Boston, MA, April. In *Working Papers.* Cambridge, MA: Harvard Project on Women's Psychology and Girls' Development, 1993.

Gilligan, J. (1996). *Violence*. New York: Putnam.

Klein, M. (1975). *The Writings of Melanie Klein*. London: Hogarth and the Institute of Psychoanalysis.

Kohut, H. (1971). *The Analysis of the Self.* New York: International Universities Press.

Linklater, K. (1976). *Freeing the Natural Voice*. New York: Drama Books.

Miller, J. B. (1988). Connections, disconnections and violations. In *Work in Progress*, #33. Wellesley, MA: Stone Center Working Paper Series.

Noel, N. (1995). Unpublished journal.

Rogers, A. G. (1993). Voice, play and a practice of ordinary courage in girls' and women's lives. *Harvard Educational Review* 63(3):265–295.

Rogers, A. G., Brown, L. M., and Tappan, M. B. (1994). Interpreting loss in ego development in girls: regression or resistance. In *The Narrative Study of Lives*. Vol. 2, ed. A. Lieblich and R. Josselson, pp. 1–36. Thousand Oaks, CA: Sage.

Taylor, J. M., Gilligan, C., and Sullivan, A. (1995). *Between Voice and Silence: Women and Girls, Race and Relationship*. Cambridge, MA: Harvard University Press.

Wharton, E. (1968). The fullness of life. *The Collected Short Stories of Edith Wharton*. Vol. 1, ed. R. W. B. Lewis. New York: Scribners.

Wolff, C. G. (1995). *A Feast of Words*. Reading, MA: Addison-Wesley.

Woolf, V. (1921). An unwritten novel. In *A Haunted House and Other Stories*. London: Grafton, 1982.

Gilligan, C., Brown, L. M. and Rogers, A. (1990) "Psyche embedded: a place for body, relationships and culture in personality theory," in *Studying Persons and Lives*, ed. A. Rabin et al., pp. [illegible]. New York: Springer.

Gilligan, C. and Rogers, A. (1993) "[illegible] resistance and courage in girls: a [illegible] and development," [illegible]. Cambridge, MA: Harvard Project on Women's Psychology and Girls' Development.

Gilligan, C., Rogers, A. and Noel, N. (1992) "Cartography of a lost time: women, girls and relationships." Paper presented at the [illegible]. Reprinted in *Working Papers*, Cambridge, MA: Harvard Project on Women's Psychology and Girls' Development, 1993.

[illegible] (19[illegible]) [illegible]. New York: [illegible].

Klein, M. (1975) *The [illegible]*. [illegible] of Psycho-Analysis.

Kohut, H. (1977) *The Restoration of the Self*. New York: International Universities Press.

[illegible] (19[illegible]) *[illegible]*. New York: [illegible].

Miller, J. B. (1988) "Connections, disconnections and violations," in *Work in Progress*, no. 33. Wellesley, MA: Stone Center Working Paper Series.

Noel, N. (1993) Unpublished journal.

Rogers, A. G. (1993) "Voice, play, and a practice of ordinary courage in girls' and women's lives," *Harvard Educational Review* 63(3): 265–295.

Rogers, A. G., Brown, L. M. and Tappan, M. B. (1994) "Interpreting loss in ego development in girls: regression or resistance?" in *The Narrative Study of Lives*, vol. 2, ed. A. Lieblich and R. Josselson. Thousand Oaks: Sage.

Taylor, J. M., Gilligan, C. and Sullivan, A. (1995) *Between Voice and Silence: Women and Girls, Race and Relationship*. Cambridge, MA: Harvard University Press.

[illegible] (19[illegible]) [illegible], ed. [illegible], pp. [illegible]. New York: [illegible].

Winnicott, D. W. (19[illegible]) *[illegible]*. Reading, MA: Addison-Wesley.

Woolf, V. (192[illegible]) [illegible], in [illegible]. London: [illegible], 1932.

8

A Multimodal Approach for Working Through a Therapeutic Impasse in the Case of Childhood Sexual Abuse

Bonnie S. Mark and Robert Anderson

This chapter discusses the treatment of an adolescent girl and attempts to resolve the underlying causes hindering her emotional fulfillment. The psychological backdrop to Lucy's persona is provided through a description of her family, focusing on both the symbolic interrelationships between the members of the family and the significant events in Lucy's development. The heart of the chapter addresses the question of the efficacy of hypnosis as an adjunct to two to three psychodynamic psychotherapy sessions a week. Hypnosis is discussed as a therapeutic option to facilitate the patient's confrontation with emotional situations that have been deeply repressed because of the trauma in their psychological history and as a strategy to overcome an impasse in treatment. The primary therapist, client, and clinical specialist work collaboratively in the hypnotic process to mediate both the depth of the experience and the content of material. The element of the client's personal control, participation, and sense of safeness balanced with the therapist's careful direction are crucial in the successful integration of hypnosis into the therapeutic situation.

After many therapeutic sessions, Lucy, a talented artist, discussed sexual abuse by her older brother that she had experienced as a young teenager. Concomitant to her reexploration of this pain in treatment, she painted a canvas unlike any she had ever created before. It depicted a pair of unfinished eyes, hands dripping blood. Unlike her other artwork, which employs muted earth tones, the image of these incomplete eyes was vivid and intense. This image is a condensed symbolic representation of the complex and paradoxical psychic world of Lucy. She came to see the unfinished eyes as her own self-portrait of her unconscious struggles. And she began the journey.

THE FAMILY ROMANCE

From her earliest days, Lucy remembers enacting the role of the family caretaker, always accommodating others. As a child, she both feared and worshiped her brother (18 months older) despite the escalated physical and sexual nature of their childhood play. She internalized the messages, constantly reiterated by her mother, that she must fulfill the multiple and contradictory qualities of a confidante, a protector, and a maid-in-waiting.

Lucy describes her mother's identity in ephemeral terms; she was "ghost-like"—an image appearing and disappearing throughout Lucy's childhood. Often preoccupied, despondent, and withdrawn, her mother presented to her New York society friends and country "clubbies" a fabulously fabricated fairy-tale life. Her mother embodied the role she played in Lucy's symbolic unconscious; she was attractive, although somewhat emaciated, an aerobics instructor who exercised religiously.

Lucy's hunger for her mother's attention is vividly described in Lucy's memory of sitting in a large field on one of the many acres that her family owned adjacent to their home. Lucy, dressed in a princess outfit, waited all day for her mother to look outside the window and notice the fairy-tale scene she created. Much to Lucy's joy, her mother looked out the window for a moment and waved.

Throughout that evening Lucy waited, hoping her mother would mention how beautiful, how much like a princess she was. Her mother said nothing for several days, explaining later that she did not want Lucy's head to swell. This incident was indicative of how Lucy's mother controlled and positioned her daughter by carefully monitoring her displays of affection. Lucy became molded and manipulated by her desire to win her mother's affection.

If her mother's presence was fleeting, Lucy's father was absent. He was a highly successful businessman whose various travels were seasoned with extramarital affairs. Although he never discussed these escapades, Lucy was well aware of her mother's knowledge and sense of helplessness in the situation. Her father rarely played with the children. When at home, he sat at an office table and paid the bills, shifting his accounts and processing paperwork, always deferring his promises to play until later. Later never came.

Lucy's memories of her brother are compelling and insightful elements in this analysis. She recalls loving the attention of her brother. In their earlier years, age-appropriate developmental sexual curiosity existed between the siblings. In later years, Lucy and her brother would sneak off and enact orchestrated sexual situations. It was a game controlled by her brother, who gradually escalated the intensity of the encounters on each occasion until Lucy felt the game grew out of control. Lucy has painful memories of being tied to a chair and forced to watch X-rated videos with her brother and a friend. Her brother insisted that she enact the characters in the movie; for example, mirroring one movie, he was the gardener seducing Lucy as the mistress of the mansion. Lucy was particularly pained by acknowledging the parts of her that did not mind this "play." Her own sense of being an active player, coauthoring the script of sexual games, mixed with her intense fear of her brother's angry, aggressive, hostile side, led to a guilty sense of responsibility that she should have resisted him and protected herself.

These sexual rendezvous were the only times when Lucy's brother avowed feelings for her. At these times, Lucy recalls that he could be kind and gentle, even as he enacted a rape scene with Lucy as his victim. Where she was active, it was out of fear and curiosity. Constricted by her brother's wrath, Lucy feared resisting, but was enthused with her brother's entire focus upon her and her body. Frequently, Lucy was displayed and "viewed" by her brother and his friends. Only at the point of penetration did Lucy refuse to perform for her brother; Lucy feels that he listened to her because he too was scared of the finality of this act. Lucy remained an object of admiration, a fantasy to be beheld, an object for her brother's eyes.

THE GAZE OF THE CROWD

Lucy desperately sought an audience where she could successfully perform to meet the expectations they desired, but constantly felt thwarted in the effort. Clearly, the message that she incorporated of performing for her brother caused psychic conflict and contributed to her unconscious resistance. Always a performer, ice-skating and dancing were significant parts of her childhood. Even in this arena, Lucy's mother insisted she never capture the spotlight, that she let others go first, that she not show off, and that she behave in a "lady-like" manner. In our sessions she came to recall these internalized messages. She sought public attention and felt awful about this desire and saw how these messages factored into her inhibition. As an example of her self-diminishing thought processes, in a recent audition for a dance performance, despite knowing that her classical training skill surpassed that of the other competitors, she could not squelch the voices that insisted that she hold back, that she not "show off." The theme of self-inhibition in her dancing and acting auditions is a pressing issue in Lucy's own measure for her growth in therapy. She holds both herself and the therapy accountable for the results.

THE LANGUAGE OF THE SKIN

The absent presence in Lucy's portrait is her body, especially her skin, which, in part because of childhood eczema, Lucy sees as loathsome. As a small child, she struggled with feeling that her father's absence and her mother's lack of affection were partially attributable to her horrid looks. For many years she actively avoided mirrors. She also recalls that she received the most physical nurturing from her mother when her mother applied ointments to her ailing skin. Lucy perceives a bodily connection between her emotions and her skin, and recognizes that the eczema, although a hereditary condition, was exacerbated by her emotions.

Until a few years ago, she reportedly would be reluctant to go out in public with a pimple and her skin has been a frequent topic in therapy sessions. As an example, at the beginning of one session, Lucy opened the session by declaring that she knew I would think it awful, but that she had gone to a tanning salon. I waited, and she expressed her projection that I would feel tanning was dangerous for her health, discouraged by her skin doctor, expensive, frivolous; she felt "vain, vain, vain." She added, however, that it made her feel different, that she *was* different with a tan. She recalled that as a teenager she could be "on"—especially in the New York club scene, where she was most confident if she was tan and where it was dark so that people could not see her face. It is important to note that even when Lucy does have some slight skin markings, she is a strikingly beautiful and unique-looking young woman.

THE STRUGGLE BETWEEN DENYING AND CONFRONTING THE TRAUMA

A pivotal turning point in Lucy's life was her 13th year when her family moved from their country home to New York City, her parents divorced, and Lucy had her first consummated sexual encounter with her young boyfriend. The incidents, all paralleling one another, triggered a series of promiscuous, dangerous, self-destructive behaviors, including the escalation of the encounters with her brother. After two years her parents placed her in a short-term adolescent inpatient treatment program, followed by placement in a residential halfway house. It was at the halfway house that Lucy first recalled the years of abuse by her brother. Lucy described family therapy sessions following her recollection of the trauma where her brother acknowledged the sexual incidents. As a young adult, however, these open wounds were sutured through time and active repression. Lucy never discussed the sexual abuse with her previous male therapist in New York City, fearing that once she had developed a safe therapeutic relationship with her therapist he would reject her for having initially lied to him.

Lucy resisted facing the trauma of her past abuse for a number of reasons, most significantly her fear that full recall and clarity—*a complete picture*—would lead to self-annihilation due to her shame. She expressed fear that she would be overwhelmed by the memories. She repeatedly stated that she was finally getting "healthy," finally functioning in Los Angeles, where she had recently moved, and that she couldn't risk slipping back into depression, beginning to lose it, and slowly falling back into her self-destructive behavior. Yet she was determined to better recall and understand the experiences that, despite her attempts to repress them, "bubbled up" and impinged on her overall well-being. I introduced the notion of hypnosis, in response to her saying that there were areas that she felt she would never be able to discuss in here, that they were too painful, that to recall these issues and relive them would interfere with *all* the progress she had made. She feared she would "curl up into a little ball and never stop crying." This fear carried over to her dancing and acting, as she was haunted with the need to hold back a part of herself during an audition or class performance out of fear that "I might lose myself" in the performance and start crying uncontrollably without the capacity to stop. A vicious cycle of admonishing herself for "holding back," while ever so fearful of allowing herself to "feel," created such imbalance that she was constantly self-critically punishing herself, both consciously and unconsciously.

THE COMMINGLING OF PLEASURE AND PAIN

Even as a teen, Lucy was a riddle of contradictions: on the one hand, during one phase of her teenage years, she describes broadcasting the abuse to anyone who would listen (conversations at a New York/Los Angeles club or cocktail party), while on the other hand she often felt unable to discuss the issues, even in therapy. There was a fundamental interplay between Lucy's dramatic, public, performing side and the private, introspective, passive, and intimidated side that was less the actor than the person acted upon. Lucy was a fusion of antagonistic forces. The severe and early onset of childhood eczema, a lasting narcissistic issue, exemplifies these opposing forces. As mentioned briefly, she recalls that her mother's primary attention in her early years was the tender application of many lotions to the body, but the experience was also always painful. Lucy experienced a commingling of pleasure and pain. The same was true in the loathing that she felt for her brother, contrasting a part of her that desired coparticipation and felt ultimately guilty and responsible. Lucy was divided—a woman at war with herself. Her persona was poised on the fault line between pleasure and pain, public and private, active and passive. Riddled with ambivalence, Lucy was unable to transcend the plateau she had achieved in her development, as when she was a little girl bound to a chair, helpless to avoid the gaze of her brother that she desired so reverently, despite the sexual dramas played out by him and his friends in which she also felt manipulated and degraded.

THE COST OF DENIAL

Lucy discussed a cyclical depression that arose at the beginning of each new year. She attributed this depression, in part, to her experiences as a young teenager. She had had her first sexual encounter in January, triggering the series of self-destructive acts, sexual and otherwise, described earlier in the chapter. Lucy commented that at the present time her current relationship was being affected by the "January depression," as she was unable to experience sex as pleasurable at that time. Lucy discussed wanting to get past this, feeling that she was being unfair to her partner, and mentioning that he indicated to her that she should get help for the problem if their relationship was to be successful. Lucy's block to working through her painful memories was, thus, ameliorated by a strong commitment on her part to her own therapeutic process and to the wishes of her partner who, Lucy felt, resembled the forceful, out-of-control brother.

It was at that time that I suggested that I might hypnotize Lucy in order to help her achieve her stated objective of lowering her defenses and accessing the memories that haunted her predominantly by "their power of being too great to be discussed." Although Lucy's fear was great, her determination to overcome it seemed greater. The strong sense that she was ready to more fully explore her known memories and also those areas of her childhood previously inaccessible was reconfirmed in her affirmation that she did not want a repeat of a previous therapy where she successfully avoided these early events and feelings. It was suggested that through hypnotism, and the more direct discussion of recollections about her brother and other incidents, the abiding contradictions in her personality could be addressed. Lucy's apprehension was fully acknowledged and she was provided a detailed and reassuring description of the careful, collaborative approach that would be used, in which she would feel safe and in control at all times. Lucy understood this as a journey we would take together and acknowledged her growing feeling of safety with me as she anticipated this new chapter in her growth.

The decision to use hypnosis as a technique in the therapeutic situation is always a delicate choice that must balance the individual psychological condition of the patient with the purpose and objectives sought through the use of hypnotic trance. The decision must always be made on the basis of the therapist's understanding of the capacities of the patient and the patient's willingness to undergo the hypnotic odyssey. Under these conditions, hypnotic trance can be invaluable in carefully reaching through the impasse of unconscious resistances in order to modify self-protecting but self-defeating repressions so that analytic work can move forward more productively. The trance can also facilitate increased awareness about traumatic situations, past and present, and often allows a less inhibited expression of related feelings. Analytic work is often remarkably effective during the trance state and, because of the inherent suggestibility of the unconscious, careful reframing of early misperceptions and faulty assumptions can be corrected, as in the case of an abused child who assumed responsibility for the abuse. This is because the conscious editing and judgmental, self-critical messages are absent or less intrusive in a trance state. Hypnosis approximates a fundamental rule of brainstorming, that there is no such thing as a bad thought or idea.

The use of hypnotic trance can often produce dramatic results when the various techniques are used skillfully with appropriate subjects. It is not a shortcut in therapeutic treatment but rather another specialized technique that can be very helpful in the ongoing regimen of treatment or analysis. Although hypnosis can often release large quantities of information and emotions, accompanied with feelings of relief as well as dismay, a therapist must be prepared to maintain the ongoing therapeutic process to integrate and adjust to the newly conscious information and reframed perspectives. At such times there is occasionally an unfortunate tendency for therapists and their patients to feel the problem is solved and the case is closed. In this case, hypnosis was neither a beginning nor an ending—it was a part of the therapeutic journey.

Lucy's need to undergo the full process of working through her psychic trauma would be facilitated with the aid of hypnosis. It was Lucy's insistent desire to confront her past, and it was her willingness to face her emotional issues that finally led to the therapeutic option of hypnosis. For Lucy, the reduction in self-consciousness (a phenomenon that the hypnotic process offers) was a most attractive feature. When the possibility of using hypnosis was first discussed, age regression was suggested to help access early memories, and suggestibility was used to allow her to gain control over some of her behaviors. To experience the hypnotic process in a safe manner, the first application was a light trance. She wanted to break the habit of picking at her face and understood this would be dealt with through posthypnotic suggestion and reframing of the emotional conflict residing beneath the behavior.

At first, given many choices, Lucy elected a reclining position on the couch and almost immediately began to experience discomfort, feelings of vulnerability, and fears that she could not protect herself. We were able to explore her difficulty in relinquishing even gradual amounts of control. She discussed her fear that I would be unable to hold her or contain her tears. These fears continued even though she ventured into several hypnosis experiences successfully and proved to be a good subject.

In these early trance states, we approached the face-picking problem by reframing, with a simplified and step-by-step story of her early attempts to gain attention, the resulting disappointments, and the childlike assumption that there must be something wrong with her, such as the eczema that actually instigated her mother's caressing attention. The story continued to show that this child found two answers, contradictory and incorrect, that could now be discarded; her parents' inattentiveness was either due to her perceived unattractiveness (eczema, shameful behavior) or because she was too attractive. A no-win situation. The reality of her parents' own problems was offered as a new truth, and her unconscious was invited to help her retire the previous assumptions as obsolete. The picking at her face would no longer be necessary because she need not be punished for being attractive. The longing for a loving caress would replace the scars of her constant picking. The reframing story forms a kind of simplified interpretation ending with a posthypnotic suggestion. Guided imagery of current-life situations where face-picking might occur opened the way for modified behavior involving stroking rather than picking.

We were both encouraged by these experiences and the improvement in the face-picking habit. She was eager to go deeper and confront her feared and shame-shrouded past but felt a significant loss of comforting strength from me through my directing the hypnosis induction and processing. It felt to her that if I was ahead of her, guiding her on the hypnotic journey, she would have no one beside her or, more significantly, to catch her when she "fell." Moreover, the therapeutic transference within our relationship felt secure, and Lucy seemed to feel concerned with the relational shift. It was clear that Lucy needed the consistency of our treatment continuing with as little shift as possible. Ambivalently, she struggled with the idea of continuing the hypnotic experience in search of clarity.

At that point, I offered Lucy the option of a series of visits by a second therapist who would accompany me and continue the hypnotic process. This would facilitate my complete availability during our sessions, while a cotherapist would induce age regression and primarily guide the trance experience. I collaborated with Dr. Robert Anderson, a psychotherapist trained in advanced hypnotic technique, and he accompanied us in our explorations of these early memories. For two months we worked jointly every other week and facilitated Lucy's exploration of areas in her unconscious that she felt were unsafe to investigate in her conscious state. Her ability to allow regression was increased by frequent reminders that she was in full control each step of the way and that she could return quickly to full consciousness any time she desired.

The setting was in my office, and our placement and proximity to the couch on which she would lie were approved by her. I sat near her supportively while Dr. Anderson sat back a bit, and she chose to cover herself with a light blanket, which eased some feelings of vulnerability and assisted the feeling of regression. The therapeutic relationship that we had built and Lucy's sense of my close presence clearly enabled her to respond well to his suggestions. Furthermore, my being in the room allowed her to experience the protective "mothering" that she needed but did not have when she was young, vulnerable, and required protection from her brother. The collaborative "team" feeling seemed to give her enough strength to confront some very traumatic memories. It was clear that Lucy felt safe, protected, and accompanied through her experience. Performance anxiety and fears of being overwhelmed by a "flood of memories" were reduced with reassurances that we would move slowly and be in constant contact with her, and that she would recall just what she could manage. She was encouraged to share whatever she wished with us along the way. She was reminded that memories return in many different ways and are usually a mixture of pleasant and unpleasant experiences. As she was guided into a deep trance state through relaxation and focusing suggestions, she was told that she could return to full consciousness at any time simply by taking three deep breaths, stretching, and opening her eyes. The nature of trance was explained again as simply a way to quiet the usual activity of the conscious mind in order to focus without distraction on the task at hand—to recall details and related feelings from her childhood. It was suggested that memories might be actual incidents and experiences, important fantasies, or informational input from the people around us. The careful intent of the therapists was simply to facilitate conditions for recall and to help Lucy process newly retrieved information without our assumptions, judgments, or preconceptions.

Lucy was able to achieve a very deep state of trance and could move quickly back to her early years. She was conversational with us throughout the experience. Detailed descriptions of her home and family suggested accurate recall.

For Lucy, issues of control and lack of power over her body were fundamental; therefore, early in the hypnosis we empowered Lucy. She saw that she could protect herself and that she could modulate the depth of her involvement throughout hypnosis with the pain of her early childhood memories. She was also helped to learn how to control the depth of her trance, physical body sensations, the pace of remembering, and the intensity of her emotional reactions. For example, at an early point in the process, Lucy appeared to be anxious and fearful of being out of control. She described herself as drowning, and it was suggested that she could control this by visualizing a measuring stick marked by feet. Initially, Lucy felt she was at the 12-foot mark or the bottom and asphyxiating under the water. Through hypnotic suggestion, Lucy was able to rise quickly to a level in the "water" where she was more comfortable. Further mastery was achieved as she found she could raise and lower herself and find comfort. In this metaphorical example, Lucy's fear of what would happen under hypnosis was alleviated somewhat. Similarly, issues of control arose in another session when certain memories made her feel pinned down, straitjacketed, paralyzed. She explored these sensations in relation to the feelings she had in her encounters with her brother, and, just as the feeling of immobilization felt unbearable, she was helped to achieve a dramatic feeling of release and reclaiming of control through reparative suggestion. By attending just to the straitjacket, she was encouraged to challenge its restraints, freeing first one arm, then the other, and then each leg, struggling and straining until she was completely free of confinement. She was able to breathe freely and felt exhilarated and amazed at her escape. She soon made her own insightful connection of these experiences with the traumatic relationship with her brother. Lucy was able to move on with more detailed memories of previously "forgotten" episodes of exploitation, abuse, and neglect. She was helped throughout these sessions not only to remember and reexperience but to express feelings long suppressed. In trance, she was helped to re-create encounters with abusers and neglectors and to place responsibility where it belonged.

For example, when Lucy tearfully recalled incidents of her brother's intrusion into the bathroom with a friend or two and pressured her to "show myself" with legs up, she spoke of her feeling of helplessness and shame that she had gone along and not resisted. We were able to remind her of her brother's power over her and the absence of any parental resource and to reach her feeling of humiliation and rage. As often happens in hypnotic trance, Lucy's body was also having memories and she had drawn her legs up and was in an uncomfortable, cringing position. This was drawn to her attention and related to her feelings of humiliation and indignation. With reassurance from us for the legitimacy of her feelings, she was encouraged to "talk back" to her brother, to protest his behavior, and to extend her legs and kick him away. She was able to tell him her feelings in later reenactments. When she spoke of her vulnerability in relation to her brother and the absence of parental protection or awareness, she was helped to focus on each parent and to confront the parent within the trance with both her anger and her longing for supportive protection. These reenactments were very difficult and accompanied with painful, emotional release of long-suppressed feelings. She felt remarkably relieved after this experience. Guilt and shame were significantly reduced in this episode and others that followed.

It became clear after our two months of collaborative work with hypnotherapy that the therapeutic impasse was greatly relieved and Lucy continued on with her primary therapist in a very productive individual therapy. Initially, Lucy entered therapy seeking support and insight, yet was frightened by the prospect of *knowing*. Through the relationship that grew therapeutically, safety was established and curiosity to *know* overpowered her mechanisms of denying or repressing painful memories and feelings. There is little doubt that continuing the therapy in the traditional manner over time might have achieved the same ends. The use of hypnosis as an adjunct to treatment expedited the process and allowed us to continue the journey with increased knowledge, insight, recollections, and the power of knowing that she could tolerate the knowledge and be freed by it instead of having it destroy her.

9

Generations after the Holocaust: Multigenerational Transmission of Trauma

Deborah Berger-Reiss

In the fifty years since the Nazi Holocaust, hundreds of books and articles have attempted to make sense of the monumental evil exacted upon the Jews in World War II and its continuing aftermath for both survivors and subsequent generations. In all the literature—clinical, historical, and even fictional—stories of individual survival pour forth. They are stories of victims and heroes, losses and triumphs trickling down from generation to generation.

The clinical studies have attempted to understand and categorize Holocaust survivors (Des Pres 1976, Lifton 1968, Niederland 1968), children of survivors (Barocas and Barocas 1973, Berger-Reiss 1980, Danieli 1992, Hass 1990, Karr 1978, Kestenberg 1972, Kinsler 1980, 1994, Nadler et al. 1985, Newman 1979, Rakoff et al. 1966, Shoshan 1989, Sigal 1982, Sigal et al. 1988), and now grandchildren of survivors (Bar-On 1995, Sigal 1982, Sigal et al. 1988). Some of these studies point out that massive psychic trauma has scarred a generation and continues to affect subsequent generations. Some articles emphasize the strength and success of the second generation (Bar-On 1995, Kinsler 1994). One study by Sigal and colleagues (1988) concludes that "grandchildren of survivors are not distinguishable from other clinic children with respect to their mood, personality, or behavioral items included in this study" (p. 210).

Yet, because many of these studies are based on either clinically or self-identified survivors, children of survivors, and grandchildren of survivors, their implications are clearly limited. What about those who never show up at a clinic? What about those who do, but do not identify themselves as affected by or even related to the Holocaust? And what of survivors who never even revealed to their own children their painful identities?

This chapter chronicles a story of one family through the lens of the parents' treatment. In this family, three generations were clearly marked by the Holocaust—the second and third with no knowledge of their roots. It began in 1994 when a colleague referred the father of a child she had been treating. The therapist reported that after a year's work and very little progress with Martha, a 10-year-old, she believed the child's problems were more strongly related to the father's free-floating anxiety and panic attacks than to any other variable. The father's panic attacks and multiple phobias prevented him from participating in normal child-related activities, such as amusement parks, school plays, and scouting trips. The child suffered from multiple fears as well, such as earthquakes, dogs, social situations, the classroom, and rather extreme separation anxiety (she would not attend slumber parties or go to a friend's house without her mother or father in attendance).

The therapist felt that all roads wended their way back to the father's anxieties, and that she could go only so far without treatment for the father. The focus of this chapter is on both the father's treatment and how his journey down the road to health paved the way for his daughter's and the entire family's parallel journeys. As the treatment progressed with both John and Martha, the family reported great benefits to them all.

Martha's father, John, a lanky, compelling, 50-year-old Australian architect, had been referred to psychotherapy every year at his annual physical examination by his physician because his constant state of anxiety was so great that the physician feared his patient might suffer a heart attack, stroke, or other stress-related catastrophe. For years, he had ignored his doctor's recommendation until his daughter's psychotherapist said it was necessary in order to help his daughter. Turning 50 also may have hastened the decision to seek treatment because his mother had died, in *her* fifties, of a heart attack.

He entered my office with a paper bag in case of hyperventilation, and said he came at the insistence of his daughter's therapist, adding that he was tired of living as he had, constantly anxious and fearful of flying, earthquakes, speaking with people, Disneyland rides, and "just about everything else." He said he did not want to die and leave his three children, who ranged in age from 10 to 16, fatherless. He desperately wanted to be free of this "monster" he'd battled since early adolescence. I asked him to start by telling me when the anxiety had begun.

John's German immigrant parents lived in a small town near Melbourne, Australia, where they were employed as factory workers and raised their three children. His father, a cold, angry man, occasionally beat the children for normal childhood behaviors such as talking too loudly or eating too quickly, and rarely spoke beyond his rages. His mother, although loving, suffered from anxiety and depression and was occasionally hospitalized for "nervous breakdowns." John and his two younger siblings were shunted into foster care two or three times as small children, and when at home walked on eggshells. Their mother died in her fifties of a heart attack. Theirs was an isolated home that company never visited. The children were taught to lay low and not draw attention by wearing bright colors or standing out in any way. John characterized his parents as "paranoid about the rest of the world."

When John was 13, his parents informed him that they were Jewish. At the time, he had no idea why his parents had kept this secret to begin with, or why they had suddenly disclosed this information to him, nor did he ask. One simply didn't ask questions or have discussions in his family. There were no Jews in their town and he didn't really understand what any of this meant. He had, after all, been baptized, and was confused and angered by this news; so he proceeded as best he could to ignore it. Soon thereafter, small symptoms of anxiety appeared—the odd tic, the small fears.

As his adolescence progressed, a rebellion grew quietly inside John, and since any blatant acts of rebellion would result in a beating from father or the threat of mother becoming "ill," he learned to express some of his feelings with his guitar in a local rock-and-roll band. Playing his guitar and singing soothed him, and, ironically, for someone taught not to draw attention, John especially relished performances before a crowd. Immediately after completing high school, he moved to the United States and was invited to live in a commune (a better, warmer, more playful family) where he continued to play and compose music. Music was the only way John felt safe to express negative emotions, and he was good enough to land a song-writing contract.

John had initially dabbled in smoking hashish and marijuana at the commune to help quell his mounting anxiety. Yet in his early twenties, as his drug use became a daily habit, its sedative effect gave way to feelings of paranoia and even more anxiety. When I asked what he feared at the time, he said, "Even the sky." It was during that period that he met the woman who would become his wife, Jane, an "angel of mercy," who swooped down and rescued him from his mounting terror and his drug use. At age 25, he moved to Los Angeles with his new wife, with whom he reports having a good and secure 25-year marriage.

Once settled in the United States, he set about starting a business and tended to his growing family. Although reasonably successful in business and fully engaged as an active participant in his children's lives, helping with music lessons, scouting activities, and sports (but only from home), his anxiety mounted. During periods of heightened anxiety, he sometimes had to turn work away and increasingly withdrew from social and public events. If, for example, he was about to walk out his front door and saw a neighbor in his front yard retrieving his newspaper, John would stay inside and wait for his neighbor to go indoors, thereby avoiding the anxiety-provoking social encounter.

He never did practice Judaism—or anything else. It was something he did not want others to really know about him. His children knew they were "half Jewish," and, despite their natural curiosity, he felt too uncomfortable to pursue it any further other than to read a few books on the subject. He felt equally drawn to and repelled by Judaism, yet, as always, the fear won out.

I asked him if he had ever found out why his parents decided not to tell him about being Jewish until he reached the age of 13. 1 asked if he knew his parents' history prior to their coming to Australia. He shook his head. He'd never asked. And it was too late to learn anything from his mother since she had passed away. "What about your father?" I asked. "Is it too late to ask him? Remember, you no longer need worry about his rage because he lives on another continent." John agreed and promptly wrote to his father, who then was in his eighties.

Within two weeks he received a five-page letter from his father explaining everything. He and his young wife did in fact escape the Nazis, yet most of the family was not so fortunate. John's four grandparents and many aunts, uncles, and cousins died in the camps. John's parents were so stunned by grief and guilt and so terrified that when they arrived in Australia they changed their names to very Christian sounding names, renounced their pasts, and vowed to protect their future children from the terrible fate their families had suffered at the hands of the Nazis.

On a countertransferential basis, I had suspected he was a child of Holocaust survivors and did not consciously know it—and suddenly the magnetic pull of this client made sense since I, too, am a child of Holocaust survivors. Although I have written a master's thesis on the subject and have facilitated many "rap" groups for children of survivors, all of my group members had always known about their parents' Holocaust histories and were strongly identified (and sometimes strongly conflicted) as Jews, and many, as children, had been used as an audience for their parents' horror stories. Yet there still was a familiar feeling of shared history with John, at first understood only countertransferentially and then confirmed upon the receipt of the clarifying letter from his father, which revealed the family's story.

To fully understand the effects of the trauma on subsequent generations, the effects of Nazi atrocities on adult Holocaust survivors are highlighted in an article by Newman (1979):

1. A prolonged state of total helplessness.
2. Deprivation of individuality and autonomy: being obliged to severely inhibit normal reactions on pain of torture or death. They were treated as things, not as people, and were numbered, catalogued, and degraded.

3. Loss of their society, reference group, family, occupation, status, possessions, language, and, of course, rights.
4. Physical and mental torture and threats that seemed unrelated to their own behavior. . . . Forced labor was combined with a starvation diet (600 calories in the later years).
5. Recurrent episodes of terror, for instance, selections in which one's own survival often depended on a family member or another being killed. As well as dreading their own death, victims were put in the intolerable position of having to decide which among their fellow victims would live or die. [p. 44]

As a result of these circumstances, after the war many survivors developed *survivor syndrome*, an amalgam of various symptoms including chronic anxiety, depression, nightmares, irritability, fear of persecution, impaired social relations, and psychosomatic disorders (Niederland 1968). Although John's parents were not in concentration camps, they still are considered to be survivors of the Holocaust because they shared many of the same losses, including home, country, language, and family, and, of course, they suffered from "survivor guilt" for having survived when so many others in their families did not (Lifton 1968).

So John and his siblings were born into a family that had been severely traumatized by the war. Both of John's siblings still live in Australia and both suffer from differing degrees of anxiety and/or panic attacks. Furthermore, the relatively unusual step of the parents renouncing their religion and not even telling their children until their teen years increased the trauma.

Some children of survivors recognize that their families are different and are able to understand why this is so. John, of course, was raised in ignorance of his history by fearful, even "paranoid" parents. He only knew there was a great deal to fear. Until he learned the truth about his family and dealt with his feelings, there would be little hope for him or Martha.

Once his story was revealed, he was able to work through feelings of rage and then sadness that so much of his and his family's lives had been wasted and driven by fear. He mourned his mother's passing and, to an even greater extent, the fact that he would never be able to hear the entire story of her childhood, World War II experiences, and subsequent life. John grieved over not having been closer to his mother during the last third of her life. She might have been able to fill in the many missing blanks in their relationship. He yearned to know why she had made the kinds of decisions she had made, and to truly "know her."

In the meantime, he decided not to make the same mistake with his aging father. They began a correspondence in which, as more and more gaps were filled, the intimacy between father and son grew. His father had retired, was more relaxed, and had begun in recent years to attend synagogue.

Only two months after the beginning of this correspondence, John's father suffered a stroke. John phoned me for an emergency session the next day. He wanted to jump on a plane to help his father, yet his fear of flying stood in the way.

By the time of the session, his sister in Australia had phoned, asking him to postpone his visit until their father's scheduled release from the hospital in two weeks, because it was then that the real need for help would begin. John agreed to this postponement, which gave us extra time for him to work on the flying phobia, as well as to prepare him for this important reunion.

During the next two weeks, John's anxiety level lifted significantly. He felt liberated by the knowledge his father had shared with him, released from a lifetime of not knowing and therefore not understanding, and relieved to have encountered a warmer, gentler father than the one who inhabited his childhood memories. Furthermore, he had a powerful desire to see his father and connect with him and help him. The veil of anxiety seemed to be lifting. By the session before he left town, the fear of flying had decreased; on a scale we had created of mild to intense anxiety, John's anxiety had dropped from a 9 down to a tolerable 3 or 4.

Although John was not aware that he was to arrive in Australia on the first night of Passover, I was, and grappled with whether or not to tell him. Suspecting that this knowledge might ultimately have important ramifications, I decided to tell him. His response was tears —tears, he said, of joy mixed with some fear and excitement.

He asked how he could learn enough about preparing a Passover seder for his father, and here I felt called upon as teacher and guide. I told him about the Haggadah, the book outlining the ritual of the seder, the story of Passover, as well as the prayers. We discussed plans for procuring matzoh (ritual unleavened bread) and kosher wine. Then, on the airplane, he would read the Haggadah to further prepare. Here, the familiar look of panic tugged at John's eyes and mouth. "What if someone on the plane sees what I'm reading and *knows* I'm Jewish?" He then paused, shrugged and laughed: "So what if they know?" This after five months of therapy.

For the first time in his life, John managed his flight to Australia without medication, although he had it with him just in case. Another first—he celebrated Passover. That this took place with his father contributed to the healing of three generations. During the Seder, his father reclined next to him on the sofa, holding his hand throughout, crying tears of joy. He said that this seder had made his life worthwhile.

John returned to Los Angeles triumphant, calm, and energized. In the subsequent three months of therapy, we talked more about his children and how his fears had affected them, especially Martha. He began to attend more outings, at first small ones, like picnics in public places. Within a couple of months he attended a ballet recital, a soccer match, and, his crowning achievement, Disneyland. The anxiety remained at a comfortable, steady 2 or 3 on our scale.

At the time of this writing, John had begun to build a future for himself and his family in a world that is no longer outlined by fear. While he and his family have begun to occasionally attend synagogue and celebrate some Jewish holidays, there is still a measure of ambivalence. John is a voracious reader of Holocaust literature, and has begun to search for relatives in Australia, Israel, and the United States. Clearly, John's religious identity is a work in progress; rather than having resolved it all, he is learning to live with an open mind sprinkled with a good dose of skepticism and a marvelous sense of humor.

After a thorough reading of the clinical literature about the Holocaust, one thing is quite clear. A unique and horrible trauma occurred that has deeply affected the survivors and the second and subsequent generations in ways that are so complex, alternately subtle and blatant, contradictory and inconsistent, that all we really know is that to categorize and define it seems at once both necessary and yet futile. When working with affected families, it is crucial to bear in mind the magnitude of what happened and its historical and social context, and the vast clinical literature is essential to that endeavor. Yet, in the end, when working with multigenerational transmission of trauma, we must set aside our knowledge and make room for the individual narrative onto which our attention must be focused like a laser beam. It is the truth and how it is perceived, reworked, and revealed through the narrative in which there are answers to be found.

Yet the color of truth is not always black and white. What were the survivors' circumstances before and during the war? What degree of success did they achieve after the war? At what point were their children born and into what circumstances? How did their postwar communities view them, and did they help with their adjustment to a new culture? How did the second generation view the parents' World War II experiences? To what degree were the survivor parents able to reveal small, appropriate parts of their stories in response to their growing children's questions? Were the parents viewed as heroes or victims? These are a few of the endless questions therapists must ponder, for the truth is composed of endless shades of gray.

Many studies point clearly to the psychological repercussions of survivors and children of survivors. In a 1992 lecture, Stanford Professor Steven Sapolsky claimed that the "traumatic hormones" that cross the placental barrier in the third trimester of pregnancy are likely to recur in "waves" over six generations (Kinsler 1994).

In John's family, the effects of his anxiety on Martha were evident. Clearly, at least some of his anxiety can be traced back to his parents' trauma as a result of the Holocaust. Yet how much of his mother's anxiety can be attributed to the war, and how much would have existed had she never experienced such trauma? It cannot be so easily measured, defined, and condensed into convenient theory. Nor does it need to be, for even without a trauma such as the Holocaust, children are always influenced by their parents' psychological impasses.

"It's not your burden, but how you carry it," goes the old saying, and John's parents went through their lives carrying a crushing burden. They carried it surreptitiously, guiltily, fearfully. It was not until the secret was revealed that the trauma that had already reached its tentacles into the third generation could be retracted and the healing could begin. And it is three generations that have begun to heal simultaneously.

The coincidence that John and I both are children of Holocaust survivors was a lucky one, because I was primed for the clues. I, too, had been raised on family secrets, a sense of loss, fear, and mistrust. I had countertransferentially sensed a sort of connective tissue with a comrade who too had been raised in the veiled shadow of great evil.

At this point in time, Martha's therapy is rapidly progressing. It is clear that her father's anxiety had a powerful effect on her, and that his dramatic and rapid recovery came as a result of facing the issues of his life: being a Jew and a child of Holocaust survivors, learning the truth behind the family secrets, reconnecting with his father, mourning his mother, and continuing the search for more answers by seeking extended family members.

Martha's improvement may be measured by the symbolic firsts, both hers as well as her father's. At the time of this writing, Martha was planning her first sleepover at her best friend's house. More pronounced is the public healing father and daughter experience together as they rehearse a musical duet to be performed in Martha's school talent show. The generations join together to heal, and it is this healing that will constitute the legacy to be passed along to the next generation.

REFERENCES

Barocas, H., and Barocas, C. (1973). Manifestations of concentration camp effects on the second generation. *American Journal of Psychiatry* 130: 820–821.

Bar-On, D. (1995). *Fear and Hope: Three Generations of the Holocaust.* Cambridge, MA: Harvard University Press.

Berger-Reiss, D. (1980). *Children of Nazi Holocaust survivors: a coming of age*. Unpublished master's thesis, Goddard College.

Danieli, Y. (1992). The diagnostic and therapeutic use of the multi-generation family tree in working with survivors and children of survivors of the Nazi Holocaust. In *The International Handbook of Traumatic Stress Syndromes, Stress and Coping Series*, ed. J. P. Wilson and B. Raphael. New York: Plenum.

Des Pres, T. (1976). *The Survivor.* New York: Oxford University Press.

Hass, A. (1990). *In the Shadow of the Holocaust: The Second Generation.* New York: Cornell University Press.

Karr, S. D. (1978). *Second generation effects of the Nazi Holocaust.* Unpublished doctoral dissertation, California School of Professional Psychology.

Kestenberg, J. (1972). Psychoanalytic contributions of the problem of children of survivors from Nazi persecution. *Israel Annals of Psychiatry and Related Disciplines* 10:(4):311-325.

Kinsler, F. (1980). The unfinished business of the family: treatment of children of Holocaust survivors: thoughts and feelings of a therapist. In *The Many Dimensions of Family Practice: The Proceedings of the North American Symposium on Family Practice*. New York: Family Service Association of America.

——(1994). *Shoah aftermath: the second generation at mid-adulthood*. Unpublished paper presented at the American Psychiatric Association, Philadelphia, PA, May.

Lifton, R. J. (1968). Survivors of Hiroshima and Nazi persecution. In *Massive Psychic Trauma*, ed. H. Krystal. New York: International Universities Press.

Nadler, A., Kav-Venaki, S., and Gleitman, B. (1985). Transgenerational effects of the Holocaust; externalization of aggression in second generation of Holocaust survivors. *Journal of Consulting and Clinical Psychology* 53:365-369.

Newman, L. (1979). Emotional disturbance in children of Holocaust survivors. *Journal of Contemporary Social Work* 60:43-50.

Niederland, W. C. (1968). The psychiatric evaluation of emotional disorders in survivors of Nazi persecution. In *Massive Psychic Trauma*, ed. H. Krystal. New York: International Universities Press.

Rakoff, V., Sigal, J., and Epstein, H. (1966). Children and families of concentration camp survivors. *Canada Mental Health* 14:24-26.

Shoshan, T. (1989). Mourning and longing from generation to generation. *American Journal of Psychotherapy* 43(2):197-202.

Sigal, J. J. (1982). The nature of evidence for intergenerational effects of the Holocaust. In *Generations of the Holocaust*, ed. M. Bergmann and M. Jucoovy, pp. 3-25. New York: Basic Books.

Sigal, J. J., DiNicola, V. F., and Buonvino, B. A. (1988). Grandchildren of survivors: Can negative effects of prolonged exposure to excessive stress be observed two generations later? *Canadian Journal of Psychiatry* 33:207-211.

10

Memory, Trauma, and Psychotherapy*

Daniel J. Siegel

Working with individuals who have experienced trauma during childhood is challenging for both the therapist and client. The ways in which the client has adapted to a trauma, both during the event(s) and afterward, can determine how the mind encodes the experience into memory. This chapter provides a concise overview of basic processes of the mind and how they may become impacted by, and used to adapt to, trauma. A clinician reading this chapter will learn about some possibly new aspects of the psyche and how to use this knowledge in evaluating and treating traumatized individuals.

---

*Parts of this chapter were first published as the article "Memory, Trauma, and Psychotherapy: A Cognitive Sciences View" in the *Journal of Psychotherapy Practice and Research*, vol. 4, no. 2, pp. 93–122. Copyright © 1995 by the American Psychiatric Press, and used by permission.

It is exciting to see how an integration of studies of the mind and the brain can lead to a deeper understanding of subjective experience. This chapter presents a view of how the inner experience of trauma and its developmental effects leads directly to a clinical approach to working with traumatized individuals and their unresolved memories. In children, adolescents, and adults, the self emerges from how our minds have encoded experiences, the essence of memory, and the source of our life stories. This chapter focuses on the heart of the relationships between memory and narrative, experience and self. It raises some basic questions that may challenge previous assumptions about what it means to remember.

This chapter integrates findings from the fields of cognitive science, child development, and trauma to address basic questions about posttraumatic stress disorder (PTSD). In the profile of posttraumatic disturbances one can see deviations in various functions, including attention, information, processing, and memory (Litz and Keane 1989, Pynoos 1993). These functions may interact, and a thorough evaluation and treatment plan should attempt to address these interactions by building on an individual's strengths. This chapter focuses on aspects of memory and trauma; however, for assessment and intervention to be meaningful, this perspective should be woven together with a consideration of the person as a whole.

OVERVIEW OF MEMORY, COGNITION, AND TRAUMA

How do traumatic experiences affect memory? How can the contrasting findings of selective amnesia and specific avoidance and startle responses, classic in certain traumatized individuals (American Psychiatric Association 1994) be understood? Why does posttraumatic stress disorder include the memory disturbances of amnesia, intrusive recollections, and flashback phenomena? How can flashbacks be understood in terms of normal memory processes? How does the "resolution" process lead to elimination of these disturbances of memory?

These questions have led to attempts to apply knowledge gleaned from basic studies in cognitive science to the clinical findings in traumatized individuals. When trauma occurs during childhood, developmental variables become important factors in the outcome of acute and chronic trauma (Terr 1991). Long-standing clinical interest and a recent upsurge in societal concern about how experiences of trauma during childhood are recalled, especially by adults, remind clinicians and researchers of the importance of scientifically informed, rational approaches to memory (Christianson and Loftus 1987).

A simple axiom about cognitive processes is that from the beginning of an infant's life, the mind/brain is organizing experiences and stimuli and attempting to make sense of them (Flavell et al. 1993, Siegel 1995a). Many studies on perception and memory suggest that the infant is capable of recognition, summation, and generalization across perceptual modalities (Stern 1985). These cognitive processes are thought to reside in the massively complex parallel processing of the neural networks that compose the architecture of the brain (with billions of neurons and many evolving interconnections between them) (Morris 1989). With development and experience, these networks acquire increasingly sophisticated capabilities to represent individual stimuli as well as to categorize objects and events. Perceptual categories and conceptual categories thus form the basis for neurally making sense of the world (Edelman 1992).

Generalizations of repeated events can be encoded into a schema or mental model for a given type of experience (Johnson-Laird 1983). Mental models are thought to be generated from past experience to bias present perceptions, and to influence future decisions. Motivational systems, such as attachment, may be organized by mental models, for example, Bowlby's (1969) notion of "internal working models" (Main et al. 1985). Memory storage may also be structured in terms of schemas or models (Alba and Hasher 1993).

What is memory? What are the normal developmental changes in memory, and how will the timing of trauma affect these processes? How does one make sense out of trauma?

Implicit and Explicit Memory

The word *memory* refers to a number of processes in which the mind/brain is able to perceive a stimulus, encode elements of it, and store these for later retrieval. Retrieval of memory may influence behavior directly (implicit memory), or it may lead to the subjective conscious experience of recalling a fact or event (explicit memory).

The approximately synonymous terms *early*, *procedural*, and *implicit* memory refer to the behavioral (and emotional and possibly somatosensory and sensory) memory processes that develop first and likely reside in the brain structures that mediated their initial encoding (basal ganglia and amygdala, and possibly motor, somatosensory, and sensory cortices) (Schacter 1987). *Late*, *declarative*, and *explicit* memory are terms referring to what people generally think of as "memory" in which an event can be recalled as if it were from the past and communicated to others as such (Squire et al. 1990).

Explicit memory requires focal (conscious) attention for processing. It is thought to be mediated via the medial temporal lobe system, which includes the hippocampal formation and related structures (Squire 1992a,b). Hippocampal processing is required for the establishment of explicit memory and is dependent on an easily disrupted neurophysiological process called *long-term potentiation*. A separate, subsequent process is *cortical consolidation*; this process takes days to weeks to months, during which time memories are made permanent in the cortex and are independent of the hippocampus for retrieval.

Certain conditions have been found to be associated with intact implicit memory and impaired explicit memory. These include benzodiazepine effects, certain organic amnestic syndromes (such as Korsakoff's), divided attention phenomena, and childhood amnesia. The latter two conditions are especially relevant to this discussion (Lister and Weingartner 1991).

Development

Studies of the development of memory (Fivush and Hudson 1990, Nelson 1993b) suggest the following:

1. Children have excellent encoding and retrieval capacities for implicit memory from early on.

2. Explicit memory encoding may be good, but retrieval strategies for especially young children are immature, and this may lead to the observed limitations and inconsistencies in cued and spontaneous recall for personally experienced events.
3. The nature of post-event dialogue regarding an experience can influence the manner and probability of recall of aspects of an experience.
4. Childhood amnesia is the normal, non-trauma-related phenomenon in which children over the age of about 5 years (the range is 3 to 7) do not have continuous explicit memories of their lives from before this age period.

The development of autobiographical memory in children has been found to be markedly influenced by the "memory talk" in which adults (usually parents) talk to children about the contents of their memory (Nelson 1993a). This enhanced recall by social interaction may be attributable to the reinforcing impact of such talk, the learning about how to remember, as well as the co-creation of a narrative about events. The term *co-construction of narrative* refers to the shared contributions to the creation of a story that may directly contribute to events in early childhood becoming a part of explicit memory.

Narrative

Narrative refers to the telling of a sequence of events. The narrative mode of cognition is thought to be a predominant mode in early childhood, developing before its counterpart, the *paradigmatic* or *logico-deductive* mode (Bruner 1986). Narrative is the most common mode in which the contents of autobiographical memory are recounted at any stage in development. Personally experienced events may be stored in a narrative structure, with sequencing, protagonists, perspectives, crises, and expectations and their disruptions. Retrieval of autobiographical memory may then be recounted in its narrative form. Some authors suggest that the self is fundamentally related to narrative (Dennett 1991), and that after the second year of life its development can be directly expressed (Siegel 1995a).

Narrative has at least three genres: fictional stories, schematic sequences, and autobiographical stories. Recounting of direct autobiographical narratives or stories requires explicit memory retrieval. However, it is useful to consider that fictional narrative may be driven by implicit memory in the absence of explicit encoding (Clyman 1991). The theoretical relationship among explicit memory, cortical consolidation, and narrative needs to be explicated by research.

A Theory of Encoding and Retrieval of Trauma

How does a traumatic experience become encoded differently from a nontraumatic event? Here are some factors to consider:

1. overwhelming emotions, including a sense of fear, helplessness, shock, and horror;
2. perceptual details that flood the capacity to sort through and selectively attend in the setting of input that has never been sensed before;
3. extreme stress and physical pain that may have been present;
4. social context and the meaning of the event (sense of loss, betrayal, abandonment);
5. cognitive adaptations during and immediately after the event that may influence encoding, including perceptual avoidance, divided attention, fantasy of escape, and somatic numbing;
6. deviations from previously established schemas or mental models for expectable occurrences.

Each of these factors may lead to a disruption in the normal processing of perceptual input toward long-term memory.

One theoretical view is that the perceptual and emotional flooding, extreme stress, and divided attention during trauma may lead to impaired hippocampal (explicit) processing of the event but intact implicit encoding. This configuration can also explain numerous findings in PTSD, including specific avoidance behaviors, startle response, and somatic symptoms (intact implicit memory) in the setting of dissociative amnesia (impaired explicit memory). REM sleep and dreams are thought to be required for cortical consolidation of memory; thus, one can view nightmares in PTSD as an attempt to consolidate (or resolve) a traumatic memory.

Traumatic reenactment, evidenced by patients' repeated behaviors and children's spontaneous play, can be seen as driven by implicit memory. Even traumatic narratives (as fictional stories involving violence and death but devoid of a sense of oneself in the past) can be viewed as implicitly derived despite being mediated by language, which is often considered expressive of explicit or declarative memory.

Memories of traumatic events that do not fit into prior schemas and that are not formed into a narrative and consolidated explicitly in the cortex may be prone to repeated retrieval. Triggers of this implicit and/or explicit retrieval may be perceptual stimuli (a car backfiring), emotional states (fear, anxiety), interpersonal contexts (separation, illness of a caregiver), and language cues (discussion about trauma-specific issues). Implicit retrieval produces a subjective internal experience of trauma-related emotions, bodily sensations, and images that are not sensed as "self in the past." Adaptations to these implicit retrievals may include specific avoidance behaviors, chronic distractibility, and difficulty with focal attention (as conscious/focal attention is bombarded by internal stimuli). Implicit retrieval also produces external manifestations such as fictional narratives, reenactment, and abrupt behavioral shifts (caused by sudden intrusions of implicit recall).

Abrupt state-of-mind shifts may not make sense and may be attributed to different "selves" as a dissociative adaptation. The intrusive implicit recall of traumatic somatosensory memory may be triggered by environmental cues or internal states (such as anxiety or fear). These retrieved implicit memories will not be experienced as "self in the past," and they may be felt as somatic complaints without attribution to past events.

Therapeutic Implications

In this view of encoding, the perceptual details of the traumatic experience and their psychosocial meaning have been encoded implicitly and are recurrently retrieved in an intrusive manner. Explicit encoding may be limited. The therapeutic implication of this view is that current accessibility of retrieval may depend on the nature of the dialogue patients have had in the past regarding their memories of the event and the stories that have evolved from those discussions.

If the symptoms of PTSD are related to the encoding of trauma, then the resolution process may need to focus directly on those processes that have been uniquely disturbed. Developmentally, patients may not yet have the metacognitive capacity to reflect on their internal, intrusive experiences and translate them into an explicit narrative (Flavell et al. 1986). However, over time this translation of experience into narrative may be an appropriate and effective therapeutic strategy to resolve these intrusive memories. An intensive effort to help patients with state and behavioral regulation in the setting of an attachment relationship with a therapist should be the bedrock of trauma work. In this relationship, patients can begin to desensitize themselves to triggers from the environment via play therapy, graded exposure with relaxation techniques, and imagery. Internal states that trigger implicit recall would be more challenging to modify, but similar techniques could be used with the goal of making the cascade of associated reactions to fear or anxiety less likely to occur. Conditioned fear due to trauma may have been broadly generalized and thus may lack context dependency. One goal of therapy is to narrow the range of cues and settings that may elicit fear responses. Narrative, imagination, imagery, play, and desensitization would be the major components in this approach.

As patients abused during childhood develop in psychotherapy, their capacity to feel attached to others, to deal with their feelings and fear of abandonment, and to translate somatization into expressible emotional states and deal directly with their triggers will all contribute to their healthy psychological development in the emotional, cognitive, and social domains. Children will need help throughout their youth in resolving the trauma and loss at different stages as their memory and metacognitive capacities continue to develop.

Although there is no sense in the trauma of childhood, therapy can help individuals make sense of their internal world and their interactions with others.

BASIC PRINCIPLES OF MEMORY

As this consolidated overview suggests, normal memory is inextricably linked to other cognitive processes, including development, consciousness, mental models, metacognition, emotions, and state of mind. Trauma may affect these processes and memory in complex ways. In reviewing the background of these basic cognitive science concepts, the following principles of memory can serve as an anchoring framework and reference guide:

1. *Memory is a process.* There is no closet in the brain in which a memory is stored like a photo in an album. Remembering, like other cognitive processes, is believed to be a product of the interactions of complex networks of nerve cells in the brain. Remembering can be thought of as the activation of a neural net profile that represents the things being recalled. Thus, memory can be thought of as a verb, not a noun.
2. *Memory is reconstructive, not reproductive.* Both the process of encoding an event (perceiving the external stimulus, internally responding to it, and registering it in some form) and retrieving the event (reactivating the neural net profile representing these encoded elements) are products of neural processing. These various stages of processing are influenced by active mental models or schemas that link together perceptual biases, associated memories, emotions, and prior learning. The details remembered may be very accurate, although not complete, or they may be biased by questioning after the event.
3. *Memory and consciousness are not the same.* Memory is not a unitary thing. There are at least two forms of memory that depend on different brain structures. Some forms of remembering involve conscious awareness; others do not. Thus, the mind can store information that is not easily accessible to the conscious but that can influence behavior. Most of cognition is nonconscious.
4. *Memory involves monitoring processes that assess the origin and accuracy of a memory.* Memory includes both experiential and correspondent dimensions of subjective recollections;

experiential refers to the sense of conviction an individual has regarding the accuracy of a memory, whereas *correspondent* refers to the correlation between the recalled information and the actual experience. These two features may be somewhat independent under certain conditions (for example, hypnosis, brain injury, intensive post-event questioning) and in certain individuals.

5. *Memory and narrative are not identical.* The language-based output that constitutes telling a story about an event is an approximation of retrieving information in memory, but it is also influenced by the social context of the teller and the listener. Thus, encoding, storage, and retrieval are often followed by the recounting of a story to another person, and this may be driven by both memory retrieval processes and social factors. Attachment experiences early in life may influence the way people remember and how they tell their autobiographical stories.
6. *The development of memory is profoundly influenced by interpersonal experiences.* Early remembering is enhanced by parent–child interactions that involve shared construction of stories about remembered events. Inhibition of this memory talk may form a part of memory disturbance in childhood trauma.
7. *Trauma may uniquely affect memory processing at the levels of encoding, storage, retrieval, and recounting.* Cognition and interpersonal experiences during and after trauma may uniquely affect the way in which memories for these events are processed and later accessed.

OVERVIEW OF COGNITIVE PROCESSES AND MEMORY

Cognitive science is an interdisciplinary field of research that has blossomed in the last decade to provide valuable insights into the functioning of the mind (Posner 1989). Cognitive psychologists, computer scientists, neuroscientists, psycholinguists, anthropologists, and philosophers are pursuing research in this field. What follows is an overview of some cognitive science concepts that are relevant to the study of memory and trauma. The fundamental ideas and research bases for cognitive science have been reviewed elsewhere and may be useful as a more intensive introduction (American Psychiatric Association 1994, Posner 1989, Terr 1991).

Forms of Consciousness and Modes of Processing

Consciousness has intrigued philosophers for centuries and is an active domain of study for cognitive scientists (Marcel and Bisiach 1988). Most mental activity is nonconscious; it is out of awareness of phenomenal experience (Greenwald 1992, Kihlstrom 1987). One way of describing conscious awareness is as a complex serial selective sampling of mental activity being processed in parallel form (Dennett 1991). Crick (1994) utilizes visual awareness to explore the cellular basis of conscious experience.

Another view, based on a biological assessment of brain function, is that of Edelman (1992). He describes two forms of consciousness that derive from the resonant interactions between groups of neurons. In this model, primary consciousness stems from the interaction between perceptual and conceptual categorizations. This form of consciousness, called the "remembered present," is also found in higher animals and is unable to transcend momentary awareness. It is embedded in the present but is influenced by categorizations from the past. In human beings the capacity to have lexical processes with language categories enables a "higher order consciousness" to exist, stemming from the resonance between these categories and conceptual categories. Higher order consciousness frees inner experience from the prison of the present and allows for views of the past and planning for the future. Included in these forms of consciousness is a "scene" of the present situation in which the self is placed in a temporospatial context.

Two relevant topics are attention and mode of processing. Focal attention (conscious attending) to a stimulus leads to a different form and degree of further processing than occurs with stimuli that are not focally attended (Lewicki et al. 1992). The latter, however, do get processed, especially with regard to gestalt features.

Some cognitive processes occur in serial mode and others in parallel (Flavell et al. 1993). Serial processing is limited in the number of stimuli it can handle at one time; it limits the number of other serial processes that can simultaneously function, and is said to have a limited capacity (Flavell et al. 1993). Consciousness is believed to be a serial process. Parallel processes, in contrast, are thought to have unlimited capacity, do not interfere with other simultaneous processes, and can handle huge amounts of data. The majority of cognition is nonconscious and may occur in a parallel process.

Notions of self and consciousness are important in examining basic issues such as the meaning of a patient's statements that "I don't remember" or "I have an image of . . ." What consciousness has access to may be a limited view of what the individual is experiencing or has experienced. Thus, studies of consciousness can help inform an understanding of a patient's capacity for self-awareness. One effect of trauma on memory processes may be to limit which aspects of experienced events are available to conscious recollection. The process of putting frightening memories into words may be important in freeing trauma victims from the prison of the remembered present, the pervasive, timeless quality of symptoms of unresolved trauma.

Learning and Mental Models

Learning requires that the brain encode experiences and then influence subsequent behaviors as a function of that encoding. The capacity to learn is basic to the central nervous system, which has elements that take in stimuli from the environment, process the data, and affect behavioral output.

Studies of perceptual abilities in infants reveal that the newborn is capable of complex cognitive operations, including amodal perception and generalizations, from the beginning of extrauterine life (Siegel 1995a). In amodal perception, the infant is able to perceive in one modality (such as tactile sensation) and then recognize in another (such as visual input), suggesting that the infant is capable of mentally representing the outside world from birth. A second cognitive capacity in early infancy is the process of generalization. Infants can note both similarities and differences across stimuli. Numerous research strategies have demonstrated that from infancy onward, the human mind is able to establish a summation of prior stimuli and experiences. This process can be thought of as the creation of a mental model for a category of objects, persons, and interactions (Morris 1989). The term *schematization* is sometimes used to describe this nonconscious cognitive process.

Mental models are thus derived from the generalizations of past experiences. They in turn can influence present perceptions and help to determine future behavior. Mental models are an example of how higher cognitive functions influence the flow of information from lower order processes such as sensation and perception. This influence of higher functions on lower processes is called "top-down" processing.

A mental model is always nonconscious. Models, however, influence perceptions, thinking, emotional reactions, and behavioral responses (Horowitz 1991, Morris 1989). Stern (1985) discusses the infant's development of a representation of an interaction that is generalized (RIG) as the summation of numerous interpersonal experiences with caregivers. These RIGs are thought to act as the building blocks of what Bowlby terms the internal working model of attachment; this view of the genesis of attachment has formed the conceptual framework for much of attachment theory and research (Edelman 1992, Johnson-Laird 1983).

Mental models can be instantiated by various control processes and environmental triggers (Horowitz 1991). Models for a particular attachment figure may be conflictual or inconsistent, leading to cognitive difficulties in adaptation that may include certain forms of insecure attachment (Main 1991) and possibly predispositions to dissociation (Liotti 1992). Models may also profoundly influence behavioral response patterns by providing a cognitive link between stimulus input and behavioral output.

Mental models or schemas are also thought to form a basis for the organization in storage and significantly influence the cognitive strategies necessary for retrieval. Learning is thus inextricably linked to schematization and memory.

In repeatedly traumatized children, maltreatment may lead to mental models that perpetuate feelings of distrust, fear, or abandonment in later life. Models may be instantiated by environmental or internal triggers and produce perceptual biases (such as perceiving a therapist's lateness as an act of hostility or abandonment) that would have been protective in youth but are maladaptive in adulthood. These mental models may be a central focus for change in the comprehensive therapy of individuals abused as children.

Metacognition and Metamemory

Cognitive processing can transform the nature of neural representations of external stimuli as well as representations of cognitive processes themselves. This latter capacity to "think about thinking" is a process termed *metacognition.* Developmental psychologists use various paradigms to study metacognitive development, and recently controversies have arisen about the timing of the acquisition of certain metacognitive capacities (Flavell et al. 1986). In general, between 3 and 9 years of age children develop the capacity and then the ability to express their metacognitive functions directly. Theoretically, the stage of metacognitive development of a child at the time of abuse may have an important influence on how the child is later able to adapt. This may especially be the case with intrafamilial abuse that involves a sense of betrayal and conflictual mental models for the same caregiver (Main 1991).

The regulation of cognition, also called *metacognitive monitoring*, involves the assessment of thinking sequences for fallacious logic, factual errors, and contradictions in context. Main (1991) has found that metacognitive monitoring may be distinctly impaired during discourse that involves the subject of an unresolved traumatic experience.

Metamemory, or "thinking about memory," includes the processing of memory processes. *Source monitoring* is the metamemory process by which "people discriminate, when remembering, between information that had a perceptual source and information that was self-generated from thought, imagination, fantasy or dreams"(Johnson 1991, p. 3). Johnson (1991) has hypothesized that this process uses perceptual information, contextual information, and supporting memories in assessing whether a memory originated in experience or is self-generated.

This model of the reality-monitoring process may be useful in the future for applying a scientifically based view of metamemory processes to the evaluation of recalled traumatic experiences in both children and adults. Further studies of the development of source and reality monitoring in children may advance our understanding of how a child's personal memory system is influenced by direct experiences, interpersonal talk about those experiences, and imaginal, dream, and fantasy processes. Understanding these influences has important clinical and forensic implications.

Narrative and Co-Construction

Narrative is the telling of a series of events. Academicians in areas ranging from literature to anthropology are concerned with this language-based, "meaning-making," theme-creating process (Britton and Pellegrini 1990). Bruner (1986) has described two basic modes of thought: narrative and paradigmatic or logicoscientific. The narrative mode begins earlier in child development and is an important way in which children perceive and make sense of the world. Narrative takes into account the teller and the listener and can thus be considered a form of discourse. Genres of narrative include the schema, personal account, and fictional story. Perspectives include first or third person, and past, present, or future tense. Narratives may include various levels of complexity, from interactional descriptions to statements about intentions and inner emotional states.

Autobiographical narrative begins with the onset of language development and appears to be a way in which the child attempts to make sense of the events of daily life (Nelson 1989). One view holds that this observed discourse is a reflection of primary, inherent cognitive processes now expressed through language. Another view is that the co-construction of stories as a family activity becomes internalized, so that narrative is actually a form of discourse with an imagined listener.

For children, narratives can be co-constructed with their parents, allowing for their joining together in the telling of a story. A similar process, *memory talk*, between parent and child focuses on the parent's interest in the views and inner experience of the child. Studies suggest that a child's ability to use language to spontaneously recall an event is greatly enhanced by and may be dependent on the shared discussion of an event with others (Nelson 1993a). Thus, narrative both establishes a sense of meaning for a child and is a shared process between parent and child that can shape the degree of importance of the content of memory.

A basic cognitive question is how narrative influences the encoding, storage, and available retrieval strategies that allow for conscious access to memory.

Traumatic experiences may have a unique place in memory in that they cannot be incorporated into a coherent narrative of one's own life. The role of linguistic processing, the application of mental models of the self ("narrativization") to encoded experiences, and the inhibition of sharing information through discourse with others may thus be important aspects of a traumatized individual's uniquely impaired cognitive processing of trauma-related information.

State of Mind, Emotions, and Memory

Cognitive studies of the effect of mood on memory have found a direct relationship between state of mind and various processes from encoding to retrieval (Bower 1987, Eich and Metcalfe 1989, MacLeod 1990). Emotional biasing of the interpretation of stimuli and the content of memories retrieved is known as *state-dependent* learning and memory.

The concept of a *state of mind* has influenced the work of a number of researchers interested in memory and in trauma (Putnam 1989, Silberman et al. 1985, Spiegel 1988). The activation of a given mental model may be determined by environmental stimuli, internal control processes, specific memories, and emotional states (Horowitz 1991). A state of mind can include perceptual biases, dominant emotional tone, behavioral response patterns, and increased accessibility of particular memories.

The state of mind at the time of encoding may determine the accessibility to later retrieval (Bower 1987). For example, if one is presently sad, it may be easier to recall events experienced when one was sad in the past. How young children's relatively labile shifts in state of mind influence their memory processing is unclear. Studies of dissociative disorder patients suggest that shifts in state of mind may be accompanied by various degrees of memory barriers (Nissen et al. 1988, Schacter et al. 1989, Silberman et al. 1985). For patients with multiple personality disorder (*Diagnostic and Statistical Manual* [*DSM-IV*] dissociative identity disorder), alter identities can be conceptualized as distinct states of mind with, to some extent, autonomous autobiographical narratives. Asymmetric access to memory across amnestic barriers raises intriguing questions about cognitive processes and dissociation (Spiegel et al. 1993). These global impairments in memory function may be different from impairments specific to memories for particular traumatic events.

MEMORY: RESEARCH AND MODELS

Information Processing

For the last three decades cognitive psychologists have conceptualized memory in terms of an information processing model (Posner 1989). Although linear in its architecture despite the parallel structure of the brain, this basic model has proved useful both for designing productive research paradigms and establishing a common vocabulary for talking about memory processes.

Figure 10-1 illustrates the following brief telegraphic overview of the basic terms and concepts that pertain to this information processing model. *Input* refers to the information or data coming into the system from the outer world. *Sensory imaging* is the ultrabrief (less than half a second) representation of sensory input. *Attention* directs the flow of informational processing from the sensation stage onward. Information is processed and placed in working or short-term memory (not necessarily synonymous) for about half a minute. *Chunking* refers to the clustering of bits of information to facilitate further processing. Working memory is said to be able to handle 7 ± 2 chunks of information. Information can be transferred from working memory to long-term memory with various rehearsal processes. The structure of long-term memory is thought to be influenced by schematizations with various associative categorizations. Emotions may play a role in the associative links forming the structure of long-term memory storage.

Encoding refers to sensory intake, perceptual processing, and working memory transfer to the storage stage in long-term memory. Once in storage, items may have various degrees of storage strength and retrieval strength. Retrieval inhibition is a crucial, normal function that prevents the voluminous (and perhaps unlimited) quantity of information in long-term storage from flooding into consciousness and working memory (Bjork 1989). Consciousness, focal attention, and retrieval are thought to be serial processes that are thus both rate-limited and capacity-limited.

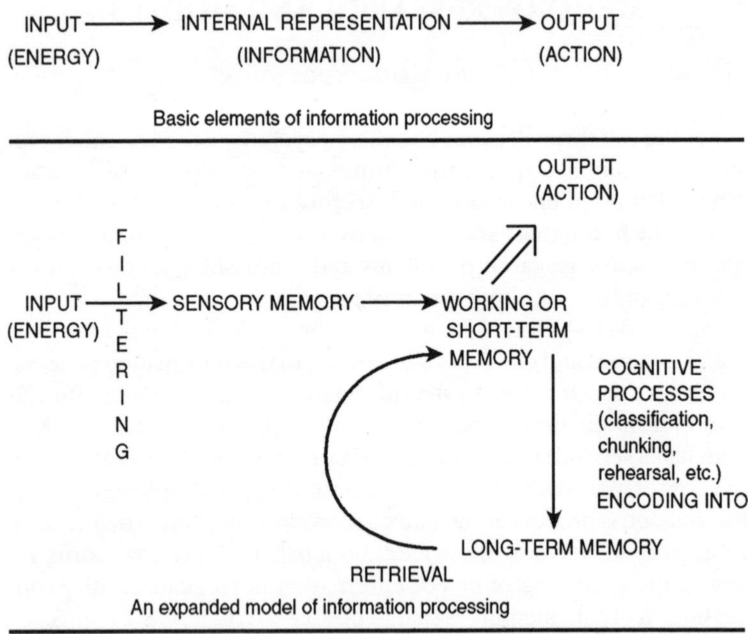

Figure 10–1. Basic elements (top) and expanded model (bottom) of information processing. Attentional processes, which can act at any of the stages shown by arrows, are thought to regulate the flow of information processing.

In this model, items retrieved from long-term memory are placed in working memory where they can be further processed and placed again, in newly altered form, in storage. Thus, retrieval acts as a memory modifier. Retrieval can be divided into direct and indirect forms. Direct retrieval can be measured by tests of spontaneous recall, cued recall, and recognition. Indirect retrieval can be measured by tests of priming effects, such as the speed of relearning a task, word stem completion, and free association. These indirect tasks do not require the subject to consciously recall having experienced the test stimulus (Richardson-Klavehn and Bjork 1988).

Differences in the probability of retrieval may be a function of various factors, including aspects of encoding, storage, retrieval, and the conditions at time of questioning. Several principles derived from experimental protocols have met with various degrees of acceptance in the field. Table 10–1 summarizes some of these principles as discussed by Kihlstrom and Barnhardt (1993). For example, the encoding specificity principle suggests that the conditions at time of encoding influence which context will facilitate accurate recall at the time of retrieval.

Models of Memory and Cognitive Neuroscience

The study of memory has resulted in the conceptualization of different systems or processes leading to two very different forms of memory. These forms have been described as implicit, nondeclarative, or early memory, and explicit, declarative, or late memory (Schacter et al. 1989, Squire 1987, Tulving 1985). Most memory theories view memory either in terms of multiple storage systems or as models with distinct forms of processing. Tulving (1985) divides memory into procedural, episodic, and semantic memory stores; *procedural* refers to learned behavioral responses, *episodic* to autobiographical memory (oneself in an episode), and *semantic* to representations of knowledge. Squire (1992a) focuses on the divisions of *nondeclarative* and *declarative* memory, the latter being accessible to verbalization. These are examples of the dominant multiple storage systems models. An influential processing model is that of Schacter and colleagues (1989), who describe

Table 10–1. Principles of Memory Retrieval

Principle	*Conditions of Encoding, Storage, and Retrieval*
Elaboration	The probability of remembering an event is a function of the degree to which that event was related to preexisting knowledge during processing.
Organization	The probability of remembering an event is a function of the degree to which that event was related to other events during processing.
Time dependency	The probability of remembering an event is a negative function of the length of time between encoding and retrieval (with reminiscence and other exceptions readily acknowledged).
Cue dependency	The probability of remembering an event increases with the amount of information supplied by the retrieval cue.
Encoding specificity	The probability of remembering an event is a function of the extent to which cues processed at the time of encoding are also processed at the time of retrieval.
Schematic processing	The probability of remembering an event is a function of the degree to which that event is congruent with preexisting expectations and beliefs. (Note: retrieval of schema-incongruent memories may also be enhanced and related to "failure-driven memory"* in which exceptions to the expected norm are noted in early infancy.)
Reconstruction	Memory of an event reflects a blend of information retrieved from a specific trace of that event with knowledge, expectations, and beliefs derived from other sources.

*See Kihlstrom and Barnhardt 1993.

memory as ***implicit*** or ***explicit***. Although the domains of these various classifications may not overlap exactly, for simplicity this chapter uses the terms *implicit* and *explicit* memory. Explicit memory is assessed with direct measures of memory. Implicit memory cannot be stated directly and is assessed via indirect measures (Richardson-Klavehn and Bjork 1988).

Squire (1992a) has described the contrasting features of these memory systems as follows (Table 10-2):

> One kind of memory provides the basis for conscious recollections of facts and events. This is the kind of memory that is usually meant when the terms "memory" and "remembering" are used in ordinary language. Fact-and-event memory refers to memory for words, scenes, faces, and stories, and it is assessed by conventional tests of recall and recognition. This kind of memory was termed "declarative" to signify that it can be brought to mind and that its contents can be "declared." Other similar terms include explicit memory and relational memory. . . . Nondeclarative memory includes information that is acquired during skill learning (motor skills, perceptual skills, and cognitive skills), habit formation, simple classical conditioning including some kinds of emotional learning, the phenomenon of priming, and other knowledge that is expressed through performance rather than recollection. Experience can cumulate in behavioral change but without affording conscious access to any previous learning episodes. . . . [pp. 232, 233]

Implicit memory is the way in which the brain encodes an experience and then influences later behavior without the use of conscious awareness, recognition, recall, or the inner subjective experience of a retrieved memory (Schacter 1987). Thus, the skill of riding a bicycle can be demonstrated even if a youngster has no recall of when he or she learned to ride. This is implicit memory without explicit recall. An extension of the usual behavioral notions of implicit memory might theoretically also include somatic, emotional, or perceptual sensations that are derived from past experiences but that contain

Table 10–2. Classification of Memory*

Declarative (Explicit)	*Nondeclarative (Implicit)*
Facts	Skills and habits
Events	Priming
	Simple classical conditioning
	Nonassociative learning

*Adapted from Squire 1992a, p. 233.

no sense of their origins in the past. Implicit memory may be fundamental to clinically observed, repeated patterns of maltreatment and to transference phenomena (Clyman 1991). Cognitive neuroscience findings suggest that the basal ganglia may play a primary role in mediation of implicit memory related to motor behavior (Squire 1992a, Squire et al. 1990). The somatosensory cortex, amygdala, and sensory cortex, respectively, may mediate the hypothesized somatic, emotional, and perceptual forms of implicit memory.

Explicit memory involves the subjective experience of remembering. It is directly accessible to conscious awareness and can usually be stated in words. Explicit memory allows for representation of the critical relationships between events and may permit inferences from memory to novel situations (Eichenbaum 1992). This can include memory for facts (semantic memory in Tulving's original model) and for personally experienced events (episodic memory). Episodic or autobiographical memory has the unique features of self and time; these features distinguish it from memory for facts, which may have no source attribution or sense of when the fact was learned.

The medial temporal lobe memory system, including the hippocampus and related brain structures, is thought to be essential for the processing of explicit memories (Squire 1987, 1992b). Lesions in the hippocampal formation can produce dissociations (in cognitive science terminology, "dis-association" in usually associated processes) with impaired explicit and intact implicit memory.

Hippocampal processing may depend on a neurophysiologic event called *long-term potentiation* (LTP), which requires simultaneous activation of presynaptic and postsynaptic neurons, the anterograde release of the neurotransmitter glutamate, and the retrograde diffusion of released nitric oxide. This process is easily impaired by specific chemical inhibitors (Nicoll 1988).

After this initial hippocampal processing, a *cortical consolidation* process, taking from days to weeks to months, occurs between the hippocampus and the cortex, making memories "permanent" and the retrieval independent of the hippocampus. This process may explain the phenomenon of retrograde amnesia seen in brain injury (Squire et al. 1990). Theoretically, cortical consolidation may also be intimately related to the language-based processing of autobiographical memory.

I propose that disruptions first in the normal processing of experiences via the medial temporal lobe (including the hippocampus) and subsequently in cortical consolidation may lead to unresolved traumatic memory. The discussion that follows explores possible causal mechanisms as well as the possibility that the resolution process may facilitate explicit memory processing and cortical consolidation.

Dissociations in Associated Processes

Studies have revealed dissociations in the normally associated memory functions of implicit and explicit recall in various mental states (Schacter 1989, Squire 1992a). The use of the term *dissociation* in cognitive science is distinct from its application in clinical settings, in which it refers to a complex set of normal and pathological subjective alterations in conscious states of mind and the normally integrative functions of identity, memory, and consciousness (Putnam 1989). In research paradigms, examining "dis-association" of usually associated cognitive processes is a scientific opportunity to learn more about the underlying mechanisms associating these processes (Schacter 1992).

Explicit memory, by definition, implies that the subject can consciously recall an item from memory and usually use language to express what is retrieved. Amnestic patients with lesions in the hippocampus and related structures showed associations between implicit (intact) and explicit (impaired) recall (Squire et al. 1990). Studies of the effects of benzodiazepines on normal subjects reveal a similar dissociation—normal functioning and awareness during testing, but impaired explicit and intact implicit recall. Similar dissociations can be demonstrated in hypnotically induced amnesia, childhood amnesia, divided-attention experiments, and cases of surgical anesthesia (Lister and Weingartner 1991, Spiegel et al. 1993, Squire 1992a). In this chapter I present the hypothesis that posttraumatic disorder may involve the blockage of hippocampal processing, producing the classic findings of amnesia (explicit impairment) in the setting of specific avoidance behaviors, startle response, and hyperarousal (intact implicit memory). Supporting this view are studies that have found abnormal hippocampal structures in patients with PTSD

(Bremmer et al. 1992) and studies that have suggested hippocampal impairment from excessive stress mediated by glucocorticoids (Sapolsky et al. 1990). Empirical research is needed to establish the roles of divided attention, emotional flooding, and stress during trauma in mediating this impairment of explicit processing.

The Organization of Memory

Memory studies suggest that the processes of encoding, storage, and retrieval have complex interrelationships. Context-dependent and mood state-dependent effects reveal that the conditions of time of encoding have a marked influence on the probability and timing of recall later on (Bower 1987, Kihlstrom and Barnhardt 1993) (see Table 10-1). These findings have important implications for mood, anxiety, dissociative, and posttraumatic stress disorders.

Anderson and Bower (1973) have described an associational network that interconnects items in memory and is responsible for activating certain items and making them more retrievable. Others have discussed a schematic organization for memory in which encoding and retrieval are determined by organized mental models (Beck 1987, Bowlby 1969). These two views have strongly influenced research into memory disturbances in various psychiatric disorders.

It is generally believed, although not proven, that long-term memory has an unlimited capacity for storage. Bjork (1989) has studied an aspect of the retrieval process called "retrieval inhibition" and argues that inhibition of recall is essential to allow currently useful data to be readily available and for outdated information to be less accessible (and less impairing). Regulation of retrieval, rather than limitation of storage, is thus what is thought to impede the excessive flow of voluminously stored bits of information into consciousness.

Autobiographical Memory

Autobiographical memory can be thought of as the memory of oneself in an experience at a given time in the past. It may include a sense of time, spatial context, and the metamemory process of source monitoring. Some cognitive scientists do not consider autobiographical memory to be a separate system (Anderson and Ross 1980, Squire 1987). Others feel that whether or not it involves a separate cognitive/neural process, autobiographical memory has unique aspects worthy of investigation (Neisser 1982, Rubin et al. 1986). Relevant findings from these studies are described below.

Childhood amnesia is the normal phenomenon whereby most people over the age of 6 or 7 have intact implicit but impaired explicit recall of events prior to the age of 3 to 5 years (Nelson 1993b, Weltzer and Sweeny 1986). Various theories proposed to explain childhood amnesia invoke different aspects of the memory process, including immaturity of narrative processes, retrieval strategies, the sense of self and time, and hippocampal development. Specific memories before the age of 5 are present in many individuals but are not usually abundant or continuous. Terr (1987) has explored ways in which traumatic memories from this age period may be recalled in the form of behavioral repetition and fantasy themes as the child develops.

Recency effect refers to the finding that people generally remember events in their lives that occurred most recently.

Reminiscence is the interesting finding that individuals over the age of 35 recall more events from childhood and adolescence when presented with neutral cues (Rubin et al. 1986).

Memory and Attachment

An important independent set of studies has fascinating implications for the development of childhood memory. Attachment theory has a long history of its own, stemming from ethologic, psychoanalytic, and developmental approaches to early parent–child interactions and subsequent behavioral patterns (Johnson-Laird 1983, Main 1991).

Attachment theory has many intriguing and controversial implications for our understanding of childhood development. For the purposes of this chapter, two general findings are especially salient. For the group of *dismissing* adults corresponding to the *avoidantly attached* children, there is a fascinating set of converging findings.

These parent–child pairs are characterized by emotional distance and parental rejection. Adults can be classified as "dismissing" by an instrument called the Adult Attachment Interview. Their children are often found to have "avoidant" attachments to them in the Infant Strange Situation Separation Paradigm at 1 year of age. The first year of life of these infants was marked by a mother–child relationship with emotional distance and rejection (Ainsworth et al. 1978). Beebe and Lachman (1994) have found that when the child is 2 years of age the face-to-face interactions of these dyads is characterized by lack of the normally present match between word use and affective facial expression. A study of 4-year-olds found that in problem-solving tasks the parents of avoidant children did not join in at the level of the child's "zone of proximal development," essentially allowing the child to do the task on his or her own rather than taking part in the requested joint effort (Crowell et al. 1988). Main's (1991) sample of avoidantly attached children at 10 years of age had a unique paucity in the content of their spontaneous autobiographical narratives. Interestingly one of the characteristics of the parents of avoidantly attached children is that they have a repeated insistence on not being able to recall their childhood experiences.

Why is this? Are these genetically related individuals merely expressing the phenotype of impaired long-term memory for attachment experiences? Or is there something about this attachment classification, characterized by emotional distance and rejection, that leads to diminished encoding or impaired retrieval accessibility? I propose that examining the roles of "memory talk" and co-construction of narrative may be important for future studies; perhaps these avoidantly attached children are not engaged by their parents in either of these two processes, with the result that the accessibility of memories for experiences is greatly diminished. This hypothesis requires research validation.

Developmental changes in memory function and their relationship to social experiences have important implications for abused children. A second salient group are adults with the attachment classification of "unresolved" (trauma or grief). In their semistructured autobiographical narratives, disorientation and disorganization occur in response to specific cues related to abuse or loss. Ainsworth and Eichberg (1991) found that the reported experience of trauma or loss alone was not significant but that lack of resolution in the parents was statistically correlated with disorganized attachment in the infants. The disorganized behavior of the infant at the time of reunion in the separation paradigm is unique in its chaotic, ineffective, and bizarre nature. The notion that frightening or frightened behavior on the part of unresolved parents is causal in this disorganized attachment status has been suggested by Main and Hesse (1990). The relationship among early conflictual attachment experiences, incoherent (conflictual) mental models (Main 1991), and potential predispositions to disassociative phenomena (Liotti 1992) need exploration.

Memory in Childhood

Research on childhood memory has yielded numerous findings potentially relevant to working with children and adolescents in the clinical and forensic arenas. Two broad academic areas in childhood memory research are basic developmental studies and applied memory investigations. Space limitations permit only a very brief outline of salient findings in each area.

Developmental studies examine the normal changes in the processes of encoding and retrieval. In general, these studies suggest that children can remember accurately, although their spontaneous recall may be incomplete and inconsistent. Immature retrieval strategies may be present in young children and may impair their ability to access information stored in memory. Interpersonal communication, such as in co-construction of narratives and memory talk, plays an important role in the creation of a personal memory system (Nelson 1993b). Normal developmental changes in memory include the phenomenon of childhood amnesia.

Applied childhood memory research attempts to answer questions important to trauma and forensics. Thus, the ways in which pre-event information, intra-experience stress and bodily contact, and post-event questioning influence children's recall are fundamental queries. Ceci and Bruck's (1993) review provides a comprehensive historical analysis of the suggestibility of the child witness. In general, these studies suggest that even young children can accurately recall events and can retain information for long periods of time. Pre- and post-event information can bias which details are reported and can even establish conviction that an event occurred when in fact it did not. Of note is the finding that repeated questioning of a young child may lead to alteration in responses, the possible elaboration of a story with fictional elements, and intense conviction in the veracity of the fictional parts. This finding of reporting with conviction details that were never present has important forensic implications regarding the interviewing of child victims or witnesses. Controversy exists among researchers, especially regarding studies that assess the recall of bodily contact (for example, a physical examination) and those in which a child is a passive witness (Goodman and Bottoms 1993, Saywitz et al. 1991). These crucial issues need further clarification and study.

Adult Recall of Childhood Experience

The issue of how childhood experiences are processed in memory and recalled in adulthood is of long-standing clinical importance as well as recent intense societal concern (Pillemer and White 1989). A fair proportion of adults—an estimated 5 to 10 percent of the nonclinical United States adult population—may have a "dismissing" attachment classification (Main 1991). The autobiographical narratives of this group of adults, as assessed by the adult attachment interview, tend to include an insistence that they do not recall details from their childhood family life. Whether they are not consciously aware of events stored in memory, have impaired encoding of these experiences, or merely are not reporting on these events is unclear at this time. There is no suggestion in attachment theory or research findings that these individuals were overtly traumatized. Another finding in adults is the reminiscence phenomenon, wherein adults after the age of 35 years tend, in response to neutral word cues, to recall events from their childhood more than in earlier adult years (Rubin et al. 1986).

These are examples of impaired and amplified explicit autobiographical recall in nonclinical adult subjects. Clinical implications of these findings are that therapists should not overzealously interpret lack of recall as a pathognomonic indicator of "repressed" trauma.

Also, an increased tendency to recall childhood in mid-life may be a normal developmental event and not a sign that something traumatic in childhood is "hidden" and is now intruding on consciousness. Given the highly suggestible nature of both children and adults (Schumacher 1991), it is crucial that mental health practitioners be aware of their own biases so as not to inadvertently influence or pressure nontraumatized individuals into believing in aspects of their histories that may not have occurred.

The recent upsurge in societal interest in adults reporting delayed retrieval of memories of childhood trauma has led to a number of publications on the subject (Briere and Conte 1983, Loftus 1993, Terr 1994). Carefully designed retrospective studies on the experience of amnesia (dissociation and repression in clinical terms, impaired explicit recall in cognitive science terms) in individuals with documented experiences of trauma in childhood are crucial. Even better would be the challenging establishment of prospective studies that would follow traumatized children as they develop.

The MEM Model and PTSD

Johnson and Hirst (1992) have proposed a model called the multiple entry modular memory system (MEM), composed of two major interrelated systems of perceptual (P) and reflective (R) processes. The perceptual processes act on either externally derived or internally created images. These are amodal processes that can act on representations across sensory modalities (vision, hearing, touch, taste, smell). The reflective processes occur independently of sensory images derived from external or internal sources and can be sustained by internal events alone. Each system contains subsystems of related processes (P1 and P2, R1 and R2). Within each subsystem, related component processes act on information from multiple levels. This division of memory into distinguishable perceptual and reflective systems has provided a model for organizing empirical data from a variety of studies, including investigations of normal memory and studies in clinical populations with amnesia due to general medical conditions, confabulation, or delusions.

In the MEM model, items are encoded with profiles of relative degrees of perceptual and reflective components. Included in these profiles are situational context and emotional states in the various levels of P and R. Very basic emotions, such as anger, fear, and joy, are present at the perceptual levels. At higher, reflective levels, the emotions become more complex; they include, in addition to the basic emotions, feelings such as jealousy, nostalgia, and remorse (Johnson and Multhaup 1991). Thus, memory retrieval contains a profile of processing data, including emotions, from the basic perceptual processes to the higher reflective functions. Reflective processing may also be useful in the control of thought processes (Bonanno and Singer 1993).

As mentioned earlier, source monitoring is a reflective process that allows the mind to determine the origin of a memory. A form of source monitoring called *reality monitoring* is viewed as the process by which people discriminate between remembered information that had a perceptual source and that which was self-generated (Johnson 1991). Research in various settings suggests that the greater the amount of reflective processing that takes place at the time of an event, and thus associated with a given memory, the more an individual is able to accurately distinguish that memory as internally versus externally generated. Although Johnson and colleagues have not yet applied this model to trauma (Johnson and Hirst 1992, Johnson and Multhaup 1991), this paradigm may become a useful framework for attempting to address how the experiential sense of conviction correlates with the correspondent accuracy in individuals with memories of traumatic events.

Source monitoring can be hypothetically extended to examine the process that allows the discrimination between ongoing sensory input and retrieved memory. How is it that an unresolved traumatic memory can be reinstated as a flashback and experienced as happening in the present? The MEM model has possible theoretical applications to the understanding of flashback phenomena as experienced by individuals with posttraumatic stress disorder. If a traumatic event is associated with overwhelming emotions (terror, betrayal, pain, shock), intense sensory input, an adaptive marked division in focal attention, and a lack of substantial reflective processing at the time of initial processing, then the encoding of that event, or portions of it, may have a predominance of perceptual processing only. An extension of reality-monitoring studies (Johnson 1991) suggests that the retrieval of that "high P, low R" memory configuration without the usual contextual cues biases discrimination as originating from external rather than internal sources.

A possible mechanism underlying flashback phenomena may be that the lack of reflective processing during and after a traumatic event, combined with a flood of perceptual input, produces a uniquely P-rich, R-poor encoding/retrieval profile. Reinstatement of this high-P, low-R profile may thus be consciously experienced as a "current experience" rather than a recalled "memory." This profile may be similar to the conceptualization of intact implicit memory with minimal explicit processing. The cognitive processing of events at the time of encoding, the state in which they are stored in long-term memory, and their "processing profile" at time of retrieval thus may contribute to how they are consciously experienced when recalled. Intact reality monitoring but trauma-specific encoding profiles (high P, low R, or intact implicit/impaired explicit memory) may thus be proposed as a mechanism to explain flashback phenomena in posttraumatic stress disorder. Experimental studies of flashback phenomena that could compare findings with those of other deviations in reality monitoring, such as hallucinations and delusions (Bentall 1990, Harvey 1985), are needed to gain insights into the cognitive bases of these disturbances in normal mental functioning. Therapeutic interventions that add reflective processing to retrieved memory may thus alter this P/R profile and halt recurrent flashbacks. Another perspective is that reflecting on highly perceptual memories may transform primarily implicit memory into an explicit form.

TRAUMA-SPECIFIC COGNITIVE PROCESSING

A cognitive understanding of mental processes and memory, combined with a clinical awareness of child abuse and its developmental sequelae, leads to a series of basic hypotheses regarding trauma and memory.

Repression and Dissociation

The specific effects of traumatic experiences on an individual depend on numerous factors, including developmental age, cognitive ability, and the interpersonal context of the trauma (Alba and Hasher 1993, Van der Kolk 1984). These factors contribute to the meaning of an event or series of events for a given individual. Terr (1991) has discussed the impact of single event versus repeated trauma in childhood. She has suggested that children may adapt to trauma by using several defense mechanisms, including voluntary suppression (leading to involuntary repression), play, fantasy, and projection. Dissociation, which may derive from divided attention and altered states of consciousness, is another defense used in childhood trauma.

Childhood trauma may thus involve several adaptations that influence memory: suppression/repression, denial, fantasy, and dissociation. Although not emphasizing trauma, Singer's (1991) volume on repression and dissociation reviews the scientific data available on these two distinct direct-memory mechanisms, which may be present concomitantly in a given individual. In this chapter I propose a basic cognitive science view of the contrast between repression and dissociation. In repression an experience is attended focally, encoded explicitly, and then stored in an elaborated form. Active intentional suppression may initially inhibit retrieval, limiting further elaborative and organizational processing (see Table 10-1). This active inhibition of retrieval may later become an automatic process called repression. Some authors view suppression and repression as using the same cognitive mechanisms (Erdelyi 1993), through which conscious awareness of this latent or potential memory becomes automatically blocked. Retrieval inhibition (Bjork 1989) is a normal and essential function of memory that makes certain data more accessible than others. In the retrieval of a previously repressed memory, this view predicts that the reactivation would be experienced not as a flashback but as a more fully processed set of images that may have already been narrativized or consolidated to some extent, although they may be intrusive.

I hypothesize that in clinical dissociation, the division of attention and/or state of mind during a traumatic experience leads to the inhibition of explicit encoding. Furthermore, the normally associated elements of perceptual modalities, context, emotions, and reflections may be differentially processed and thus may have segregated associative linkages (Siegel 1996). Their storage and subsequent reinstatement will reflect this "dis-association" and be experienced consciously as a set of disjointed perceptual and reflective components. The depersonalization, time distortion, and intrusive subjective experiences in clinically dissociative patients reflect this trauma-specific form of cognitive dissociation in processing (Siegel 1995b).

Thus, the recall of a memory reflects the quality of processing during *and* after trauma. The hypothesis presented here is that repressed memories are explicitly processed more fully than dissociated memories. When retrieved, repressed memories are subjectively experienced as a "past" form; this contrasts with the disjointed nature of recall, with distortions in both self and time and a predisposition toward flashbacks, found with dissociated memories.

Although numerous authors (Erdelyi 1993, Kihlstrom and Barnhardt 1993, Spiegel et al. 1993) maintain the clinical reality of repression as a memory process inhibiting conscious access to encoded and stored material, others (Holmes 1991, Loftus 1993) question the scientific evidence for repression as a cognitive mechanism and the claims of its widespread prevalence. Recent retrospective studies of undocumented cases of trauma (Briere and Conte 1993, Herman and Schatzow 1987) and preliminary findings from cases of documented trauma in a single study (Williams 1992) suggest that one-third to one-half of adults may have amnestic periods for childhood trauma. Clearly, more documented and prospective studies are required to confirm these findings.

Cognitive psychological studies not directed at trauma have shown that most cognition is nonconscious (Greenwald 1992) and that inhibition of retrieval and motivated forgetting are fundamental processes in blocking conscious awareness of items stored in memory (Bjork 1989). Studies of suppression and other forms of mental control also support the concept of active inhibitory processes that, under stress, may lead to increased retrieval of a blocked item (Wegner and Pennebaker 1993). Even recent cognitive neuroscience conceptualizations of brain function and consciousness support the functional possibility and evolutionary benefit of selective inhibition of access of memories to consciousness (Stern 1985).

Disruption in the normally integrative functions of identity, memory, and consciousness, known clinically as dissociation, has been described from various perspectives (Putnam 1989, Singer 1991, Spiegel et al. 1993, Van der Kolk and Van der Hart 1989). Dissociative amnesia has been contrasted with proposed mechanisms of repression. In dissociative amnesia, disrupted encoding and storage of information lead to blocked accessibility and distorted forms upon retrieval, including dissociations in any of a number of features of episodic memory. Distortions may encompass perceptual segregations and displaced sense of self, time, cause-and-effect relationships, and context.

Thus, cognitive science "dis-associations" at encoding and storage may produce clinical dissociations at impaired retrieval. Dissociative amnesia thus refers to the blocked retrieval of interpretable memory data. Empirical research is needed to establish the role, as proposed here, of divided focal attention, stress, and emotional flooding in forming intact implicit but impaired explicit memories. The inhibition of hippocampal processing and subsequent cortical consolidation may uniquely impair conscious access to these dissociatively processed data.

Developmental level of metacognitive capacities (such as reality monitoring), social context (including attachment, safety, and betrayal), and the use of projection, denial, and fantasy may influence accuracy of recalled events. These developmental and adaptive factors, combined with the altered encoding or retrieval of memories in repression and dissociation, affect the evolving personal memory system and autobiographical narrative in traumatized children. The prohibition against talking openly about traumatic experiences in abusive families may also play an important role in blocking traumatic events from becoming a part of the child's personal memory system.

Although trauma during childhood has broad and lasting effects on development, the general concepts discussed here may be applicable to trauma victims at any age. Intratraumatic cognitive processes may produce specific effects on memory in both children and adults.

Divided Attention and Differential Processing

What actually makes an experience traumatic? Numerous investigators have attempted to address this question (Alba and Hasher 1993,

Herman 1992, Lindemann 1944, Pynoos 1993, Van der Kolk 1984). Possible factors proposed include overwhelming emotions; the sense of being out of control; helplessness; threat of severe injury or death to self or other, especially by the negative intentions of another human being; betrayal by someone who is in a relationship normally based on trust; the meaning of the experience; and the inability of the person to escape from continued harm or threat. Given these factors, one can imagine that the cognitive processing of the data will be different from, say, the processing of a walk on the beach. Why should it be different? The emotional context will create a hyperaroused state of mind. This arousal may impede focal attention, which is needed to process incoming data and is already limited in its processing capacity. A cognitive adaptation during trauma, as described by patients with posttraumatic stress disorder, may be the focusing of serial, focal attention on a limited portion of the traumatic experience or on a nonthreatening aspect of the environment. The parallel, nonfocal attentional processing of the majority of the traumatic elements thus may be a primary mechanism of cognitive encoding during trauma. Serial processing can handle only a limited amount of input; therefore, of cognitive necessity only a selected portion of the traumatic experience can be processed via "conscious" focal means. Focal attention appears to be required for explicit processing. This cognitive adaptation may thus explain the impaired explicit and yet intact implicit memory seen in various forms of PTSD.

Emotional Features

The need to diminish emotional flooding during trauma may lead to attention being focused away from traumatic elements of an experience. Excessive stress, as mediated by glucocorticosteroids, may also directly impair hippocampal functioning (Sapolsky 1990). Furthermore, associated emotions during trauma may influence control processes and the instantiation of specific mental models. For example, fear may lead to instantiation of a flight schema, which in turn may intensify a "threatened" sensation. Overwhelming sensory stimuli, in addition to flooding serial attention, may also produce an emotional experience of being "out of control" during traumatic encoding. These emotional features of a trauma may become integral to the memory trace for that experience.

Betrayal represents a unique interpersonal interaction that is contrary to the basic purpose of attachment relationships and may lead the traumatized child to develop conflictual, incoherent models for the same caregiver (Main 1991). Forms of chronic PTSD in childhood, including dissociative disorders, may have their psychopathologic origin in these conflictual mental models (Liotti 1992). The maintenance of inherently contradictory schemas and associated memories may be viewed as an attempt to maintain attachment to caregivers in spite of maltreatment (Freyd, in press).

Memory Storage and Retrieval

How does adaptation during the experience of trauma influence the form in which the event is stored and eventually retrieved? In dissociation, intact implicit and impaired explicit memory may be present. There may be a minimal amount of reflective processing at the time of encoding, leading to the storage of the event primarily in perceptual form. This P-rich, R-poor profile will also include a flood of intense emotions. The retrieval of this configuration may produce mistaken source monitoring, resulting in a flashback. Repressed memories may result from the active suppression of retrieval, which may impair subsequent elaborative and organizational processing. Both dissociative and repressed memories may not meet category requirements to fit into the associational network of previously laid-down memory (unless trauma has been chronic) and also may not fit into an acceptable self-schema (see Table 10–1). Thus, in both mechanisms of repression and dissociation, the memory may not be easily retrieved in either an associational or model framework of memory storage.

Neurophysiologic Correlates

Squire (1992a) and Squire and co-workers' (1990) reviews of the role of the medial temporal lobe structures, including the hippocampus, in amnestic patients suggest the crucial role of the hippocampus in the mediation of declarative or explicit forms of memory. Lesions involving the hippocampus and related structures can result in impaired explicit memory encoding and recall. Nondeclarative or implicit memory appears to be encoded and retrieved via brain structures that are related directly to the motor and emotional processes involved at the time of encoding (including the basal ganglia and possibly the amygdala) (Goldman-Rakic et al. 1990, Schacter 1992, Squire et al. 1990).

The hypothesis proposed here is that the explicit processing of traumatic experiences may be specifically inhibited. This inhibition may be mediated by at least two mechanisms. Extreme stress may inhibit hippocampal functioning via release of adrenocorticosteroids (Sapolsky et al. 1990). Also, divided attention, as revealed in studies involving such nontraumatic conditions as dichotic listening experiments (Greenwald 1992, Lewicki et al. 1992), is associated with impaired explicit yet intact implicit memory retrieval. Thus, the mechanisms of trauma-specific encoding resulting from extreme stress and the division of focal attention during a traumatic event may result in impaired hippocampal processing of certain features of the experience.

Research with organic amnestic patients also has suggested a consolidating process over weeks to months, in which explicit memory encoded via the hippocampus becomes embedded in the associational cortex and, after consolidation, does not require the hippocampus for retrieval (Squire et al. 1990). In this way, permanent or longer term long-term memory can be intact in certain amnestic patients. By extension, in trauma processing the unresolved quality of traumatic memory might be explained by the impairment of the consolidation process normally occurring between the hippocampus and associational cortex. Thus, blockade of hippocampal processing during and after trauma may result in both impaired explicit recall and lack or inhibition of subsequent cortical consolidation. Dreaming and REM sleep may be important in this long-term memory consolidation; thus, nightmares and sleep disturbance, frequent in traumatized individuals (Ross et al. 1989), may represent the subjective experience of this impaired cortical consolidation process.

Recent work in cognitive neuroscience (Nicoll et al. 1988) suggests the central role of long-term potentiation (LTP) for hippocampal (as well as amygdala) functioning and the learning process leading to long-term memory. LTP is dependent on the action of pre- and postsynaptic neurons firing simultaneously to produce a specific associative pathway. Studies have demonstrated the importance of timing in the induction of LTP and have shown that elements of the process can be specifically inhibited with particular chemical antagonists. If trauma does specifically inhibit explicit processing, perhaps it is through a mechanism that produces a selective disruption of LTP in the hippocampus. Future studies might examine how conditions of trauma may impede LTP via alterations in the timing and chemical milieu of the hippocampus and thus may specifically impair explicit processing.

Joseph LeDoux (1992) has demonstrated that conditioned fear or emotional memories may be mediated primarily through the amygdala, the part of the brain that has a central role in emotional behavior. The amygdala receives direct sensory input from connections via the thalamus, which then sends projections on to the sensory cortex. In contrast, the hippocampus receives input later, after processing by the sensory cortex (Davis 1992). Thus, the amygdala may process sensory data and encode fear independent of any input from the hippocampus. Animal studies demonstrate that, indeed, conditioned fear can occur without any hippocampal functioning. This arrangement allows for a rapid response to potentially life-threatening situations and hence has significant survival value.

The hippocampus appears to play a role in determining the specificity and context dependency of conditioned fear. Without hippocampal input, conditioned fear has broad generalizability and becomes context-independent (Davis 1992, LeDoux 1992). A clinical illustration of this is the Vietnam veteran victim of a helicopter crash with an excessive fear of all flying vehicles (lacking specificity) in many situations, such as in airports or while watching television (context independency).

Thus, PTSD may be understood to be pathological conditioned fear with broad generalizations and context-independent responses to trauma-related stimuli. The proposed mechanism for these phenomena is impaired hippocampal (explicit) processing during and after trauma while amygdala (implicit) processing remains intact. Conditioned fear may be very difficult or impossible to extinguish. Neural circuits established via the amygdala are tenacious. Behavioral change that may be achieved through various forms of therapy is thought to be due to cognitive override mechanisms rather than elimination of basic learning in the amygdala (LeDoux 1992). These mechanisms may rely on hippocampal and cortical processing to override established amygdala circuits. This may involve making fears more specific and context-dependent, thus rendering them less disabling. This picture of neural components suggests a central role for the hippocampus and associational cortex in the treatment of fear responses, which may be necessary to reduce the symptoms of posttraumatic stress disorder.

Intrusive Memories in Unresolved Trauma

Posttraumatic stress disorder is also characterized by recurrent, intrusive recall. This clinical finding of selective hypermnesia may include the activation of "total scenes," partial episodes, or small components of an experience (which might involve emotions, isolated perceptions, and somatic sensation, respectively). These phenomena may be on a continuum with flashbacks but are distinguished by the inclusion of a sense of past and an identification of source. The disjointed quality of these memories also may include a sense of depersonalization and timelessness.

Several cognitive science findings may be relevant to these clinical phenomena. The finding that recurrent recollections are triggered by neurophysiological changes in hormonal milieu and receptor sensitivity associated with PTSD (Bremmer et al. 1993), as well as the cognitive phenomena of hypermnesia (Kihlstrom and Barnhardt 1993) and reminiscence (Rubin et al. 1986), may provide insights into mechanisms of increased accessibility. The studies of suppression (Wagner and Pennebaker 1993) and its release under stress may also prove useful in understanding the mechanisms underlying intrusive recall.

Trauma may also produce an inhibition in the subsequent cortical processing of an explicit memory. Given this lack of subsequent higher cortical processing, the intact implicit memory may be retrieved as the reactivation of perceptual, somatosensory, emotional, and motor structures (Schacter 1992) without explicit recall and thus may lack the subjective sense of past. Unresolved traumatic memories would remain "in limbo," prone to flashback reinstatement (due to their P-rich, R-poor form), and would lack the cortical processing that would place them in a larger associational network. Their reinstatement may thus be dependent on triggers from the environment or noncortical structures. Triggers could include emotional states (via the amygdala), physiological arousal conditions, and perceptual contexts. These mechanisms may be out of conscious control of the individual and may create the "intrusive" quality of traumatic memories.

In addition, one may see dissociations in the normally associated sensory input. That is, different sensory modalities may be segregated in perception and stored and retrieved separately. This is a significant problem for retrieval in that only one sensory channel may be recalled at a time. On top of all of these other memory disturbances, the recall thus may have an eerie quality of disjointed sensory modalities (only hearing a scream, only feeling somatic pain, or only seeing an intruder's face looming, rather than remembering the experience as a whole). Furthermore, traumatic memories may have dissociations between episodic and semantic memory, so that the factual context of an episode may be accessible while the sense of self, time, and interpersonal context is absent. Thus, subjective experience of depersonalization (non-self), disorientation, and intrusiveness may be parts of the initial reinstatement of memories of trauma. These are classic symptoms in patients with dissociative disorders.

Metacognition and Narrative

The timing of child abuse with respect to cognitive development is significant. If the child has immature metacognitive knowledge or monitoring capacity, he or she may be particularly prone to negative consequences of abuse experiences. These capacities develop beginning at about age 3 and mature significantly by 7 or 8 years of age. With the abusive parent perpetuating the trauma by not acknowledging either the experience (Main and Hesse 1990) or his or her role in the behavior, the pre-metacognitive child may be particularly vulnerable to cognitive distortions and conflictual mental models. Theoretically, this may be a precursor of dissociative adaptation (Liotti 1992) and may explain the research findings that multiple personality (*DSM-IV* dissociative identity disorder) usually occurs only in cases of reports of early child abuse (Putnam 1989). Adults with unresolved histories of trauma may have impaired explicit but intact implicit recall, with repetition of learned behavioral responses. Without explicit awareness of prior abuse, metacognitive monitoring may be impaired. As a result, these adults may be prone to repeat disorganized or frightening parental behavior (Ainsworth and Eichberg 1991) and thus perpetuate intergenerational patterns of maltreatment.

In narrative processes one attempts to construct a coherent theme from events of one's life. With victims of abuse, the distorted experiences of childhood abuse and the need to maintain attachment may affect the narrative process. In these individuals, narrativization may require segregated themes with separate narratives—as may be postulated for dissociative identity disorder—or a general inhibition of the narrative process. Narrative may also be used to regulate the flow of thought (Meichenbaum and Fong 1993); therefore, developmental disturbance in narrative may affect cognitive adaptive capacities. As suggested above, impairment in cortical consolidation due to inhibited hippocampal processing during trauma may explain these inhibitions in narrativization.

Clinical dissociation may permit separation of emotional conflicts as well as memories from conscious experience. The process of psychotherapy, resolution of trauma, and healing from the developmental wounds of child abuse may intimately involve metacognitive and narrative processing of previously inaccessible memories.

Painful Memories and Memories of Pain

The perceptual profile of reinstated memory includes the neural activation of somatic pain or emotional pain (betrayal, shame, guilt, loss). In an unresolved traumatic memory, these sensations may be relatively raw and unprocessed, so that their reinstatement may feel as if it were happening all over again. Distinct from memories of pain are painful memories, in which the awareness of a recalled event is painful because of the present meaning of the event to the person.

In the flood of perceptual details accompanying sensory pain and painful emotions, the patient in treatment may feel totally overwhelmed and may be at risk of being retraumatized by the act of retrieval. What is different in the recalling versus the actual experiencing, however, is that the patient can now reflectively process the experience and co-construct a narrative with the therapist. This processing includes emotionally responding in the present to what happened in the past. By drawing this distinction between remembered pain and the pain of remembering, the patient can begin to gain a sense of mastery in the present by beginning the process of grieving that has been impaired for so long.

Cognitive Models of PTSD

Studies of PTSD, extending findings of information processing abnormalities in the anxiety disorders, have revealed attentional biases toward fear- or threat-related stimuli (Ingram and Kindall 1987, Main et al. 1985). Most subjects studied to date have been combat veterans, and further work is needed to establish the generalizability of these findings to forms of acute and chronic trauma in childhood (Pynoos 1993). PTSD is clinically characterized by both intrusive processes (memories, images, emotions, thoughts) and avoidance elements (psychic/emotional numbing, amnesia, behavioral avoidance of environmental cues resembling the initial trauma) (Ingram and Kindall 1987). This syndrome may have some adaptive aspects. Cognitive attentional biases that are primed to detect fear-related stimuli might permit early detection of threatening situations that, if not avoided, would produce excessive, incapacitating psychophysiological arousal.

I proposed that impairment of explicit memory may be fundamental to PTSD. For example, a combat veteran with chronic PTSD may have no direct recall (explicit memory impaired) of a helicopter crash. Years later, continued avoidance of airports, amnesia for combat, general apathy, and social withdrawal (avoidance elements) combined with startle response, panic attacks, intrusive images, and nightmares (intrusive components) suggest intact implicit memory for the combat trauma. This individual is emotionally, behaviorally, and cognitively impaired.

Controlled research studies are needed to clarify which elements of treatment are essential for effective therapy for PTSD. Approaches to treatment generally include the view that the impaired emotional processing of the traumatic event makes it necessary for interventions to involve active recollection, in explicit terms, of the details of the experience (Foa and Kozak 1986, Greenberg and Safran 1989, Harber and Pennebaker 1993, Herman 1992, Pennebaker et al. 1988, Putnam 1989). Effective treatment of unresolved trauma usually involves the active cognitive processing of specific memories; the memories in question are those that include emotional responses and psychophysiological arousal that may have been present at the time of the traumatic event. Why does this occur? The following discussion provides a possible explanation.

IMPLICATIONS FOR PSYCHOTHERAPY

Basic Principles

The principles of a psychotherapeutic approach to patients with posttraumatic stress disorder include the following general areas:

- The core self: agency, coherency, affectivity, and continuity
- Affect regulation and self
- Attachment: secure base and safe haven
- Consciousness, mental models, and states of mind
- Metacognition, awareness of thinking
- Memory and narrative
- Traumatic memories and their resolution
- Body and mind
- The experiential role of the therapist
- Choice and continuity: healing and the whole person.

This chapter focuses primarily on the aspect of working with traumatic memories and their resolution. It is crucial to treat the whole person, not just their recollections of horrifying events. How the core sense of self, affect regulation, and sense of secure attachment develop within therapy is the bedrock of healing. Cognitive functions that develop as therapy progresses include flexibility of mental models, consciousness and states of mind, and the increased capacity for self-reflection or metacognition. Autobiographical memory and narrative, as proposed in this chapter, are the central processes impaired in posttraumatic memory. Resolution of these memories facilitates the integration of body and mind, emotions and logical thought, and allows the patient to achieve a sense of choice and continuity in life.

The overall goal in the treatment of an individual who has experienced trauma is to allow the person to function as fully as possible and to have a subjective experience in life that is characterized by a sense of well-being, choice, and dignity. One of the most important principles is that of a therapeutic alliance. Given that many forms of childhood trauma involve mistreatment by adults, the issue of trusting authority/parental figures often becomes a crucial therapeutic area with these individuals. The patient will be developing new metacognitive capacities, memories, narratives, and models of the self. This is no simple or painless process.

The patient's narratives and manifestations of mental models of self and others can be revealed both in descriptions of present relationships and in the therapeutic relationship itself. The patient's metacognitive knowledge and metacognitive monitoring will become evident in self-reflection during therapy. Developmental adaptations to trauma may involve the avoidance of thinking about thinking. These adaptations may have preserved the child's capacity to take part in the flow of "normal" family life. Effective therapy may catalyze the development of metacognitive knowledge and monitoring, which can then become more coherent and functional.

It is crucial for the clinician to be aware of the highly suggestive nature of human memory (Pettinati 1988, Schumacher 1991). Memory is reconstructive. A memory may consist of an emotional gist or theme (Christianson and Loftus 1987) with only vague details accessible to conscious recollection. Over time, specific memories may become more complex. Normal human discourse may lead one to fill in the gaps, elaborating a story so that it makes sense. The listener's bias can shape the nature of the unfolding story. The therapist's bias may be manifested as subtle nonverbal cues, verbal emphases, or repeated questioning about a given topic.

Delayed recall of repressed or dissociated memories of childhood trauma is a phenomenon (Terr 1987) with a plausible theoretical cognitive mechanism. Clinicians need to be aware that partially distorted or wholly false memories of traumatic events are also theoretically plausible; the possibility of distortions in recollection is supported by studies on the suggestibility of human memory (Ceci and Bruck 1993, Schumacher 1991) and by case examples (Terr 1987).

Every human relationship has its influence on each member. It is wise for clinicians involved in evaluation and treatment to be aware of their own biases, and they should be mindful of the potential authority/parental role they may play that may make patients particularly vulnerable to suggestive influence. Within the therapeutic relationship, it is important to be supportive, empathic, and concerned without leading. This delicate balance is a challenge to all therapists. The basic principles of clinical interest, compassion, and open-mindedness can help optimize therapeutic progress and minimize iatrogenic distortions.

Working with Traumatic Memories

Several authors have written about various techniques in the treatment of traumatized individuals (Freud 1914, Harber and Pennebaker 1993, Ingram and Kendall 1987, Putnam 1989, Spiegel 1988, Van der Kolk and Van der Hart 1989). *Abreaction* refers to the reinstatement of a memory, including its concomitant emotional responses from the time of the event. A patient may recall some of the details of an event, including its time, place, and context, but may lack recall of what it was like to be there. There are no definitive data suggesting that abreaction must occur for therapeutic response, but it is a widely held belief among traumatologists from various schools of thought. Clinically it has been noted that the symptoms of an unresolved trauma—startle response, avoidance behaviors, psychic numbing, amnestic periods, nightmares, flashbacks, intrusive images, and somatic sensations of traumatic content—are prone to recur if intervention has not involved some form of therapeutic abreaction.

The retrieval of a memory by itself is not therapeutic, nor does it necessarily alter the form in which the memory is stored. A flashback or abreaction that does not involve therapeutic processing only exposes the patient to a repeated experience of being overwhelmed, helpless, and in pain. A therapeutic abreaction emphasizes processing, both cognitive and emotional, of dissociated elements of a previously inaccessible or partially accessible memory.

Two basic axioms based on the hypotheses presented in this chapter are as follows:

1. Therapeutic interventions that allow implicit memories to be processed in an explicit manner, including desensitization, self-reflection, and narrativization, will be essential in the resolution process.
2. Self-reflection during an abreactive experience will provide additional reflective components to a previously perceptually rich and reflectively poor memory profile. This increase in reflective processes will then permit source monitoring to assess the source of the memory accurately and not misinterpret it (as in a flashback) as a presently lived experience.

The symptoms of unresolved trauma are themselves traumatizing; the patient may not be aware of why they are occurring and may again feel helpless to control them. In addition, the content of memory may be frightening. When the patient is ready, there may come a time when he or she needs to recount the details of the experienced trauma. This may be a frightening and painful experience. Therapeutic abreaction strives to bring disparate pieces of memory together for the first time. It is the separation of perceptual modalities and sense of self from explicit reflective processes that allows the memory to be kept from conscious reinstatement for what may be decades. These segregated cognitive representations of the experience can be brought together to make a coherent, although painful, mental picture and narrative of what occurred.

This process often involves asking the patient gently and at appropriate times about some of the details of the experience: What was seen, felt, and heard at the time, and what was the interpersonal context? These elements can help the patient focus on the sequence of events from the beginning to the end of an episode of traumatic experience. Possible feelings of shame or guilt over having caused the trauma, especially in cases of sexual abuse, should be raised directly at certain times. The patient may enter a form of flashback, in which source monitoring assesses the reinstated memory as an event occurring in the present. In some way this immersion may be a fundamental part of the emotional experience of abreaction. The patient should not be left to merely reexperience this memory, but should be encouraged in the present to cognitively process this newly assembled set of perceptions, emotions, and reflections from the past.

For this purpose, various schools of psychotherapy may be drawn upon. Therapeutic tools for psychological distancing, such as those derived from imagery or hypnosis, provide a number of helpful techniques for use during abreactive sessions (Spiegel 1988). Psychodynamics also provide a wide array of helpful tools to facilitate listening, empathy, and the therapeutic relationship. Active use of supportive techniques based on a knowledge of how emotions and thoughts interact can be very useful. Understanding the complex developmental effects of trauma on the growing mind of the child is an important basis for working with the adult patient. Judicial use of psychopharmacologic agents may be helpful at specific times in treatment when autonomic hyperarousal becomes incapacitating (Nagy et al. 1993, Silver et al. 1990).

In the setting of a supportive and empathic therapeutic relationship, the patient carries out the cognitive processing on these previously unavailable data that did not occur during or after the trauma. Processing may help override conditioned fear responses and make them less broadly generalized, more context-specific, and hence less disabling. This explicit processing will also lead to the establishment of hippocampal and cortical circuits and thus to the storage of a different form of memory. As noted earlier, it is not known whether newly associated explicit and implicit memory actually replaces prior forms or merely become a more accessible form, making reinstatement of the original, implicit-only form less likely. Clinical experience suggests that traumatic memories can in fact be fully resolved so that flashbacks and other symptoms of lack of resolution never occur again (Herman 1992).

Resolution

The following is a brief clinical example illustrating a composite case history:

A patient who was raped at 10 years of age by a group of schoolboys focused her attention during the trauma on a picture of a waterfall on the wall. Having been abused repeatedly by a relative between the ages of 3 and 8, she had developed the capacity for dissociative adaptations to overwhelming situations. Her ability to place her focal attention on the waterfall allowed her to block explicit processing of the rape itself.

After the trauma at 10 years of age, she seemed to cope well in school and told no one of her experience. She later stated that she "just forgot it." However, in high school whenever a group of boys would gather near her she would feel a sense of panic, have the urge to run away, begin to get a bodily sensation of pain in her groin, and hear screaming voices. These are examples of implicit memory for the rape: emotional, behavioral, somatosensory, and perceptual, respectively. The reactivation of these implicit memories does not feel like a recollection; rather, it feels real and present. Her inability to recall, at that time, the rape itself is called dissociative amnesia and can be understood as blocked explicit memory.

As therapy progressed, this adolescent was able to begin to reflect, consciously, on these reactivations of implicit memory. She had had no story about the rape, only the avoidance impulses, hyperarousal, and sensory experiences, which she could not explain. As the implicit memories were allowed to be activated simultaneously, she was able to begin to process them explicitly and develop a narrative about the rape experience. Not surprisingly, recalling this event then brought up other times, earlier in her life, when she had to dissociate, to focus her conscious attention away from a traumatic experience, as an adaptation. Her emerging narrative, although now incorporating painful aspects of her life experiences, began to have a newly acquired sense of flexibility and coherency. Her ability to tolerate a wider range of emotion in herself and in others also developed as therapy progressed. When the direct memory work was completed over many sessions, she no longer experienced the intrusive and disabling perceptions, sensations, or behavioral impulses around this traumatic event that had paralyzed her functioning before therapy. The emotional sequelae of trauma—the psychological meaning of having been abused, helpless, or betrayed—may have persistent effects.

The working-through process is the overall therapeutic growth in which an initial trauma is recalled, abreacted (which may take numerous sessions), processed, and incorporated into the ongoing mental models and narrative of the patient's present life (Freud 1914). The working-through process invariably involves grieving as the advent of the new knowledge that destroys an often idealized sense of a significant other or of the self. Depression also commonly accompanies this grief and can be seen as a part of the acceptance of what before was an event unavailable to explicit awareness. The incorporation of the knowledge of the traumatic events into individuals' views of the self, others, and the world around them can lead to profound changes in their experience of life. This change can itself be disorienting. Fortunately, the relief from the torment of flashbacks, intrusive images, and nightmares can help in the face of transient depression and disorientation.

Enhancing the ability of patients to reflect on their internal processes, including memories, expands their experience of self. In Johnson's (1991) terms, the self can be seen as reflections on reflective processing. Dennett (1991) considers the self as the center of narrative gravity and regards consciousness as greatly influenced by language-based interpretations of experienced events. Kegan (1982) views this meaning-making process as central to the development of the self throughout the life span. Narrative and self-reflection are considered important aspects in the development of a sense of self (Siegel 1995a). In fact, traumatized children may experience severe impacts on their core sense of self, including agency, affect, coherence, and continuity (Siegel 1995b). Psychotherapy as a whole can be seen as facilitating the development of these disturbed aspects of a patient's core self. The working through of traumatic memories thus enhances patients' sense of agency, comfort with their own emotional experience, sense of bodily coherency, and narrative continuity.

Working with the memories of trauma within this cognitive science framework requires approaches that are specific to the nature of traumatic memories and also to the therapy of the patient as a whole person who must incorporate this new knowledge into the sense of self (Siegel, in press). Working through the trauma can lead to resolution. The process of grief and healing, like other forms of learning and psychological change, takes time. Although it is a difficult and often painful process, the rewards for patient and therapist can be deeply gratifying.

REFERENCES

Ainsworth, M. D. S., Blehar, M. C., Waters, E., et al. (1978). *Patterns of Attachment*. Hillsdale, NJ: Erlbaum.

Ainsworth, M. D. S., and Eichberg, C. G. (1991). Effects on infant-mother attachment of mother's unresolved loss of an attachment figure or other traumatic experience. In *Attachment Across the Life Cycle*, ed. P. Marris, J. Stevenson-Hinde, and C. Parkes, pp. 160–183. New York: Routledge.

Alba, J. W., and Hasher, L. (1993). Is memory schematic? *Psychological Bulletin* 93:203–231.

American Psychiatric Association (1994). *Diagnostic and Statistical Manual of Mental Disorders*, 4th ed. Washington, DC: American Psychiatric Association.

Anderson, J., and Bower, G. H. (1973). *Human Associative Memory*. Washington, DC: Winston.

Anderson, J. R., and Ross, B. H. (1980). Evidence against a semantic-episodic distinction. *Journal of Experimental Psychology: Human Learning and Memory* 6:441–446.

Beck, A. T. (1987). Cognitive models of depression. *Journal of Cognitive Psychotherapy* 1:15–37.

Beebe, B., and Lachman, F. (1994). Representation and internalization in infancy: three principles of salience. *Psychoanalytic Psychology* 11:127–166.

Bentall, R. P. (1990). The illusion of reality: a review and integration of psychosocial research on hallucinations. *Psychological Bulletin* 107:82–95.

Bjork, R. A. (1989). Retrieval inhibition as an adaptive mechanism in human memory. In *Varieties of Memory and Consciousness: Essays in Honor of Endel Tulving*, ed. H. L. Roediger and F. I. M. Craik, pp. 309–330. Hillsdale, NJ: Erlbaum.

Bonanno, G. A., and Singer, J. L. (1993). Controlling one's stream of thought through perceptive and reflective processing. In *Handbook of Mental Control*, ed. D. M. Wegner and J. W. Pennebaker, pp. 149–170. Englewood Cliffs, NJ: Prentice-Hall.

Bower, G. H. (1987). Commentary on mood and memory. *Behavior Research Therapy* 25:443–456.

Bowlby, J. (1969). *Attachment and Loss, vol. 1. Attachment*. New York: Basic Books.

Bremmer, J. D., Davis, M., Southwick, S. M., et al. (1993). Neurobiology of post-traumatic stress disorder. In *American Psychiatric Press Review of Psychiatry*, vol. 12, ed. J. M. Oldham, M. B. Riba, and A. Tasman, pp. 183–204. Washington, DC: American Psychiatric Press.

Bremmer, J. D., Seiby, J. P., Scott, T. M., et al. (1992). *Decreased hippocampal volume in post-traumatic stress disorder* (NR155). New Research Program and Abstracts: American Psychiatric Association 145th Annual Meeting, Washington, DC, May.

Briere, J., and Conte, J. (1993). Self-reported amnesia for abuse in adults molested as children. *Journal of Traumatic Stress* 6:21–31.

Britton, B. K., and Pellegrini, A. D., ed. (1990). *Narrative Thought and Narrative Language*. Hillsdale, NJ: Erlbaum.

Bruner, J. (1986). *Actual Minds, Possible Worlds*. Cambridge, MA: Harvard University Press.

Ceci, S., and Bruck, M. (1993). Suggestibility of the child witness: a historical review and synthesis. *Psychological Bulletin* 113:403–439.

Christianson, S. A., and Loftus, E. F. (1987). Memory for traumatic events. *Applied Cognitive Psychology* 1:225–239.

Clyman, R. B. (1991). The procedural organization of emotions: a contribution from cognitive science to the psychoanalytic theory of therapeutic action. *Journal of the American Psychoanalytic Association* 39(suppl): 359–383.

Crick, F. (1994). *The Astonishing Hypothesis*. New York: Basic Books.

Crowell, J. A., Feldman, S. S., and Ginsberg, N. (1988). Assessment of mother–child interaction in preschoolers with behavior problems. *Journal of the American Academy of Child and Adolescent Psychiatry* 27:303–311.

Davis, M. (1992). The role of the amygdala in fear and anxiety. *Annual Review of Neuroscience* 15:353–375.

Dennett, D. C. (1991). *Consciousness Explained*. Boston: Little, Brown.

Edelman, G. (1992). *Bright Air, Brilliant Fire*. New York: Basic Books.

Eich, E., and Metacalfe, J. (1989). Mood dependent memory for internal vs. external events. *Journal of Experimental Psychology: Learning, Memory, and Cognition* 15:443–455.

Eichenbaum, H. (1992). The hippocampal system and declarative memory in animals. *Journal of Cognitive Neuroscience* 4:217–231.

Erdelyi, M. H. (1993). Repression: the mechanism and the defense. In *Handbook of Mental Control*, ed. D. M. Wegner and J. W. Pennebaker, pp. 126–146. Englewood Cliffs, NJ: Prentice-Hall.

Fivush, R., and Hudson, J. A., eds. (1990). *Knowing and Remembering in Young Children*. New York: Cambridge University Press.

Flavell, J. H., Green, F. L., and Flavell, E. R. (1986). Development of knowledge about the appearance reality distinction. *Monographs of the Society for Research in Child Development* 51(1):212.

Flavell, J. H., Miller, P. H., and Miller, S. A. (1993). *Cognitive Development*. Englewood Cliffs, NJ: Prentice-Hall.

Foa, E. B., and Kozak, M. J. (1986). Emotional processing of fear: exposure to corrective information. *Psychological Bulletin* 99:20-35.

Freud, S. (1914). Remembering, repeating and working through. *Standard Edition* 12:145-156.

Freyd, J. J. (In press). *Betrayal-Trauma: Theory*. Cambridge, MA: Harvard University Press.

Goldman-Rakic, P. S., Funmahashi, S., and Bruce, C. J. (1990). *Neocortical Memory Circuits*, vol. 55. Cold Spring Harbor, NY: Cold Spring Harbor Symposia on Quantitative Biology.

Goodman, G., and Bottoms, B. (1993). *Child Victims, Child Witnesses: Understanding and Improving Testimony*. New York: Guilford.

Greenberg, L. S., and Safran, J. D. (1989). Emotion in Psychotherapy. *American Psychologist* 44:19-29.

Greenwald, A. G. (1992). New look 3: unconscious cognition reclaimed. *American Psychologist* 47:766-779.

Harber, K. D., and Pennebaker, J. W. (1993). Overcoming traumatic memories. In *Handbook of Emotion and Memory*, ed. S. A. Christianson, pp. 359-387. Hillsdale NJ: Erlbaum.

Harvey, P. O. (1985). Reality monitoring in mania and schizophrenia. *Journal of Nervous and Mental Disease* 173:67-73.

Herman, J. L. (1992). *Trauma and Recovery*. New York: Basic Books.

Herman, J. L., and Schatzow, E. (1987). Recovery and verification of memories of childhood sexual trauma. *Psychoanalytic Psychology* 4:1-14.

Holmes, D. S. (1991). The evidence of repression: an examination of sixty years of research. In *Repression and Dissociation*, ed. J. L. Singer, pp. 85-102. Chicago: University of Chicago Press.

Horowitz, M. J., ed. (1991). *Person Schemas and Maladaptive Interpersonal Patterns*. Chicago: University of Chicago Press.

Ingram, R. E., and Kindall, P. C. (1987). The cognitive side of anxiety. *Cognitive Therapy and Research* 11:523-536.

Johnson, M. K. (1991). Reflection, reality monitoring and the self. In *Mental Imagery*, ed. R. G. Kunzendorf, pp. 1-2. New York: Plenum.

Johnson, M. K., and Hirst, W. (1992). Processing subsystems of memory. In *Perspectives in Cognitive Neuroscience*, ed. R. G. Lister and H. J. Weingartner, pp. 197-217. New York: Oxford University Press.

Johnson, M. K., and Multhaup, K. (1991). Emotion and MEM. In *Handbook of Emotion and Memory*, ed. S. A. Christianson, pp. 33-46. Hillsdale, NJ: Erlbaum.

Johnson-Laird, P. N. (1983). *Mental Model: Towards a Cognitive Science of Language, Inference, and Consciousness*. Cambridge, MA: Harvard University Press.

Kegan, R. (1982). *The Evolving Self*. Cambridge, MA: Harvard University Press.

Kihlstrom, J. F. (1987). The cognitive unconscious. *Science* 237:1445-1452.

Kihlstrom, J. F., and Barnhardt, T. M. (1993). The self-regulation of memory: for better and for worse, with and without hypnosis. In *Handbook of Mental Control*, ed. D. M. Wegner and J. W. Pennebaker, pp. 88-125. Englewood Cliffs, NJ: Prentice-Hall.

LeDoux, J. E. (1992). Brain mechanisms of emotion and emotional learning. *Current Opinions in Neurobiology* 2:191-197.

Lewicki, P., Hill, T., and Czyzewska, M. (1992). Nonconscious acquisition of information. *American Psychologist* 47:796-801.

Lindemann, E. (1944). Symptomatology and management of acute grief. *American Journal of Psychiatry* 101:141-148.

Liotti, G. (1992). Disorganized disoriented attachment in the etiology of dissociative disorders. *Dissociation* 5(4):196-204.

Lister, R. G., and Weingartner, H. J., eds. (1991). *Perspectives in Cognitive Neuroscience*. New York: Oxford University Press.

Litz, B. T., and Keane, T. M. (1989). Information processing in anxiety disorders: application to the understanding of post-traumatic stress disorder. *Clinical Psychology Review* 9:243-257.

Loftus, E. G. (1993). The reality of repressed memories. *American Psychologist* 48:518-537.

MacLeod, C. (1990). Mood disorders and cognition. In *Cognitive Psychology: An International Review*, ed. M. W. Eysenck, pp. 9-56. West Sussex, UK: Wiley.

Main, M. (1991). Metacognitive knowledge, metacognitive monitoring, and singular (coherent) vs. multiple (coherent) models of attachment: findings and directions for future research. In *Attachment Across the Life Cycle*, ed. P. Marris, J. Stevenson-Hinds, and C. Parkes, pp. 127-154. New York: Routledge.

Main, M., and Hess, E. (1990). Parent's unresolved traumatic experiences are related to infant disorganized attachment status: Is frightened and/or frightening parental behavior the linking mechanism? In *Attachment in the Preschool Years: Theory, Research and Intervention*, ed. M. T. Greenberg, D. Cicchetti, and E. M. Cummings, pp. 161-182. Chicago: University of Chicago Press.

Main, M., Kaplan, N., and Cassidy, J. (1985). Security in infancy, childhood and adulthood: a move to the level of representation. In *Growing Points of Attachment Theory and Research. Monographs of the Society for Research in Child Development* 50(1-2):66-104.

Marcel, A., and Bisiach, E., eds. (1988). *Consciousness in Contemporary Science.* New York: Oxford University Press.

Meichenbaum, D., and Fong, G. T. (1993). How individuals control their own minds: a constructivist narrative perspective. In *Handbook of Mental Control*, ed. D. M. Wegner and J. W. Pennebaker, pp. 473-490. Englewood Cliffs, NJ: Prentice-Hall.

Morris, R. G. M., ed. (1989). *Parallel Distributed Processing: Implications for Psychology and Neurobiology*. New York: Clarendon.

Nagy, L. M., Morgan, C. A., Southwick, S. M., et al. (1993). Open prospective trial of fluoxetine for post-traumatic stress disorder. *Journal of Clinical Psychopharmacology* 13:107-113.

Neisser, U. C., ed. (1982). *Memory Observed: Remembering in Natural Contexts*. San Francisco: Freeman.

Nelson, K. (1989). *Narratives from the Crib*. Cambridge, MA: Harvard University Press.

——— (1993a). Events, narratives, memory: what develops? In *Minnesota Symposium in Child Development: Memory and Emotion*, ed. C. A. Nelson, pp. 1-24. Hillsdale, NJ: Erlbaum.

——— (1993b). The psychological and social origins of autobiographical memory. *Psychological Science* 2:1-8.

Nicoll, R. A., Kauer, J. A., and Malenka, R. C. (1988). The current excitement in long-term potentiation. *Neuron* 1:97-103.

Nissen, M. J., Ross, J. L., and Willingham, D. B. (1988). Memory and awareness in a patient with multiple personality disorder. *Brain and Cognition* 8:117-134.

Pennebaker, J. W., Kiecolt-Glaser, J. K., and Glaser, R. (1988). Disclosure of traumas and immune function: health implications of psychotherapy. *Journal of Consulting and Clinical Psychology* 56:239-245.

Pettinati, H. M., ed. (1988). *Hypnosis and Memory*. New York: Guilford.

Pillemer, D., and White, S. H. (1989). Childhood events recalled by children and adults. *Advances in Child Development and Behavior* 22:297-346.

Posner, M. I., ed. (1989). *Foundations of Cognitive Science*. Cambridge, MA: MIT Press.

Putnam, F. (1989). *Multiple Personality Disorder Diagnosis and Treatment.* New York: Guilford.

Pynoos, R. S. (1993). Traumatic stress and developmental psychopathology in children and adolescents. In *American Psychiatric Press Review of*

Psychiatry 1993, vol. 12, ed. J. M. Oldham, M. B. Riba, and A. Tasman, pp. 205–238. Washington, DC: American Psychiatric Press.

Richardson-Klavehn, A., and Bjork, R. A. (1988). Measures of Memory. *Annual Review of Psychology* 39:475–543.

Ross, R. J., Ball, W. A., Sullivan, K. A., et al. (1989). Sleep disturbance as the hallmark of post-traumatic stress disorder. *American Journal of Psychiatry* 146:697–707.

Rubin, D. C., Wetzler, S. E., and Nebes, R. D. (1986). Autobiographical memory across the life span. In *Autobiographical Memory*, ed. D. Rubin, pp. 202–224. New Haven, CT: Yale University Press.

Sapolsky, R. M., Uno, H., Robert, C. S., et al. (1990). Hippocampal damage associated with prolonged glucocorticoid exposure in primates. *Journal of Neuroscience* 10:2897–2902.

Saywitz, K. J., Goodman, G. S., Nicholas, E., et al. (1991). Children's memories of a physical examination involving genital touch: implications for reports of sexual abuse. *Journal of Consulting and Clinical Psychology* 59:682–691.

Schacter, D. L. (1987). Implicit memory: history and current states. *Journal of Experimental Psychology: Learning Memory and Cognition* 13: 501–518.

——— (1989). On the relation between memory and consciousness: dissociable interactions and consciousness. In *Essays in Honor of Endel Tulving*, ed. H. L. Roediger and F. I. M. Craik, pp. 335–390. Hillsdale, NJ: Erlbaum.

——— (1992). Understanding implicit memory: a cognitive neuroscience approach. *American Psychologist* 47:559–569.

Schacter, D. L., Kihlstrom, J. F., Kihlstrom, L. C., et al. (1989). Autobiographical memory in a case of multiple personality disorder. *Journal of Abnormal Psychology* 98:1–7.

Schumacher, J. F., ed. (1991). *Human Suggestibility: Advances in Theory, Research and Applications*. New York: Routledge.

Siegel, D. J. (1995a). Cognition and perception. In *Comprehensive Textbook of Psychiatry*, 6th ed., ed. B. Kaplan and W. Sadock. Baltimore: Williams & Wilkins.

———(1995b). Dissociation, psychotherapy and cognitive sciences. In *Treating Dissociative Identity Disorder*, ed. J. Spira, pp. 39–79. San Francisco: Jossey Bass.

——— (1996). Cognition, memory and dissociation. *Child and Adolescent Psychiatric Clinics* 5:509–536.

——— (In press). *Emotional Relationships and the Remembering Mind*. New York: Guilford.

Silberman, E. A., Putnam, F. W., and Weingartner, H. (1985). Dissociative states in multiple personality disorder: a quantitative study. *Psychiatry Research* 15:235–260.

Silver, J., Sandberg, D. P., and Hales, R. E. (1990). New approaches in the pharmacotherapy of post-traumatic stress disorder. *Journal of Clinical Psychiatry* 51(10 suppl):33–38.

Singer, J. L., ed. (1991). *Repression and Dissociation*. Chicago: University of Chicago Press.

Spiegel, D. (1988). Dissociation and hypnosis in post-traumatic stress disorders. *Journal of Traumatic Stress* 1:17–33.

Spiegel, D., Frisholz, E. J., and Spira, J. (1993). Functional disorders of memory. In *American Psychiatric Press Review of Psychiatry*, vol. 12, ed. J. Oldham, M. Riba, and A. Tasman, pp. 747–782. Washington, DC: American Psychiatric Press.

Squire, L. R. (1987). *Memory and Brain*. New York: Oxford University Press.

——— (1992a). Declarative and non-declarative memory: multiple brain systems supporting learning and memory. *Journal of Cognitive Neuroscience* 4:232–243.

——— (1992b). Memory and hippocampus: synthesis from findings with rats, monkeys and humans. *Psychological Review* 99:195–231.

Squire, L. R., Zola-Morgan, S., Cave, C. B., et al. (1990). Memory: organization of brain systems and cognition. *Cold Spring Harbor Symposia on Quantitative Biology* 55:1007–1023.

Stern, D. N. (1985). *The Interpersonal World of the Infant*. New York: Basic Books.

Terr, L. (1987). What happens to early memories of trauma? A study of twenty children under age five at the time of documented traumatic events. *Journal of American Academy of Child and Adolescent Psychiatry* 27:96–104.

——— (1991). Childhood traumas: an outline and overview. *American Journal of Psychiatry* 148:10–20.

——— (1994). *Unchained Memories*. New York: Basic Books.

Tulving, E. (1985). How many memory systems are there? *American Psychologist* 40:385–398.

van der Kolk, B. A., ed. (1984). *Post-traumatic Stress Disorder: Psychological and Biological Sequelae*. Washington, DC: American Psychiatric Press.

van der Kolk, B. A., and Van der Hart, O. (1989). Pierre Janet and the breakdown of adaptation in psychological trauma. *American Journal of Psychiatry* 146:1530–1540.

Wegner, D. M., and Pennebaker, J. W., eds. (1993). *Handbook of Mental Control*. Englewood Cliffs, NJ: Prentice-Hall.

Weltzer, S. E., and Sweeny, J. A. (1986). Childhood amnesia: an empirical demonstration. In *Autobiographical Memory*, ed. E. Rubin, pp. 191–201. New Haven, CT: Yale University Press.

Williams, L. M. (1992). Adult memories of childhood abuse: preliminary findings from a longitudinal study. *The Advisor: American Professional Society on the Abuse of Children* 5(3):19–21.

PART III

Treatment Issues in Working with Adolescents

INTRODUCTION TO PART III

Working with adolescents therapeutically has often been described as challenging, and the literature is replete with examples of the difficulties as well as the rewards of this work. The Reiss-Davis Child Study Center has always served the mental health needs of adolescents as well as children. Over the past year we have broadened our age level from 18 to 25 to include older adolescents and young adults in need of diagnostic and therapeutic services. Knowing that one cannot work the same way with 13- to 25-year-olds, we have developed different methods and approaches to coincide with different phases that adolescents and young adults move through. This section focuses on new directions in working with specific issues facing these very interesting and often challenging patients.

Chapter 11, "Joys and Pains in Treating Adolescents in Psychotherapy," by Irving H. Berkovitz, looks at both the transference and countertransference issues that may arise when working with adolescents in group therapy, especially focusing on the range of feelings that can occur in working with this population. Group therapy with adolescents is compared with that of adults, and issues such as communication of feelings as expressed in younger versus older adolescent groups are discussed.

Chapter 12, "Snow White: The Treatment of a Young Woman with Crohn's Disease," by Rita Lynn, examines the relationship between the mind and body when illness arises. Through case illustration of the treatment of an adolescent with Crohn's disease, the emotional components affecting symptomatology of the disease are described along with the psychodynamic treatment factors that, in conjunction with medical intervention, proved successful.

Chapter 13, "The Death of a Parent: The Spirit of Healing through Individual and Group Therapy," by Bonnie S. Mark, examines the dimensions of reactions experienced by children and adolescents during the illness and death of a parent. This chapter presents a framework for working in depth with clients who are dealing with issues of death and loss, as well as treatment implications through the case description of a teenage boy who experienced various defensive phases as he worked through conscious and unconscious reactions that haunted him throughout his high school and college years.

Chapter 14, "The Unborn Mind of the Therapist: Psychotherapy and the Buddhist Traditions," by Shelley Alhanati, examines the difficulties of adolescents who operate in life as if they have never been drawn into a true world of self and other, rather spending their energies counteracting an underlying deadness. The author, using a case illustration, addresses treatment issues where there is an early infancy bonding failure that results in the child's attempts to compensate by prematurely providing a sense of aliveness when in fact the true experience is a yearning for peaceful non-aliveness.

Chapter 15, "Treating Shame in Adolescence: Integrating Intersubjectivity, Object Relations, and Mind-Body Healing," by Nancy P. VanDerHeide and Ronald A. Alexander, explores the issue of shame in adolescence—a time that a patient is critically involved in the tasks of identity formation and development of healthy self-esteem, both of which can be impacted by shame. The authors look not only at the theoretical roots of shame but also at the relationship of mind-body healing to psychodynamic psychotherapy, and how the integration of these two approaches is effective in dealing with the treatment of shame in adolescent patients.

11

Joys and Pains in Treating Adolescents in Psychotherapy

Irving H. Berkovitz

Most of the literature about countertransference, attunement, empathy, and intersubjectivity pertains especially to the feelings and thoughts that occur in a therapeutic interaction between therapists and adult patients. This chapter focuses on therapists' feelings when treating adolescent patients. While many of the feelings to be described may occur in the treatment of adults as well, there are important distinctions when treating adolescents.

REVIEW OF THE LITERATURE

Brandell (1992) provides an excellent historical review of the concept of countertransference. Marshall (1979) observes that countertransference is more intense in treating children and adolescents than in treating adults. He notes that "the violent and concrete projections of the child into the analyst may be difficult to contain. The intensity of the child's dependence, of his positive and negative transference, the primitive nature of his fantasies, tend to arouse the analyst's own unconscious anxieties" (p. 411).

It is soon evident to therapists of patients of this age group that there is a rekindling of one's old experiences or desires (or of lost opportunities) and even envy or pity of youth. So often when supervising therapists of teenagers, the supervisor will hear statements such as, "I was like that when I was a teenager," "Today's teenagers certainly are different," or "I'm glad I'm no longer a teen." This also could relate to the fact that the child or adolescent is on the way up, while the caregiving adult is on the way down.

Kernberg (1976) refers to two basic concepts of countertransference, the classical and totalistic. The *classical* comprises only the analyst's reaction to the patient's transference. The *totalistic* comprises the total emotional reaction of the therapist to the patient in the treatment situation, both conscious and unconscious. This view, to my mind, gives value to all feelings in the therapist and allows for a positive and helpful use of such feelings in the therapy.

Giovacchini (1992) distinguishes homogeneous and idiosyncratic countertransference reactions. The *homogeneous* "is regarded as a reaction that is somewhat predictable" and "most therapists . . . might be expected to react in a certain way"; for example, "if a patient reveals homicidal fantasies and then behaves threateningly, most clinicians would feel fearful. . . . *Idiosyncratic* reactions are defined as reactions that arise from the 'unique qualities' of the background of the therapist" (Brandell 1992, p. 10). For example, a therapist who had experienced divorce in his own childhood could identify or empathize with his adolescent patient being stressed by the same event, or might need to control painful memories in both the patient and himself.

While some authors have seen countertransference as an indication of residual psychopathology in the therapist (Friend 1972), others view feelings about the patient more positively as normal growth and development that the patient induces in the therapist. In describing therapy with adults, Natterson (1991) states, "The subjective life of the therapist is coequal to that of the patient in creating the therapeutic transaction. The therapist's subjectivity is not merely countertransference, but an indispensable component of the therapeutic process" (p. 15).

Burke and Cohler (1992) prefer the use of the concept *counter-resonance* to describe the process through which the patient's transferential enactments are absorbed, subject to analytic reflection, and finally made available to the patient as the therapist's empathic resonance. This comes close to recent emphasis on intersubjectivity where processes in the therapist need review as they impinge on and give rise to the patient's productions (Stolorow et al. 1987). I feel this is also close to Kernberg's totalistic concept. However, I will discuss this issue in terms of the feelings of the therapist rather than the theoretic nuances of the various authors in the countertransference literature. Also, I will be describing the context of office treatment of the adolescent rather than treatment in institutional or residential settings where other ancillary personnel become involved with and arouse transferential and countertransferential currents in the patient and the therapist.

SOURCES OF FEELINGS

Feelings aroused in the therapist when treating teenagers may have several sources: (1) unconscious or conscious feelings rearoused by the patient related to significant persons in the therapist's past (parents, siblings, friends, etc.), including the therapist's own children, grown or still teenagers; (2) conscious reactions to the personality and actions of the teen patient; (3) activation in the therapist of feelings about teenagers in general, including negative (or positive) cultural biases toward teens; (4) the reality of being an older person relating to a younger person, and feelings about one's own aging; (5) unconscious feelings in the therapist from his or her own teenage years, including experiences with peers at that period.

JOY AND PAIN

I classify the array of therapists' feelings toward teen patients into two broad categories—those that involve the therapist's feeling pleasure, joy, delight, and approval of the teen patient, and those that involve the therapist's feeling pain, fear, anger, and disapproval of the teen. These feelings can often influence the choice of therapeutic technique, as will be discussed later (Zaslow 1985). Certainly the joys influence why some therapists, including myself, choose to continue working with adolescents despite the special difficulties encountered in working with this age group.

Positive or negative feelings toward a patient are inevitable and unavoidable in any significant therapeutic interaction, especially one where a young person is challenging, frustrating, causing concern, or being sexually provocative. The therapist has to have feelings of reaction and empathy, especially with young persons (and often with their parents), in order to respond appropriately and effectively. In the effort to understand and be attuned to a teenager's rapid and sometimes baffling productions, the therapist may be intellectually and emotionally preoccupied and not be able to pay full attention to how the young person is making the therapist feel and how these feelings can be of help in the therapy. The pace and change of topics during sessions, especially with younger teens, can be taxing. In addition, the unconscious feelings are more difficult to determine at a particular moment.

A critical aspect of therapy is what one feels about the patient, and how these feelings are, or are not, conveyed to the patient. This is especially crucial with adolescent patients. Most adolescents, especially those in treatment, have experienced intimidation, mistrust, suspicion, or defiance regarding the adults in their lives. These feelings often recur with their therapists. In reality, adolescents do have less power relative to adults, and each reacts to this disproportion. Their sensitivity to wounded narcissism and feelings of shame can be extremely acute and traumatic. The feelings of hurt after an even unintended nonempathic comment from the therapist can be so deep that the teen's evasive or angry actions are instantaneous and often are correctable (if discerned) only after strenuous efforts. Yet the therapist often must "retain his interpretive stance while being provoked or while being loved one moment and hated the next" (Van Leeuwen 1977, p. 272).

The feelings thus aroused in the therapist can be considered the therapist's contribution to the therapeutic situation, and thus a normal, natural interpersonal event. When *countertransference* is used as a pejorative term to label such reactive feelings as indicating bad therapeutic technique, there can be interference with optimal awareness and use of these feelings in the therapy. For example, a hospitalized 14-year-old boy said to his therapist, "I know where you live and I could come to your house and rape your wife and kill your children." While the therapist might have felt some concern, his knowledge of the youngster allowed him to process this so that he did not react punitively or defensively, by threatening removal of pass privileges, for example. He did respond with, "That would be terrible." He may have interpreted the boy's anger and provocativeness at a later time. To my mind, this exemplifies the ability to process countertransference feelings and consider the murderous feelings on a larger superego and empathic level than just as a communication of patient–therapist anger (Bleiberg 1994).

ABSTINENCE AND SILENCE

An important question relevant to therapy with adolescents (and with many adults) is, When is it appropriate to use abstinence (or silence) as a therapeutic stance? Often the silence may be used as a respite for when a therapist is confused or angered by events in the session. The silent interlude may give the therapist a chance to think and work out an appropriate response or to get control of her or his feelings. Some analysts question the role of abstinence generally. Lindon (1994) states that at times "the analyst's silence can be an optimal provision," but it is necessary to determine "what provision is optimal for facilitating the analytic work at *that moment with that particular patient*" (p. 552).

With an adolescent, the therapist's abstinent posture can often be (mis)interpreted as indifference, hostility, or the wish not to be involved. Yet, for the therapist to be constantly actively involved can interfere with objectivity and the opportunity for reflection by patient and therapist. Some middle path of interactivity and neutrality is needed. Silences with this age group often need to be shortened by the empathic therapist to keep anxiety within tolerable limits and to convey caring. Moments of silence can arouse feelings of terror, threat, and implications of inadequacy, especially to younger teens. Certainly, exploration of what preceded the silence or of feelings during the silence are relevant and are topics for discussion if the teen is ready for that degree of inquiry. The silence may be protective, or even hostile, when used by the teenager.

A therapist can be sorely vexed by and concerned about long periods of silence. A unique example of such prolonged silence is provided by Sarles (1994). He describes the therapy with a moderately anorexic 16-year-old girl.

"Cheryl did not talk with me again [after the fifth visit] in her twice-a-week therapy from Thanksgiving to Easter [five months]. But she always showed up on time even after she got her driver's license and the drive was ninety minutes to my office and ninety minutes' return" (p. 65). In the silent sessions, Sarles was "frustrated, weary, puzzled, angry, disappointed and stumped" (p. 65). All his interpretations about her silence were met with silence. To reduce her (and his) anxiety, he read to her books on repair of Volkswagen automobiles (her parents had bought her one), books on horsemanship, articles from *Time* and *National Geographic*, and even Bruch's *The Golden Cage*, a classic text on anorexia. "One day (after 5 months), Cheryl stood up, hit the arm of the chair and said, 'OK, Dr. Sarles, that's it!' She left and never returned" (p. 65). The parents remained in therapy the remainder of the school year. Sarles learned from their therapist that Cheryl continued to do well academically, developed several new close friends, had a part-time job, and her spirits and behavior at home were fine. This helped to contain his anxiety. He received a high-school graduation announcement, and seven years later an engagement announcement.

After a seven-year absence, Cheryl returned one day, unannounced. She talked continuously, including about the silent sessions. She said, "I really tried to get you and sometimes I did. I know I did. But you always let me come back. It gave me a chance to look at my family, at myself, at my friends (or lack of friends). You could have gotten very angry, but you didn't. You were tolerant" (p. 66). Sarles ventured several speculations, including that he provided a "holding environment" (Winnicott 1949, p. 72), where she had a feeling of control and power. She needed the time and space to grow, and "she did feel fed and nourished without needing to put on weight" (Sarles 1994, p. 71). Not all therapists (or parents) will tolerate this long a duration of silent sessions. Sarles did not discuss what process within him allowed his tolerance and endurance, but he did state, "The therapist should have a gleam or twinkle in his eye for the patient and serve and act as a parent but not *the* parent" (p. 71).

If the therapist is open and subscribes to the concept of counterresonance (Burke and Cohler 1992), he or she can learn and change from interactions with some patients, especially as a result of direct suggestions or criticisms. At times, for example, the teen may be using criticism of our style of dress or office decor as a defensive distraction from being under scrutiny or to try to create equality. At other times, the teen may be trying to be sincerely, but tactlessly, helpful, or to relate as he or she might to a peer, or to invest a part of her- or himself in the decor and, therefore, the therapy. At times though, the intent can be truly hostile and a wish to hurt and/or test the tolerance and reactions of the therapist. More directly, some perceptive teens (or adults) may make a comment about the therapist's personality or therapeutic style; children of therapists are frequently more apt to do this.

The subject of treating children of therapists or of colleagues warrants separate consideration. Often, these teens have more sophistication, real or surface, having heard the vocabulary of therapy at home. They may pretend knowledge, or may have been subjected to valid interpretations from parent(s), thus reducing the value of these same interpretations by the therapist. If the therapist knows the parents, feelings may enter as if the parents were in the room judging the therapist. Or the therapist may regard the teen as a member of the therapeutic family, almost as his or her own child.

Occasionally, an articulate teen's comments may be accurate and uncomfortably surprising. Zaslow (1985) describes therapy with a bright 16-year-old boy who focused on the therapist's "oversolicitousness and seriousness which replicated in large measure his experiences with anxiously concerned parents" (p. 529). Zaslow validated his perceptiveness about "oversolicitousness and seriousness being character traits of mine, not all generated by him. I resolved to change, to 'lighten up,' to see if I could change the tone of therapy. In sessions I labeled and laughed at absurdities without exploring or belaboring. As I changed, he changed. Therapy became fun and playful—no longer obsessional, though we still worked at clarifying" (p. 530). This may seem to some to be excessive overaccommodation and yielding, even to the point of avoiding hostility that might have ensued from deeper examination of the patient's anger with his parents and the therapist. Many teens may say "You're just like my parent(s)." The therapist may need to evaluate the truth of this and discuss it, or possibly alter his style as Zaslow did. Not all therapists can, or will, change this easily. Not all teens can be articulate or objective enough to point out a therapist's personality traits. Also, might grandiose, omnipotent feelings be encouraged by empowering the adolescent in this way?

On the other hand, other kinds of pain can be aroused in the therapist, for example, when the teen will have nothing of what the therapist has to offer, and spits at, or derides, his or her best efforts. Often this rejection will not be overt but more passive, indicated by missed sessions, dropping out of treatment, or other evasive tactics. It can be even more painful to deal with the more narcissistic, arrogant, manipulative, or scheming teen patients. They may twist and turn every which way to outwit the therapist's attempts to make contact or to advocate some protective measures to avoid self-damaging actions, such as car accidents or unwanted pregnancy. Yet, even while being provoked, one can marvel at the creativity and inventiveness that may enter into some of these negative actions.

USE OF HUMOR

Humor in therapy with all age groups can be effective in improving perspective, reinforcing insight and self-awareness, and bringing a refreshing tone to the interaction for both parties. However, there often may be the danger of humor made at the patient's expense, an unconscious piece of hostile countertransference. This is especially possible with teenagers whose views of the world can at times strike the therapist as naive, bizarre, childish, or ludicrous.

Schimel (1993) feels that humor permits "a broader perspective from which to view the patient's concerns," that humor lightens "the gloomy, overly serious and dark outlook on life that characterizes many adolescents and some therapists" (p. 53) (cf. Zaslow 1985). Some therapists may be reluctant to mention examples of humor, perhaps because of Kubie's (1971) warning against the possible destructive use of humor. Schimel states that later in his life Kubie felt humor could be used in a nondestructive manner.

Schimel (1993) offers the following vignette:

> A very competitive prowess-oriented adolescent, who happened to be both a great athlete and an intelligent youngster, started the hour in a gloomy mood and recounted a number of personal defeats.
>
> *Patient:* And not only that, but I'm feeling lousy. I had to go to the doctor.
> *Therapist:* What's wrong?
> *Patient:* I have Victor's disease.
> *Therapist:* Congratulations. What did you win this time?
> *Patient:* I didn't win anything. I have sore gums, ulcers, the doctor said. He was surprised. He said only poor people who are malnourished get it.
> *Therapist:* Oh, that's Vincent's disease.
> *Patient:* I can't believe it. You've been telling me I'm too busy with who's on top. Victor's disease. So that's my problem. [p. 52]

Presumably, the patient laughed at this point. Schimel reports, "In my experience, few adolescents are so damaged that they cannot appreciate humor or cannot laugh, even at themselves" (p. 52).

PROJECTIVE IDENTIFICATION

A relevant concept for understanding feelings caused in the therapist by patients is projective identification, in which patients can stimulate the same feelings in the therapist that they have in themselves, or feelings their parents had toward them, such as helplessness, frustration, or admiration. Wallace and Wallace (1985) describe such a case.

Carole, aged 13, was "silent in many sessions, sometimes even falling asleep, reading magazines, or writing letters to her friends" (p. 473). The therapist felt overwhelmed and defeated. She learned from the parents' therapist that Carole's mother had felt overwhelmed at Carole's birth. The therapist then identified her countertransference with these feelings of Carole's mother. She began to feel less overwhelmed. Nine months later, Carole's functioning had changed dramatically. She no longer slept in the sessions and was performing better in all areas of her life. There was no indication that the therapist had communicated any of her knowledge of mother's feelings explicitly to Carole.

COMMUNICATING FEELINGS TO ADOLESCENTS

Should the therapist verbally make known to the adolescent his or her joy, pain, or other reactions? With some adolescents, communicating approval or disapproval after some trust has been established can be useful feedback. With others, it can be hurtful or threatening. Some positive or negative feelings are undoubtedly communicated nonverbally, for example in facial expressions. Communicating pleasure or approval directly to a patient has risks. Yet, many patients, adult as well as adolescent, have had little experience with receiving praise (or calm, nonangry criticism) from authority figures, and need to be helped to accept this comfortably. Disapproval or criticism of behavior is more difficult and needs to be communicated with great care and discretion and not in moments of anger.

Perhaps my use of the word *pain* in the therapist seems inappropriate to the stereotype of the "good therapist." We are, after all, not expected to feel pain with patients, but are expected to concentrate on providing help with minimum discomfort. Yet, some adolescents have adapted to dysfunctional family situations by learning to inflict pain in self-defense, whether to validate their own presence or by identifying with aggressors in the family. This may be so especially in cases where physical or sexual abuse of the teenager has occurred. Certainly, suicidal or other self-damaging behaviors by the teen will arouse pain and appropriate concern in the therapist. The therapist may feel relief and offer congratulations after the survival, even though this may risk reinforcing secondary gains from such actions (Berkovitz 1981).

Some therapists are prone to share events from their own adolescence as a way of trying to universalize the teen's experiences or to improve the therapeutic alliance. This self-disclosure needs monitoring since it may at times represent a desire by the therapist to join the adolescent in his or her youthfulness or narcissistic joy. Occasionally, sharing a commonality may reduce the adult–child gap, but few lives are identical and important differences may be overlooked.

GENDER AND SEXUAL ISSUES

A perennial question is whether the therapist should be of the same or different gender as the teenager. Young girls (ages 11 to 14) may feel embarrassed or even blocked about discussing with a handsome young male psychiatrist their anxiety about the approaching menarche or concern about flat-chestedness. The male psychiatrist, especially if he is young, unmarried, or sexually uncomfortable, may be equally embarrassed. The pleasure in working with a sexually attractive and flirtatious nymphet can be a risky trial for some male therapists. Reminders of the attractive adolescent females one did, or did not, get to know or get involved with in one's own adolescence may be revived. Or feelings and actions toward or from an attractive sister or mother may be rearoused. Vicarious pleasure and titillation may occur in a male or female therapist hearing details of adolescent sexual activities. Undue intensity of this vicarious pleasure may justify referral to another therapist. Yet, each teen has sexual anxieties and misinformation that need to be discussed with an older person. Risks of undue anxiety in the teen may give rise to accusations of sexual harassment, which may need the therapist's awareness and protection as well.

On the other gender axis, in my experience of supervising female therapists of younger adolescent boys, I have noted awkwardness in some therapists in their dealing with the male aggressive urges or the early male sexual curiosity and experimentation. Similarly, some boys may flaunt sexual questions or remarks and even overtures, testing the controls and countertransference, especially of young, attractive female therapists. However, secure, skilled therapists of either sex can often surmount these difficulties and provide an empathic, useful therapy. In this era of more frequent absent fathers, a male therapist for many adolescent boys (and girls) may be crucial to try to repair the lack of a father.

PARENTAL FEELINGS

The occurrence of the therapist's parental feelings toward the teen patient has already been touched on explicitly and implicitly as some of the joyful or painful feelings a therapist may have. When a therapist is helping a younger person, positive or negative parental feelings toward the patient are likely, especially if the therapist is also a parent. However, as a parent, an adult has expectations, ongoing mutual dependencies, and narcissistic involvements with a child. This relationship is similar to but significantly different from the time-limited, financially involved connection of the therapist to a young patient. Yet some therapeutic connections may at times become extended, even lifelong relationships with letters, phone calls, and visits, providing many parent-like functions for the young person. This is still not usually with the full commitment of the parental relationship.

Many patients, of any age, in the heat of transference feelings may wish to be adopted and parented by the therapist. Perhaps young patients have this wish more often than adult patients. Some young patients have overwhelming needs for nurturance because of the loss of the parents, or of having been adopted, or of living with unavailable or dysfunctional families. A concerned therapist will often be deeply touched and even have the fantasy of wanting to reparent or adopt the young person and supply the missing nurturance. Occasionally, these fantasy wishes may represent competitive feelings with the patient's parents or even with one's own parents. These feelings can at times aid the therapy and convey a sincere sense of caring, which can help establish a positive therapeutic alliance. But at times these feelings can also interfere, and frighten the young person who may be trying to separate from or find a way to express anger to his or her parent. In these cases, the frustrated reparenting impulse may expose the therapist to feeling hurt, unappreciated, and disappointed, especially when the angry side of the teen's ambivalence comes to the surface.

MONITORING FEELINGS

The chronically depressed, suicidal teen can arouse pain and distress, as a difficult, anxiety-laden, therapeutic challenge. Unconscious reactions to such pain may well influence our actions unless we can monitor those reactions carefully, such as by first self-monitoring, or using ongoing supervision by, or consultation with, a trusted colleague who is able to point out interfering countertransference events in a sensitive, nonjudgmental way. The results of effective supervision have been discribed in several studies (Alonso 1985, Myers 1992). Audiotapes or videotapes of the sessions, if not too disturbing to the therapy, provide an excellent in-depth view of the interaction and, especially with videotapes, the nonverbal elements. Reporting from notes is prone to omissions and censoring, but can still be very useful.

Self-monitoring procedures can include writing notes about feelings immediately after the session, including free associations to features of the patient and/or interactions. Dreams by the therapist in which the patient may appear, literally or disguised, can provide clues about past parts of the therapist's life being activated. Rachman (1975), writing about group therapy with adolescents, has suggested associating colors or animals to patients. Depending on the meaning of the particular color or animal, this can provide a clue to the emotion being stirred in the therapist by the adolescent.

PARENTS

Another perennial issue in the treatment of teens is the therapist's type of alliance or battle with the parents. The parents' natures can influence the joy or pain of the therapy significantly. If the parents are likable, famous, wealthy, or otherwise influential, these factors may sway some therapists to be biased toward the parents, especially in familial conflict situations. In other cases, parents may resent the therapist's building a close, trusting relationship with their child when they could not do so. These parents may sabotage the therapy in numerous subtle or overt ways, even breaking it off despite possibilities of suicide or serious destructive action by the adolescent. One of the most painful situations is where the parents are divorced but are still fighting. Often, one of the parents supports the therapy and the other, usually the father, does not, occasionally to the point of not paying the bill and not being receptive to parenting advice.

In younger teens, the need to be driven to the appointments allows the parents' ambivalence to enter, often influencing the punctuality in arriving at the appointments. These emotional conflicts may give a clue to the teenager's family problems, but also arouse feelings in the therapist. These feelings may cloud or interfere with objectivity, biasing the reaction to the teen or the parents. Ideally, the conflict can give the therapist some idea of how the teen patient feels about the parents' habits, and a chance to share victimhood.

HATE

It has been reassuring to several generations of therapists to read Winnicott (1949):

> However much he [the therapist] loves his patients he cannot avoid hating them and fearing them, and the better he knows this, the less will hate and fear be motives determining what he does to his patients. In certain analyses, the analyst's hate is actually sought by the patient. It seems that he can believe in being loved only after reaching being hated. [p. 71]

I do not believe Winnicott is advocating indiscriminate expression of anger to the patient, but rather our ability to admit to ourselves that we may feel hate toward some patients. We should be honest enough to analyze ourselves to try to learn from and lessen the hate, or to consult about it with a colleague, or, if need be, to transfer the patient. Resuming one's own therapy may be a necessary step in some cases as well.

In a more extended self-revealing point, Anthony (1988) reports,

> Over the years that I treated him, Fred's reactions often made me squirm within myself. I reminded myself that there were at least twenty-one good reasons why the "good enough" therapist sometimes hated his adolescent patient and, at times, toyed with the idea of annihilating him. That the patient is creative in no way implies that he is easy to deal with or that he follows the therapist's line rather than his own idiosyncratic path of therapeutic progress. [p. 201]

JOYS

Much of this chapter has been concerned with the painful interactions with teens. These are obviously the ones that prompt families to bring teen offspring to our offices for our therapeutic attention and assistance. However, there are also many satisfactions and joys that keep many of us (including myself) working with teens. Moments of joy are fortunately unavoidable while treating most adolescents. The teen may delight us with a happy sense of discovery or the naive enunciation of an insight after weeks of seeming stalemate. Or a youngster finally has the courage and knowledge to speak up to a dominating sibling, or to assert him- or herself appropriately to a parent or employer, or understand an aspect of self-functioning that has been elusive. Or a delinquent, gang-involved youngster gradually gains a more empathic awareness of others' pains and leaves the gang. There is the joy of seeing a depression lift and the adolescent begin to experience some of the opportunities open to other less disturbed adolescents, such as experiencing awakening sexual feelings, or feelings of mastery with learning new information or solving problems rather than hiding in fear. There can be a special joy of achieving a unity between adolescent, parents, and therapist. The idealism and optimism of many adolescents, especially after depression is relieved, can refresh and gladden a sometimes weary and jaded therapist.

However, there may be mixed pleasure in seeing an adolescent graduate from high school to go off to college and terminate therapy, especially when a point of resolution has not been achieved. Successful participation in an after-school sport or job often requires missing sessions or flexibility in scheduling appointments. The boost to self-esteem, social skills, and feelings of mastery attained in these activities can supplement and advance the therapy rather than contribute to avoiding necessary self-exploration. Also, the therapist often has the dilemma of whether to try to keep in contact after the teenager has left town, or instead wait for the teen to call. At times, further therapy can be conducted in phone calls or, occasionally, if a teen is phobic about coming to the office (Lindon 1988).

Joy in seeing young patients grow validates our skills and appropriately pleases our narcissism. This same pleasure does occur in therapy with adults, but differently. With adolescents, is it more like a parent's satisfaction? Yet, unlike with a parent, successful therapy usually means loss of the ongoing connection with the teen.

YOUNGER TEENS

Perhaps a greater amount of pain occurs when treating teens younger than 16, especially the 13- and 14-year-olds. Their knowledge of reality is less than that of 16-year-olds, and their actions more often are impulsive and expressive of a demanding, even reckless independence that is often difficult for adults to accept. If psychopathology and/or drug use is mixed with this approach, therapist anxiety about risky, dangerous actions may be more prevalent.

The average adult, even a well-trained therapist, may feel alien to the age period of 12 to 15. Here, action so often prevails over reason. These impulsive actions may need monitoring to protect the teen, but also the teen may be discovering the joys, pains, and complexities of peer-group relating, with its frequent disappointments, changes of friends, and alternating passions. The therapist may have to sit through uncomfortable silences, or hear endless accounts of details about friends whose names are difficult to remember from one session to the next. Most adults have repressed the memories of this painful period more than of the period age 15 to 18. The earlier years of 12 to 15 see the most intense, almost inchoate, moments of feeling alone, abandoned, or betrayed, but also often of feeling happy and exuberant.

To be effective with teens the therapist needs to review memories of his or her own former teen pleasures, especially when one first began to learn self-assertion, even if it included pleasure in thwarting adults. Many training programs wisely include trainees' bringing in photos, diaries, or other memorabilia from their teenage years to make more vivid the empathy with teen patients. If the therapist never rebelled as a teen, might this preclude sufficient empathy with teens who are in major rebellion? Most of us in the mental health field were well-behaved students earning good grades to get into college and graduate school programs. Perhaps there was little chance or wish for rebellion, or we suppressed the wish. A therapist need not have experienced all the same travails and problems of his or her patients to be an effective therapist. But in working with this younger age group some congruence of earlier difficulties may be especially helpful.

WHEN THE THERAPIST ATTENDS A PATIENT'S GRADUATION, CONFIRMATION, OR BAR/BAT MITZVAH

The therapist will often be invited by the youth or the parents to attend one of these milestones in the development of the teenager, such as graduation, stage performance, bar/bat mitzvah, confirmation, and so on. Attending these events can have significant effects on the treatment relationship and its effectiveness. The decision of whether or not to attend needs consideration as to consequences for the therapeutic relationship. If the therapist does attend, there is the opportunity to witness firsthand the dynamics of the extended family more vividly than has been encountered in the office. One may witness the impact of parents, siblings, and extended family members on the patient and her or his coping skills with these persons who may or may not have been described in the sessions. This information often can advance the therapy and enrich the relationship with the youth. Rejection of the invitation may inflict hurt and be taken as not caring by the therapist. The caring therapist would usually want to go to share the teen's feelings of triumph or anxiety. In my many years of working with teens, it was expeditious to attend the ceremony as part of the audience, and not the family party that usually followed. The party may involve more compromising social/familial ramifications. Family members will often make comments or ask questions about the therapy, which cannot be answered without betraying confidentiality. Occasionally, negative reactions occur because the therapist is seen now in a human context and not only as the savant in the office.

On another level, but also representing a significant rite of passage for the teen, is the acquisition of the first car. The therapist may be invited to admire and share the pride or even to be taken for a ride. There may be some hesitation by the therapist because of concern about the expertness of the teen's driving ability. Yet, refusal again may be taken as lack of interest in the youth's growth and entry into adulthood. Each instance needs consideration.

Other activities outside the office, such as taking walks and visits to snack shops or playgrounds, may be appropriate. These are useful at times to help the teen relax and talk more freely away from the formality of an office setting. At times, however, these activities can be used to reduce tension more in the therapist, which may also be desirable.

More often self-monitoring is necessary to distinguish the source of the stress. If the therapist participates in extraoffice activities, there may then be the dilemma of how to avoid fostering expectations of continued less formal and intimate interactions that the therapist won't or can't provide later. Such activities may also give an action tone to the therapy, especially with younger teens, and make it difficult to reestablish a focus on examining motivation and feelings. Yet relating in a less verbal mode may be very useful for some adolescents, the younger ones especially.

SUMMARY

This brief overview of a large subject has considered the range of feelings that may arise when treating adolescents. The emotional lability of many teens, especially the younger ones, and the different sense of time, commitment, and respect for space of the other person make this therapy very different from that with most adults. A knowledge of treating children can be helpful since so many of the behaviors and attitudes are evolving from earlier ones. Despite some pains in the process, there may be joys and the satisfaction of working with young persons who will for a few moments or longer allow themselves to join our helping efforts. In addition, work with this age group gives the therapist a chance to recontact and review his/her own adolescent history.

Therapists treating or contemplating treating adolescents need to pay attention to, respect, and learn from their own feelings rather than reject them as coming only from unanalyzed parts of themselves. Such feelings can give clues to feelings raging in the teen and enhance self-understanding as well as the therapy of the teen. Awareness and acceptance of these feelings can help preclude unknowingly influencing the treatment in an untoward way. With troubled teens, the treatment is difficult enough without this added complication.

ACKNOWLEDGMENTS

I am grateful for the early learning opportunities I received when working as a volunteer therapist at the Reiss-Davis Child Study Center during the years 1954 to 1960. I want to thank Max Sugar, M.D., John A. Lindon, M.D., and Heiman Van Dam, M.D., for their assistance.

REFERENCES

Alonso, A. (1985). *The Quiet Profession.* New York: Macmillan.

Anthony, E. J. (1988). The creative therapeutic encounter at adolescence. *Adolescent Psychiatry* 15:194–216.

Berkovitz, I. H. (1981). Feelings of powerlessness and the role of violent actions in adolescents. *Adolescent Psychiatry* 9:477–492.

Bleiberg, E. (1994). *The borderline adolescent.* Presented at the meeting of the Southern California Society for Adolescent Psychiatry, Los Angeles, CA.

Brandell, J. R., ed. (1992). *Countertransference in Psychotherapy with Children and Adolescents.* Northvale, NJ: Jason Aronson.

Burke, N., and Cohler, B. J. (1992). Psychodynamic psychotherapy of eating disorders. In *Countertransference in Psychotherapy with Children and Adolescents*, ed. J. R. Brandell, pp. 163–189. Northvale, NJ: Jason Aronson.

Friend, M. R. (1972). Psychoanalysis of adolescents. In *Handbook of Child Psychoanalysis*, ed. B. Wolman. New York: Van Nostrand Reinhold.

Giovacchini, P. L. (1992). The severely disturbed adolescent. In *Countertransference in Psychotherapy with Children and Adolescents*, ed. J. R. Brandell, pp. 141–162. Northvale, NJ: Jason Aronson.

Kernberg, O. (1976). *Borderline Conditions and Pathological Narcissism.* New York: Jason Aronson.

Kubie, L. (1971). The destructive potential of humor in psychotherapy. *American Journal of Psychiatry* 127:861–866.

Lindon, J. A. (1988). Psychoanalysis by telephone. *Bulletin of the Menninger Clinic* 52(6):521–528.

———(1994). Gratification and provision in psychoanalysis, "Should we get rid of the Rule of Abstinence?" *Psychoanalytic Dialogues* 4(4):549–582.

Marshall, R. J. (1979). Countertransference with children and adolescents. In *Countertransference*, ed. L. Epstein and A. H. Feiner, pp. 407–444. New York: Jason Aronson.

Myers, W. A. (1992). *Shrink Dreams.* New York: Simon and Schuster.

Natterson, J. (1991). *Beyond Countertransference.* Northvale, NJ: Jason Aronson.

Rachman, A. W. (1975). *Identity Group Psychotherapy with Adolescents.* Springfield, IL: Charles C Thomas.

Sarles, R. M. (1994). Transference and countertransference with adolescents: personal reflections. *American Journal of Psychotherapy* 48:64–74.

Schimel, J. L. (1993). Reflections on the function of humor in psychotherapy, especially with adolescents. In *Advances in Humor and Psychotherapy*, ed. W. F. Fry, Jr. and W. A. Salameh, pp. 47–56. Sarasota, FL: Professional Resource Press.

Stolorow, R., Brandchaft, B., and Atwood, G. (1987). *Psychoanalytic Treatment: An Intersubjective Approach.* Hilldale, NJ: Analytic Press.

Van Leeuwen, K. (1977). Adolescent's countertransference in adolescent psychoanalysis. *International Journal of Psychiatry, Psychology, Psychoanalysis, and Neurology* 1:271–275.

Wallace, N. L., and Wallace, M. E. (1985). Transference/countertransference issues in the treatment of an acting-out adolescent. *Adolescent Psychiatry* 12:468–477.

Winnicott, D. W. (1949). Hate in the countertransference. *International Journal of Psycho-Analysis* 30:69–74.

Zaslow, S. L. (1985). Countertransference issues in psychotherapy with adolescents. *Adolescent Psychiatry* 12:524–534.

12

Snow White: The Treatment of a Young Woman with Crohn's Disease

Rita Lynn

There has always been a variety of approaches to the treatment of Crohn's disease, and a dispute about whether there is an emotional component in its etiology or in the exacerbation of the symptoms. This chapter describes a psychodynamic treatment of this illness, working in conjunction with the available medical treatment.

Hope had the thickest medical file I had ever seen. She had been to the hospital many, many times and had innumerable investigations. Even after Crohn's disease had been diagnosed, investigations continued as every symptom was examined and treated individually, *not* as a whole picture. It later became clear just why her notes continued to expand with such alarming speed. There was an emotional correlation. When I first met Hope on the ward she looked like Snow White. She had milk-white skin, very black hair, very red lips and her clothes, which were too large for her, looked like something a wicked queen might have made her wear. She was a young adult when I first saw her but looked much younger. She was shaking and perspiring and told me that she was on the ward because she had terrifying panic attacks, blurred vision, disordered sensations in various parts of her body, a severe shortness of breath, and agoraphobia for a duration of six months, the onset of which occurred after she had broken up with her boyfriend and had smoked hash (she was not a habitual user).

She was an only child. She was born when her father was 41 and her mother was 30. When she was 2 years old her mother had a miscarriage. Her father was a retired rabbi who appeared to be timid and dominated by the mother, and Hope seemed to feel cold toward him.

Mother was extremely loud and dominating, and extremely possessive of the patient. She would answer questions addressed to the patient and would arbitrarily change the subject in an intrusive and aggressive manner whenever she felt like it. She also demanded help and answers but never paused for breath or for a response; she was a help-demanding help-refuser.

I met both parents when Hope was first admitted to the hospital. There was tremendous conflict between the parents about practically everything and this sad state had apparently been present for as long as the patient could remember. The conflict could encompass anything—money, food, religion, work, child-rearing, politics, or personal behavior. It is not surprising that the family was severely isolated, with no friends. Upon his retirement the congregation asked the rabbi to leave the house in which they had lived all their married life. This was also cause for dispute, with Mother taking the matter to court and flying into a constant temper with all and sundry.

After Hope's admission to the hospital, the family reluctantly contracted to have four focal family sessions with the psychiatric intern. The reluctance is particularly significant in that despite their ambivalent feelings about coming, the mother and father were furious when the intern missed one of the interviews. The patient said it was okay, but had tears in her eyes and then was passive.

During these sessions it emerged that the patient saw her father as a cold, inadequate man, unable to give anything, who protected himself from attack with his role of rabbi. The patient saw him as of "no therapeutic use to me." It was not clear what she meant by that, but I guessed that she meant that she could not get the response she required from him. I hoped that I would be of therapeutic use. Mother, the patient thought, was better but still of "no therapeutic use." In a way, the patient was right. Any therapeutic help was not going to come from mother or father, but from herself.

During these first few interviews the patient's symptoms dominated the sessions. The family was prepared to talk about them and wanted the symptoms "stopped" immediately—after all, we were in a hospital, were we not? In the meantime, Mother brought vitamins to the ward and visited every day. Father also visited every day but at a different time than Mother. The patient telephoned her parents at least five or six times a day between the visits.

I have introduced the family in some detail not only because I am sure that many therapists have had similar experiences of families presenting in this denying way, but also to give some picture of the system that existed in this family: while the patient was constantly complaining about how she wanted her parents to leave her alone, she constantly contacted them.

Although it is obvious how much anger was present in this family, Mother was the only one who expressed it. Hope and Father were remarkably controlled and both claimed an inability to lose their tempers. When asked what she might lose her temper about if she were to lose it, Hope said, "About how people, not just my parents, have walked all over me. Friends as well." She went on, "I feel unreal, like in a dream. I've felt like this for about 6 months and it has made me unable to take a job or to find my own place to live." She spoke in a flat, unfeeling way. I wrote in my notes at the time: "Her name is Hope but she has none."

Let us look at her history, which emerged gradually over the next few weeks. Hope was born in the East End of London and it was a normal birth. Hope was the source of conflict in the home. Mother was always taking Hope to the doctor for minor health matters, from infancy onward. The myth of a fragile, sickly child was established. There was one short period of separation from Mother when she had a miscarriage. Hope remembered being very upset by this separation.

Hope went to school from age 5 to 19, and was a good student. Mother kept her home from school often, due to all sorts of ailments, and finally kept her at home entirely, for weeks on end. In her early years Hope remembers sitting on the bed like a doll in a pretty dress and being told that she was not well enough to play outside, although she felt quite well.

Mother called her Dolly. Her clothes were always too large for her—Mother said "to grow into"—but in effect they made her look smaller. "I was angry about being kept in bed; there was nothing wrong with me." When she was kept home from school, the inspector visited and made her go back and she passed all her examinations and got her three advanced "A" level examinations (the equivalent of a high school diploma).

Hope wished to go to college but Mother thought that this would be too great a strain on her. It was only because a schoolteacher pushed her parents that Hope was allowed to attend a local teachers' training college (three-year course). Hope passed her teaching diploma at age 22 having had one year off at age 20 with Crohn's disease. This attack of Crohn's disease at age 20 brought her to my hospital and into the care of a very enlightened internist. He started to control her Crohn's with medication and suggested that she see a psychiatrist. This caused great consternation in the family, as anything "physical" was totally acceptable while anything "mental" was shameful and frightening. However, she saw the psychiatrist, who wisely suggested that the best treatment for her would be to leave home and go back to college. She improved.

Crohn's disease, which presents with painful abdominal spasms and both obstruction and chronic diarrhea, is a disease of unknown etiology. It is defined as a chronic granulomatous inflammatory disease, commonly involving the terminal ileum, with scarring and thickening of the bowel wall. It frequently leads to intestinal obstruction and fistula and abscess formation. In Hope's case the symptoms of Crohn's had been present in milder form since age 18 and had finally become acute when she went to college.

Since age 11 (puberty), Hope shared a bed with Mother and did not like it. Mother did not sleep in the same room as Father. Nominally, Hope had been living away from home since leaving college, but she had actually gone home to eat dinner most nights and spent a lot of time there. When she left college she became a primary school teacher. She worked for one year but she was ordered about by another teacher, and left. The next year she tried dental nursing but was ordered about by a dentist, and left. She was, at the time of this episode, a primary school teacher again. She liked her job and had a good work record but she often complained that the "aggressive boys" were "too much" for her.

Her psychosexual history was as follows: menarche at age 12, and regular periods until the onset of Crohn's. She had her first boyfriend at age 18, and then several casual boyfriends. Father wanted her to mix with religious Jews but Mother did not. This caused further conflict. Six months before I saw her, she had broken up with a boyfriend with whom she had been for several months. She had sexual intercourse with him, but she was not sure about her feelings toward men. She had not had any homosexual experiences but had had some positive bisexual fantasies.

Although she had not been a habitual drug user, she had smoked marijuana occasionally and six months earlier had taken some hash with friends. She became euphoric and dizzy; she panicked and went to the hospital, but was all right by the next day. Four weeks later she took some more hash and a few days after that she developed various symptoms such as blurred vision, disordered sensations of various kinds in her body, and agoraphobia. The agoraphobia persisted.

She had just broken up with her boyfriend and so she returned to live at home with her parents, and over the subsequent months she had never been free of symptoms. She had not been out except in a car, afraid to use public transport or to walk. She stayed at home in her room and occasionally would rush out to the emergency department of our hospital, asking for reassurance that she had not been physically damaged by taking hash. She had been miserable, crying at times. Her appetite was poor, there was some loss of weight, and her sleep was disturbed during the night. When examined, she veered from being convinced that "it" was physical to saying, "I think 'it's' due to the hashish but in fact I think 'it's' due to trying to break away from home and 'it's' due to stress." This mixture of denial and insight continued to happen throughout her treatment.

I began seeing her once a week on the ward but she also attended the rest of the groups on the ward. Since it was run as a therapeutic community, these were plentiful. I doubt that I would have been able to get as far as we did without the additional support of ward work.

INDIVIDUAL PSYCHOTHERAPY

While she was in the hospital, I saw her once a week for six months. Then, after a short break, she was transferred to my group at another hospital where she remained for three years.

In the individual sessions the first month was characterized by shaking, crying, and saying things like, "I'm falling to pieces. I'm afraid I'm crumbling." She also talked in detail about the hash incident in which she had "intense blurring" of vision and described her terror at "running in the streets and shouting." The terror increased when all the symptoms returned, having gone entirely, exactly one month later, without the hash. Hope then began to say things like "It was there under the surface—the drug just brought it out." I asked about her parents' reaction. Father had said nothing. Mother was upset at first but now was saying, "Forget about the drug, it was obviously bound to come out." When talking about the drug she cried with real feeling, "It was my own fault. I feel so guilty I damaged myself."

Gradually, over the first two weeks, her symptoms of shaking receded and only returned subsequently as signposts that we were touching some difficult or painful area that she needed time and help to express. For example, when anyone talked about her returning to work or put any pressure on her to find somewhere to live, she began to shake. Yet this was precisely what she wanted to do. It was like watching someone being pulled in two directions—one to stay still, one to move. The shaking had the Parkinsonian quality to it that Oliver Sacks (1982) describes so well in *Awakenings*. He says of the shaking: "It conveys a sense of impatience, impetuosity and alacrity, as if the patient were very pressed for time, and in some it goes along with a feeling of urgency and impatience, although others, as it were, find themselves hurried against their will" (p. 9). The shaking is described by Charcot as a "cruel restlessness." These words often occurred to me as I sat with Hope in sessions. There seemed at times to be a fight going on inside her. At the same time I felt that I was starting to get a mixed message. She sat passively and wanted to know what was expected of her and yet complained constantly that her friends "bossed me around," "took over my life," and "made decisions for me," which she said she did not want. She did the same to me, both asking for something in a helpless way and threatening with her symptoms if that something was about to be given to her. She described her fear at seeing me, saying that she was afraid that therapy would be painful. But she gradually stopped shaking except when we spoke about her parents.

At the end of the second month, she was showing considerable improvement on the ward, had virtually stopped phoning her parents, and had confessed that the hash smoking that had started her present panic had taken place the night before she was to move back to her parents' home. The incident that caused the recurrence of symptoms had happened while driving back to London with an old friend. The friend called her "cold, boring, and depressed." This had rankled her and had remained in her mind all week. Gradually the symptoms had taken her over—the symptoms, not the anger.

As she phoned her parents less, she became angrier with them. She was resentful of phoning but frightened of stopping. She began to shake the most when the topic of death came up in the session, and she related this to her own murderous feelings. However, the shaking subsided when she verbally expressed her conflict at separating from her family or staying as she was. She also started to realize how much she colluded with her mother in keeping her father in his place—isolated, alone, separate, in his room with his books. But they also kept him alive, since father had already had one heart attack and was now being protected from an upset of any kind.

In the third month of therapy Hope became really angry with her parents, with herself, with other patients and with staff, and simultaneously she was ashamed of being angry. When with me, she would shout, "This is not me; every time I open my mouth, I don't know what's going to come out. How much more is there?"

But she could not express anger to her parents. When they visited she got angry but could only tentatively and indirectly express it. Once, when her father said "smile," she snapped back angrily. Once Mother was deliberately late. Hope felt angry and insecure but only sulked.

When we looked at what her fantasy was if she did express her anger, she said she was afraid they would stop loving her or might die. The two appeared to be the same. She cried when talking about their dying. Somehow she felt that the repression of her anger kept them alive and happy and, as they were only pleased if she looked happy, she had to pretend more and more. As more and more was demanded of her by her parents, she was both afraid to refuse and unable to give in any longer. She told me she was forbidden to cry in the house. "So," she said, "I developed Crohn's disease."

The next group of sessions were characterized by crying, lots and lots of it. She would shout through her tears of sadness, frustration and anger. "Here I am falling apart at your feet and there you sit and it doesn't bother you." This transference was just what was required. I felt a great many feelings from her in the sessions but whenever I interpreted any transference at all, Hope would get very secretive and would close down.

When she cried she acknowledged that she was putting off thinking about casually leaving home and telling her mother about it. "My mother will probably get ill; she is very overweight and will eat even more."

Meanwhile, Mother kept telling the patient that she thought all this psychotherapy was "a load of lies and nonsense" and "it is always the poor mother's fault, according to the psychotherapist." Although Mother could see that Hope was getting better, she continued to abuse psychiatry and continued to say that all Hope really needed was vitamins. Mother also made desperate efforts to see me privately and to telephone me, even though the therapeutic team made it clear that it was inappropriate. It was explained to her she could talk all she wanted to the rest of the team, but that I was Hope's therapist and therefore she would have to consult Hope about seeing me.

Hope's traveling phobia was also interesting. She appeared to have a desperate fear of trains, particularly as we began to look at the sexual material. I suggested that she practice going on a train with a member of staff. The next day she got on a train, alone. Then she went home for her car, insured it and brought it back to the hospital. She did not even want to discuss it. So much for the traveling phobia. Apparently she no longer had a sense of unreality in the car—she was now in control.

She also started saying no to patients' requests for lifts or favors. She was surprised when people would first get angry with her and then, to her amazement, behave quite normally toward her. She took this in. She also got very angry with me and about no longer having me all to herself when she was discharged from another hospital and joined my group.

Finally, Hope realized that if she denied all her failings and allowed none to come out, they would inevitably come out in other ways—through her symptoms.

I had been encouraging her to go out with friends. She went out with them, but quickly wanted to leave. She forced herself to stay and immediately began to feel unreal and depersonalized. From this she understood that her feelings might be producing the symptoms. She still demanded answers from me and reassurances but was not brought down or disappointed by my reticence; indeed, she was pleased because she then answered and reassured herself.

When she left the hospital she found herself a room quite far from her parents' home and was looking for a job. By the end of the six months, the separation from the parents did not seem to be the great issue that it had been, and although she still visited them every week it seemed to present no problems for her. She said she felt trapped when there, but felt fine when she left and this followed her initial success—her initial separation from me.

CROHN'S DISEASE AND ANGER

The etiology of Crohn's is clearly connected to repressed anger. During those first few months of intensive therapy and reconstitution on the ward, Hope's symptoms settled down and, although she was still on a high dose of steroids, she was managing to control the symptoms. Three months later, by the time she came into the outpatient group, living alone and holding a job, the steroids had been reduced and continued to be reduced gradually for the next year. Except for three or four very specific and dramatic incidents, Hope was free from symptoms and steroids for the last two years of the group.

The group that Hope joined was made up of four men and four women, and all her issues of sexuality and sexual relating emerged in her relationship with the men in the group. However, although she was able to relate and flirt, she was not able to be angry in the group. Anger was always the issue: its expression, its repression, and (when repressed) where it went.

One of the men in the group was extremely angry and potentially violent. He particularly frightened her, and all of us to a greater or lesser degree. But Hope was also fascinated by his rage and had extraordinary insight into his "child." After one of his outbursts she felt a return of her panic and, although free from Crohn's, felt a curious and frightening tightness in her chest and diaphragm. She, inevitably, rushed off to the nearest emergency department of the hospital. They found nothing, but the feeling persisted. A few weeks later Hope came in unable to speak and through whispers explained that she felt she had inhaled some poisonous fumes, had been poisoned and had been to the local hospital emergency department, where nothing was found. According to the hospital, there was no damage and no lump, although she felt a real lump in her throat.

This continued on and off for a few weeks. The group described "something" rising, and then Hope came in with a springy step and a lot of energy.

She told us the following: She had been driving her car in the East End of London and had suddenly stopped at a green light even though she had accelerated toward it. She just felt like stopping. Unfortunately, the cars and drivers behind her had not had the same feeling and they smashed into her and each other. The man behind her was furious and jumped out of his car and rushed over to her window, where he put his hands on the top of her half-open window and berated her for her stupidity, as only an enraged Cockney can do, in very flowery language. At this point, Hope told us, her eyes shining, instead of being frightened and cowed, she had rapidly closed her window, trapping his hands and, jumping out of her car, she had run around to him and berated him like a fishwife. So much so that he had asked for mercy and apologized and asked her to let him go. She did, and on driving to group she had an enormous lifting of all her symptoms at once. She never again had any full-blown symptoms of Crohn's.

I wish I could say that all one needs to treat Crohn's patients is to get them to explode with rage in the East End of London and then it will all be over. It's not quite like that. It took nearly a year of difficult work to get to that point and nearly two years of working through to internalize all that her body had taught her. But the Crohn's never returned and the steroid treatment was discontinued. She is, to the best of my knowledge, still clear of symptoms now many years later. The inference, not only from this patient's etiology but also from the many other cases that her psychiatrist and I collected during my 9 years at the hospital, is that anger and its suppression ("pushed down" was how Hope put it) is at the heart of the etiology of Crohn's disease.

Hope became adept at reading what her body told her and, even though she went through numerous difficult and traumatic situations in her personal life and sex life, a small twinge of former symptoms was all she needed to signal that her feelings, particularly her sadness and her anger, were "being bottled up and pushed down my body to my colon." This is her description and her own realization. Rarely in my practice have I seen a more dramatic or more clear relation between illness and internal object relations.

APPLICATIONS TO OBJECT RELATIONS THERAPY

Let us look at Hope in terms of object relations. Given a history of the unhappiness of the marriage into which Hope was born, a marriage that was truly a disappointment to both of her parents, a marriage that could only be saved for Hope's mother by having a child, a child that she had great difficulty in conceiving since her antipathy for her husband was enormous—one can clearly see that there was tremendous anxiety and depression in the home, in the marriage and, indeed, in the very breast which fed Hope in her early months of life.

Even in those early months she started her service to her parents: for her father, to protect him from further abuse and to distract her mother's attention from him; for her mother, to serve as her dolly and willingly to accept, like a transitional object for her mother, all of Mother's projections and feelings that Mother could not or would not carry herself. Hope reflected Mother's needs and wants, not knowing which were Mother's or which were hers, certainly not in those early years. Mother often took her to the doctor with all sorts of aches and pains. Mother needed attention and care—she felt she did not get this from her distant, cold, studious husband, but she got a lot of attention if she took her baby to the doctor. The baby girl was thin and did not sleep. Winnicott (1975a) described this in his note on normality and anxiety: "Undoubtedly, ever-present anxiety is the chief cause of thinness" (p. 14). He describes children who may be anxious all day, scared of any show of hostility, as a result of quarrels between parents. In such cases the cause of the debility is obvious to any observer. But not if observers see themselves not as the impinger on the child but as an extension of them. The child experiences the impingement but the impinger does not, parents experience an expansion—as if they had moved into a larger apartment, psychologically speaking—and therefore have more storage space to expand and put some of their needs on show without owning them.

Winnicott says that although the anxiety state is always present or latent in such children, symptoms do not necessarily appear all the time. Symptoms tend to appear in attacks, recurring at more or less regular times, with intervals of health. In this way the recurrence of colic in these children may produce a picture closely simulating that of smoldering appendicitis and has led to the removal of a large number of healthy appendices. Or the intestinal *hurry* of these patients leads to a false diagnosis of colitis, and colonic washouts can convert such innocent colon irritability into serious colon disease. If the proper diagnosis were known, such a colon would be left without local treatment.

Early in Winnicott's career a little boy came to the hospital by himself and said to him "Please, doctor, my mother complains of a pain in my stomach." This drew Winnicott's attention to the part mother can play. In his paper "Reparation in Respect of Mother's Organized Defense," Winnicott (1975b) could be talking about Hope's early days. He says that a child who is supposed to have a pain has often not yet decided where the pain is. If one can catch him before his mother has indicated what she is expecting, one can find him bewildered and simply wanting to say that the pain is "inside." What is meant is that there is a feeling that something is wrong, or that there ought to be.

Probably Winnicott got an especially clear view of this problem in a children's outpatient department because such a department is really a clinic for the management of hypochondria in mothers. This is not the pejorative statement that it sounds for there is no sharp dividing line between the frank hypochondria of a depressed woman and mother's genuine concern for her child. A doctor who knows nothing of psychiatry, or knows nothing of the counterdepressive defenses, or who does not know that children get depressed, is liable to tell a mother off when she worries about a child's symptom, and fail to see the very real psychiatric problems that exist. On the other hand, a child psychoanalyst, fresh from newly discovered understanding of childhood depression, could easily fail to notice when it is the mother who is more ill than the child.

Winnicott thought that the depression of the child could be the mother's depression in reflection. When there seems to be special talent and even an initial success, as with Hope's school results (which were indeed a success given her large number of absences), there still remains an instability associated with dependence of the child on the mother; inside the child's self, deep inside, there is both a recognition and a resentment of this remarkably responsible job of keeping Mother alive by containing Mother's depression. However, in Hope's case, when the disinhibition of the hash brought her feelings to the surface, there was a sudden but sporadically repetitive realization that there was a personal sadness there. "I could not cry so I developed Crohn's," she said, and experienced a huge anger at being so used and at allowing herself to be so afraid. When thinking about returning Mother's depression to her, Hope said, "My mother will probably get ill; she is overweight and will probably eat even more and it will be my fault."

It is interesting that Hope left both her jobs because of the same dynamic as the one at home. Somewhere along the line she internalized enough good objects from her teachers that she at least was finally able to recognize, and try to escape from, that subservient role.

Winnicott describes the children who carry Mother's depression as children who in extreme cases have a task that can never be accomplished. Their task is first to deal with mother's mood. If they succeed in the immediate task, they do no more than succeed in creating an atmosphere in which they can start on their own lives. He says that this situation can be exploited by the individual as a flight from that acceptance of personal responsibility that is an essential part of individual development. But where the child has the chance to dig down to personal guilt through analysis, then the mother's (or father's) mood is also there to be dealt with. Hope had made herself responsible for her mother instead of for herself.

The usual observation in these cases is that the child's mother or father has a dominating personality. Instead, as analysts, we should say that the child lives within the circle of the parents' personality, and that this circle has pathological features. In Hope's case, the very thought of removing herself from this circle had disastrous consequences. In Hope, the intelligent, attractive girl I have described, the mother's need for help in respect to the sadness, deadness, blackness and fury in her inner world finds containment in emotionless, painful illness and, in looking after the child's painful symptoms, the mother is able to nurse her own pain.

It is possible to get astonishing clinical success by actively displacing the parent in the early part of psychotherapy. In this case it was possible to take the patient's side against the parent and at the same time gain and keep the parents' confidence. We are able to do this because most parents, including these parents, want their children to thrive and when they recognize that their own unmet needs, carried by the children, are indeed killing their children, they can recognize the truth. They continue to say, "We have done everything and will do anything for our child," but when, instead of saying it's your fault, the analyst says, "Do more, take back your own sadness" some gladly do this. I eventually made an alliance with Hope's mother and was able to provide some help for her. If the parents do not take back their own internal projections and moods then, in order to survive, the children distance themselves and everyone loses. Alternatively, the children fail to distance themselves and either live as emotional cripples or break down.

Winnicott says that some of the most spectacular successes in his professional work have been due not to the interpretations but to the really important thing—that the analyst has displaced a good but depressed parent. Initially, the important thing is that the analyst is *not depressed* and the patient finds herself because the analyst is not needing the patient to be good, or clean, or compliant, and is not even needing to be able to teach the patient anything.

Winnicott (1975b) says that a patient can proceed at her own pace. She can fail if she wishes, and should be given time and a sort of local security. These external details of management are the prerequisites for the patient's discovery of her own love, with the inevitable complication of aggression and guilt, which alone makes sense of reparation and restitution.

Clinically, however, we meet with a false reparation, which is not specifically related to the patient's own guilt. This false reparation appears through the patient's identification with the mother and the dominating factor is not the patient's own guilt but the mother's organized defense against depression and unconscious guilt. Hope's mother miscarried when Hope was 2 years old. The subsequent guilt and depression would have permeated the household and Hope would have taken responsibility for making Mother happy.

Snow White's story teaches that just because one has reached physical maturity, one is by no means intellectually and emotionally ready for adulthood, as represented by marriage. Considerable growth and time are needed before the new, more mature personality is formed and the old conflicts are integrated. Only then is one ready for a partner of the other sex, and the intimate relationship with them, which is needed for the achievement of mature adulthood.

But before the "happy" life can begin, the evil and destructive aspects of our personality must be brought under our control. And those parents, who, like the Queen, act out parental oedipal jealousies, nearly destroy their child and certainly destroy themselves.

The ups and downs of adolescent conflicts are symbolized by Snow White's twice being tempted, endangered, and rescued by returning to her previous latency existence (like Hope going home, and being rescued from destructive sex).

In Snow White's story, the Father huntsman fails to take a strong and definite stand. He neither does his duty to the Queen, nor meets his moral obligations to Snow White to make her safe and secure. Like Snow White, who seemed endlessly prepared to accept poisonous presents from the Queen, Hope also accepted Mother's guilt and anger. Like Snow White, Hope spent time with the dwarfs—with children at school (safe and not threatened).

Hope's mother expressed her anger everywhere, but Hope did not have this privilege. The way her anger was controlled at home was by Mother's constant threat that Hope's anger, not Mother's, would provoke Father into a second and fatal heart attack, which would destroy him. But unlike the wicked Queen, Hope's mother was grateful for her daughter's emotional growth, even though it meant owning her own projected bad objects and allowing Hope to learn to take control of her own sadness, guilt, and disappointments. Both learned a capacity for reparation and their anger decreased.

I wish I could say "and they lived happily ever after." I can say that they lived separately ever after, with Hope's success being enjoyed by her parents and her sorrows mourned by them. Hope's worries still remain her own, there is still no Crohn's, and there is occasionally true HOPE.

REFERENCES

Sacks, O. (1982). *Awakenings*. London: Picador.

Winnicott, D. W. (1975a). A note on normality and anxiety. In *Through Paediatrics to Psycho-Analysis*. New York: Basic Books.

——— (1975b). Reparation in respect of mother's organized defense. In *Through Paediatrics to Psycho-Analysis*. New York: Basic Books.

13

The Death of a Parent: The Spirit of Healing through Individual and Group Therapy

Bonnie S. Mark

I am thy father's spirit,
Doomed for a certain term to walk the night.
Shakespeare, *Hamlet*

The therapeutic process involved in coming to terms with the death of a parent is often a ghost story—the psychological work is haunted by the spirit of the parent who has died. This chapter addresses some of the experiences adolescents face with the death of a parent. While the recommended reading list at the end expands upon issues illuminated here, the chapter is unique in its elucidation of the benefits of integrating group therapy as an adjunct to individual therapy.

When Nick entered therapy at age 20, it was in order to uncover, discover, and recover from the shadow of his father, whose gradual deterioration and subsequent death from cancer had possessed him from the age of 15. At the beginning of treatment Nick had very long, curly hair, a rarely shaven face, and unconventional apparel, all of which were statements about how he desired to be perceived. He spoke of his long hair as a sign of autonomy from a more traditional style, especially that of his mother, who felt his hair was a symptom of Nick's prolonged *shiva*, the Jewish mourning period, over the death of his father. His wild hair seemed to be a representation of the wildness of his internal inferno, a bodily manifestation of his inner demons whose possession Nick was unable to sever. Nick reported that he simply hadn't gotten around to cutting his hair, suggesting that there were many things he wasn't getting around to and that he felt he wasn't cutting it in life.

At the same time, Nick did not feel he knew what specific statement of himself he was making through his appearance. His nonconformative clothing matched his hair in spirit; it marked Nick's ambivalence, which was defined only in his resistance to his mother's attempt to get him to look "normal" by going to The Gap, a clothing store, with her.

In our initial meetings, Nick had difficulty making eye contact and occasionally struggled with words. He commented that my looking at him intensely both intrigued and distracted him. These issues dissipated over the years, and Nick's hair eventually took on a short look with pronounced sideburns, which were stylish at the time.

Nick's childhood and young adolescence were described as relatively happy, and left him completely unprepared for his fifteenth year, when he, his mother, and his older half-sisters began the waiting process as they watched their father struggle for two years with cancer, the effects of chemotherapy, and, finally, the slow death of a terminal illness. His performance at his highly demanding college preparatory high school did not reflect the inner trauma over witnessing his father's deterioration and eventual death, which occurred at the end of his junior year.

Nick coped in his final year of high school by attempting to elude the overwhelming feelings that flooded him. He described anger as the dominant emotion that bubbled up when he allowed himself to feel. This natural reaction to his situation became the gauge of his feelings, his own barometer of how he was coping with the experience of the death of his father. Nick remembered closing off the vocalization of his feelings and modifying his responses in order to constantly suppress the torment he experienced as a result of his father's slow decay.

A vivid example of Nick's torment as a teenager was evident in Nick's reaction to his father's choking and throwing up at the dinner table after he began his chemotherapy treatment. Nick remembered feeling the range of emotions, from initial disgust, moving to guilt, and finally to anger. He recalled going to his room and kicking a hole in his door. His mother's response was to tape a poster over the door to hide the hole. Little was discussed, except that Nick should not let his father know about how angry he had become. The opening, which was created by Nick's display of anger, allowed him both literally and symbolically to vent his feelings. Taping that opening shut was a sign of the foreclosure of his expression, the sealing off of the emotional wounds that needed to be shared in order for the healing to begin.

Nick did not enter therapy at that time, nor did he have an outlet to deal with his feelings, which were simmering from his inner tumult. Instead, he wore a mask to shield his mother from signs that he wasn't holding up under the strain of watching his father's health deteriorate, which would lead to eventual death. He played the role of his mother's "strong little warrior," which served a dual function. He perpetuated an image of himself in which he struggled to conquer the torment of the emotions generated by the illness of his father. After his father died, Nick waded in conscious and unconscious pools of anger through fantasies of death and destruction, even considering suicide as a final gesture to destroy the unbearable conflict with his inner and outer demons, all manifestations of his father, whose ghostly presence eluded Nick's attempts to end the battle.

After high school, Nick was accepted by an elite university in the Midwest where he eventually surrendered to a lengthy depression. His depression began with his separation from his home and his mother, and was intensified as Nick confronted the need to face everyday responsibilities, such as paying his bills, completing his course work, and so on. He felt isolated, alone, and vulnerable, caught in a battle with a spirit world that he was invariably at a loss to control. A darkness descended upon him during these months. College was marked by this shadowy emptiness that defined Nick's existence. Unable to see clearly through his emotions, Nick often tripped over himself, sabotaging his own efforts. Mired in a haze of feelings that he refused to acknowledge, he found himself unable to perform academically or personally.

He described little spurts of motivation, generally accompanying the beginning of a school term, but deteriorating as class requirements became more substantial. Nick's vacillation between momentary eruptions of activity and periods of stagnation was principally affected by the constant conflicts between what he thought he "should" do and what he emotionally felt he could do. As this internal rupture widened, self-defeating behavior became the norm. For example, Nick described feeling that he "should" have a roommate (a notion encouraged by his mother). He would advertise for a roommate, only to find himself "trashing" his apartment and "acting like a maniac," effectively discouraging all prospective roommates.

He took recreational drugs, having used them occasionally since high school, which offered an illusory escape, but instead exacerbated his confusion, and in turn depressed his functioning, including his ability to resist more drugs. Throughout this period, his social life began to wither; his time was spent in isolation. He was stalked by feelings he could neither control nor understand, and in response he wrote poetry, began screenplays, and listened to music, which enabled him to access the ambiguity of his emotions, albeit in a veiled form.

Nick's ambivalent relationship to his own feelings intensified his inner turmoil. The split between Nick's coping mechanisms and the insistent emotional turbulence that was progressively disrupting all aspects of his social life shattered his academic performance. Nick bargained with his university's administration and had a real sense of accomplishment when he convinced them, time after time, to grant another probationary period until, eventually, there was no latitude given for his recurring failures, and he dropped out of college.

Early in our treatment sessions, we identified that Nick had tried to kill off his emotional life with the death of his father. As out of touch as he was with his own emotions, his dream world was haunted by chaotic and bloody visions. Night after night, he used a multitude of weapons to annihilate assailants that attacked in a myriad of horrific forms. Nick remembered many of the dreams vividly and our sessions focused on the dichotomy of control versus helplessness, which was the dominant theme of these nocturnal revelations. For example, he described dreams of being attacked in a coffeehouse or a police chase, and how he would eventually "blow them all away." Nick was being attacked by everything that he most feared, especially his loss of control, exemplified by his father's inability to master his physically debilitating state. This resulting sense of helplessness was compounded by his conflict-ridden inner world.

Nick's dream world was experienced in vivid color, which cut a stark contrast with the gray and colorless world of his everyday existence. To deal with his feelings, Nick strove to compartmentalize his feelings, which he found unbearable, as well as to sever himself from the associations produced by his emotional responses, which were experienced as overwhelming. This process of internal separation always failed, leaving Nick frozen in an emotional battle with the ghost of his father.

Freezing his painful emotions had been Nick's only mechanism for dealing with his pain, and he subsequently found that he had lost access to his pleasurable feelings as well. As we worked through his issues, Nick came to see therapy as an ice pick—a process of chipping away the frozen traces of his past experiences that kept him from moving forward with his life. Nick's thawing process began in our sessions by his sitting in the sadness created by the unexpected tragedy, pain, and loss of his relatively good childhood. He could see that only as he gained insight into the terrain clouded by his emotional fog could he begin the "thawing process."

The following dialogue illustrates how the therapeutic process proceeded:

Therapist: You freeze away the bad feelings, but when you do that all the other feelings get frozen, too.

Nick: I fear you're taking an ice pick and chipping away at me.

Therapist: Maybe it's you who is using the ice pick to chip away at your own defenses.

Nick: You know how hard this is—I can talk about the sadness and my anger but it's difficult to face the feelings of fear—I'm scared of their overwhelming quality. When Dad was dying, Mom kept saying I had to be strong—keep a positive attitude, think good thoughts, and Dad would be okay.

Therapist: Magical thinking—that if you deny your own feelings, and you don't feel the fear, Dad will survive.

Nick: Yeah. I was so scared of Dad's leaving me and disgusted by my anxiety of seeing him deteriorate. As Dad was deteriorating, I had nowhere to turn. A few years ago, I found out there was a teen group at the hospital that I could have gone to. But, NO! Mom never mentioned it until long after Dad died. I had to be the strong one, the positive thinker. Just keep trying good thoughts and Dad won't die. I couldn't "need" help.

Much of treatment served merely to permit Nick access to his emotional reality, which was "taped" shut or "frozen solid" in order to avoid the overwhelming feelings. Nick's fear of being overwhelmed by his own feelings increased and was prevalent throughout treatment. He was afraid of being smothered by the blanket of depression that had engulfed him. He connected his fear of being enveloped by depression to the immobilization that left him isolated and nonfunctioning. He recognized that for years he felt erroneously that if he shut off feelings and coped, he would survive. A similar misconception developed in our treatment. Nick's perception of the therapeutic process was that healing meant no longer feeling pain or the other difficult emotions; he perceived health as not being sad.

After one year of treatment, Nick began to measure his progress by establishing goals that he hoped to achieve and that he knew would please his mother, who consistently pressured him to find direction in his life. At first, after initial enthusiasm and determination to accomplish these ambitions, he would sabotage his goals, just as he had in college. This would put him into a deep depression and he would reexperience a familiar feeling of hopelessness. At times, he also seemed to be testing therapy and my response to his failure. His self-defeating behavior was exemplified in his application to a few highly competitive specialty training programs for which he did not have the prerequisites for admission, particularly since he had dropped out of college. Yet he refused to lower his standards because he felt that he didn't want to attend a second-rate school. He felt the schools should be able to see beyond what appeared on his application and recognize his inherent excellence. Nick felt entitled to a place in these schools, that he should be accepted even though he had not taken the necessary steps to get in. In his denial of the reality of the process that needed to be followed, he went from feelings of entitlement and omnipotence to devastation and despair. Over time, he came to see this pattern as self-defeating, propelling him back into precisely the depth of depression that the initial goals had been devised to combat.

The pattern of goal definition, and the self-sabotage that tended to bring these aspirations quickly crashing to a halt, was related to Nick's ambivalent relationship to his mother. His mother at times overcompensated for the loss of Nick's father by attempting to assume his role in Nick's life. She persistently provoked Nick to accomplish tasks she deemed important, an attitude that Nick resisted. Her own self-concept was strongly fused with Nick's achievements and his ability to succeed at the endeavors she considered consequential. Nick sardonically stated that in her attempt to be both Mom and Dad, his mother followed him from room to room, asking, "Did you finish your homework? Did you complete your assignments? Is everything done?"

At times, the relationship between Nick and his mother allowed for fertile transference issues to arise. In our sessions I was caught in the web of countertransferential desire to encourage Nick, yet any attempt to get Nick to move forward in his career, to explore the options of school, or to fulfill the goals he discussed or established during sessions were met with resistance. Any encouragement potentially contaminated the therapeutic dyad, was confused with his mother's attempts to directly involve herself in Nick's development, and unconsciously served as a familiar reminder of his mother's unrealistic imperative to "think positive" even as his father was dying.

An enactment of this struggle ensued on the occasion when Nick tentatively agreed to visit his college in order to decide whether he was ready to reenter. Even as he and his mother drove to the airport, ambivalence about his motives arose. At that point, he couldn't access his mixed emotions, yet his overwhelming feeling that he was doing this for his mother generated fury. At the airport, seeing Mom "take over" and open and repack his suitcase (reportedly packed satisfactorily) resulted in an anger so blinding that he was immobilized. He found himself unable to board the plane and described sitting at the airport crying for hours filled with shame over the hated exposure. For the subsequent month, he cut off all communications with his mother, including her not-so-subtle attempts to reconnect both directly and through friends and family members who called to make sure he was still breathing. Moreover, as Nick struggled through this period, I had to override her propensity toward encouraging him to communicate his anger directly with his mother instead of ostensibly punishing his mother through the wall of silence he had created. Nick viewed any exploration of this in our sessions as a violation—in the transference, his "therapist-mother" was repacking his emotional suitcase.

As Nick completed a year of therapy, he elected to join a young-adult therapy group that I facilitated as an adjunct to his individual treatment. His stated goals were to experience feedback and connections with others his age, but he also acknowledged both wanting to please me, since I strongly encouraged his joining the group, and to feed his curiosity about who else was being seen by me.

Nick was accepted readily by the group members and quickly fell into the role of "co-therapist." He displayed an interest in others, always asking questions about their experience, but had difficulty getting beyond this safety mechanism to explore issues about himself and his own pain. Nick attempted to play the role of the "good patient" in group and in his interaction with other members. His efforts at being a "good" patient were, in part, his unconscious attempt to hide his "bad bits" from the group, from the therapist, and from himself. He also acknowledged how much he wanted to impress me and the other group members.

After a year in group Nick went through periodic moments of acting out by coming late, not paying, or forgetting individual sessions. There were profuse apologies and lofty explanations, as well as much introspection, which included discussion of his desire to see how I would react if he was not a "good" patient, and to see what it would be like to make it without therapy. For example, following my summer vacation Nick resisted suggestions that he was angry about the vacation break and acknowledged that he did not want to feel that he had come to rely on treatment. His more mature drive for autonomy—his wish to grow up and to be self-motivating and self-reliant—was in conflict with the childish part of him that feared growing up and continued to need support. This was especially pronounced as he reached his twenty-first birthday, an event that he felt mandated the assumption of responsibility and direction over his life—expectations that were terrifying to Nick.

Nick's group experience was exemplary of how group treatment offers possibilities that individual treatment often cannot. Socially, he could experience himself and his processes with others, and he had the opportunity to look at and listen to feedback from others and experience their acceptance. When reflecting with the group, he could understand his need to make the group work and to hold it together as a symbol of his own process of "getting it together."

In addition, Nick stated that growth came from his connection with other group members. On one occasion, one member of the group encouraged Nick to "get going" by clapping one hand into another and saying, "You gotta just do it." The physical action of slapping her hands together corresponded to Nick's own struggle to take responsibility for his actions and get things together. That interaction had a profound impact on Nick and significantly altered his behavior. "You just gotta do it" became a representation of his own ability to take action. This interaction recreated pressures placed upon Nick by his mother, yet the imperative to take action triggered his working through the walls he had erected.

It must be noted that at that moment in the group the comment seemed to have a judgmental tone that potentially might have narcissistically wounded Nick. The group members, however, had created a safe place for each other so that the comment could be taken as an inspirational suggestion, instead of as a critical comment. As the group leader, I had to respect the space the group created without feeling the need to intervene when an individual might be hurt. I had to rely on and trust the power of the group, which was occasionally a challenge when the material approached areas of individual vulnerabilities.

A major breakthrough in Nick's therapy occurred when he realized that his decision to enter therapy meant that he was no longer struggling alone. One of the primary issues in treatment was Nick's sense of isolation and his fear of being misunderstood by the critical eyes of the world—both the external world and the internal world he created for himself. Early in treatment, he surmounted his initial resistance (putting up guards and boundaries) when he saw that he could return to therapy even after experiencing and sharing the raw emotions of anger, shame, confusion, hostility, and helplessness. Once Nick internalized that his feelings would not destroy me or the therapeutic relationship, the emotion flooded into the office, eventually leading to relief and a sense of safety.

It was shortly thereafter that we had a therapeutic session at his father's grave. The decision to visit the grave was both practical and symbolic. We would revisit the site where the specter that haunted Nick was manifest in its most concrete form and thus directly confront the source of his unresolved conflict. Nick experienced anguish whenever he passed by the cemetery. The anxiety produced by the locale of his father's phantom was escalated by the fact that the grave site was on the way to the airport. Thus, every time Nick left for school in the Midwest after a visit home, he was both abandoning mother and reexperiencing being abandoned by father. Since Nick's mother had come to rely on Nick in many ways after the death of his father, the abandonment issues this separation provoked were particularly pronounced. The grave was, therefore, the central symbol that wove together the various strands of Nick's psychic trauma.

By meeting at the cemetery for a session, Nick was able to reexperience the cemetery and what it had come to represent, enabling him to directly confront the source of his unresolved conflict and to have a reparative experience. Upon first arriving, we began searching for his father's burial site. Nick had difficulty orienting himself in the cemetery, getting lost when trying to make his way back to the source of his original wound. When his father's plot was located, the context provided the stimulus for Nick to reexperience and reveal many of the deep emotional memories that haunted him.

Neither Nick nor any other family member had been at the hospital at the moment when his father died, which for Nick had meant that his father had died alone. Even though Nick knew that his father's death was inevitable, he was overwhelmed with the force of the feelings that arose. Nick recounted the moments leading to the funeral and following it, when he sat *shiva* with his mother and felt that they were separated from everyone else—isolated, except for one another.

We moved from the grave site and entered a chapel nearby, which was empty, except for the sound of the funeral music. Nick disclosed how invaded he felt by the entire ambiance of death that danced this dirge around him. In encountering, discussing, and assessing each of the elements woven into the experience of his father's passing, Nick could continue to connect to the painful loss of his father. Nick's fragile selfstructure became more solid as a result of seeing that he had the ability to tolerate painful emotions that heretofore had been too painful. He could demystify the cemetery and the ghosts that haunted it. The visit to the cemetery, therefore, proved to be a pivotal experience in Nick's healing process.

CONCLUSION

The dominant issue of Nick's treatment, his inability to access his feelings due to his sense that they would be overwhelming, was perhaps most clear as we approached the time when Nick decided he would return to school to complete college. Even though the thawing of his feelings had been an expressed goal of his, Nick also acknowledged coexisting needs to disown the parts of him that seemed intolerable. This need to cut off his negative feelings centered on the emotions experienced due to loss: initially father's and grandfather's deaths, then the loss of his self-esteem, and finally the loss of his childhood. Now, a new loss was to be the therapy he had engaged in while healing.

Termination issues were explored months before he was accepted to reenter school. As the date grew closer, Nick experienced a pronounced fear of feelings that would sneak up and overwhelm him, thus risking the destruction of what he had been trying to achieve all these months.

Together, the importance of his looking at the feelings of loss and sadness was examined. As hard as this was for him, he came to see that not doing so would have amounted to his remaining trapped with the unresolved emotional conflicts, fighting phantoms that could never be exorcised because of the unknown elements conjured by his environment.

In the month prior to his return to the university, he forgot to come to sessions and resisted interpretations that these absences were correlated to our pending separation. Interpretations that he was continuing to sever himself from his many feelings—excitement, fear, happiness, sadness—was met with recalcitrance. Since he would no longer have the twice-a-week sessions, which provided a safe place to heal and to feel, he had a hard time in his remaining sessions.

Nick said it was safer and more controllable to think his emotions (pointing to his brain) as opposed to feeling them (pointing to his heart). Once again, we looked at how unsafe it was for him, on his own, to feel the feelings, but that our work could offer a foundation of strength to work through these feelings differently than he had in the past.

Much of his pain was projected outward in order to buffer him. For example, as the moment of separation came closer, I would feel sad at the end of the sessions. Nick, on the other hand, seemed to feel little emotion. He struggled to feel only positive feelings so as to ward off entering the once too-familiar black hole of sadness and anger from which he had come, and into which he feared he would descend if he let himself feel anything negative about his decision to return to school. Only in response to the comment, "There are a lot of sad feelings here and they are not all mine," was Nick able to embrace the sadness. We worked to resurrect feelings buried in the past—feelings that he had not felt safe experiencing as his father was dying—concomitant to the reexperiencing of loss, anger, and sadness at our imminent ending. My ability to tolerate his feelings allowed him, over time, to reintegrate the full range of his feelings resulting in a transmuting internalization of the structures of his core self and a major change in his capacity to relate both inwardly and outwardly.

Nick's experiences in group therapy as an adjunct to his individual sessions allowed him to connect to his feelings by experiencing similar emotions in other members of the group and then by feeling the acceptance of others as he touched his own cut-off emotions. Slowly the deadened feelings reemerged and he was able to integrate the feelings that immobilized him as he recognized and addressed the impact of his traumatic experience throughout his father's illness and after his death. His struggle continued to be one of self-regulation of his emotions, where the complete range of his feelings could flow more easily through him. His positive feelings became more accessible as he experienced himself as someone who had developed the power to overcome obstacles of an inner world by which he no longer felt haunted.

SUGGESTED READINGS

Anthony, S. (1971). *The Discovery of Death in Childhood and After*. New York: Basic Books.

Bloom-Feshbach, J., and Bloom-Feshbach, S. (1987). *The Psychology of Separation and Loss*. San Francisco, CA: Jossey-Bass.

Cook, A. S., and Dworkin, D. S. (1992). *Helping the Bereaved*. New York: Basic Books.

Furman, E. (1974). *A Child's Parent Dies*. New Haven, CT: Yale University Press.

——(1986). When is the death of a parent traumatic? *Psychoanalytic Study of the Child* 41:191–208. New Haven, CT: Yale University Press.

Grollman, E. A. (1990). *Talking About Death*. Boston, MA: Beacon.

Kübler-Ross, E. (1983). *On Children and Death*. New York: Macmillan.

Lonetto, R. (1980). *Children's Conceptions of Death*. New York: Springer.

Moriarty, D. M. (1967). *The Loss of Loved Ones*. Springfield, IL: Charles C Thomas.

Schowalter, J. E., Patterson, P. R., Tallmer, M., et al. (1983). *The Child and Death*. New York: Columbia University Press.

Worden, J. W. (1982). *Grief Counseling and Grief Therapy*. New York: Springer.

Zeligs, R. (1972). *Children's Experience with Death*. Springfield, IL: Charles C Thomas.

14

The Unborn Mind of the Therapist: Psychotherapy and the Buddhist Traditions

Shelley Albanati

There is a time in an infant's life that is not only before words but before vocalizations of any kind, and even before movements. This is a time when the infant, who has no language and barely even has gestures, absolutely depends on the presence of another who is able to be quiet, inactive, and noncommunicative, but very much present and alive. Unfortunately, the temptation to focus on the active, on the communicative, on the verbal, and on the vocal is so strong that this quiet infant easily gets the shaft.

There is also a grammar to the silent communications that occur between patient and therapist. It is a grammar that we rarely understand consciously, but that is regularly understood unconsciously, and which, when understood, we ascribe to the domain of intuition or the uncanny.

Part of the training program at the Reiss-Davis Child Study Center is to do year-long, weekly infant observations according to the method described by Esther Bick (1964). In doing infant observations, I have been very much struck with the feeling that there seems to be very little that the just-born infants actually do to reassure their mothers that they are, in fact, alive. At this stage, they are dependent on their mothers to have live internal objects (that is, to not confuse stillness with deadness).

Winnicott (1965) describes the experiences of infants with depressed mothers (which I think can be expanded to include a wide range of situations, such as infants with schizoid or narcissistic mothers, and infants with birth traumas).

> In certain cases, the mother's central internal object is dead at the critical time in her child's early infancy, and her mood is one of depression. Here the infant has to fit in with a role of dead object, or else has to be lively to counteract the mother's preoccupation with the child's deadness. Here, the opposite to the liveliness of the infant is an anti-life factor derived from the mother's depression. The task of such an infant is to be alive and to look alive and to communicate being alive; in fact it is the ultimate aim of such an individual. . . . It is a constant struggle to get to the starting point and keep there. No wonder there are those who make a special business of existing and turn it into a religion. . . . Liveliness that negates maternal depression is a communication of a reassuring nature, and it is unnatural and an intolerable handicap to the immature ego. [p. 181]

I have also seen several cases in which this state of quietude was traumatically disrupted even before birth due to serious medical emergencies. As a result, these babies miss out on that very precious time of one's life that has been variously described by psychoanalysts as basic unity (Little 1960), primary maternal preoccupation (Winnicott 1956), and maternal reverie (Bion 1962).

Bion (1992) writes about the function of dream alpha as being something like allowing oneself to be pregnant with the patient, and the importance of developing the analyst's intuition through the discipline of trying to rid oneself of memory, desire, and understanding.

I think the difficulty we often have in emptying our minds of preconceptions lies in the difficulty many of us have had during that period of life when the predominant experience was one of stillness and emptiness. If this stillness didn't go well (and it rarely does, due to a variety of factors such as birth traumas, feeding difficulties, problems in utero, maternal depression, narcissism, and so on), then the empty, quiet solitude that could be a wellspring of peacefulness, nourishment, and creativity gets filled instead with anxiety, depression, deadness, boredom, isolation, mania, disintegration, panic, hate, greed, envy, intellectualization, arrogance, and violence.

When there is no tolerance for mental space, it does not become a source of potential that is lived with, but rather a source of dread that is, at best, lived through (painfully tolerated, withstood) and, at worst, avoided altogether.

Tustin (1986) wrote about the need that certain patients have to adhere to hard surfaces and sensations as a way of ameliorating the terror they feel about falling forever into an unintegrated state. One thing I have noticed in patients who have had traumatic disruptions in this state is that they often have an intense need for the therapist to understand how they feel without having had to describe it in words. They seem to have a need to have the therapist actually relive the experience with them, and to absolutely require a profound counteridentification with them that the therapist can then verbalize. However, it seems to me that the importance of the therapist's verbalization is not so much because it has given the patient words to put to the experience (although this is part of it), but more because it has demonstrated to the patient the level and accuracy of the counteridentification that has occurred, and reassures the patient that a state of "primary maternal preoccupation" (Winnicott 1956) and a "psychic skin" (Bick 1968, Mitrani 1994b) have been established within the therapeutic relationship.

I think it can be a grave mistake to misinterpret the patient's silence and reliance on the counteridentification of the therapist as a destructive attack on verbal communication, as an unwillingness to be born. I have made this mistake myself, and found that it only created a greater sense of despair in these patients. What I have found is that rather than being motivated by a resistance to the therapeutic process and to growth, it seems to be the patient's way of determining whether the minimum emotional conditions for therapy exist. I think, in these cases, the communication through introjective counteridentification has been crucial to being able to move forward into other kinds of object relating.

Bion (1992) talks about the importance of "dreaming" the patient, carrying them in our womb, so to speak. Is this the level at which patients are being carried when unintegration is allowed and uncanny experiences begin to occur in the therapy? Is this a sign of success of a convergence of the preinfantile parts of both the patient and the therapist? The verbalizations, symptoms, behaviors, and experiences we notice are something like a hieroglyphic tablet whose meaning is unknown to us. Both of us are in the dark as to the rules of decoding the message. The original writers of the message (the patient in the past, the infant, the fetus, the ancestral infants) are long gone. There is no direct link to the original communicator of the message. There is no child inside the adult who can talk to us directly. There are only footprints of where the child has walked to guide us.

I believe there are times in every therapy when we need to be able to enter into something like a countertransference psychosis with our patients. The therapist must be prepared to get hypnotized. Bion says this in a slightly different way when he states that the failure to establish a normal projective identification relationship between the mother and infant precludes the development of alpha function.

However, despite all of the attention that the subject of countertransference has gotten recently, there still remains a remarkable difficulty in allowing ourselves to be empty and vulnerable with our patients.

I would like to introduce a new term, *adhesive counteridentification*, to distinguish an aspect of the countertransference in which there is no tolerance for emptiness, from *introjective counteridentification*, in which emptiness is lived with as a normal and necessary part of establishing the nonverbal link with the patient.

Mitrani (1994a) states,

> While normal/narcissistic object relations prevail, anxieties defended against by the subject are either paranoid-schizoid, manic, or depressive in nature, anxieties which have been well-defined by Melanie Klein. However, she goes on to state, that those "anxieties evaded through autosensual/adhesive maneuvers may be more accurately conceptualized as states of raw and unintegrated panic, equated with the elemental fear of falling forever, of discontinuity of being, of nothingness, dissolution, and evaporation—of being a 'no-body' nowhere, anxieties described in the work of Winnicott and Tustin." [p. 364]

It is this second class of anxieties that is evaded through adhesive maneuvers in therapists as well as patients. Adhesive maneuvers are those that serve to obliterate the unintegrated panic in the awareness of emptiness that is inherent in unborn states of mind. Without emptiness, there can be no unborn mind; without an unborn mind, there can be no real relationship; without a relationship, there can be no psychic skin contact; and without psychic skin contact, communication through projective identification cannot take place.

Just as projective identification is often met up with introjective counteridentification in the countertransference, I believe that adhesive identifications (Bick 1968) often stimulate adhesive counteridentifications in the therapist.

A common example of this is a situation I recently found myself in, in which the patient was in an unintegrated state, experiencing panic and terror, but unable to speak. I was stimulated to panic as well, but was unaware of this, and instead of experiencing it with the patient and allowing the meaning of it to emerge, I began to adhere to rigidly formulated theoretical constructions, shoving them into the patient instead of making contact. One must be able to have psychic skin contact established before considerations of "into" and "out of" can even be entertained. This drove the patient into premature verbalization and greater dread of remaining forever alone with no psychic skin container for these feelings. Luckily, this patient was able to point this out to me and help me correct my mistake.

I think it is extremely important for us to cultivate a state of mind that allows for the greatest sensitivity to being able to feel these subtle distinctions in the types of counteridentifications that are occurring within us during the session. It is only through noticing these subtle distinctions in the way we are feeling in the session that we will be able to notice when the patient's verbalizations feel premature (more like mimicry), and to be more aware of when we have shifted into areas of unintegrated panic as opposed to normal/narcissistic terrors.

This is a session from the therapy of an adolescent boy dealing with unintegrated states related to a traumatic birth history, in which there are shifts from premature verbalization to raw panic to adhesive maneuvers to the beginnings of psychic skin formation to projective identification. I will resist the temptation to label specific points in the session, because these shifts are rapid, complex, and nonlinear in nature.

The patient starts off talking for about 15 minutes in a laborious and detailed way about different types of bicycles. I am having a difficult time making sense of this. Suddenly, I notice a very sharp, intense pain on the right side of my head, sort of in my ear. It is getting to the point of being unbearable, and I am contemplating whether or not I should interrupt the session, and maybe leave the room. Just at that point, as if out of nowhere, the patient says:

P: When I was born, I had to have surgery on my ear. My mom said I was screaming for hours. She thought it would kill me.

(Countertransference—my pain disappears.)

(Long silence. Then, the patient starts convulsing and trembling.)

T: What's happening?

P: I feel sick. . . . My head is killing me. . . . I'm sweating. . . . My head is going to explode. . . . I never talked about the surgery before . . . I never really thought about it.

T: Maybe you were afraid it would kill you if you thought about it or talked about it.

(Patient falls asleep for about 5 minutes.)

P: I dreamt my mind was all cluttered. Then you started to talk to me. I don't remember what you said, but it calmed me down.

T: My words were reassuring to you?

P: The sound of your voice.

(Long silence. At first, the atmosphere feels quiet and reflective, but after awhile I start to feel disconnected and impatient. He also seems to be getting frustrated.)

P: Close your eyes.

(Countertransference—I do. I begin daydreaming about holding him like a little baby, rocking him, cuddling him. I imagine that we are floating in some kind of liquid, as if the air in the room is made of baby oil, or something.)

T: Wanting to be held?

P: Now you understand. . . . I had a dream last night that I asked you to sit next to me and you did and you held me. I don't know how to explain this, but we were kind of blurry, like liquid.

T: Your body flowing into mine, and mine flowing into yours, like we are one.
P: Yes, like you are a part of my soul.
T: And you are a part of mine?
P: I hope so.

Buddhism has very deeply developed traditions on how to train people to handle the difficulties that one encounters when trying to be fully empty (*sunyata*, which originally means the hollow of a pregnant womb) (Epstein 1995). They train their students to let go of attachments to intellectual understanding and preconceived notions (adhesive maneuvers), and thereby to leave themselves open to their own vulnerability (and terror), and to cultivate their mind or *citta*, which literally means heart/mind in Sanskrit—they do not distinguish the two. In this tradition, it is felt that "aversion or fear of demonic states is itself a demonic state" (Cleary 1994, p. 21). It is through the discipline of silent meditation and facing the primal terrors and panic in the experience of emptiness that true compassion for all sentient beings is felt to develop.

Bion's alpha function describes the mental state of tolerating what is unknown and unknowable long enough to be able to digest, make meaning of, and return to the person something that is in a more tolerable form. The function of the Zen koan is to confront people head on with this "unknowability" in such a way as to both bind patients and free them within their own subjectivity and existential aloneness. Psychotherapy adds a crucial element in that it is done within the context of a relationship with another human being.

Wu-men Hu-k'ai, the Sung period master of the Rinzai school of Zen, discusses the problem of adhesive identification in the study of Zen koans: "For subtle realization it is of the utmost importance that you cut off the mind road. If you do not pass the barrier of the ancestors, if you do not cut off the mind road, then you are a ghost clinging to bushes and grasses" (Aitken 1990, p. 12).

In the same vein, metapsychology, metaphysics, and scientific research are often misused as adhesive maneuvers against unintegration, which inevitably take us away from the fundamental quality of psychotherpy and dilute the experience, distracting rather than enlightening us. They take us into our heads and away from our minds, into our bodies and away from our perceptions.

Psychoanalysis is a way of being. Talking about psychoanalysis can be quite detrimental because it colludes with our desire to be able to believe that we can skip over the fundamental experience of terror and substitute knowledge for experience (or to put it in Bionian terms, it keeps us in the realm of K versus O). We cannot actively seek out this state of mind. We can only learn through discipline and practice how to become better receptors, vessels, or conduits of experience.

The Tibetan Buddhist monk Chogyam Trungpa (1993) describes the process of opening our hearts and minds to allow for greater receptiveness in this way:

> Examine the nature of unborn awareness. When you look beyond the perceptual level alone, when you look at your own mind (which you cannot actually do but you pretend to) you find that there is nothing there. You begin to realize that there is nothing to hold onto. Mind is unborn. But at the same time, it is awareness, because you still perceive things. There is awareness and clarity. . . . When you begin realizing non-existence, then you can afford to be more compassionate, more giving. A problem is that we would like to hold onto our territory and fixate on that particular ground. . . . But however confused we might be, however much of a cosmic monster we might be, still there is an open wound or sore spot in us always. . . . That is very nice—at least we are accessible somewhere. . . . That sore spot is known as embryonic compassion, potential compassion. . . .
>
> Not only that, but there is also an inner wound, which is called tathagatagarbha or buddha nature. Tathagatagarbha is like a heart that is sliced and bruised by wisdom and compassion. When the external wound and the internal wound begin to meet and to communicate, then we begin to realize that our whole being is made out of one complete sore spot altogether, which is called "boddhisattva fever." That vulnerability is compassion. . . . It's very harsh treatment, in some sense; but on the other hand, it's very gentle. The intent is gentle, but the practice is very harsh. By combining the intention and the practice, you are being "harshed" but you are also being "gentled" so to speak—both together. That makes you into a boddhisattva. [p. 31]

In a similar way, when we treat our own wounds (derived from traumatic experiences with states of emptiness) in this way, we are becoming psychotherapists.

However, there are also many misconceptions about this aspect of Buddhism as well as of psychotherapy. Muso Kokushi, the ancient master of both Japanese and Chinese Zen, has this to say about these misconceptions,

> To say that Zen is not done physically, verbally, or intellectually does not mean that it consists of absence of thought, extinction of sense, or mortification of the body. The point is that the ordinary ideas of body and mind are illusions. . . . Ordinary people attribute perception to the senses, but Buddhism speaks of sensing independently of the ordinary sense organs. It is those who are unfamiliar with this principle who are disturbed by the statement that real Zen practice has nothing to do with acts of body, speech, or mind. . . . To think that Zen practice means abandoning all understanding is a big mistake. As an ancient said, "It cannot be sought consciously, yet it cannot be found in unconsciousness; it cannot be comprehended by silence." Even among Zen students there are those who make literal interpretations of ancient sayings about nonattachment and think that the message of Zen is to ignore all meaning and principle, not define distinctions in stages, and not keep either Buddhism or wordly realities in mind. The ancients ridiculed this, calling it "spade Zen," because a spade is used to dig things out, representing the misconception that the teaching of Zen is to abandon all understanding. [Cleary 1994, p. 117]

Zen aims to dissolve dualistic thinking and to look for the primordial unity underlying fabricated dualities.

It also teaches that "It is better to practice a little than to talk a lot." Therefore, I am purposely stopping now to allow the ideas to have the space to dwell in the reader's mind.

REFERENCES

Aitken, R. (1990). *The Gateless Barrier: The Wu-men Kuan (Momonkan)*. San Francisco: North Point Press.

Bick, E. (1964). Notes on infant observation in psychoanalytic training. *International Journal of Psycho-Analysis* 45:448–466.

———(1968). The experience of the skin in early object-relations. *International Journal of Psycho-Analysis* 49:484–486.

Bion, W. (1962). A theory of thinking. *International Journal of Psycho-Analysis* 43:306–310.

———(1992). *Cogitations*. London: Karnac.

Cleary, T. (1994). *Dream Communications*. Boston: Shambala.

Epstein, M. (1995). *Thoughts Without a Thinker*. New York: Basic Books.

Little, M. (1960). On basic unity. *International Journal of Psycho-Analysis* 4:377–384.

Mitrani, J. (1994a). On adhesive pseudo object relations, part I. *Contemporary Psychoanalysis* 30:348–366.

———(1994b). Unintegration, adhesive identification, and the psychic skin. In *Melanie Klein and Object Relations*, December, pp. 65–88.

Trungpa, C. (1993). *Training the Mind*. Boston: Shambala.

Tustin, F. (1986). *Autistic Barriers in Neurotic Adults*. London: Karnac.

Winnicott, D. (1956). Primary maternal preoccupation. In *Collected Papers: Through Paediatrics to Psycho-Analysis*, pp. 300–306. New York: Basic Books, 1958.

———(1965). On communicating and not communicating leading to a study of certain opposites. In *The Maturational Processes and the Facilitating Environment*, pp.179–192. New York: International Universities Press.

15

Treating Shame in Adolescence: Integrating Intersubjectivity, Object Relations, and Mind–Body Healing

Nancy P. VanDerHeide
and Ronald A. Alexander

Gretchen enters the office with a mixture of aplomb that is remarkable in a 16-year-old and tentativeness that resembles a child on the verge of a painful confession. Punctual as always, she hands me payment for her biweekly therapy sessions, a check (from her own checking account).

"I was almost late," she admits apologetically. "I had to rush but I just made it here on time. I had to get the invoices ready to go out at work and I didn't want to leave my desk a mess. I was really nervous that I wouldn't get it done on time and my boss would come in and see it all over my desk."

Gretchen's sessions are scheduled to give her time in the evening for homework after having spent the afternoon at a local florist shop where she handles the bookkeeping duties. A high school student with a 4.0 grade point average, Gretchen has the pretty, fresh-scrubbed appearance of a small-town homecoming princess.

What is wrong with this picture? Why is Gretchen spending two hours a week talking to her therapist when she could be talking on the phone with her girlfriends about the new guy in her English class?

> The third time Rick was expelled from school, his mother and stepfather brought him to therapy. At 15, he had an ongoing history of drug use, fighting, and running away. Rick maintained his cocaine habit by selling marijuana and other drugs to classmates and kids outside the schools he attended. His schoolwork, however, did not receive that level of attention and his grades suffered accordingly. Rick presented in therapy a tough-guy bravado that quickly faded to depression and anxiety.

Gretchen and Rick present superficially different pictures, but both are suffering the insidious devastation of shame. By adolescence the foundation has been laid for the formation of a shame-based identity and at no other time since the rapprochement crisis has the individual been so vulnerable to cementing feelings of worthlessness into the fabric of his or her being.

For Gretchen, every grade of A she receives is merely a reminder of the possibility of failing next time and a burden that must be lived up to. The pressure to achieve and maintain an outward appearance of perfection is so great that there is no time available to internalize such success. That her teachers and employer find her delightfully competent is not merely lost on Gretchen, but is in fact another source of stress, another source of impossible expectations she feels she must fulfill.

Fueling Rick's classroom acting out and running away behaviors is a pervasive sense of inferiority. Difficulties in forming friendships resulted in an isolation breached only by drug deals with other "loadies," an isolation reinforced by mortifying interactions with peers and family members. Beneath his seemingly callous and distancing behaviors toward others is a deep longing to feel a part of something, to belong.

In its least disruptive form, shame brings to consciousness some as yet unrealized component of the self, expanding self-awareness and contributing to healthy identity formation. This painful, innate affect signals the involvement of the self in some behavior unacceptable or injurious to the self (Tomkins 1963). As a temporary experience, shame can prevent one from continuing to engage in a potentially dangerous interaction by promoting withdrawal. The tendency for some individuals, however, is to perpetuate the shaming process well beyond an adaptive boundary and into the development of an identity based on pervasive, low self-esteem.

It is more accurate to look at shame as a range of feelings existing along a continuum of intensity rather than as a single emotional entity. Shyness and embarrassment, for example, are milder in intensity than humiliation and mortification. Kindred feelings include despair, self-contempt, chagrin, disgrace, and dishonor. Central to each of these feelings is the experience of exposure of the self as in some way diminished or inadequate. And it is not just a part of the self that is felt to be so reduced; rather, it feels as though the entire self suffers a small to tremendous loss in value. There appears to be a fusion between whatever element was exposed to view and judged to be bad, and the self as a whole, rendering the self as bad.

SHAME IN THE PSYCHOANALYTIC LITERATURE

Freud's most important contribution in the area of shame was the introduction of the notion of the ego ideal as the forerunner to the superego, in his 1914 paper "On Narcissism." The ego ideal in this formulation contains the sense of perfection that existed in infancy and measures the ego's actual control over the drives, which is compared with perfect control over the drives. Shame results from the failure to live up to the ideals created both through the original infantile narcissism as well as through the later internalizations and identifications that compose the ego ideal as represented phenomenologically by the shape of an ideal self.

Although Freud did not pursue the line of thought he proposed in the 1914 paper, ego psychologists such as Hartmann and Loewenstein (1962) continued to grapple with the concept of the ego ideal and its relationship to the superego. They position the development of the ego ideal within the oedipal phase, postulating it to contain those aspects of the superego that form in response to oedipal conflicts.

The ego ideal, with its escalating demands for perfection, becomes that toward which the ego strives. The superego also integrates within itself the moral code, thus becoming the holder of both perfectionistic standards and prohibitions.

Maintaining the ego ideal as a part of the superego makes it difficult to distinguish between shame and guilt. Hartmann and Loewenstein, in fact, specifically questioned the existence of such a distinction. However, both clinical material and later research on affect states (Tomkins 1962, 1963) provide evidence to the contrary. Schafer (1960) attempts to maintain the superego as the structure responsible for generating shame as an affect distinct from guilt by separating the loving functions of the superego from those that are hostile. The superego is seen to function in a loving manner by protecting the ego from abandonment by important objects. Identification with the ideals of the parental superego provides this protection. Schafer posits the notion that the ego experiences inferiority feelings (shame) upon failure to live up to those ideals; thus, "inferiority feelings correspond to feelings of loss of the superego's love, just as guilt corresponds to feelings of the superego's hatred" (pp. 178–179). Thus, Schafer maintains both the structural constructs delineated by Freud and the ego as the psychic agency experiencing shame.

Building on Hartmann's (1950) definition of narcissism as "the libidinal cathexis not of the ego but of the self" (p. 85), Schafer (1967) focuses attention on the self and its representations, specifically those involving ideals. He proposes the ideal self as the form of self-representation that reflects the successful matching of the actual self to the desired goals of the ego ideal. The affect of shame, experienced as a sense of defeat, inferiority, or weakness, arises out of the failed attempt to match the self to the shape of the ideal self.

The transition from conflict theories to theories that give greater consideration to narcissism makes necessary the inclusion of the object. Reich and Jacobson both include in their works primitive object relations, narcissism, and self-esteem in considering the creation of ideals. Reich (1960) observes oscillations in self-esteem arising from narcissistic injury and proposes merger of the self with idealized objects as a significant attempt to restore self-esteem. Idealization of the object takes place through the activities of the ego ideal, which then becomes fused with the idealized object.

Jacobson (1964) retains a firm commitment to structural theory and conflict in her conceptualizations of shame and guilt, yet includes narcissistic vulnerability and destructive, primitive object relations in delineating conflicts leading to shame. For Jacobson, the narcissitically invested ego ideal serves as a bridge between the ego and superego and is an entirely separate structure. By viewing the ego ideal as outside of the superego, itself embodying grandiose fantasies and ideals, the ego ideal can then function with shame as a central affect while the superego retains guilt as its central affect.

Theorists who consider shame from an object relations perspective focus primarily on the relationship between shame and the presence of unstable self-other boundaries arising from the incomplete internalization of introjects and split-object representations. This leads to poor autonomy and identity development. Shame is then an affectual response to perceived rejection and/or hostility from both internal and external objects.

Kinston (1983) posits that a painful awareness of one's separate yet dependent nature arises from difficulties in relating to important others. This self-conscious realization produces extreme discomfort (shame) followed by movement away from awareness of needs, conflicts, or imperfections. In this way, according to Kinston, shame acts as signal anxiety. Merger of the self with the significant object reduces the anxiety and, thereby, the shame experience. This is accomplished through compliance with the demands and needs of the other—in other words, through the development of a "false self." Winnicott (1960) first developed the notion of the false self as a move by the self to protect its true essence from the impingements of the environment. Although he did not include shame per se as an impetus in the development of the false self, the interpersonal nature of many shame experiences qualifies the affect as arising, at times, from impingements of the environment.

Self psychology places the self as a structure firmly in the center of the individual's psychic life. The central facet of the theory is the supraordinate role of the self and its deficits. The place of shame in self psychology has evolved even as the theory has.

Kohut's (1966) early work in the field of self psychology retained elements of Freud's drive and conflict-oriented structural theory. In this work, he relates shame to the frustration of the narcissistic self's exhibitionistic demands. The sensation of failure that occurs when the grandiosity of the narcissistic self overwhelms the ego is experienced as shame. Later, Kohut (1971) focused on inadequately mirrored and neutralized (and thereby, disavowed) grandiosity, which threatens the integrity of the self. Thus, shame "is due to a flooding of the ego with unneutralized exhibitionism and not to a relative ego weakness vis-à-vis an overly strong system of ideals" (p. 181).

With *The Restoration of the Self* in 1977, Kohut's perspective moved completely away from object relations and the relationship of the ego ideal to shame, and toward a line of narcissistic development involving the interaction between self and selfobject. This and later work (Kohut 1984) emphasize the importance of structural defects resulting from early self-object failure. Defects occur in either the self, arising from mirroring self-object failure, or in the self structures that arise in response to the primary defect in the self. Kohut termed such structures compensatory, as they are an attempt to repair the damage done in the early phase of development by seeking cohesion through merger with an idealized selfobject. Defects in the compensatory structures are the result of failures in the attempt to merge with an empathic, idealized selfobject. Although his writing includes many allusions to shame-related phenomena and the failure of the self to reach particular goals and ideals, Kohut maintains that shame itself is the result of inadequately mirrored grandiosity that becomes overwhelming to the self.

Morrison (1989) builds on Kohut's work, expanding the explanation of shame to include the failure of the self in its pursuit of ideals, that is, in failures in the compensatory structure. Failure in any realm of self-object relatedness confronts the self with its inability to meet its ideals and narcissistic expectations of perfection. Shame then develops in response to any experienced need for the selfobject, proportional to the inability of the selfobject to meet those needs. The unmet selfobject needs that most significantly pertain to the experience of shame, according to Morrison, are those related to the self's attempts to achieve vigor through the attainment of ideals.

Whereas Kohut abandons the notion of the ego ideal along with object relations in general, Morrison (1989) proposes the development of an ideal self, composed of the qualities of Kohut's (1971) idealized parental imago. Rather than forming psychic structure as an idealized superego, Morrison sees the idealizing selfobject functions as becoming "attached to the basically firm self in the process of attaining structuralization, and to its vigorous, esteemed qualities" (p. 79). The ideal self becomes the internal representation of the goals and ideals of the self. Failure of the self to manifest the aspirations represented by the ideal self results in the experience of shame. Acceptance of the self with all its weakness and inadequacies as compared with the ideal self is the basis of therapeutic healing of shame in this model.

Kaufman's (1985) and Kaufman and Raphael's (1991) formulation of an interpersonal origin for shame integrates the interpersonal theory of Sullivan, object relations theory as understood by Fairbairn and Guntrip, and the affect theory of Tomkins. The interpersonal theory of the origins of shame rests on the foundation of a fundamental human need for relationship. Many theorists have previously emphasized the importance of the need to feel loved and wanted by a significant other (Fairbairn 1966). And self psychology bases healthy development on the presence of adequate self-selfobject ties (Kohut 1977). A critical part of the need for relationship is mutuality of response. In addition to being loved, an individual must be allowed to give love in return, and to experience the uncritical acceptance of that love as valued and desired. Over time the young child develops trust in the existence of this two-way relationship. A relationship develops between having a need and having it met such that expecting a response occurs in tandem with having a need.

Kaufman calls this emotional bond the interpersonal bridge and maintains that any disruption to it evokes shame. A major source of disruption is the awareness that one's most basic expectations of the other are wrong. An important caregiver who refuses to relate to the child or who actively withdraws love violates the child's expectations that this significant person values him or her. Other parental responses that break the interpersonal bridge are expressions of contempt, blame, and ridicule. Conveying disappointment in the child will also sever the bridge and trigger shame, as will any communication of parental belief that the child has inherent deficiencies.

Shame, however, is not an affect confined to early developmental years. People continue to respond with shame to events throughout life. Less intense inducers of shame are interpersonal occurrences such as lack of sensitivity, criticism, and oversight. More intense are experiences of contempt, humiliation, disparagement, and blame.

The process of shame internalization expands the sense of exposure from involving simply an aspect of the self seen as deficient to the whole self as being that which is exposed as defective. The internalization of shame plays a major part in the formation of identity. Prior to internalization, shame is the result of an interchange in which someone else does something to the self. It is a transient experience, readily dispatched through repair to the interpersonal bridge. This degree of shame is thought to be central to the development of conscience and dignity. A reprimand in place of the delighted mirroring expected both evokes shame and alerts the self to differentiating between right and wrong. After the process of shame internalization, however, the shame experience itself is greatly magnified, and what is more, it becomes autonomous. The individual no longer requires an external shame-inducing event. The self begins to shame itself perpetually for a myriad of perceived inadequacies. This can lead to the development of a shame-based identity.

The sequence of events involved in the process of shame internalization consists of an inappropriate response to a child's need or expression of affect, the conversion of the need or affect into a bad feeling, and the consequent decision that it is the self that is bad. Kaufman (1985) posits three main aspects of internalization in general, which forms the conscious experience of the self. One aspect is the internalization of attitudes about the self, which can include verbal messages. These are taken in to form the basis of the emerging sense of identity. Furthermore, one internalizes the way one is treated by others, which becomes the way one treats oneself. Finally, identifications in the form of parental images are internalized and provide specific guiding images. These are usually unconscious but are frequently accompanied by auditory messages. The imagery of the parental identifications is the way in which aspects of the parent's attitudes and behaviors are taken into the self. When these messages are essentially shaming in nature, the inner experience becomes based on shame. Internalized shame is basic to the sense of identity.

The need for relationship is a primary human need, and the feeling of not being a valued member of a significant relationship induces shame. When a parent treats a child as an extension of him- or herself rather than as a separate and uniquely valuable person, the child's essential nature is rejected. Similarly, if the child is expected to fill the parent's needs rather than vice versa, the normal flow of care-giving is disrupted and insecurity results. This occurs also when the child receives communications from the parents not to expect needs to be filled by the parents. The extreme insecurity generated by such interactions easily generalizes and ultimately the self is found to be deficient. The need for relationship, as well as the self, is then experienced as bad, because it engenders intolerable feelings of shame.

SHAME IN ADOLESCENCE

Adolescence is a time of intense sensitivity—to pain as well as to joy and beauty. Experiences imbued with such deep meaning contribute to the definition of who one is at a core level. As teens do their job of trying on and discarding various identities, they incorporate those that strike the loudest chords of resonance to some as yet unmanifest sense of who they really are. Children for whom shame has been a pervasive self-experience find their feelings of low self-worth exacerbated by encounters with others whose scornful evaluations are magnified in importance during this exquisitely sensitive time. At no other age is the longing to belong felt with such poignant force, and teens who are predisposed to feel doubtful about their desirability will feel a special urgency to adapt accordingly.

SHAME AND NARCISSISM

The ability to adapt to standards set by others is a well-honed skill for Gretchen, the 16-year-old discussed above, as it is for many whose early survival was felt to be dependent on accommodation to the needs of significant caregivers. The narcissistic cathexis of the child by the mother leaves the child with few alternatives but to display only those characteristics that maintain the connection between the two. The intrinsic relationship between shame and narcissism has been illuminated by numerous writers since the 1971 publication of Helen Block Lewis's *Shame and Guilt in Neurosis*. Few theoreticians before that time made that relationship explicit in their work, although some did imply a connection. For instance, in observing the oscillation of feelings between grandiosity and worthlessness, Reich (1960) is noting the relationship of narcissism to shame.

Among more recent contributions to this subject, Chasseguet-Smirgel (1985) considers the place of shame in narcissistic merger. She posits the development of the ego ideal as separate from the superego, arising out of primary narcissism. In an attempt to regain the lost infantile sense of being its own ideal, the self projects the ego ideal into the idealized object, and attempts from then on to merge with it. Chasseguet-Smirgel considers these attempts at reunion to be regressive in nature and prone to the development of shame due to the passive dependence on the object for maintenance of self-esteem. Shame results from the recognition of the self's unworthiness for reunion and the fear of the loss of love of the idealized object. The fear of loss of love arises out of the unacceptable nature of the self's libidinal longings and judgments about the dependent nature of the longings.

Another perspective is offered by Broucek (1982), who elaborates on the work of Tomkins (1962, 1963) in considering shame to be the primary affect in narcissism. The disappointing failure to receive the expected response from the parent for the infant's expressed interest or pleasure is a narcissistic injury reflecting the infant's "inability to influence, predict, or comprehend an event that the infant expected . . . to be able to control or understand" (p. 370). It is Broucek's contention that shame both instigates the development of the grandiose self and is itself a response to the grandiose self. Narcissistically vulnerable patients deal with the grandiose self by either devaluing the object and glorifying the self, or, alternatively, by splitting off and projecting the grandiose self onto an idealized other and retaining a devalued sense of self.

A developmental perspective is offered by Johnson (1987), who integrates the conflict model of classical psychoanalysis with a deficit model consisting of aspects of object relations, self psychology, and ego psychology. His formulations trace the inability of the environment to meet the changing needs of the developing child, attributing the different character disorders to environmental failure and subsequent arrest at specific developmental stages.

Following Mahler and colleagues' (1975) developmental schema, Johnson places the development of narcissistic difficulties in the rapprochement subphase of separation-individuation. The phase immediately prior to rapprochement is the practicing subphase, wherein the child enjoys a "love affair with the world," exhibiting the grandiosity and euphoria that Johnson posits to be the developmental analogue to grandiose narcissistic behavior in adulthood. Under optimal conditions, this grandiosity is neutralized during the child's encounters with reality and limits in rapprochement. Rapprochement is a period of reconciliation between grandiosity and vulnerability. The other pole to be reconciled is that of symbiosis and separation. Successful negotiation of this developmental phase involves nontraumatic confrontation with the realities of separateness and limitation, as well as adequate mirroring of the child's magnificence by the admiring parent (Kohut 1971). The result of a successful rapprochement is a true sense of self, and, compensating for the loss of omnipotence, increased ego strength and the pride of relative autonomy. Failure to integrate the poles of grandiosity and vulnerability leads to a developmental arrest at the stage of grandiosity and the symptom pattern of narcissism.

Narcissistic injury to the child's attempt to develop his or her real self, combined with the challenge of rapprochement, is the guide here to understanding narcissism. Unresolved narcissistic needs of their own incite parents to respond to the child in one of two nonaffirming ways. One damaging response is idealization and nonacceptance of the true vulnerabilities of the child. The other is humiliation, out of envy for the child's magnificence. Both of these responses convey the message that the parent requires the child to be who the parent needs him to be rather than who he truly is. The occurrence of this injury during the child's attempt to reconcile grandiosity and omnipotence with his or her new awareness of vulnerability is significant in the development of narcissistic symptoms.

The child must compensate for the narcissistic injury and does so through the development of an idealized false self. The false self is the child's attempt to be who the parent wants him or her to be, and is an adaptation geared for survival via maintenance of badly needed contact and love. Concomitant with adoption of false-self attributes is the child's rejection of his or her real self in a manner reflecting the environment's rejection of real self expression. The rejected aspects are then disavowed and hidden from experience. Failure to provide the mirroring that the grandiose self requires in order for the grandiosity to be neutralized leads to developmental arrest at that point. The child then attempts, as part of the false-self compensation, to live up to the grandiosity by attaining perfection.

The relationship between shame and narcissism in this conceptualization has to do with the polarization between grandiosity and worthlessness. The compensatory, idealized false self develops out of the pole of grandiosity. The false self exhibits grandiosity, entitlement, striving for perfection, inability to accept failure, reliance on achievement for self-esteem, manipulation, pride, and arrogance. These manifestations are frequently disavowed by the individual, who then has little awareness of the grandiose nature of the false self's demands. As the false self is not based in reality, it is extremely vulnerable.

The failure of the grandiose false self releases the affects of the symptomatic self, which is formulated around the pole of worthlessness. Associated feelings are humiliation, depression, the sense of not being enough, isolation, loneliness, worthlessness, and envy.

Both the false and symptomatic selves are split horizontally from the denied real self. Arrested at so early a developmental phase, the real self is a reservoir of pain and rage arising from unmet needs. Captured along with disavowed feelings of emptiness and despair are the innate capacities of the real self, its identifications, ambitions, and ideals. Many individuals have extremely well developed false-self defenses and have manipulated their environment to support their grandiose self-concepts. For these people, dismantling the false self is neither appealing nor simple. The real self will resurface only upon the failure of the false self and the resolution of the symptomatic self's painful affects.

Thus, the horizontal split serves a defensive function. The false-self manifestations protect against awareness of the extreme pain associated with the unmet, archaic demands of the real self. The symptomatic self protects against the affective demands of the real self, as well as against awareness of the false self's grandiosity.

Shame enters this picture of narcissism through the symptomatic self, and is indeed a key aspect of the symptomatic self. The shame can be understood to fill a signal function, indicating the underlying injury to the self and the archaic demand for mirroring. Shame also signals the unrealistic nature of the false-self demands. Overall, the pain of the symptomatic self is a signal that the needs of the real self are not being met.

Thus, although there exists no consensus regarding the actual nature of the relationship between shame and narcissism, there is significant accord as to its existence. The two primary notions involve matching the actual self with some ideal self image, together with the various strategies for coping with the inevitable discrepancy, and the ways with which the self deals with unneutralized grandiosity.

CASE STUDIES

Gretchen

Gretchen's early history reads like a primer on the development of narcissism. A striking number of incidents Gretchen recalls from childhood indicate a blatant disregard on the part of her parents for their children's sensibilities, feelings, and age-appropriate needs for consistency and predictability. The oldest of three siblings, Gretchen recalls being left in charge while her parents locked themselves in their bedroom for hours watching television on Sunday afternoons. Later, when Gretchen was 7 years old, her mother developed a chronic and debilitating illness. Even at that young age Gretchen performed such tasks as the family cooking and shopping, as well as looking out for her younger siblings. She reported feeling very ashamed of having to do these tasks, because other kids had a mother who could do them. Her mother made it clear that any problems, or behavior that was less than exemplary, was a tremendous burden for her to bear. Although Gretchen was a model student, she felt as if nothing she did was ever good enough. Additionally, she perceived her mother as taking her accomplishments for granted, that nothing less was expected of her, and, moreover, that they took no effort. She feels that people will view her as inadequate if she has to work at something in order to do it well. In fact, she feels inadequate if she has to make an effort, as accomplishments should come with little or no work. Mother often included herself in Gretchen's scholastic accomplishments, co-opting credit for what could have been self-enhancing experiences for Gretchen.

A series of particularly impacting events occurred as Gretchen began her emergence into adolescence. An altercation between her mother and the teacher of one of Gretchen's siblings culminated in the abrupt withdrawal of both children from a school in which Gretchen was doing extremely well, surrounded by a strong support system of friendships. Gretchen was subsequently, and without input into any of these decisions, enrolled in another school in the middle of the ninth grade, her freshman year of high school. Her ability to regulate her self-esteem was seriously compromised as she felt hopelessly out of place both socially and academically. Whereas school had felt relatively easy for her and she had maintained both her grades and the high regard of her teachers, suddenly she was in the position of needing to catch up in her classes. Not only was her previously certain site of narcissistic supplies cut off, but she was also required to exert a tremendous effort to regain her standing on the dean's list, an effort that for her was a self experience tantamount to failure. Additionally, within a year of this transfer, Gretchen's parents became embroiled in a particularly venomous divorce, whereupon Gretchen felt compelled to provide cohesion for her mother's fragmented state. As this was a task inherently doomed to failure, Gretchen's sense of identity in these formative years was organized around experiences of doubt, failure, and pressure to perform well beyond her ability.

In therapy, Gretchen demonstrated a number of unconscious organizing principles that are basically narcissistic in nature. A primary way Gretchen has of interacting in her environment is to discern and then provide for the needs of significant others in order to continue receiving necessary supplies from them. In the therapy, she attempted this by being a "good client" who adhered rigidly to all the normal aspects of the frame, such as punctuality, attendance, and payment. She had a great deal of anxiety about breaking any of these rules. It was also important to her that she bring up "interesting" material, as I might be comparing her to other patients and find her less attractive and less worth my time. Gretchen expressed considerable distress when she interpreted my comments to mean that she was not "working hard enough." Additionally, she was very worried about disappointing me by letting me know that she was not "cured" of issues we had already discussed.

A second organizing principle concerned Gretchen's belief that she should be able to do everything by herself. This was evident in her concern that she needed to do something immediately with whatever interpretation I might make. She had a fair amount of difficulty taking something in, and felt pressured to do something with it immediately. In one session she reported an exhausting dream about the necessity of carrying many people from one place to the other, and that she accomplished this on her own. Associations to this dream pointed to her belief that there is no help available to her, thus, she has to do everything for herself. Additionally, her tendency to experience most interpretations as judgments rather than as valuable aids in the restoration of her self pointed to narcissistic injury at not being entirely self-sufficient.

Also, Gretchen operated under the assumption that she must appear competent at all times. She had tremendous shame about revealing any weak or needy aspects of herself during the sessions. Slowly she became able to unveil the relatively undifferentiated self underneath the competent front, terrified of being scorned and rejected. Her experience of such exposure was of being extremely small and vulnerable, and very alone. It was very hard for her to believe that I could tolerate her presence when she was in that state, and frequently followed such vulnerable sessions with a return to extremely intellectual material. She held a strong belief that others expected her to easily perform tasks that she considers to be impossible to accomplish, placing her under tremendous pressure. This belief was so strong that she seldom questioned the reasonableness of the expectation. This came through in the transference when she finally expressed her frustration and anger that she was unable to do what she presumed an interpretation was instructing her to do.

Gretchen's competent appearance and impressive accomplishments belied the extremely chaotic and frightening nature of her internal world. It was as though she constantly walked a thin line between being open to receiving longed-for attention for that unacceptable, vulnerable part and being exposed as a fraud who will lose the love and care of people who are important to her if she reduced her tight control on her external appearance of competence and perfection.

Rick

The predisposing factors in Rick's case stem from more blatantly abusive experiences. An only child, Rick was 4 years old when his father abandoned the family. His alcoholic mother attributed the desertion to the burden of having a "whiny" child in the family. She remarried shortly after the divorce. Rick's stepfather was also alcoholic and Rick recalls frequent exposure to frighteningly explosive and violent fights. As Rick's mother desperately needed a relationship with a man for the regulation of her own self-esteem, she seldom protected Rick from his stepfather's scathing verbal attacks. Rick remembers also being required to stand before large gatherings of family members reciting poetry and answering questions about his schoolwork posed, as a game, by his stepfather. Reserved by nature, Rick felt humiliated and physically ill as a result of these performances.

Sexual abuse at the hands of a 21-year-old male neighbor further compromised Rick's already precarious sense of self. Rick continued to suffer a crippling level of shame about his genitals at least into his twenties. The shame around his sexuality was intensified by unfortunate incidents in the dating arena. For example, Rick approached a girl who had agreed to date him only to have her ridicule him in front of her girlfriends, saying that she never had any intention of going out with him, that her acceptance of his invitation was simply a joke to amuse her friends. The mortification evoked in Rick compelled him to run away from home for an entire year.

Rick appears to have employed a full spectrum of defense reactions to the devastation of shame. Kohut (1984) points out that narcissistic rage is analogous to the fight component of the fight-or-flight reaction to attack employed by biological organisms. Similarly, the flight reaction corresponds to narcissistic withdrawal and avoidance of injury. Rick's tough-guy acting out in class and his frequent fights with other kids demonstrates displaced narcissistic rage; the heavy drug use and running away are manifestations of flight from disorganizing experiences of worthlessness and humiliation.

There is another important aspect of Rick's flights from home related to the development of his shame-based sense of identity. The critical human need for relationship with others, when frustrated, touches off a number of responses. The need to belong, to be a part of something, can manifest in the formation of false-self defenses that will enhance the possibility of acceptance by others. In this regard, Rick's use of drugs and alcohol both increased his sense of being "okay" and provided him with a social life. As per Erik Erikson (1968), the shame of feeling like a social misfit can be rectified through the development of a negative identification. Rather than struggling with the pain of not belonging, Rick identified with it by joining the cadres of "Deadheads" that followed the counterculture band the Grateful Dead around the country. His year as a Deadhead helped solidify a sense of self based on not being a "normal" member of society.

In therapy, Rick responded surprisingly quickly to the therapist's stance of nonjudgmental, empathic attunement to the traumatic injuries beneath his seemingly antisocial exterior. His extreme vulnerability to slights of any kind, coupled with his truly mortifying encounters with others, resulted in sudden reversions to his fight-or-flight defensive patterns, and Rick's attendance in therapy was sporadic for the first several years.

TREATMENT

Shame is a window opening onto the needs of the self. Like most pain, shame signals the presence and proximity of the injuries to be healed. Carefully tracking the course of this affect throughout the process and content of the therapy session leads to invaluable opportunities for healing through the emergence and reintegration of split-off needs and affects.

As explored above, shame is an integral part of narcissism. The omnipotence of narcissism precludes the acceptability of needs; thus, need is considered to be bad and is split off. Need becomes associated with shame and the self as a whole is considered to be defective. Shame must become the aspect of this process valued for its special place as an entrance to the needs of the self.

An integration of psychodynamic and mind–body healing is useful when focusing on treating shame. Psychodynamic interventions focus on bringing disavowed and otherwise unconscious processes to awareness, as well as providing therapeutic acceptance of the patient's self. The transference is also an invaluable area for working through shame dynamics and developing a more positive self-identity. Mind–body healing approaches depotentiate shame through experiences in trance that interrupt limiting patterns and allow the reintegration of real-self expressions and resources in a healthier pattern. The particular kind of contact and attention available through mind-body interventions are healing in and of themselves. And, as individuals learn to value their internal experiences of comfort and safety, and become familiar with their own rhythm for being, self-valuation increases.

Psychodynamic Approach to Treating Shame

Analyzing the course of shame affects, rather than shame's self-denigrating content, is a key aspect of the treatment. Understanding the various forms that shame feelings can take increases an individual's ability to cope with shame. Bringing the various manifestations of shame to consciousness can be done largely through interpreting the pain that drives them. This is an empathic approach to facilitating incorporation of relatively uncomfortable material. As Rick came to understand his baffling behavior as manifestations of shame and defenses against it, he was able to begin the long process of separating his sense of self from his behaviors. His ability to understand the pain driving him into self-defeating patterns gave him more compassion for activities triggering self-contempt.

Normalizing the incredible intensity of shame reactions to seemingly insignificant events is often critical to the treatment. A lifetime of shame experiences fuels these seemingly out-of-proportion reactions. Initially, for Gretchen, the shame reactions themselves were highly shame inducing. This exemplifies the shame-internalization mechanism, wherein shame is autonomously produced in a seemingly never-ending cycle. It was first necessary to break into this cycle, indicating the extent to which the cycle was understandable in light of the pervasively shaming atmosphere of the environment in which she was raised. It is also helpful for the patient to recognize the signal function of the shame feeling. By realizing that having the feeling meant something, Gretchen was able to shift her focus from the experience of self-deficiency to the needs underlying it.

The therapist supports the patient's growing acceptance of her self through empathic mirroring and respectful attendance to her feelings and needs. It is critical here that the therapist understand the patient's deep fear of exposure. For Gretchen, this fear coincides with her experience of less-than-perfect aspects of her self as indicating deficiency of her self as a whole. Shame signals injury and a need for mirroring; however, the mirroring of patient needs and feelings must be done with sensitivity to the possibility that the patient considers those needs and feelings to be bad. Gretchen frequently interpreted the mirroring of a need to be a judgment pronounced by the therapist; a shame-based rupture such as this requires immediate repair for treatment to continue.

The time and attention that the therapist devotes to understanding the patient at a deep level allow him or her to feel valued as a person. In therapy, Rick had his first experience with an individual who actually sought to understand his inner world, and who seemed to find him worth taking the time to know. His idealization of his male therapist gave him a long-missing ideal other with whom to merge and a chance to restore development based on positive identifications.

Acceptance of the patient's self with all its perceived and realistic weakness and imperfections gives the patient the opportunity to learn to be self-affirming. This is especially so when the therapist is able to convey the notion that differences are both acceptable and valuable. For the shame-prone person, differences have typically been used to measure the deficiencies of the self against the strengths of others, and as such are experienced as threatening. Valuing differences is a difficult and important achievement for this kind of patient.

Becoming aware of and owning her propensity for self-criticism allowed Gretchen to develop new ways of responding to self-attack. Frequently, such patients are unaware of their ubiquitous self-devaluing attitudes until this pattern has been consistently and repeatedly pointed out by the therapist. It took considerable time for Gretchen to recognize that this "default setting" of self-criticism was not yet another indication of her failure as a human being. Eventually, though, recognizing and replacing the harsh self-attacks with curiosity led to her development of new ways of relating to the "bad" parts, primarily by divesting these parts of their severely negative valence.

The therapist's emergence as a highly significant person in the patient's unconscious formulations makes it critical to be alert to undischarged shame and rage arising from interactions within the therapy setting. The therapist is a natural source for patient shame responses by virtue of the exposure inherent in the setting. Disruption of the interpersonal bond due to the therapist's misattunement can also trigger shame. For Rick, these inevitable occurrences were injuries reminiscent of his abandonment by his father. The loss of that interpersonal bridge was understood to reflect on his badness and undesirability. Tracking the course of shame was essential both to illuminate it and to prevent the discharge of hostility toward the self that occurred when Rick found it too threatening to direct it at a much-needed person. It also gave the therapist a basis from which to understand the intensity of the rage when it was expressed in his direction. Working in the transference not only grounds the projections so intrinsic to the shame-based personality, it also draws the patient's attention inward, to the real source of pain and potential for healing. Mind–body healing expands on the patient's ability to make use of those inner potentials.

Mind–Body Healing of Shame

Depotentiating the powerfully painful affect of shame through mind–body healing involves reconnecting individuals with their own, intrinsically healing inner resources for well-being. The suspension of ordinary states of consciousness provides unusual experiences of safety and comfort that are in themselves contrary to the self-devaluing feelings of shame. Within the trance state, attention and support are given to particular unconscious healing processes, engaging them and allowing them to unfold naturally. Many of the interventions facilitate unlearning limiting patterns of behavior and developing underutilized abilities and resources. The internally generated nature of these processes, which are discernible by the patient, engender feelings of self-worth.

Development of therapeutic trance entails taking advantage of those moments in which the patient's attention is fixed on some compelling inner sensation or external source of fascination. Such fixation often occurs spontaneously, as in response to an interpretation that articulates an awareness very near the surface of consciousness. These moments of suspended consciousness are supported and allowed to expand into sustained altered states of consciousness. The many ways of facilitating the development of the trance or mind-body healing states are well outlined in other sources (especially Erickson and Rossi 1979, among other works).

Even without the intentional encouragement of the unconscious hypnotic processes and responses, these periods of reverie have the value of allowing the unconscious to process spontaneously whatever interventions the therapist may be using. Such states of mind are similar to the infant states of alert inactivity described by Demos (1982), which appear to be the periods of time in which the sense of self is organized. The work of Daniel Stern (1985) supports this observation. He contends that the infant in this state is responding creatively to both internal and external stimuli. Bion (1963) recognizes the reverie that accompanies the mother's (and the analyst's) containment of the individual's frustrations as being important in the development of thought processes. Actively expanding periods of reverie through mind–body healing interventions allows experiences in trance that can be useful in treating shame.

By providing containment, the therapist is holding for the patient a space of trusting that it is worthwhile to go inside, that there is something of value within. This kind of holding provides the unusual experience of someone having tolerance for the patient's inner moments. Trance-time can be experienced as either passing extremely quickly or as having been greatly expanded. These experiences are directly counter to narcissistic pressures around time, and as such are extremely healing. As with most other needs, the need for time has been split off in the narcissistically injured individual and that need must become first valid, then acceptable, and then valuable. Once the need for time is valued, the time can be used to explore other split-off needs.

Comfort is another important real-self resource that is accessed during mind–body healing. Experiencing the unconscious as a source of self-soothing and comfort provides a means of self regulation and reduces some of the narcissistic strivings toward receiving externally the supplies available internally. False-self reliance on achievement for worth is mitigated.

Gretchen and Rick both developed the facility for entering a trance state relatively easily. Rick's musical talent provided a natural conduit to the creativity of his unconscious. He was able to generalize the altered state of consciousness that developed when playing his guitar to a therapeutic trance state. Experience in the trance state helped ameliorate the considerable anxiety that was a crippling and pervasive self state, rendering him more available to therapeutic intervention.

Many of the trance experiences have been very meaningful for Gretchen, particularly one in which she experienced the presence of something worthwhile existing within her. She said it was the first time she had ever had such a sensation. This is significant at a number of levels. It is during similar periods of alert inactivity that infant experiences of a cohesive, valued, and valuable self occur. It is unlikely, given the traumatic self-state of Gretchen's mother, that this developmental avenue was thoroughly pursued. In addition, this kind of therapeutic interaction helped facilitate a therapeutic alliance by overcoming Gretchen's skepticism about caregivers providing anything of value. And these sessions gave Gretchen repeated experiences of being with a significant other who mirrored for her that these feelings of self-worth are valid and worth taking the time to attain.

The comfort available in the trance state was very valuable for Rick in providing an alternative method of self-soothing. Whereas drugs helped regulate his affect states at some cost to his ego strength and self-esteem, the comfort he was able to connect with was entirely ego-syntonic and, in fact, increased his ability to feel good about himself by releasing previously unavailable vitality.

Spending time accessing and exploring the resources within the unconscious of safety, trust, and comfort lays the foundation for the emergence of another key resource, curiosity. Curiosity is a healing resource because it fuels the patient's interest in staying with the issue, rather than avoiding it in some way. As the opposite of the pressure to know, curiosity is a healing element for narcissism. Curiosity allows exploration and learning to take place relatively free from pressure. Many of the patient's traumas around learning and taking in new things began when childhood curiosity was shamed, punished, not encouraged, or devalued in favor of learning instantly. Narcissistic parents in particular are less able to tolerate the "not knowing" that curiosity implies, either in themselves or in their child. Consequently, the child develops fear as a response to feeling curious and quickly shuts it down. It takes the presence of a solid base of security and trust for this individual to begin to access curiosity. The therapist can model curiosity in nonthreatening ways and mirror its gradual emergence in the patient. Treating the narcissistic pressure to know everything immediately facilitates the availability of curiosity as a resource for healing. By becoming capable of maintaining curiosity about the symptom or problem, Gretchen and Rick later became curious about the nature of their healing processes. In time, enough safety developed that they could sustain curiosity about their feelings, leading ultimately to curiosity about the needs underlying those feelings. Having enough curiosity to sustain exploration of the needs is an important factor in their reintegration into the self.

As the focus of intense attention and evaluation, the shame-based self is the subject of paralyzing self-scrutiny. Often the source of evaluation is felt to be external as the scrutinizing actions are projected onto others. The self, however, remains the center of attention. Developing the ability to focus attention firmly on any sensory experience, or visually on something in the environment, interrupts the autonomous shame activities. Gretchen developed the ability to shift attention fully from one thing to another during the trancework. Additionally, she developed sufficient familiarity with a relaxed state of mind that now it can be accessed almost at will. She has learned to use the signal generated by emergence of a shame state to focus attention outwardly and shift into a mildly altered state for long enough to move into a third, self-valuing state of mind.

For the shame-prone individual in particular, doing is especially favored over being. Being, in fact, is bad. It is only through accomplishment and by manipulating things and people in the external world that the patient is able to connect to any sense of validation. Nearly all of Gretchen's sense of value was based on her achievements, the compliments she elicited, and her ability to provide the persona she perceived others as requiring from her. Time spent in the internal reverie of therapeutic trance provides some healing of the traumas associated with just being. Rick, too, was impacted positively through time spent without pressure to have to do anything. The therapist can encourage this experience and generate a surprising amount of comfort through such phrases as: "And you don't need to do anything at all." As are many such individuals, Gretchen was particularly prone to worrying about whether she was "doing it right" when in the trance state, and needed considerable reassurance that there was, in fact, nothing to do. The conscious mind can be allowed to do whatever it needs to do, and at the same time the unconscious mind can activate in its own, spontaneous, undirected fashion.

The resource of allowing is closely related to being, and its development will enhance the individual's ability to value his or her sense of being. When the patient can distance herself from her need to have active, conscious control over every aspect of her life, she can begin to allow her unconscious the time to reorganize experiences, resources, and learnings, and generate new associations leading to resumed growth and healing changes. Split-off parts lose their negative charge and become available for incorporation into the whole.

By staying with the patient's explicit experience, real-self expressions can be validated in areas that were repeatedly invalidated in childhood. As the individual's real self activates at the points of developmental deficit, careful attunement to experiences occurring within the trance allows the appropriate developmental course to resume where it was derailed.

REFERENCES

Bion, W. R. (1963). *Elements of Psycho-analysis*. London: Heinemann.

Broucek, F. (1982). Shame and its relationship to early narcisstic developments. *International Journal of Psycho-Analysis* 65:369–378.

Chasseguet-Smirgel, J. (1985). *The Ego Ideal*. New York: Norton.

Demos, V. (1982). Facial expression in young children—a descriptive analysis. In *Emotion and Interaction: Normal and High Risk Infants*, ed. T. Field, pp. 127–160. Hillsdale, NJ: Erlbaum.

Erickson, M., and Rossi, E. (1979). *Hypnotherapy: An Exploratory Casebook*. New York: Irvington.

Erikson, E. (1968). *Identity: Youth and Crisis*. London: Faber and Faber.

Fairbairn, W. R. D. (1966). *Psychoanalytic Studies of the Personality*. London: Routledge & Kegan Paul.

Freud, S. (1914). On narcissism: an introduction. *Standard Edition* 14:73–102.

Hartmann, H. (1950). Comments on the psychoanalytic theory of the ego. *Psychoanalytic Study of the Child* 5:42-81. New York: International Universities Press.

Hartmann, H., and Loewenstein, R. (1962). Notes on the superego. *Psychoanalytic Study of the Child* 5:42-81. New York: International Universities Press.

Jacobson, E. (1964). *The Self and the Object World*. New York: International Universities Press.

Johnson, S. (1987). *Humanizing the Narcissistic Style*. New York: Norton.

Kaufman, G. (1985). *Shame: The Power of Caring*. Cambridge, MA: Schenkman.

——(1989). *The Psychology of Shame: Theory and Treatment of Shame-Based Syndromes*. New York: Springer.

Kaufman, G., and Raphael, L. (1991). *Dynamics of Power: Fighting Shame and Building Self-Esteem*, 2nd ed. Rochester, VT: Schenkman.

Kinston, W. (1983). A theoretical context for shame. *International Journal of Psycho-Analysis* 64:213-226.

Kohut, H. (1966). Forms and transformations of narcissism. *Journal of the American Psychoanalytic Association* 14:243-272.

——(1971). *The Analysis of the Self*. Madison, CT: International Universities Press.

——(1977). *The Restoration of the Self*. New York: International Universities Press.

——(1984). *How Does Analysis Cure?* Chicago and London: University of Chicago Press.

Lewis, H. B. (1971). *Shame and Guilt in Neurosis*. New York: International Universities Press.

Mahler, M., Pine, F., and Bergman, A. (1975). *The Psychological Birth of the Human Infant*. New York: Basic Books.

Morrison, A. (1989). *Shame: The Underside of Narcissism*. Hillsdale, NJ: Analytic Press.

Reich, A. (1960). Pathologic forms of self-esteem regulation. *Psychoanalytic Study of the Child* 15:215-232. New York: International Universities Press.

Schafer, R. (1960). The loving and beloved superego in Freud's structural theory. *Psychoanalytic Study of the Child* 15:163-188. New York: International Universities Press.

——(1967). Ideals, the ego ideal, and the ideal self. *Psychological Issues Monograph* 18/19:131-174.

Stern, D. (1985). *The Interpersonal World of the Infant*. New York: Basic Books.

Tomkins, S. S. (1962). *Affect/Imagery/Consciousness: Vol. 1. The Positive Affects*. New York: Springer.

———(1963). *Affect/Imagery/Consciousness: Vol. 2. The Negative Affects*. New York: Springer.

Winnicott, D. W. (1980). Ego distortion in terms of the true and false self. In *The Maturational Processes and the Facilitating Environment*, pp. 140–152. New York: International Universities Press, 1965.

PART IV

Treatment Issues in Working with Parents and Families

INTRODUCTION TO PART IV

The Reiss-Davis Child Study Center has always incorporated a family model in working with patients. Although family therapy is offered as needed, the majority of treatment cases are addressed through an individual child–parent model that simultaneously addresses the issues and problems of the child, including his or her symptomatology, and the issues and problems of parenting, including individual and family symptomatology. This model, while dealing with current problems of both the child and parent, also allows for parental growth that is reflected in the parents' reaction to other children and adolescents in the family, and thus becomes preventive in nature. This section's chapters reflect both remedial and preventive work with parents and families.

Chapter 16, “The Transmission of Womanhood from Mother to Daughter,” by Bertrand Cramer, illustrates how parental problems are often displaced and/or projected onto the children as they tend to re-create their own childhood dynamics with their children and with their parents. The author notes that very often a child’s symptoms may really be parental issues being played out by the child who is expressing the family pain. Treatment suggested for a child’s problems may never include the child, as the approach suggested requires resolution of family-of-origin issues, a family therapy approach, and more typically direct work with the parent couple.

Chapter 17, “The Father-Infant Toddler Group,” by S. Robert Moradi, looks at the development of psychological connections between father and child and the benefits for fathers of attending groups designed specifically for fathers and their young children. The author addresses issues of shame, rage, gender, paternal empathy, and a range of intrapsychic issues unique to men.

Chapter 18, “Parenting as a Function of the Adult Self,” by Paul Ornstein and Anna Ornstein, illustrates how infant and child development studies have become central to the human behavior research endeavor. The authors discuss how a group of patients who suffer from discrete structural deficits can be related to equally discrete and subtle failures in parental responsiveness to the patient’s developmental needs for affirmation and validation as a child. They also indicate the mutuality of the parents and the biological anlage for human psychological development that resides within the infant as a capacity to elicit certain responses from the environment. Their chapter further suggests that parental empathy is not only a mode of observation but an emotional nutrient as well, and its absence in parenting can create pathology in the child.

Chapter 19, “A Wrinkle in the Sheets: An Overview of Parent Treatment through Couples Therapy,” by Walter E. Brackelmanns, develops a model for marital therapy based on an idea that in all relationships there are four levels of interaction. The goal of marital therapy is to move the couple from level one to level four. The author suggests that a good indication of when a couple is in need of marital therapy is when the couple is in conflict and experiencing psychic pain rather than assuming responsibility for their intrapsychic problems.

Chapter 20, "Chronic Disconnections: Three Family Contexts," by Irene Pierce Stiver, looks at the families of alcoholics, families with incest, and families of survivors of the Holocaust in order to illustrate different contexts in which chronic disconnections occur. Some of the salient features characterizing these families are identified as well as the different strategies used by people growing up in such families to stay out of the negative relationships.

Chapter 21, "A Multigenerational Inquiry into the Relationship between Mothers and Daughters," by Barbara Zaks and Stephan Poulter, explores how many women experience their mothers during various stages of life. The struggles of daughters in love and work relationships reflect family dynamics, especially with maternal figures. The authors point out a set of symptoms that often present in women with this conflict as well as their effects on personal, work-related, and intimate relationships.

Chapter 22, "Perpetually Battling Parents," by Carl F. Hoppe, focuses on custody evaluation litigants who have an underlying "relationship disorder" and belong to a distinct clinical group that uses primitive psychological defense mechanisms and has distorted perceptions. The author describes how this relationship disorder intensifies the triangular relationship between the divorcing parents and the child where inner vulnerabilities of each parent become confused with the needs of the child. The chapter then focuses on how this disorder affects custody evaluations in the court setting.

16

The Transmission of Womanhood from Mother to Daughter

Bertrand Cramer

In psychotherapeutic work with parents and infants, the therapist cannot help to be awestruck by the powerful influences of parental representations about the infant's motivations and especially about his future image as an adult. Parents react not to the child only, but to what he is supposed to become later on. Parents predict, and their anticipatory thinking (Trad 1990) orients in a profound way attitudes, play, and thinking in the child. Most of these expectations are strongly colored by parental values, either positive or negative.

The more familiar type of expectations are made of highly desirable characteristics; the infant is expected to be smart, strong, and so on. It is ego ideal contents that shape those predictions, and we know that this narcissistic cathexis powerfully influences a positive parental attachment to the child. The child is thus under contract to fulfill ideals of the parents, which makes him or her a promise of future gratification. The child is then invested as a powerful source of pleasure and pride.

But frequently, consultations about babies are due to the impact of highly *negative* expectations about the child, that he or she will become delinquent, or perverse (the fear of homosexual development of boys being a frequent anxiety). It is therefore important to carefully study expectations parents have about the future of their infant, and to analyze this material in terms of their value systems (i.e., ego ideal characteristics).

This chapter focuses on a specific aspect of the expectations mothers have about the future of their daughters—that is, their view of womanhood. I will demonstrate that all mothers orient their daughters' development according to their value system concerning the role of women, particularly in their relationships to the other sex. Mothers relate to their daughters with a constant reference to the future woman they are supposed to become. These expectations are conscious, reflecting as well cultural trends concerning the popular representations of womanhood. But they are also based on unconscious fantasies about the feminine body, about the relations between the sexes, and about a large spectrum of feminine attitudes and functions. Among those functions, motherhood plays a predominant role. Its importance is paramount when one treats a woman who brings her infant daughter for therapy. The main focus of treatment is almost always centered on the representations of the maternal role, and this always brings back images of the past relationship between daughter and mother, one generation before. Thus, in conjoint therapy, when one treats mother and daughter, one has the opportunity to study the transmission of representations of womanhood (and simultaneously of motherhood) through three generations. The values determining representations of womanhood, as well as the anxieties linked to feminine imagery, are revealed in the concerns mothers have about their daughters. As in a cameo, one can grasp in the microcosm of mother-infant interactions the representations of womanhood inherited by mothers from their own parents, and their guiding influences on the budding female identity of a baby. As in the picture of a snake biting its tail, one can observe how the grown woman that is the baby's future links with old images, carried by her grandmother, thus joining the old and the new in a circle.

FEMININITY AND CULTURE

One of the basic tenets of infant psychiatry is that a baby's experience can only be understood within its context. The baby's development of experiences is largely codetermined by shared meanings within his familial-cultural environment. When adulthood is reached, the individual's inner *working models*, understood here very much as Bowlby (1958) defined them, are fed by two main sources. The first is representations that were accumulated since infancy, resulting in a gestalt or schema that is fixed and repetitive, made up of memories of things felt, heard, and learned, resulting in cognitive shapes, and of emotions (excitement, anxiety, guilt, and so on), desires, and fantasies (in the psychoanalytic sense). The result is not a simple storage of recollections, but a construction summarizing and synthesizing these many features in a *mean representation* that is characterized by cognitive features, emotional tone, values, intensity, and personal style. For example, the word *woman* will have a myriad of personal connotations, such as powerful or weak, beautiful or ugly, live or dead, desirable or awesome, while referring simultaneously to cognitive features that can be shared with the human community, such as anatomical, social, and psychological characteristics.

The second source of these inner models is the store of representations typical for a culture. The concept of social desirability (Boszormenyi-Nagy and Spark 1973) illustrates this cultural source. Each cultural group proposes representations of characteristics, some of which are connoted by positive, ideal values, while others are disqualified as bad. Margaret Mead (1935) studied three primitive societies and stated that standardized personality differences between the sexes are cultural creations. Moreover, each generation, male and female, is trained to conform. Erik Erikson (1950) showed in his remarkable clinical studies how each social group shapes the images one should tend to resemble. Many feminist studies also emphasize that womanhood is a cultural creation. In their efforts to deconstruct images of femininity, they berate the weight applied by social-cultural forces such as men's needs to keep women in the kitchen and caring for children. They focus on how men want to maintain women in submission and avoid their intrusion into the economic, political, and cultural fields (Bassin et al. 1994). "You are not born as a woman, you become a woman," wrote Simone de Beauvoir (1949), a philosopher and a major pioneer in feminine studies. This point of view summarizes the powerful role of cultural values as they shape sexual identities, with the mediation of parental education as the main instrument in this creation.

THE STUDY OF SEXUAL ROLES AND IDENTITIES

While we emphasize the influences of cultural factors on the development of femininity, many other determinisms need to be taken into account. Constitutional and congenital factors have as yet not produced strong evidence for sex differences at birth. But the advances in molecular biology in neurosciences and in genetics will possibly determine sex-related characteristics that affect psychological functioning.

Sociological influences have been widely studied, first in what is called anthropological sociology (see for example the pioneering work of Levi-Strauss 1956), and later in a wealth of feminine studies. Historical studies have demonstrated the influences of current socioeconomic and cultural values on the definition of womanhood (Atkinson 1991, Knibiehler and Fouquet 1980). Historical studies of education have demonstrated the powerful influence of advice by experts on maternal practices (Ehrenreich and English 1979).

Psychoanalytic studies have emphasized that sex differences play a crucial, organizing role in shaping psychic conflicts ever since Freud's "Three Essays on Sexuality" (1905). Psychoanalytic observation of infants and young children showed that early relationships (especially with the mother) powerfully determine gender identity (Roiphe and Galenson 1984, Stoller 1985).

It appears that long before the crucial influence of the Oedipus complex the predeterminants of sexual identity had been laid down, and this encouraged researchers to study infant observation and, more recently, mother–infant interactions.

If one looks at the wealth of data accumulated in the field of early interactions, one sees the power of reciprocal communication in the dyad. All interactive behaviors can be interpreted as messages, as intentions, or as actions on the partner. A behavioral vocabulary and syntax is developed in common. Mutually organized scenarios become a precious, precise and repetitive social convention used by the parent to orient the infant's experience and behavior. It is through this behavioral semiology that mothers indicate to the infant which attitudes are welcomed and which are not. Thus, mothers create beacons that will show which paths to follow in order to create an identity that suits the mother's prerequisites, while serving simultaneously the infant's interests.

One of the more potent beacons in this search for identity models concerns sex-linked attitudes. Each culture carries a more or less rigid representation of womanhood. In so-called primitive societies, this code is strictly enforced, while in the modern world a diffusion of gender identity prevails. Mothers in traditional societies make sure to reproduce the feminine model they were exposed to. In our society, they have to improvise such models, since cultural indices of womanhood have become multiple.

Yet, a secret, unconscious tradition of stereotyped feminine models remains active, and is transmitted from generation to generation. One of the main challenges of young mothers today is reconciling these unconscious, old models with modern ones. Women are no longer determined by their biology alone. Until the nineteenth century, the definition of women was simple: "*Tota mulier in utero*," a woman's destiny is entirely reducible to her uterine function. But now contraception allows them to control their fecundity. Mothers are no longer totally dependent on their husbands since they can produce their own income. The conflict between traditional and modern models is apparent in consultations with young mothers who worry about their babies. While they want to accomplish their ambitions, in terms of career and personal achievements, they also want to be good mothers, often according to models that were handed down from previous generations. The infant's symptom is often the visible sign of this quandary concerning maternal identity.

MOTHER–INFANT PSYCHOTHERAPY

Infants cannot be treated alone. It is the relationship between the partners in the dyad that becomes the focus of observation and therapy. During the sessions the therapist listens to the mother's complaints and anxieties, while observing the infant in interactions with her (Cramer 1995b). This format allows the uncovering of maternal conflicts and representations as they are mobilized by the infant. Specific shapes of interactions appear that are linked to maternal core conflictual relationships and to the mother's values, prohibitions, and anxieties. They are also linked to the infant's temperament, gender, and burgeoning psychic structure. The resulting exchanges and maternal verbalizations open a window into the modes and contents of transgenerational transmission.

In the following discussion we focus on the transmission of messages concerning specifically gender identity in the exchanges between mothers and daughters.

CASE PRESENTATION: TRANSMISSION OF REPRESENTATIONS FROM MOTHER TO DAUGHTER

To illustrate the means by which a mother orients her daughter's gender identity, I will summarize a mother–infant psychotherapy case that is presented in more detail in the first volume of this book (Cramer 1995a). This mother and infant developed a pathological interaction destined to inhibit the baby's appetite and pleasure. I will summarize the case and present the follow-up, as it documents the penetration and permanence in the girl's functioning of her mother's constraining ego-ideal messages focused on sexual identity.

The daughter, Jane, 12 months, presented an oppositional anorexia. Her mother, Ann, was upset because she was a gourmand and indulged in eating binges. Her core conflict centered around her eating impulses because she unconsciously confused them with unbridled sexual orgies, based on memories (or fantasies) of her parents' sexual activities. Moreover, she berated herself for her obesity. She called herself a "fat slob" and repeatedly swore that she would start a diet, which she never managed to do. Unknowingly, she wanted now to check her wayward impulses through her daughter, by controlling strictly her intake and her appetite. What is important to stress is that she indeed succeeded in developing an opposition anorexia in Jane, and that we could observe how she instrumented this prohibition in symptomatic interactions. When Jane grabbed a chocolate bar, Ann applied a systematic barrage of verbal and behavioral prohibitions against eating. She thus coached Jane in renouncing her wish to eat and trained her in the practice of self-control. In fact, she trained her so well that Jane overcontrolled her appetite and developed anorexia.

Ann's training effort fulfilled a double agenda: while she focused on eating control, she simultaneously (and unconsciously) coached her daughter to develop a vigilant control of all impulses, and especially sexual impulses. She explained that she did not want her daughter to develop the voluptuous shape "that wakens men's desires." Ann announced that she never wanted to succumb to a man's seduction, because she felt that she had had to submit to her father's seduction. She thus wanted to reinforce Jane's capacity to oppose all forms of intrusion or submissiveness.

When we observed video recordings of their interactions, especially centering on feeding episodes, we realized that the principal aim of Ann's educative practices was to inculcate an ideal of self-imposed censorship on all impulsive desires, and a vigilance against all forms of seductiveness and masculine authority. She instrumented this aim by a multitude of actions, both verbal and interactive. This was so systematic that one could conclude that it was a very complex system, a kind of philosophy of life. All interactions between mother and daughter were infiltrated by this system, which contained clear (while unconscious) directives about such basic issues as how to deal with pleasure seeking, how to behave toward a man, how to impose one's will, and how to consider one's body. The model of joint therapy was ideally suited to reveal simultaneously the mother's unconscious and conscious representations about these issues, the strategies through which these meanings were conveyed and transmitted to the child, and the way Jane reacted to these injunctions. In fact, a great deal of what is considered as infant pathology can be deciphered in terms of mismatches between parental expectations and the willingness or capacities of the infant to adapt to them. The infant can accept and internalize these modes through compromise formations, but he or she can also either reject them or totally submit to them, which causes pathology.

Follow-up

This dyad was seen again four years later when Jane was 5 years old. Ann was very annoyed to observe that Jane was excessively attached to another girl. They played with dolls, mothered each other, and were altogether too engrossed in affectionate feminine games. "I hate the idea that she restricts herself to an identity of a conventional little girl," exclaimed Ann, who was frankly anguished by these signs of female development. She would prefer if she rode a bicycle!

When I saw Ann and Jane together, I was struck by the child's behavior toward me, which I considered symptomatic. Over several sessions, she remained totally mute, hiding behind her mother, and systematically avoiding any contact with me. The more I tried to involve her, the more she retreated. I found in this avoidant behavior the same oppositional strength as I had witnessed four years before, when she avoided food by tightly closing her lips. Now she was refusing me, and I explained to these two partners that Jane was now materializing the suspicion her mother had about men's seductiveness. Jane was refusing contact with me, as if she were following her mother's directives, designating men as dangerous seductors. Ann was probably afraid that she had so well succeeded in making her daughter afraid of men's advances that she was now concerned that Jane developed a homosexual attachment to her girlfriend.

As we discussed once again Ann's fear of men (as oversexed, and as wanting women to submit to them), she revealed that she had wanted to be a boy; in fact, she had a very precise fantasy in which she wished to fulfill the ideal of becoming a man called Robert, with green eyes. As she elaborated this fantasy, it proved to contain a complex ideal of being an androgynous being without a womanly shape, thus not arousing men's libidinous desires. During adolescence, she had been very attached to a girlfriend who presented a severe case of anorexia nervosa. "Her largest round shapes were her knees," she said, and added, "I know that she nearly died, but to die thin must be wonderful!" She then explained that her main wish concerning Jane was to turn her into an androgynous being, thus enabling her to avoid what had caused so much pain to Ann: her submission to bestial men. By fostering her daughter's anorexia, Ann had begun at the earliest stages to prepare her to refuse the imperative pressures of her desires, and to coach her to become thin and unshapely. Her goal of protecting Jane against men's seduction had already been realized when the little girl, at age 5, opposed strenuously my efforts to make contact with her. Jane had then evidenced in her behavior her mother's anxious need to avoid men and make them feel rejected and helpless. In psychoanalytic terms one could say that Ann's preventative against men had powerfully oriented Jane's oedipal conflict; Jane had made hers a suspicion of men and an alliance with women, which contributed to what is referred to as a negative oedipal solution.

One would need to do a psychotherapeutic investigation of the child alone to establish how this maternal coaching simultaneously protected Jane against intrapsychic anxieties in the oedipal conflict, and entered in collusion with the child's own, subjective fears. In the joint, mother-child psychotherapy, the evidence that appeared first and with greatest clarity was the transmission of the maternal philosophy about the relations between the sexes, and its impact on the infant, and later the child, while she is developing her sexual identity. This transmission from mothers to daughters of basic themes (or representations) about womanhood and about relations between the sexes will be now discussed at a more theoretical level.

THE CONSTRUCTION OF PSYCHIC STRUCTURE

Many epistemologies seeking to understand how the mind functions look for answers in its origins. It was classically done in psychoanalysis, following the lines of genetic reductionism (all psychic functions are determined by their earliest antecedents). More recently, the influence of early childhood is seen rather in a dialectical interplay with the individual's present reconstruction of his past, according to his prevalent working models—see for example, Green's (1979) radical formulation that, in psychoanalysis, childhood is only a metaphor. My contention is that there is a theoretical model that mediates these two opposed viewpoints concerning the role of early childhood. If one considers that parental transmissions of thinking models systematically orient, modify, and give meaning to early childhood experiences, one can conceive that early subjective models are always interpreted through the lens of adult, parental thinking systems. "There is no such thing as an infant," as Winnicott said. This is certainly the case in the early parent–infant interactions from the point of view of what could be called the creation of shared meanings (Cramer 1995a).

This may be too radical an image, because there is enough evidence in clinical work for the maintenance throughout the life cycle of areas of the mind that remain secret, noncommunicable, and cut off from social exchange. But the importance of the shared-meaning concept lies in the window it provides in the field of parental and cultural influences on the childhood development of fantasies, working models, and representations of identity.

To return to the clinical example, it seems clear that Ann and Jane share a representation of the relations between the sexes, a concept of the female body, and a suspiciousness about excesses of gratification. That this orients, at age 5, the child's sexual identity and attitudes toward men seemed apparent.

TRANSMISSION, AND THE PERMANENCE OF CULTURE

While early psychoanalysis focused on the individual, considering him in his own creation of his world through fantasy production and conflict resolution, there is now much attention paid to his interface with external forces that help shape his psychic structure and experience.

This interface has been studied from several angles. Anthropological works showed how the individual is molded by culture-linked prohibitions and obligations. This trend was most notably illustrated in Erikson's (1950) influential book, *Childhood and Society*. More recently, a discipline called ethnopsychiatry found its theoretical underpinnings (Nathan 1994). Developmental studies illustrated the powerful, structuring role of parent–infant interactions, whether it is in the fields of affect regulation (Emde and Sorce 1983), or cognitive development (Berger 1992).

Family studies proved the permanence of ideals, relational styles, and pathologies through the generations (Boszormenyi-Nagy and Spark 1973). Attachment studies revealed a relationship between maternal modes of representation and attachment styles in infants (Main et al. 1985).

In psychodynamic psychiatry, a transgenerational approach to the study of development and psychopathology has become an area of intense research, especially in the field of infant psychiatry (Lebovici 1988). It has convincingly shown how selected modes of relating, of conflict solution, and of ideals and values are transmitted through the generations.

Referring to these various models, one can conclude that parents hand down to the next generation very complex mental contents and styles of functioning from birth on. Mother–infant psychotherapies are a good framework from which to observe these transmissions. They are instrumented with gestures, glances, affect, the regulation of distance and proximity, voice intonation, and so on. In other words, one can see how interactions are the vehicle of this communication, allowing for the transmission of a familial style, and, through these microscopic exchanges, for the acculturation of infants. Mothers introduce children, from birth on, to a maze of meanings that convey the essence of a culture. It is through education that parents support the child with a form of cultural scaffolding. All gestures, prohibitions, and rewards convey with force a philosophical system, which contains instructions about basic life issues such as what it is to be a girl or boy, how and why to regulate aggressive and selfish desires, what the highest and lowest motivations are, and how to deal with others in terms of domination, submissiveness, the gratifications of egotistic versus altruistic desires, and so on.

Ethical coaching is thus introduced to the child, and this starts with the implementation of feeding. The first teacher is the wet-nurse, said Rousseau (1782). Two centuries later, Benjamin Spock (1946) the world-famous pediatrician whose work had enormous influence on postwar generations of parents, pronounced the similar precept: that feeding is learning. These authors had already perceived that the earliest ministrations practiced by mothers contained an educational project and a learning experience for the child.

While Ann regulates how chocolate should enter into baby Jane's mouth, she concentrates on this small orifice her way of entering culture into her daughter. Ethics first penetrate through the mouth!

THE REGULATION OF SEX ROLES

Traditional culture has strict standards about sex roles. Many present-day families do too. But, in clinical work and in sociological studies of womanhood, one perceives acutely the upheavals that have been affecting and transforming cultural criteria of feminine and maternal roles. In the last twenty-five years, women have become more autonomous as they have entered the work force. A career gives women more financial freedom and an alternative to exclusive involvement with family issues.

Women also have more control over their reproductive lives because of modern contraception. Moreover, laws have been enacted in several countries to support more equality between spouses. Higher divorce rates have turned many mothers into heads of families. The feminist movement and feminist studies have contributed to developing new ideological concepts of womanhood and motherhood.

Joint mother–infant psychotherapies are an ideal situation for the observation of the collision (or collusion) between these new models of womanhood and traditional ones inherited from generation to generation, which remain unconscious until pregnancy and birth bring them to the fore, often traumatically, creating conflicts and symptoms in the mother. A revolution has occurred in the collective representations of women and mothers, but a compulsion to repeat images of motherhood retained since infancy enters in conflict with the aspirations of present-day women. They want to foster their career but at the same time want to be ideal mothers, and this ideal has its roots in ancient images and early experiences. This contributes to a dilution of identity themes for women, who then seek consultation because they cannot reconcile motherhood tasks and personal aspirations.

Several anxiety-laden concerns are presented when mothers consult about a baby; they feel insecure, even incompetent in their maternal role, because they feel torn between the demands of their work and the equally pressing need to be a good mother. They feel guilty when they go to work, and enslaved by the baby when they cater to its needs. The compulsive need to take care of the baby is often perceived as a humiliating submissiveness, which is then rationalized with precepts such as "mothers have to sacrifice their needs in order to respect those of the baby."

A particularly frequent offshoot of this situation is expressed by mothers who complain then about their husband, and, by extension, about all men. The classic complaint goes as follows: "My husband leaves to me all responsibilities concerning the baby; he focuses on his work. I am enslaved by domestic chores. The baby has taken all my freedom away." And this is generally followed by a generalization: "Life is much easier for men; they make money and when they come home, they expect that everything should be ready for them. Women have to accept this lower status when they become mothers." This theme can develop into various subthemes, and into states of revolt of various intensity. A sort of war of the sexes can develop, to which mothers often adapt by entering into a masochistic solution that plays a key role in the appearance of depressive features; 10 percent of women present with postpartum depression (Murray 1992). The pleasures of baby care are then replaced by endless complaints of pain, of having to submit, and of having to confine themselves to the lower status of domestic chores. In these circumstances, the child is seen either as a persecutor who cripples the mother's freedom, or as partner used—in a symbiotic mode—as a therapeutic agent against depression (Cramer 1993).

MOTHER–DAUGHTER RELATIONSHIP

With an infant daughter, mothers follow various modes of relationship. They tend to create a new edition of their infantile tie to their own mother, either in order to recapture (and repeat) their longed-for relationship to their mother, or in an effort to establish now an idealized relationship that they did not have. They may also reverse their original relationship if they had felt that their mother had been too frustrating, too authoritarian, or too distant. Now they want to provide their daughter with what they had missed and longed for in their past. They become overly gratifying, and are unable to place any limit on the infant. This brings about progressively a tyrannical disposition in the child, thus validating the fantasy that mothers need to be sacrificed and abused. This type of scenario is very frequent nowadays, especially in socially ascending families. Many different variations of this theme are possible. But how does the transmission of a womanhood identity theme occur?

Let us first return to our clinical vignette, which illustrates both *what* is being transmitted and *how* this is instrumented. Ann, the mother, had many misgivings about being a woman. She confused her eating binges with a wayward, unrestrained sexuality, which she could not control. She was still frightened by the vision of her parents' sexual antics, and wanted now to protect baby Jane against such excesses, which she made sure to tame from the onset, choosing appetite as her target for impulse control. This need to develop in Jane a powerful self-control was the first and most pressing issue in her educational system. In taming Jane's appetite, she taught her highly valued behaviors in century-old, Christian education: the child needs to curb its own egotistic, perverse tendencies. This need to control the child's innate "bad" tendencies was a cornerstone of traditional education before the twentieth century. It was intimately linked to precepts of certain religious figures, among which one of the most respected authorities was St. Augustin (1855) who suggested that allowing the child to do what he desires would result in his running headfirst into all sorts of crimes.

In developing Jane's capacity for self-imposed ascetic control, Ann unknowingly perpetuated an old tradition of education based on self-denial, which had been handed down through the generations.

Simultaneously, Ann had been powerfully influenced by the feminist movement's liberation of women from adherence to traditional sex roles. She did not accept that her daughter should identify with the stereotyped image of a dainty, frail girl playing with dolls. This representation was unacceptable to her as it heralded weakness and submissiveness to abusing men. She thus promoted in her daughter all characteristics that would ultimately lead to the realization of an androgynous identity—neither girl nor boy but both sexes intertwined. This would provide the utmost power, and especially protection against men's desires and authority. She partially succeeded in her endeavor, as Jane at age 5 exhibited a marked suspicion of me and avoided all seductive advances of men.

It is thus a complex, multilayered construction of womanhood that Ann conveyed to daughter Jane; a bedrock of self-control against appetite laid the foundation for a suspicion against unbridled impulses, which served simultaneously for a watchful stance toward men's seductiveness. The androgynous fantasy developed on that base and completed Jane's protection against the eruption of desires; just as she had been armed to resist opening her mouth (the anorexia), she was now prepared to resist the temptation to be open to desires for men. An androgynous identity is indeed a guarantee for narcissistic self-sufficiency as the need of the female for completion by a male counterpart is erased. The realization of an abrasion of sex differences and of an androgynous identity is often found as a major goal in traditional feminist writings (Badinter 1992).

It is thus a complex construction of an identity that is being transmitted. This amounts to a life project, or even to a philosophy whose most influential concepts concern a definition of womanhood, of the relationship between the sexes, of the seeking of gratification, and of the regulation of power in social exchange.

When mothers educate their daughters, they are like philosophers who explain the world to the child. To produce this epistemological system they rely on their personal store of memories, ideals, anxieties, and conflicts. They find their sources in an inheritance of traditional precepts, carried from one generation to the next, thus framing the infant in the continuation of very old life strategies. This is then internalized in the child's superego and ego-ideal structures. As Freud (1938) wrote, a person's superego represents the total civilization of the past that—as a child—he or she was forced to relive. But mother's ideals are also remodeled by present-day cultural trends. A recent move toward an undifferentiation or dilution of sex roles feeds an androgynous fantasy that pulls young mothers toward new educative precepts, where autonomy, refusal of submissiveness, and the fulfillment of personal ambitions become paramount.

These two sources of sex role definitions may create conflicts that are brought to therapy. The therapist can observe what constellation of feminine values and characteristics are being handed down.

MOTHER'S SECRETS

All mothers ask themselves fundamental questions when a daughter is born: "What type of woman is she going to become? How am I going to bring her to this female identity?" In this quandary, today's mothers have to improvise more than their mothers and grandmothers did, since sex roles are now so difficult to define. We must acknowledge that experts and therapists also are confused about the criteria of gender identity, as cultural precepts have become so vague on this subject. Yet, one issue remains paramount for all mothers: they have to provide their daughters with strategies that will help them in dealing with the other sex. All women have their own view of this problem. Relations between the sexes can be an armed confrontation, a highly idealized meeting promising complementarity, or a utilitarian partnership. In all cases, mothers will indoctrinate their daughters, providing them with representations of men that vary from highly idealized to contemptuously debased. This form of coaching is often clandestine and forms a secret message that daughters have to contend with in their own construction of sex differences. This indoctrination starts from birth and relies on subtle exchanges that are often nonverbal. By co-creating their daughter's femaleness, today's mothers have a chance to produce new models of woman and of mothers. This is one of their major contributions in the building of new cultural and collective representations. A clinical illustration of symptomatic modes of female transmission can be found in Cramer (1996).

Fathers contribute heavily to their daughter's representations of gender identity and of relations between the sexes. They co-create the parental couple that will serve as reference for the daughter's representations of relations between the sexes. They, too, carry an image of women and of men and will contribute to daughter's views on sex differences and on relations between the sexes. The degree of cohesion or of conflict between female images carried by mother and father will in great part determine the future woman's fate.

CONCLUSION

This chapter discussed the role played by transgenerational transmission in the construction of representations of womanhood from the earliest phases of the mother–daughter relationship.

For the clinician-therapist, the main imports of this approach are as follows:

Evaluation of infants' psychic development needs to be done within their interactions *with* their parents.

Attention should be paid to maternal implicit thinking models about womanhood and relations between the sexes.

These models are multilayered. They contain inherited, traditional representations of womanhood and motherhood, but they also convey present-day cultural values about gender issues. Special attention should be paid to intrasystemic conflicts between various, often opposite, models of womanhood, exacerbated by new cultural and social developments.

Mother–infant psychotherapy is an appropriate format for the study of cultural transmission and of the development of ethics.

REFERENCES

Atkinson, C. W. (1991). *The Oldest Vocation: Christian Motherhood in the Middle Ages.* Ithaca, London: Cornell University Press.

Badinter, E. (1992). *XY de L'Identité Masculine.* Paris: O. Jacob. [*XY, On Masculine Identity*. New York: Columbia University Press, 1995]

Bassin, D., Honey, M., and Kaplan, M. M. (1994). *Representation of Motherhood.* New Haven, London: Yale University Press.

Berger, M., (1992). *Les Troubles du Developpement Cognitif.* [*Disorders of Cognitive Development*] Toulouse, France: Privat.

Boszormenyi-Nagy, I., and Spark, G. M. (1973). *Invisible Loyalties.* Hagerstown, MD: Harper & Row.

Bowlby, J. (1958). The nature of the child's tie to his mother. *International Journal of Psycho-Analysis* 39:350–373.

Bruner, J. (1979). Early social interaction and language acquisition. In *Studies in Mother–Infant Interaction*, ed. H. R. Schaffer. London: Academic.

Cramer, B. (1993). Are postpartum depressions a mother–infant relationship disorder? *Infant Mental Health Journal* 14(4):283–297.

——— (1995a). The beginnings of psychic life. In *Handbook of Infant, Child, and Adolescent Psychotherapy*, vol. 1, ed. B. S. Mark and J. A. Incorvaia, pp. 5–16. Northvale, NJ: Jason Aronson.

——— (1995b). Short-term dynamic psychotherapy for infants and their parents. *Child and Adolescent Psychiatric Clinics of North America* 4(3):649–660.

——— (1996). *Secrets de Femmes.* [*Secrets of Women*] Paris: Calman-Levy.

De Beauvoir, S. (1949). Le Deuxieme Sexe. Paris: Gallimard. [*The Second Sex*. New York: Knopf, 1953]

Ehrenreich, B., and English, D. (1979). *For Her Own Good: 150 Years of the Experts' Advice to Women*. London: Pluto.

Eiser, J. R. (1980). *Cognitive Social Psychology*. London, New York: McGraw-Hill.

Emde, R., and Sorce, J. (1983). The rewards of infancy: emotional availability and maternal referencing. In *Frontiers of Infant Psychiatry*, ed. J. Call, E. Galenson, and R. Tyson, pp. 17–30. New York: Basic Books.

Erikson, E. (1950). *Childhood and Society*. New York: Norton.

Freud, S. (1905). Three essays on sexuality. *Standard Edition* 7:125–248.

——— (1938). An outline of psychoanalysis. *Standard Edition* 3:139–207.

Green, A. (1979). *L'enfant Modele*. [*The model child*] *Nouvelle Revue de Psychanalyse*. Paris: Gallimard.

Knibiehler, Y., and Fouquet, C. (1980). *Histoires des Meres du Moyen Age a Nos Jours*. [*Stories of Mothers from the Middle Ages to the Present*] Paris: Montalba.

Lebovici, S. (1988). Fantasmatic interaction and intergenerational transmission. *Infant Mental Health Journal* 9(1):10–19.

Levi-Strauss, C. (1956). In *Man, Culture, and Society*, ed. H. L. Shapiro. New York: Oxford University Press.

Main, M., Kaplan, N., and Cassidy, J. (1985). Security in infancy, childhood and adulthood: a move to the representational level. In *Growing Points of Attachment Theory and Research. Monograph of the Society for Research in Child Development*, ed. I. Bretherton and E. Waters, pp. 66–104. Chicago: University of Chicago Press.

Mead, M. (1935). *Sex and Temperament in Three Primitive Societies*. New York: William Morrow.

Murray, L. (1992). The impact of postnatal depression on infant development. *Journal of Child Psychology and Psychiatry and Allied Disciplines* 33(3):543–561.

Nathan, T. (1994). *L'influence qui Guerit*. [*The Healing Influence*] Paris: O. Jacob.

Roiphe, H., and Galenson, E. (1984). Infantile origins of disturbances in sexual identity. In *Frontiers of Infant Psychiatry*, vol. 2, ed. J. Call, E. Galenson, and R. L. Tyson, pp. 435–440. New York: Basic Books.

Rousseau, J. J. (1782). *L'Emile, ou de l'Education*. Paris: Gallimard, 1966. [*Emile, or, On Education*. New York: Basic Books, 1979]

Spock, B. (1946). *The Pocket Book of Baby and Child Care*. New York: Pocket Books.

St. Augustine (1855). *La Cité de Dieu*. [*The City of God*.] New York: Modern Library, 1983.

Stoller, R. (1985). *Presentations of Gender.* New Haven, CT: Yale University Press.

Trad, P. V. (1990). *Infant Previewing: Predicting and Sharing Interpersonal Outcome.* New York: Springer-Verlag.

17

The Father–Infant Toddler Group

S. Robert Moradi

This chapter looks at the formation and process of a group of fathers and their infants and toddlers. The structure of the group, staffing, and therapeutic format are described, and some observations of empirical differences between mother–infant groups, and father–infant groups are presented. One of the culturally determined roles, that of the father as protector, is examined, with its manifestations in terms of the father's role in the care of young children. A central proposition of this chapter is that psychological connection between father and child can serve as a preventive measure against the acting out of repressed rage. Clinical observations as to the nature of the father's intrapsychic processes around issues of envy of mother–child intimacy and projection of rage are presented, and data and hypotheses are analyzed to show how groups that are designed for fathers and their children benefit the father in a profound way.

STRUCTURE AND COMPOSITION

The majority of the fathers are referred by their wives through Mommy and Me groups. The men are married, Caucasian, and educated, and socioeconomically in the upper middle class. The research draws upon interactions observed through a father–toddler group that was established in June 1995. The group meets on alternate Sunday mornings for an hour and a half in a playground under the sponsorship of the Early Childhood Center, a community resource program of the Division of Child and Adolescent Psychiatry of the Department of Psychiatry at Cedars Sinai Medical Center in Los Angeles, California. Group members sign up for eight sessions with the option to continue thereafter.

The staffing and format of the group is as follows: The fathers and their children spend the first 15 to 20 minutes in the outdoor playground with each other until the children are at ease in the setting. Fathers talk casually with each other and staff. This period provides opportunities for staff to view the father–child relationship and interactions. The observations are then used in making interpretations of behavior and clarifications for the child and the father. The time together is followed by two or three group greeting songs for the children while they all sit around a table and eat a snack. This time at the table provides opportunities for modeling limit setting. The fathers then sit together in a semicircle within fifty feet of the children. The children freely roam, play, and touch base with their fathers as needed. The child development specialists provide narration for the children and work within brief interactions between fathers and children as situations arise.

The group consists of eight fathers ranging in age from 28 to 54 and ten toddlers (including two sets of twins). The staff's orientation is psychodynamic. The staff consists of two male group facilitators and three female child development specialists (a 12-year-old daughter of one of the group facilitators assists the child development specialists). Fathers engage in group discussion for one hour, at which time the children and the child development specialists join the fathers for feedback regarding their observations of the children and provide opportunities for dialogue between staff and fathers. The entire group ends with a few closing songs. The staff then meets alone for an hour of group processing. (Total staff time adds up to 3 hours, i.e., ½ hour pregroup set up and discussion, 1½ hours of group time and 1 hour of postgroup discussion and processing of the group by the staff.)

DESCRIPTION OF THE GROUP PROCESS: DISCUSSION OF ISSUES

Fathers talk of not knowing their child as well as they wish, and not being known by their children. A common fear expressed is not being an adequate provider and protector of their child. Most fathers share the burden of having to work full time and not having energy and playfulness by the time they get home. Once home, they feel responsible to relieve the mother, but it involves stepping into an arena not familiar to them: what to feed, how to change, how to soothe, and how to play and engage their children. Fathers find themselves coming home in a condition similar to their children, that is, they too need their rest, are hungry, and need to be soothed and engaged. Many fathers report, "After I spend 2 or 3 hours with her, she's finally in bed. This is my life and I have no time to myself. I am totally exhausted." The men grieve the loss of the life they had before their children were born. A repeated phrase heard in the group is, "I never have a moment to talk with my wife." Often they feel in competition with the baby. They feel deprived and inadequate at the same time. They juxtapose how impotent they feel at home and how competent at work. Fathers struggle together and talk about how they are incompetent to comfort their babies, how they can't differentiate cries. They talk of their resentment of the child waking them in the middle of the night, of the loss of intimacy with their wives since the baby was born, and of their guilt and shame when they find themselves angry and they "lose it" with the child. They are angry for being blamed for not caring enough. They are angry for not having "quality time" with their children. As the fathers talk to one another they find the commonality of their anger and frustration and this aids in the reduction of their shame.

DISCUSSION

Shame and Rage in Fathers

An underlying construct of the psychodynamic process with father-child groups is that the protective task of fathering should include protection of the family against the unconscious destructiveness within the parents. A psychodynamic group for fathers attempts to identify the projections and confront the denial of the "beasts" and "evils" inside the family. The exploration of this idea can occur by the connection of the men to each other and their healthy transference toward the group facilitators. As clinicians, when we observe an excessive focus on the dangers from the outside we begin to wonder about the possibility of projection of the person's unconscious internal rage and fear. An example is the father who protects his family by building fences, putting signs up, even buying a gun. He hires the best lawyers to defend his family against unfair accusations by outsiders. The family continues to find itself in repeated battles. This is when the clinician wonders if the outside enemies might be an unconscious displacement for the rage inside the home. The child grows up in such family systems not only mistrusting others, but also fearing a potential explosion inside the family or implosions inside his own psyche. The protective task of the father could be identified and worked with in the group as his role in handling the day-to-day fears, inadequacies, and conflicts that are inevitable inside the home. The protective role of the father then serves to create a sense of internal safety and security within the psyche of the members of the family. Father's task is to bring conflict to discussion without fear of retaliation from those with more power. Without this protective shield, the family will be in chaos. Unfairness can go unchecked and a fertile environment is created for neglect and abuse of the weaker members of the family.

Frequently, by the nature of his relative objectivity and time outside the home, the father can protect the child from the subjective misunderstandings by the mother. He can recognize the differences as well as the similarities of the child to the mother. He can help the child develop an identity separate and independent from the mother. He can nurture a relationship with the child that is separate and unique and, therefore, build rapport with his child's world.

There are intrapsychic blocks unique to men that interfere with the father's participation in child rearing. These blocks have their foundation in feelings of humiliation, shame, and repressed rage. Boys and young men in postindustrial Western culture are separated from older men. Young men are left to find their path without guides or mentors. Close physical and emotional bonds have been with the mother, but staying attached to her or returning to her is filled with societal humiliation. Men, in their relationships with their wives, find a form of mother and cling to her or defend against the need for connection with her by being distant. When a baby enters this system it is not unusual that the father experiences the baby as a rival. The father is unconsciously reexperiencing the emotions connected to these losses of his early childhood, that is, the loss of the mother and the absence of the father. The new father may feel excluded, unsafe, and angry, but he is often unconscious and/or ashamed of these feelings. The unconscious feelings of anger can be acted out in the community in the form of abuse and/or neglect of the weak and the needy. Within the family the victims are often the children. The most central target of this destructive force, however, is the psyche (soul) and inevitably the soma of the person who carries the unconscious conflict and rage.

The deep-seated feelings of inadequacy about how to become a man and how to protect the family are other sources of internal rage in many men, a rage that can be projected to the outside world. The false-self man, now the father who carries the childhood feelings of being unwanted, is frightened of his inability to survive, and ashamed of his inadequacies as the one who should "protect" his family. A condition of suppressed or repressed rage applies to both parents. Fathers are more identified with rage, but mothers, especially if oppressed by the father or society, pass on the seeds of repressed rage to their children.

THE CLINICAL VALUE OF FATHER–CHILD GROUPS

The closer the father is to the intimate aspects of fathering, the more aware of his role and the more in touch with his children the father will be. This connection to the child also provides a significant second chance for the father to revisit his own experience as a vulnerable child, a child who might have been "forgotten" or abandoned. Abandonment begins with the cultural pressure for young boys to separate from their mothers while girls can continue to be part of the "kitchen" in the maternal world. As mothers push their young sons away to learn their maleness, there is neither a father nor any other male to catch the rejected boy. The main defensive reaction from the discarded boy is detachment from the needy self inside and the donning of a mask of invulnerability. This mask shields the boy from the humiliation of having been abandoned. A false self begins to emerge to counteract the intense emotions, such as fear of physical disintegration or the dread of psychological humiliation. The false self is culturally reinforced by the positive approval and social value assigned to emotional detachment in men in favor of their pursuit of power and wealth.

A psychodynamically oriented group format for fathers and their young children is valuable for fathers because of the possibility of a corrective emotional experience. The universality of the experience of humiliation, abandonment, and creation of a false self can be understood and felt in the group. The group process can be an effective measure reducing shame and providing a safe space for expression of unconscious rage. The men's connection to each other and a healthy transference toward the group facilitators provides a context for exploration of the emotional deprivation that then is reduced by the compassion from paternal substitutes.

VIGNETTES: SOME PRELIMINARY OBSERVATIONS OF CLINICAL OUTCOME

The Overprotective Father

Bill, 49, is a father who overprotects. Jasmine, 18 months, is his first (probably last) child. Bill hovers over every little movement of hers. Jasmine appears flat in her mood; she is hesitant in joining the other kids and playing with toys. There is little joy in her face. She is like a bird in a cage—she is adored and certainly protected, but she'd better not "fly." Her independence threatens to leave her father feeling betrayed and rejected. Jasmine has seldom slept through the night. She comes to her parents' bed almost every night and wakes them several times each night. Bill is happy with Jasmine clinging to him. He has no concern about her poor initiative. They already have an implicit agreement; the question is not whether she will protest or not, the question is how will she do it. Right now she is reacting by being passive, dependent, and joyless. Her childhood will provide many critical points through which she might react and ultimately rage against her father's overprotectiveness. For example, at age 2 toilet training might become the battlefield; at age 3 separation and going to preschool might create an emotional upheaval. Her adolescence might bring about serious conflicts around individuation issues. As an adult, she could continue with emotional crises around issues of autonomy, attachment, and dependency.

The group intervenes by identifying Jasmine's passivity and clingingness. The other fathers frequently ask Bill if Jasmine is not feeling well physically. The group addresses Bill's indifference or even pleasure in Jasmine's dependency. They begin to voice concern about Jasmine's sense of autonomy, now and in the future. Bill gradually hears the other men's observations. He begins to talk about his own needs for Jasmine's proximity, his dread of her growing up and leaving. He fears that Jasmine might be embarrassed by her father's age and distance herself from him. Bill began to recognize that Jasmine needed his help to gain autonomy. He talked about his own parents' ambivalence about his existence. The working through had begun for this dyad.

Who is the Angry Member of the Dyad?

Chris is frustrated by his inability to comfort his son David, 3 years old. David wakes up in a bad mood almost every morning. He refuses the bottle, screams with anger, and does not respond to any physical or verbal attempts to comfort. The only way to stop him is for his father to scream back so loud that David is frightened. He then stops and comes to his father for a long, comforting hug. In other words, Father scares him out of his rage. Why is David so mad every morning? He has a younger brother who is favored by everyone, and an older sister who bosses him around and punishes him if he disobeys. His mother is overwhelmed and can't protect him, and his father is struggling to make a living, stuck and unhappy in a job he doesn't like.

Over a period of many sessions the fathers in the group began to identify that David's rage is about the injustices of his life. He has to suppress the rage out of fear of annihilation. He is not protected against his jealousy of his younger brother, the unfair treatment from his sister, or neglect by his overwhelmed mother and distant father. The parallel is drawn between the father's life circumstances and that of his son. This creates an empathic bond between the father and child. Father begins to see his son's early morning tantrums in a different light. The child calms down, allows the father to comfort him in the group and outside. Seven months into the process, David wakes up in a good mood in the mornings, and he is no longer as jealous of his younger brother. With his father's assistance he holds his ground against his sister's behavior. Chris, observing his son's changes, states, "He was screaming for both of us. I do my own screaming now."

Identity Conflict

Maria, age 2½, has announced to her parents that she doesn't want to be called Maria, her name is Ann. She became very agitated if anyone called her Maria. This went on for a few weeks to the puzzlement of us all. Maria began exhibiting other behavior problems, such as defiantly urinating on the furniture.

In one of the group sessions one of the fathers asked Maria's father if he thought that Maria may not like her name because of certain associations with that name. In response to this, father recalled that he in fact had changed his name from Steven to Joseph at the age of 7. He associated everything negative to Steven and good things with Joseph. He expressed and remembered many of his feelings as a child that led to his name change. He had never talked with anyone about this. In the next session Maria introduced herself as Maria, and her father reported that Maria's defiant behavior had also ceased. One can hypothesize that the father's empathy with his daughter created a deep enough connection between them, which aborted the potential of a dissociative phenomenon in Maria.

CLINICAL JUSTIFICATION FOR FATHER–CHILD GROUPS

It is well documented in the social and psychological literature that the degree of intellectual competence, empathy, acceptance of diversity, and self regulatory mechanisms of a child have a direct positive correlation with the extent of psychological involvement of the father. In this father-child group the fathers expressed their needs to know, be known, and to father their children. The following comments are a sample of what fathers said was their reason for joining a father-child group at the initial phone contact:

"Deep down I want to get to know my daughter and her to know me."
"I have no place where father issues are discussed."
"I've had to take a back seat to the mother-daughter duo. I want to be closer to both of them."
"A place where I can talk about difficult stuff and see what's on other dad's minds."
"My son lets himself be pushed around by other kids. I want to learn how to teach him to stand up for himself."
"I am very busy. I need to learn how to find time to be with my kid."
"I want to be a better father."
"My child is very Mommy-oriented and my ego is getting in the way; it hurts my feelings when she rejects me."
"I don't want my son to feel rejected by me. I want to learn how to discipline him."
"How can I be a parent, but not a Mom?"
"I'm concerned about my child's reaction when the second baby is born."

"My son has become very aggressive. Sometimes he walks up to me and hits me in the head. I need to know how to handle him. I don't want to act like my father did."

The researchers in the field suggest that two highly involved parents provide for diverse stimulation. Increased paternal involvement makes both parents feel more fulfilled, and this makes for warmer and richer relationships within the family. Father's involvement creates a family context in which parents feel good about their marriage and the shared parenting arrangements they have been able to work out. What seems clear is that what matters is not so much who is at home (primary caregiver) but how that person feels about being home. In this context, the father is taking responsibility for ensuring that the child is appropriately and compassionately cared for at all times, which is more significant than being available to help out when it is convenient. The mother's facilitation of father's involvement with the child seems to be related to the degree of gratification of the mother's involvement with her own father.

The staff of father–child groups who also work with mother–child groups observe that in general fathers give more room to the children to move away. The children do not check in with their fathers as often as they do with their mothers. Social and psychodynamic hypotheses about the reasons for these differences ought to be studied further. Fathers raise fewer nuts-and-bolts issues of child rearing but place more emphasis on the psychological components of the relationship. This may in part be due to the psychodynamic orientation of the facilitators of the current father–child group.

CLINICAL GOALS

Father–child groups may set the following clinical goals:

1. Strengthen the empathic connection between father and child.
2. Facilitate the empathic connection of the father to vulnerable aspects of his own psyche.
3. Provide a format for identification of projections in service of reduction of the risk of unconscious acting out of rage against

mother, child, and the father himself, reducing potential for abuse.

4. Reduce the father's shame through the realization that many of the experiences among the fathers are universal.
5. Identify the encountered maternal resistance in sharing the territory of child rearing. Father's understanding of this phenomenon can facilitate his entrance into the mother–child dyad.
6. Consolidate the father's masculine gender identity through identification with the paternal role.

A primary benefit of father–child groups accrues to the father. The group can enhance the father–child connection, making it less likely for the father to abandon the child and additionally provide a context in which unconscious rage can be identified. The father, in learning how to care for his child, can concretize his own internal child and thereby care for these infantile needs, developing empathic responses instead of responding to feelings of shame and possibly acting out aggressively.

THE DETERMINANTS OF FATHER INVOLVEMENT

The staff looks for the following indications of improved father involvement:

1. The ability to read the child's signals and responding appropriately, knowing what expectations are realistic.
2. The degree to which father is a "playmate" versus a primary caregiver.
3. The extent and frequency of initiating fantasy games.

FURTHER STUDIES AND WORK

A shortcoming of this work is its limitation in racial, cultural, and socioeconomic diversity. All fathers in the group were middle to upper middle class professional Caucasian married men. Most are referred to the group through mother–child groups. The group is also a rarity; there is only one other ongoing father–child group known to the author in the Los Angeles area. There is a need to find ways of introducing fathers of varying socioeconomic groups to the benefits of father–child groups. Designing studies in future groups to measure the change in the fathers and their children will be a natural next step.

CONCLUSION

As Michael J. Diamond (1996) eloquently puts it, "It is through parenting that fathers develop an empathic connection to their own vulnerabilities and those of the children for whom they provide a watchful protectiveness. It is within this empathic connection learned by fathering that men have the chance to develop their own sense of mature masculinity."

Father–child groups can become a format in which fatherhood is affirmed, compassion enhanced for the weak and needy (both within men and for the community's children), and a context provided for the renewal of the father–child bond.

REFERENCE

Diamond, M. J. (1996). *Boys to men: the maturing of male identity through paternal watchful protectiveness*. Presented at the Los Angeles Institute for Psychoanalytic Studies, December 9.

SUGGESTED READING

Diamond, M. J. (1986). Becoming a father: a psychoanalytic perspective on the forgotten parent. *Psychoanalytic Review* 73:445–468.

——(1992). Creativity needs in becoming a father. *Journal of Men's Studies* 1:41–45.

——(1995). *Fathers and sons: psychoanalytic perspectives on "good enough" fathering throughout the life cycle*. Unpublished manuscript, Los Angeles Institute for Psychoanalytic Studies.

Pruett, K. D. (1983a). Infants of primary nuturing fathers. *Psychoanalytic Study of the Child* 38:257–277. New Haven, CT: Yale University Press.

——— (1983b). *Two year follow up of infants of primary nurturing fathers in intact families*. Paper presented at the Second World Congress on Infant Psychiatry, April.

——— (1985). Oedipal configurations in father-raised children. *Psychoanalytic Study of the Child* 40:435–456. New Haven, CT: Yale University Press.

——— (1987). *The Nuturing Father*. New York: Warner.

——— (1993). The paternal presence. Families in society. *Journal of Contemporary Human Services* 74:46–50.

Pruett, K. D., and Litzenberger, M. (1992). Latency development in children of primary nuturing fathers: eight-year follow-up. *Psychoanalytic Study of the Child* 47:885–1011. New Haven, CT: Yale University Press.

18

Parenting as a Function of the Adult Self*

Paul Ornstein
and Anna Ornstein

Once human behavior became the legitimate subject of scientific inquiry around the turn of the twentieth century, infant and child development studies had become central to these research endeavors. Today, there is a great deal of literature related to the study of infants, young children, and the early phases of mothering. Indeed, the most revealing and dependable data on mothering currently available are from the burgeoning literature on infant research. The findings on parenting in these mother–infant studies are of great significance because they fairly consistently support an evolutionary-biological an-

*Condensed version of a paper published in *Parental Influences in Health and Disease,* ed. J. Anthony and G. Pollack. Boston: Little, Brown, 1985. Translated into German in *Kinderanalyse*, August 1994.

lage for mothering. In the early phases of mothering, a biological readiness appears to complement the infant's "built-in" capacity to solicit social responses from the environment. "The mother is involved in a natural process with her baby, a process that unfolds with a fascinating intricacy and complexity for which she and her baby are well prepared by the millennia of evolution" (Stern 1977, pp. 8–9). Klaus and Kennell (1976), Ainsworth (1973), and Bowlby (1969) have also maintained that only civilization and technology obscure the mother's instincts that could otherwise guide her in successful bonding and attachment to her infant.

However, this biological readiness, the capacity for bonding and attachment, remain disputed motives for parenting even during infancy and certainly beyond the earliest phases of the infant's life (Brady 1980, Chess and Thomas 1982). For example, Benedek (1956) maintains that in the human female mothering behavior has two sources; one is rooted in her biology and the other evolved as an expression of her personality, developed under environmental influences that could modify her motherliness. We add that the biological roots of motherliness of the human female may be outweighed by psychological factors. While biological factors may still be in evidence in relationship to the infant, it is the mother's psychology that determines her responsiveness to the increasingly more complex developmental needs of her growing child.

In addition to the biological and psychological, we need to consider also the cultural factors. In our modern Western society, the mother may be only one member of a group of adults engaged in the care of her child. From the child's perspective, it is more appropriate to speak of a "parenting unit" composed of one person (e.g., either parent) or a group of persons from whom the child can receive the responses he needs for his development; to be a "mother" or a "father" is not synonymous with parenting.

The concept of a parenting unit is particularly useful in assessing the development of children who grow up in multiple foster homes, in divorced or "reconstituted" families, or under other unconventional circumstances. Clinicians cannot readily find an explanation for the capacity of these children not only to cope with some very obvious life stresses, but to continue their progressive development. Rather than attributing such resiliency to unidentified constitutional factors, we suggest that children are able to extract developmentally needed responses from an environment that, to an external observer, may appear to have no redeeming features. And the opposite may be true as well—an environment that, to an external observer, may be "average expectable," may nevertheless not be responsive to a particular child's developmental needs.

We propose that parenting can only be assessed in conjunction with the assessment of a particular child; it is only through the immersion into the child's inner world that the clinician can appreciate what has become genetically significant for a particular child from the many, possibly significant parental influences. Kohut (1979) differentiates the etiological from the genetic approach:

> The genetic approach in psychoanalysis relates to the investigation of those subjective psychological experiences of the child which usher in a chronic change in the distribution and further development of the endopsychic forces and structures. The etiological approach, on the other hand, relates to the investigation of those objectively ascertainable factors which, in interaction with the child's psyche as it is constituted in a given moment, may or may not elicit the genetically decisive experience.

ADAPTATION, DEVELOPMENT, AND PATHOGENESIS

The question as to what external or internal factors account for pathogenicity has been with psychoanalysts ever since Freud's time. Freud's (1916–17) original answer to this dilemma was to introduce the concept of the *complemental series*. This concept was to explain the pathogenesis of the adult forms of psychoneuroses; it meant that traumatic events in a child's life created libidinal fixations, which, when reactivated later in life, lead to neurotic compromise formations. Such neurotic compromises had been traditionally differentiated from *deficiency illnesses*, which have been related either to gross parental neglect, physical abuse, institutionalization, or other, as yet unknown, factors that have prevented children from using the environment effectively.

In clinical practice, child therapists have long recognized a third group of patients—children who do not suffer from the consequences of an unresolved Oedipus complex, that is, from a psychoneurosis, nor do they exhibit gross structural defects because of severe parental neglect or abuse. This third group of children suffers from the consequences of various degrees of *discrete structural deficits* that can be related to equally discrete and subtle failures in parental responsiveness to the child's developmental needs for affirmation, validation, and to be merged with an idealizable adult. It was Kohut's (1971) discovery of the selfobject transferences that has alerted child therapists to these parental functions that, because of their silent presence, used to be taken for granted. These parental functions do not simply facilitate a drive-determined sequence in development, but rather, they themselves are responsible for the building up of psychic structures by becoming transmutedly internalized. This is a form of internalization in which the caregiver's selfobject functions become depersonalized and become the infant's and child's permanent psychic structures (capacities).

Infant research had repeatedly demonstrated that the capacity to elicit life-sustaining environmental responses that are crucial for the building up of permanent psychic structures is inborn. The infant, born with "a predictable genetic ground plan" (Lichtenberg 1982) has to be assured of phase-appropriate environmental responses, which in self psychology are referred to as *selfobject functions*. Sander (1975), for example, spoke of a "fitting together" of the endogenous (infant-determined) and exogenous (caregiver-determined) influences. The fitting together is a developmental accomplishment that requires the caregiver's ability to "read" the infant's clues. Sander used the model of adaptation to account for the two major aspects of personality development: integration and differentiation. These two, seemingly opposing directions in the development of the individual, occur within the same contextual unit. For example, the increasing differentiation of the child's emotional, cognitive, and perceptual capacities has to become integrated into the very same system in which this differentiation has taken place in order for these capacities to achieve functional freedom. In other words, functional freedom is not achieved by the child extricating himself from a symbiotic fusion with the caregiver but by achieving new levels of adaptation with increasing complexity within the same interactive regulatory system.

Our focus on the caregiver's capacity to respond to the rapidly growing and, therefore, rapidly changing psychological organization of the child, ought not be interpreted as placing the sole responsibility of a child's development on the caregiver's ability to pick up the growing child's clues for what should be a perfectly empathic response. We agree with Greenspan (1981) that each organism has its "individual way of processing, organizing and differentiating experiences . . . and that the final common pathway is unique to each individual . . . suggesting something fundamental about the organism's manner of organizing its experience of the world, internal and external, animate and inanimate."

Infant researchers we have cited so far and others whose work is relevant but too numerous to be quoted bring into serious question the primacy of the drives as motivators of development and as providers of psychic energy. Instead, the biological anlage for human psychological development appears to reside in the infant's capacity to elicit certain responses from the environment that are crucial for his development. In addition, these researchers, in their careful attention to the infant's and child's emotional environment, have expanded our view of development from one in which we could simply trace the acquisition of psychic functions to one in which we can also trace the source of the qualities of these functions (i.e., whether or not the acquired functions are executed with joy or only mechanically).

If emerging capacities in sensorimotor and affective areas are not systematically responded to, developmental progress in the most vulnerable areas may slow down or cease, simply because there is no opportunity for repetitive action sequences or practice (i.e., there is a lack of repetitive minimal stimulus nutriment necessary to consolidate these capacities) and we may observe cognitive and interpersonal delays. Secondary apathy, withdrawal, disorganization, and/or other regression may follow. The process of "fitting together" (Sander 1962), the need to maintain emotional connection between parent and child at all costs and exploring the nature and ontogeny of the specific fit of particular parents and babies across time to see how they navigate the hurdles of various developmental milestones together are not only useful conceptualizations of the complex processes of development but are fundamental to the clinician who has to understand the child's "fit," or adaptation or maladaptation, to a particular emotional environment.

THE SELF-SELFOBJECT UNIT AND PARENTAL SELFOBJECT FUNCTIONS

Child psychotherapists have found with increasing frequency that they treat children who live under varied, more often than not unfavorable, circumstances and not—as Hartmann (1958) assumed in his theory of adaptation—in "average expectable environments." Child therapists therefore are repeatedly confronted with the question as to how to set up a treatment plan that will optimally address those aspects of the emotional milieu that most crucially impinge on the child's development and on the already existing symptoms. It is no longer sufficient to ask the question whether the weight of the pathology resides primarily within the child or within the environment. Rather, we now need a conceptual tool that addresses the question of the *fit* between the child and his or her emotional environment. We suggest that this conceptual tool is provided by the model of the *self-selfobject unit*. This is a conceptual framework that can facilitate the recognition of the various degrees of failures in caregiving abilities. In the clinical situation, we can either focus on the child's developing self and assess the manner in which the environment is meeting the child's selfobject needs, or we can reverse the model and determine to what extent and in what manner the parents may be using the child to meet their own selfobject needs. Self and environment constitute an experiential unit; the self cannot be conceptualized without the selfobject environment, nor can the functions of the selfobjects be assessed without taking into account the effect that these functions have on the self.

The usefulness of the self-selfobject model is related to the fact that in the parent–child relationship, both parties, parent and child, fulfill selfobject functions for each other. While the central importance of parental selfobject functions for the child's development can readily be appreciated, the selfobject functions that children serve for the enhancement of the parent's adult self are more difficult to recognize. The difficulty lies in the fact that a parent's "average expectable" narcissistic investment in a child may not be readily distinguishable from the subtle ways in which a child may be "used" for the maintenance of the parent's self-cohesion, or more frequently, for the regulation of the caregiver's self-esteem. Erikson (1980) spoke of "generativity" that is a constituent of the adult self. "Generativity is concerned with new beings as well as new products and new ideas and which, as a link between the generations, *is as indispensable for the renewal of the adult generation's own life as it is for that of the next generation*" (p. 213).

Kohut (1971, 1977), on the basis of his observation of the various selfobject transferences, postulated a process of transmuting internalization that occurs in relation to the environment's empathic selfobject responsiveness. Examples of such selfobject responses are the merger experiences in infancy that have primarily psychophysiological functions (the establishment of physiological homeostasis, eating, and sleep-wakefulness patterns), the validating responses that affirm the toddler's initiative and self-assertiveness, the validation of the legitimacy of the rivalry and jealousy of the oedipal age child, and the mirroring that affirms the adolescent's strivings for independence. These validating experiences are combined with innumerable experiences in which the child is merged with the parents' (idealized) strength and power. The firmness of a parent's arm (or voice) as it calms the agitated child represents a selfobject function that, through repetition and optimal responsiveness, becomes the child's own ability to calm and soothe him- or herself. Repeated, innumerable merger experiences account for the development of the child's capacity to reduce tension and to tolerate anxiety. At later phases of development, these experiences concern themselves less with the child being merged with the parents' physical strength than with their moral strength and ideals. However, parental responses that are not in keeping with the child's actual abilities, skills, and talents do not have structure-building properties. For example, praise and enthusiasm in response to a particular behavior that is not experienced by the child as an expression of his or her nuclear self are more likely expressions of the parents' own expectations than an affirmation and validation of the child's own self.

PARENTAL SELF-DEVELOPMENT AND PARENTAL EMPATHY

Parenting, especially during infancy and the early years of the child's life, requires emotional resources that are not required by ordinary life stresses. Parents may be well-functioning adults in other ways, but discrete deficits in their own self-development may become manifest only when they become parents. The parent who is capable of parental attunement is one who developed an adult form of empathy—a capacity in which an adult man or woman can immerse him- or herself in the inner life of a child without this threatening his or her own sense of separateness and without the parent injecting his or her own needs into the interaction with the child. This is a more complicated and difficult task than is generally acknowledged. The difficulty is related primarily to the determination of a small child's motives regarding a particular behavior. Virginia Demos (1984) gives an example of a toddler approaching a dangerous object such as a pair of scissors to which the caregiver can have various possible responses. In view of the danger that the scissors represents, the caregiver may have difficulty recognizing the child's motive in reaching for the scissors—namely, the wish to explore and to express curiosity. Since in the case of a young child only the behavior is available for observation, it is more likely that this will be interpreted in terms of the meaning that it has for the caregiver rather than the meaning that it has for the child. This is particularly true once the child's motive has been partially or completely ignored and the behavior has been responded to only in terms of its meaning to the caregiver. By the time the child becomes demanding, hits, or bites because his intent has originally been misinterpreted or ignored, an interaction has been set into motion that precludes the possibility of recognizing and responding to the child's original motives. Understanding and appreciation of the child's internal state has to be distinguished from the manner in which a parent may respond to this state; "giving in" to a child is frequently mistaken for empathy. Parental responses can only be considered empathic when they encompass the child's reality above and beyond his momentary and, at times, imperative demands. Understanding and validating the child's inner state (i.e., appreciating his wish to explore, to touch, and to feel objects in his environment) does not have to exclude a response that is guided by mature judgment.

The question is frequently asked whether or not empathy means that a state of fusion exists between subject and object. This question appears to be related to the observation that empathy, an innate capacity of the human psyche, unfolds in the early years of psychological development. And while the infant indeed appears to be "fused" with the adult (e.g., the infant experiences the calmness or the anxiety of the adult as if this were his own), the requirements for adult empathy are the opposite of fusion. Adult empathy depends on the adult's capacity to retain his own sense of separateness. Fliess (1942) spoke of "trial identification," and Schafer (1959) spoke of "generative empathy" to indicate that empathy is a complex and high-level mental functioning. Norman Paul (1970) is most explicit about the need for the achievement of the sense of separateness in relation to an adult, that is, in relation to parental empathy. He says that an empathizer, or subject, accepts for a brief period the object's total emotional individuality, not only his simple emotions but also his whole state of being—the history of his desires, feelings, and thoughts as well as other forces and experiences that are expressed in his behavior. Further, empathy presupposes the existence of the object as a separate individual, entitled to his own feelings, ideas, and emotional history; the empathizer makes no judgment about what the other should feel and, for brief periods, experiences these feelings as his own. The empathizer oscillates between such subjective involvement and a detached recognition of the shared feelings. Secure in his sense of self and his own emotional boundaries, the empathizer attempts to nurture a similar security in the other.

With each child, the parent's empathic capacities are tested anew. Each child "creates" his or her own caregiver as the caregiver's empathic responses become "dovetailed" to the specific needs of the particular child. Herein lies the essence of parental empathy. "The parents do not respond out of their own needs, nor do they respond in keeping with prescriptions as to how to be a good parent, but their responses are determined by the needs of the particular child at a particular time in the child's life" (Ornstein 1981, p. 435). Some parents are able to be in empathic contact with young children readily, while others do not communicate meaningfully with their children until they are older or until the children reach adolescence (Olden 1953). Such variations in parental empathic capacities are generally nontraumatic, so long as other members in the parenting unit readily substitute for the temporarily unavailable one.

However, even under the most optimal circumstances, when adults become parents with a well-consolidated self, the reliable, ongoing presence of their empathy still depends essentially on two major factors: (1) the support of their social milieu, and (2) the child's ability to affirm their parenting. The mother's "motherliness," her capacity for empathic responsiveness, needs to be affirmed also. Feeding, cleaning, and handling that calms and comforts the baby promotes the integration of caregiving capacities; an unhappy, discontent infant, unable to mirror the caregiver because of congenital or acquired disability, interferes with such an integration.

Impaired babies may elicit extremes in caregiver responsiveness from overprotectiveness and oversolicitousness to overt or covert rejection. Contradictory responses may occur in the same caregiver. In considering the impact of the impaired infant on the caregiver, we are not only referring to the cases of grossly defective or handicapped infants in which parental responsiveness is usually fairly clear-cut—namely, either increased parental compassion, love, and tolerance, or obvious signs of rejection. The problem is more complicated in relationship to subtle, subliminal impairments in a child without demonstrable clinical findings. These are infants whose subtle neurological impairments interfere with the execution and mastery of their daily routines (e.g., frequent vomiting interferes with eating, sensitivity to noise and general irritability interfere with sleep, and poor motor coordination interferes with the phase-appropriate development of speech and locomotion). The parent, unable to feel effective in the care of the child, does not feel affirmed, and a slow erosion of his or her empathic capacities may follow.

What needs to be emphasized is that the feedback mechanism is not restricted to infancy. The need for adequate mirroring of the parent by the child continues throughout the parent's life and becomes of particular importance to the parent with grown children. Children who have successfully mastered their various developmental tasks affirm the parents in their parenting ability and contribute to the enhancement and esteem of their adult self. The reverse is true as well: children, who, for whatever reason, encounter difficulties in the course of their lifetime, create shame and guilt that adversely affects the caregiver's self-esteem.

PARENTAL DYSFUNCTIONS: DIAGNOSIS AND TREATMENT

In the clinical situation, psychotherapists are rarely consulted because of parental dysfunctions. These have to be assessed when parents bring their symptomatic children for treatment. Not understanding the nature, or rather the meaning, of the symptomatic child's behavior, the caregivers react with anger and disappointment, which in turn creates new problems accentuating the original difficulties. In their attempts to deal with the child's symptomatic behavior, caregivers may become increasingly more rigid and punitive or appeasing and placating. Such parental attitudes are responses to the child's symptoms and ought not be considered the cause of the child's original difficulties. What the professional sees at the time of the diagnostic assessment is the end product of years of pathological interactions that have had serious consequences not only for the child's development but for the parent's parenting capacities as well.

Parental dysfunctions are difficult to diagnose unless they take overt forms such as physical or sexual abuse, neglect, or abandonment. Failures in parenting that we have been describing are silent and usually subtle, such as the caregiver's failure to express pride through a gleam in the eye or the tone of the voice. Failures in these subtle but active parental responses easily elude the clinician and are never reported because they are, more often than not, unconscious to all parties involved. Also, empathic failures may be "hidden" behind claims of love and material indulgences. Under these circumstances, children find themselves emotionally trapped; they experience their rage in response to subtle empathic failures of the caregivers as unfounded, and may use their own body to inflict pain on those, who because of their inability to comprehend and respond to them empathically, have emotionally abandoned them. These are children who attempt or threaten to commit suicide or whose self-destructive behavior may take covert forms such as reckless driving, indiscriminate use of drugs, and running away. The self-destructive behavior represents both the expression of revenge on the nonempathic or only partially empathic caregiver, as well as an expression of the inadequate narcissistic investment in their bodies; they don't experience their bodies as being worth saving. The caregivers, sensitive to the element of revenge toward them but not able to perceive the child's psychic pain, experiences the child's self-destructive behavior as an indictment against themselves.

Kohut (1971) warns that the complexity and the limitless varieties of interplay between parent and child defy attempts at a comprehensive description. However, in reconstructing the genesis of his patients' psychopathology, he describes a spectrum of parental disturbances that may extend from mild narcissistic fixations to latent or overt psychosis, and it is his impression that "a specific type of covert psychosis in a parent tends to produce broader and deeper fixations in the narcissistic and especially in the prenarcissistic (autoerotic) realm than does overt psychosis" (p. 42). Overt psychosis in the primary caregiver has its own pathogenic impact on a child. The child "adapts" to the often bizarre, frightening behavior, the repeated need for hospitalizations, and the particularly dulling effects of many of the antipsychotic medications in such a way that symptoms may be manifested not in childhood but only later in life. However, the fact that the parental disturbance is overt appears to protect the child from the kinds of internal compromises that children whose parents suffer from various degrees of discrete forms of self-pathology have to make. In the case of an overt disturbance of a caregiver, children's own perceptions are more readily validated and they can turn more freely to other members in the parenting unit to provide the developmentally crucial selfobject responses. This assures the child of adequate consolidation of his self and the capacity to be resilient to the behavior of the disturbed caregiver.

In a child therapist's everyday practice, the largest group of dysfunctional caregivers suffers from relatively discrete forms of self-pathology. These are caregivers, who, because of self-absorption, are not available to perceive their children's states of mind and who frequently project their own moods into their emotional environments, including their children. It is also the caregiver with the discrete forms of self-deficit who may selectively respond to certain aspects of the child's personality—aspects more in keeping with their own needs for self-enhancement than in keeping with the child's own talents and temperament.

In diagnosing the degree and nature of self-disorder that underlie the various forms of parental dysfunctions, it is useful to distinguish between caregivers who emotionally distance themselves from the child whom they can no longer fit into their self-regulatory system (especially when another child has a more successful fit) from those who insist on remaining in the center of the child's universe. This latter group of parents unconsciously creates a sense of responsibility in the child for their own self-cohesion and/or for the maintenance of their self-esteem. Parents who use their children to maintain either self-cohesion or self-esteem are particularly vulnerable to rage reactions since the child is likely to frustrate their infantile, now highly intensified, selfobject needs. This explains the frequently violent attacks with which these children may be physically or verbally abused.

The child-abusing caregiver who suffers from a form of self-pathology in which the child is expected to be responsive to an exaggerated and imperative parental demand ought to be distinguished from the caregiver who had failed to develop a selfobject tie with the child altogether. The latter form of parental dysfunction is expressed in abandonment or in chronic physical and emotional neglect. Such chronic indifference is likely to result in various forms of childhood depression, low self-esteem, and lack of initiative. This is in contrast to children who have been physically abused. Such children are more likely to be subservient to the abusing caregiver, but become aggressive and provocative with younger children and animals.

In addition to considering the various forms of self-pathology that facilitate the clinician's understanding of parental dysfunctions, it is also important to recognize how a particular developmental period may become stressful to a particular caregiver. For this reason, we shall describe a few clinically important instances in which the specific features of a particular developmental period may interfere with parental empathy.

THE TODDLER YEARS

In terms of childhood and adult psychopathology, no other developmental phase appears to be as heavily implicated as the toddler years. Mahler and colleagues (1975) in their extensive work with toddlers and their mothers, note that many mothers at this time "make a sharp turnabout in the overall quality of their maternal care in response to maturational events." Mahler and colleagues' explanation for this sudden change in the mother's responsiveness rests on their observation that some mothers are unable to promote separation and individuation because of their own need to retain symbiotic fusion with the child. This need for symbiosis, in turn, they write, was determined by the fact that the baby frequently represented a part of the mother's body, specifically the phallus.

In our view, which differs fundamentally from Mahler and colleagues, there are various reasons that explain why the toddler years are so heavily implicated in childhood psychopathology. The toddler's increasing self-assertiveness and autonomy as well as a more forceful introduction of individual characteristics, especially temperament, bring new qualities into the "interactive regulatory system" (Sander 1962). A new level of the infant's self-organization requires something from the environment that is very different from that of the crib infant. From the emphasis on the establishment of homeostasis in the first year of life, for which the clues may not have been easy to pick up but that, on the whole, could still be readily "accommodated" into the caregiver's own self-regulatory system, the toddler actively demands recognition and admiration for his/her initiative, which may dramatically oppose the caregiver's own purposes and values.

Toddlers experience themselves in the center of the universe; they are filled with a sense of initiative and healthy vigor. They want those around them to see, recognize, and acknowledge their intoxicating sense of what they have discovered to be their own powers and abilities. To an environment that is fearful of losing its control over the toddler's developmentally exaggerated sense of power, this behavior will be threatening. Under these circumstances, the environment anxiously attempts to reinforce its control. Battles ensue, and a child's self-assertion disintegrates into the aimless and frequently destructive form of aggression. Still, children who respond to the increased control with aggression appear to maintain their self-assertiveness to a greater degree than those who give up their initiative and become withdrawn and apathetic. The "divergence" (Sander 1975) or the "sharp turnabout" (Mahler et al. 1975) that so commonly occurs between the toddler and his or her emotional environment may result in overt symptoms during childhood, or the divergence may remain latent and lead to some form of self-disorder later in life. In terms of overt symptoms, we witness an increase in the intensity of separation anxiety; the toddler becomes clingy and whiny and develops nightmares and other forms of sleep disturbances. Tolpin (1971) and Kohut (1971) maintain that the usual childhood anxieties (e.g., fear of the dark, noise, animals, and robbers, or the development of compulsive rituals) are the manifestations of "disintegration" and "depletion" anxiety created by the child feeling "unplugged" from the life-sustaining connection with his or her primary selfobject.

The significance of the emotional presence of caregivers of both genders in the development of children of both sexes has been repeatedly asserted (Abelin 1975, Herzog 1982, Ornstein 1983). The father or another male in the parenting unit may be available as a primary selfobject when the mother's self-pathology prevents her from being optimally responsive to the infant's merger and mirroring needs. This not only provides an opportunity for the building up of compensatory psychic structures,[1] but the child can also experience the father as strong (independent of the mother) and therefore idealizable. The developmental significance of the boy's idealization of his father can be derived from the reconstruction of transferences of adult patients as well as from the treatment of boys whose fathers

[1]The distinction between primary, compensatory, and defensive psychic structures is a useful one (Sander 1962). Primary structures develop in relation to optimal, phase-appropriate responses to narcissistic developmental needs. These are the structures that are responsible for the healthy functioning of the self, for the consolidation of both poles (ambitions and ideals), and the full utilization of innate skills and talents; the self is experienced as cohesive and vigorous. But if the developmental unfolding of the grandiose self meets with traumatic dysfunction of empathy on the part of the primary selfobject, the resulting defects in the self will be covered over with defensive structure that will prevent further unfolding and structuralization of the pole of the ambitions. However, if the child has an opportunity to turn to other available selfobjects, this will ensure the building up of psychic structure at either of the two poles and lead to the development of compensatory structures. If well consolidated, these structures will afford the self sufficient functional freedom, safeguard its cohesiveness, and allow the progression of further development.

have been out of the home in the early years of the child's life or emotionally not available to them (Herzog 1982, Kohut 1979).

To discuss the specific importance that the idealization of the same-sex parent has for a child's development, we have selected the case of a boy who was raised by his mother and who had become symptomatic after a man had moved into their home. The case shall also illustrate the challenges that are faced by single parents and how impingements or compromises to the child's self-development that occur early in life may be responsible for symptoms at a later point in development.

CASE HISTORY: DEAN AND HIS MOTHER

Dean was 9 years old when he and his mother came to the clinic. The mother complained of a major change in Dean's personality since her lover, Mr. Hillard, had moved into their home and the two had decided to get married. Dean, who up until now had been a fairly even-tempered and pleasant child, had become sullen and rebellious; his schoolwork deteriorated rapidly and he refused to go to school on a number of occasions.

Dean was an illegitimate child. His mother was 17 years old when she became pregnant, and by then she had a history of alcohol and drug abuse. However, during her pregnancy she did not drink or smoke and after delivery she surprised her welfare worker with the natural competence with which she cared for the baby. The first two years the mother devoted herself completely to the care of the child. She took good care of him and their small apartment. When Dean was about 2 years old, the mother took a job as a janitor in an office building. With her work, she resumed some of her drinking. She took Dean to the bar with her and the patrons there took to the bright-eyed youngster. They would take him on their laps and play with him; he was definitely the center of attention. Dean "entertained" these people to his mother's great delight. By the time the child was 6 years old, his acting skills were considerable and his mother enrolled him in a special school where he could study acting. He liked school and did well in all his subjects but particularly in acting, securing parts in school plays and some television commercials for which he was paid. The only thing that indicated that not all was well was Dean's shoplifting behavior. Otherwise, his engaging manner and polite behavior did not reveal that the child was suffering from any form of childhood emotional disorder.

However, this attitude and behavior changed rather drastically when, for the first time in his life, a man moved into their small apartment. Not only had Dean's disposition changed, but so did his mother's; she demanded that he be nice to the man who wanted to marry her. Mr. Hillard, too, who at first took kindly to the child, began to demand that Dean show him respect by calling him "Daddy." Dean refused, insisting that since this man was not his father, he should not have to call him that. Violent fights ensued in which Dean felt betrayed by his mother, who consistently belittled and challenged him. After he ran away from home several times and threatened suicide, he was placed by the court into a group home. Here he did somewhat better, but he remained suicidal and refused to return home and to his previous school.

Child-Centered Family Treatment: Dean, His Mother, and Mr. Hillard

The most impressive feature of the joint interview with mother and son was the total absence of the mother's empathy in relation to the child's predicament. Whatever the child's motives were for feeling and behaving the way he did, the mother could not appreciate this; she could not understand why Dean wouldn't do something that was so important to her. In his individual sessions Dean spoke earnestly about suicide. The loss of interest in acting was the first sign of his depression. Acting had been the major connection between Dean and his mother; now, he was no longer sure if it was he himself who wanted to go to this special school, or if it was his mother who wanted him to go into acting and he had done so only to keep her happy.

What emerged in the treatment of this very articulate little boy was a picture we see rather frequently in children who, after relatively adequate early nurturing during the first two years of life, "discover" a particular mode of behavior that secures for them the echoing and approving responses of their environment, which permits the consolidation of their self structures at least in a narrow area. But in the case of Dean, as in children similar to him, the growing self remained vulnerable to traumatic disappointments because its consolidation was only partial and related rather rigidly to one particular segment (namely, acting) of his personality. This segment, importantly, was one that established the connection between the child and his mother and assured adequate selfobject responsiveness from her as well as from the people at the bar.

From the time of conception, Dean fulfilled important selfobject functions for his mother. Being able to carry and give birth to a child made her feel, for the first time in her life, that she was a worthwhile human being. However, once she went back to work and began to drink again, her responsiveness to him became capricious and dependent on how well Dean was able to please her. Dean, with the hyperalertness of a child who had to extract from the environment what he needed for his emotional survival, was able to establish a workable "fit" with his mother. The mother's lack of empathy became obvious only when the demand on Dean for adaptation exceeded his psychological reserves; the child was not prepared to deal with feelings of rivalry, jealousy, and possessiveness that the arrival of the mother's boyfriend demanded of him. Because of the inadequate consolidation of his self, he experienced profound despair and disintegration anxiety that was followed by a serious suicide attempt.

The aim of the child's individual treatment was to enable him to experience the affects that this triangular relationship demanded of him. This treatment approach was based on a self-psychological perspective on the Oedipus complex—a perspective according to which the presence of a firm self is a precondition for the experience of the Oedipus complex. The treatment plan included regular meetings with his mother and Mr. Hillard so that the therapist could understand their backgrounds and their psychological makeup as well as help them understand the child's motives for his running away and his suicidal behavior. In the meetings with mother and Mr. Hillard, the mother soon focused on her own childhood, especially on her adolescence when she began to drink and when she became pregnant with Dean. The mother, crying most of the time, spoke of the emptiness she felt during those years, how easy it was for her to find relief in alcohol, and how, for the first time in her life, she felt she did something worthwhile when she gave birth to her child. She felt that Dean had "cured" her; she did not need to drink—he filled her up with his smile and by being such a good baby. She did not seriously consider marriage until she met Mr. Hillard, who, somewhat older than herself, was tender and affectionate toward her. And now she felt betrayed and let down by the child as he appeared to block her in her effort to make a better life for both of them.

We will not detail this family's treatment here further but wish to emphasize that it was crucial for Dean's recovery to mobilize the mother's empathy in relation to his predicament. This occurred by the therapist's appreciation of the mother's need to have Dean be responsive to her now as he had been in the past. By linking the mother's need for the child's responses to the emotional deprivation of her childhood, the mother was able to recognize that Dean's behavior was not in defiance of her; rather, it expressed the child's fear that unless he is the only one who can please her, he will lose her altogether. Dean was a parenting child; meeting his mother's selfobject needs assured that she would not abandon him.

The question could be raised whether or not the child's reaction to his mother's wish to marry represented the reaction of a "cheated lover." Was Dean's reaction so devastating because he could not give up his "oedipal victory," and Mr. Hillard's presence activated murderous feelings in him? In that case, the therapeutic work would have had to focus on helping the child accept the reality that with Mr. Hillard's arrival he was replaced by a bigger and more successful rival. However, from a self-psychological perspective, the important aspect of this child-centered family treatment focused on the reestablishment of the connection between mother and son and the establishment of one with the new member of the family. It was the therapist's empathic response to the mother's own mental state and the fairly consistent interpretation of her own sense of deprivation and need for then child's responsiveness to her that enabled the mother to focus her attention on the child's inner life, rather than on her own needs. The mother's increasing capacity to grasp empathically Dean's reasons for behaving the way he did provided the selfobject matrix that sufficiently firmed up the child's self to experience the jealousy, rivalry, and possessiveness that had previously overwhelmed him.

We are not stating here that Dean, on his return from the group home, entered the oedipal phase of development, but that the mother's understanding and acceptance of the child's feelings made it more likely that he would be able to experience these affects without becoming overwhelmed by them. Importantly, it appeared that Dean's relationship with Mr. Hillard helped the child not to feel sole responsibility for his mother's emotional survival. Thus, Dean had a chance to resume his self-development, in which oedipal experiences played an important part. In addition, Dean now had an opportunity to experience Mr. Hillard as an idealizable male, which was a necessary aspect for the development of his own masculine self.

SUMMARY: CONCEPTUAL ADVANCES IN PARENTAL FUNCTIONS AND DYSFUNCTIONS

In this chapter, we have suggested that (1) parental behavior is flexible (e.g., it changes even in relation to the same child in terms of the child's increasingly complex and constantly changing psychic organization); and (2) the structural changes in the adult in relation to parenting are intimately related to the narcissistic (selfobject) nature of the parent–child relationship.

Our conceptualization of parenting is based on Kohut's self psychology, which recognizes the central importance of empathy as a mode of observation as well as an emotional nutrient and its absence in parenting to be of major pathogenic significance. We have emphasized that parental empathy requires not only a temporary immersion into the inner world of the child, but a sustained capacity to perceive the child's affects and his particular manner of protecting himself from the potentially destructive impact of his emotional environment. In the course of development, parental empathy will expectedly fluctuate since it is subject to ordinary life stresses. However, such ordinary fluctuations are nontraumatic; only prolonged absence or faulty empathy indicate a defect in the parent's self-development and may become pathogenic for the child.

The concept of the selfobject permitted a fresh approach to the study of parenting by bringing together what in the past has been separated as internal or external in relation to development and pathogenesis. Since the parent as a selfobject is always viewed from the vantage point of the experiencing self of the infant or child, the external environment may thus be consistently studied as part of the inner world of the particular child. The selfobject concept helps appreciate that it is not the overt psychopathology of the parent (which is visible to the external observer and in response to which the child may find various modes of coping), but it is the more subtle, invisible deficiency or absence of certain key functions that will have pathogenic influence. The impact, for instance, of the absence of the gleam in the mother's eyes or the lack of firmness in her arms when she holds her baby can only be discovered from within the experience of the child or, reconstructively, in the treatment of an adult patient.

We have suggested that the inherent reciprocity in the caregiver-child relationship is most aptly expressed in the model of the self-selfobject unit. This model is useful because the clinician can either focus on the child's self and examine it in relation to the parental selfobject or he or she can focus on the parent's self in order to examine the nature of parental dysfunctions and determine the manner in which the child is being used as the parent's selfobject. We have demonstrated our approach to treatment with the case of Dean. We have illustrated that a child whose self has not attained adequate consolidation is not able to experience the passions traditionally associated with the Oedipus complex, namely, rivalry, jealousy, and possessiveness. However, it needs to be recognized that even when the child has attained adequate consolidation of the self and could experience these affects without adverse consequences, he or she still needs the caregiver's affirmative responses to these affects. In other words, it is not only parental seductiveness, counteraggression, or counterrivalry that may create the pathogenic conditions; the very absence of affirmative acceptance of a child's rivalry and possessiveness directed at the parents has pathogenic significance.

REFERENCES

Abelin, E. (1975). Some further observations and comments on the earliest role of the father. *International Journal of Psycho-Analysis* 56:293.

Ainsworth, M. (1973). The development of infant-mother attachment. In *Review of Child Developmental Research*, vol. 3, ed. B. Caldwell and R. Ricciuti, pp. 1-94. Chicago: University of Chicago Press.

Benedek, T. (1956). Toward the biology of the depressive constellation. *Journal of the American Psychoanalytic Association* 4:389.

———(1959). Parenthood as a developmental phase. *Journal of the American Psychoanalytic Association* 7:380.

Bowlby, J. (1969). *Attachment and Loss*, vol. 1. New York: Basic Books.

Brody, S. (1980). *The concept of attachment and bonding*. Paper presented at the First International Congress on Infant Psychiatry, Estoril, Portugal, May.

Chess, S., and Thomas, A. (1982). Infant bonding: mystique and reality. *American Journal of Orthopsychiatry* 52(2):214.

Demos, V. (1984). Empathy and affect: reflections on infant experience. In *Empathy*, vol. 2, ed. J. Lichtenberg, M. Bornstein, and D. Silver, pp. 9–34. Hillsdale, NJ: Analytic Press.

Erikson, E. (1980). On the generational cycle: an address. *International Journal of Psycho-Analysis* 61:213.

Fliess, R. (1942). The metapsychology of the analyst. *Psychoanalytic Quarterly* 11:211.

Freud, S. (1916–17). Introductory lectures on psychoanalysis. *Standard Edition* 16.

Greenspan, S. I. (1981). *Psychopathology and Adaptation in Infancy and Early Childhood: Principles of Clinical Diagnosis and Preventive Intervention.* Clinical Infant Reports Series of the National Center for Clinical Infant Programs, No. 1. New York: International Universities Press.

Hartmann, H. (1958). *Ego Psychology and the Problem of Adaptation.* New York: International Universities Press.

Herzog, J. M. (1982). On father hunger: the father's role in the modulation of aggressive drive and fantasy. In *Father and Child: Developmental and Clinical Perspectives*, ed. S. H. Cath, A. Gurwitt, and J. M. Ross, pp. 163–174. Boston: Little, Brown.

Klaus, M., and Kennell, J. H. (1976). Human maternal behavior at the first contact with the young. *Pediatrics* 46:187.

Kohut, H. (1971). *The Analysis of the Self.* New York: International Universities Press.

———(1977). *The Restoration of the Self.* New York: International Universities Press.

———(1979). The two analyses of Mr. Z. *International Journal of Psychoanalysis* 60:3.

Kohut, H., and Seitz, P. (1963). Concepts and theories in psychoanalysis. In *The Search for the Self*, ed. P. Ornstein, pp. 337–374. New York: International Universities Press, 1978.

Lichtenberg, J. (1982). Reflections on the first year of life. *Psychoanalytic Inquiry* 1:695.

Mahler, M. S., Pine, F., and Bergman, A. (1975). *The Psychological Birth of the Human Infant.* New York: Basic Books.

Olden, C. (1953). On adult empathy with children. *Psychoanalytic Study of the Child* 8:111. New York: International Universities Press.

Ornstein, A. (1981). Self-pathology in childhood: developmental and clinical considerations. *Psychiatric Clinics of North America* 4:435-452.

——— (1983). An idealizing transference of the oedipal phase. In *Reflections on Self Psychology*, ed. J. D. Lichtenberg and S. Kaplan, pp. 135-148. Hillsdale, NJ: Analytic Press.

Paul, N. L. (1970). Parental empathy. In *Parenthood: Its Psychology and Psychopathology*, ed. E. J. Anthony and T. Benedek, pp. 337-352. Boston: Little, Brown.

Rutter, M. (1972). *Maternal Deprivation Reassessed.* Middlesex, England: Penguin.

Sander, L. (1962). Issues in early mother-child interaction. *Journal of the American Academy of Child Psychiatry* 1:141.

——— (1975). Infant and caretaking environment: investigation and conceptualization of adaptive behavior in a system of increasing complexity. In *Exploration in Child Psychiatry*, ed. E. J. Anthony, pp. 129-166. New York: Plenum.

Schafer, R. (1959). Generative empathy in the treatment situation. *Psychoanalytic Quarterly* 28:347.

Stern, D. (1977). *The First Relationship: Infant and Mother*. Cambridge, MA: Harvard University Press.

Tolpin, M. (1971). On the beginnings of a cohesive self: an application of the concept of transmuting internalization to the study of transitional object and signal anxiety. *Psychoanalytic Study of the Child* 26:316. New Haven, CT: Yale University Press.

19

A Wrinkle in the Sheets: An Overview of Parent Treatment through Couples Therapy

Walter E. Brackelmanns

Marital Therapy, or couples therapy, is not quite as simple and does not function quite as smoothly as appears in written description. In reality, it is imperative for a marital therapist to have a conceptual model to work from, a framework upon which to hang the complex data being obtained from the couple. Understanding leads to resolution. A framework also is a road that the therapist and couple can travel that has a beginning, a middle, and an end.

The framework, or model, that I have developed is an understanding that in all relationships there are four levels of interaction. Level One is the "I want" level. If things are going well at this level, the couple is getting their needs met and they are happy. If things are not going well, they are frustrated, angry, and are in the conflict sphere of criticizing and defending, arguing and fighting. There is more concern about who is right than about having a loving relationship.

Level two is the "I am" level. "I am always trying to figure out who I am, what I feel, and what I need in the context of a relationship with you." The word *re-lation-ship* comes from the Greek and Latin and means "to connect again." All of our lives, in our relationships, we are consciously and unconsciously trying to form a oneness with another person while at the same time trying to maintain a separateness. I believe that this is the core issue in all relationships. At the time of marriage, at the time that we bond, we form an *unconscious contract against closeness.* In effect, we set a distance regulator for the level of closeness we can tolerate. This second level of interaction has to do with these issues of closeness. Closeness is defined as the ability of one person to unconsciously come together and form a oneness with another person, while at the same time maintaining a separateness. If things go well at this second level, there will be bliss and contentment. If one has significant problems with closeness, there will be fears of abandonment and feelings of engulfment.

Level three is the "You are" level. We each bring to a marriage unconscious unresolved problems from childhood that we unconsciously transfer onto the other person. We distort who that person is based on repressed childhood conflicts with our parents. We unconsciously seek a person with whom we can reconstruct the early conflict, so that we can get *now* what we wanted as children. Freud called it repetition compulsion, and more recent theoreticians have referred to it as Six People Getting Married Instead of Two. The name of the game is to get those parents out of bed and out of the house as soon as possible. If people are operating well at this level there is a capacity for intimacy. Intimacy, as I define it, is the ability to transmit who you are to another person, as well as understanding who that person is in his or her context.

Level four is the level of "We are." Couples operating at this level have managed to move from a level of conflict to a level where they are able to relate to each other as two separate individuals. Practically speaking this means they have moved from level one self-absorption and selfishness to being empathic, understanding, and giving.

The task of marital therapy often begins at the wedding. In many marriage ceremonies there is a ritual. The couple lights two individual candles depicting the two people and then together light a central candle indicating their union. After the central candle is lit, the two people blow out the individual candles. Two have become one.

The extinguishing of individual candles is meant to be a statement of the importance of the union and the central focus the marriage should and will have in the lives of these people. Unfortunately, this also graphically illustrates the major problem in marriages and the primary function of marital therapy. The major problem is that unless there is much attention paid to it early in the marriage, the two people disappear. They begin to relate to each other not as two special individuals with special needs but as an entity that feels or does not feel satisfaction. "If you function the way I want you to, I like you. If you don't, then I'm angry with you."

The goal in marital therapy is to move from level one to level four, to deal with conflict not in a way that excludes the essence of the other person, but in a constructive interaction that considers the other person as separate, unique, different, and special. The focus is on understanding, not criticism, and on giving, not getting.

There are a number of marital therapies—premarital, postmarital, affair, separation, divorce, and remarriage. Marital therapy is indicated when a couple is in conflict and experiencing psychic pain, and each sees the other person as the cause of the pain rather than assuming responsibility for one's own intrapsychic problems. In a conflictual relationship, we see three things:

1. There is pain at the level of 7 to 9 on a scale of 10.
2. The needs are not being met by both people, at the level of 7 to 9 on a scale of 10.
3. The two people have little or no capacity for an empathic connection. They are unable to talk and listen to each other and are unable to consider each other as separate people to be understood in that context.

Distressed couples, in trying to solve their own problems, only repeat the same psychopathological and destructive pattern over and over again. Therefore, an outside "unconscious watcher" is needed. The therapist is an unconscious watcher because he must identify and bring to the attention of the couple the ways and whys of their unconscious interactions. The therapist must show them how their inner worlds are clashing and give them hope and alternative ways of resolving their difficulties.

There are at least two requirements for marital therapy to work. The first is love. It is important that each person is able to declare with as much conviction as possible that he or she loves the other. Therapy is often successful if one person is ambivalent, but it does not work if one of the pair definitely does not love the other.

A second requirement is commitment. Commitment is conscious and should be distinguished from bonding, which is unconscious. After we meet, and as we move toward marriage, we progress through increasing levels of commitment until finally there is marriage. Some of these stages are meeting, dating, sex, exclusivity, living together, and engagement. At the time of marriage an unconscious bond between the two people is formed. This bond cannot be experienced directly, but is felt indirectly when there is a threat or reality of dissolution. It then feels like one is being cut in half by a band saw. There are severe feelings linked to fears of abandonment. Some people feel desperate if they cannot have the other person; they feel as if they will die.

How does marital therapy work? A woman calls and says that she and her husband want marital therapy. I invite them to come in together. I prefer that they are in individual psychotherapy with their own respective therapists, but it is not necessary. If indicated, we will work together toward that end. I meet with the two people and take a brief history of the problem and the marriage. Initially, I am focused on the interactional process. Usually when a couple comes in, they are in conflict. They are criticizing and defending, operating at level one, and they are not at all connected to each other, that is, not tuned in and aware of the other person as a separate and unique person apart from oneself. Until the two people become connected, nothing else really matters. I spend a tremendous amount of time in the early stages of marital therapy helping the two people to recognize that they do not have a dialogue of intimacy, that is, they are unable to effectively communicate. I teach them this dialogue. I teach them to talk and listen. Talking is telling the other person about yourself in the context of who you are, what you feel, what you need, and where your "soft spots" are, with no expectations of the other person other than that he or she will try to understand. By "soft spots,"

I mean your vulnerabilities and deepest feelings about self. Listening is hearing what the other person says in the context of that person with no reference back to oneself, without taking it personally.

During the sessions, when the people are interacting, I demonstrate how they violate my principles of communication as taught in the dialogue of intimacy, the art of talking and listening. Here are the most important ones, which are most commonly violated:

1. Acceptance: We must accept who our mate is, without in any way trying to change him or her. It is impossible for one person to change another person. The only person we are capable of changing is ourselves. We try to change another person because unconsciously we are attempting to fix our childhood. Unfortunately, this is impossible. Instead of change, the focus should be on listening and understanding. If the other person loves and cares, he or she is likely to move toward you and meet your needs.
2. Trustworthiness: If one person bares his soul, the other person cannot come back at a future time and use that information about his self spots against him.
3. Perceptual disagreement: If one person states something and the other person disagrees, there is a perceptual disagreement. Person A accuses person B of always being angry. B disagrees. This usually leads to a level-one marital battle. A better way to handle this is to cross over the perceptual disagreement line. In this way B accepts A's perception. This does not mean that B accepts the reality of what A says. B becomes a listener and becomes very interested in how A feels about the anger that B does not really believe he has. In this way B is demonstrating sensitivity and caring and will learn about A in a way that will foster understanding and a greater connection between the two people.

During therapy, as we walk through these, and other, principles of effective communication and the couple begins to learn how to communicate and begins to establish a more empathic connection, become very interested in past history and the inner worlds of the two people. This is where level-two issues of closeness, abandonment, and engulfment start to emerge. These issues are dealt with through the process of talking and listening—the dialogue of intimacy—and by interpretation.

I give an exercise to the couples I see. I ask them to set aside 15 minutes two times a week. One person is to talk and the other person listens. They are to stay in place for the full 15 minutes. There is to be no criticizing, defending, demanding, or uncontrolled anger—anger that so overwhelms the person that he or she is unable to talk or listen. The listener has four instruments to aid him.

1. Silence
   The listener can be quiet and this will allow a psychological vacuum to form. The pressure will build up and the talker will feel the need to talk.
2. Facilitating statements
   These are comments like "oh," "I see," "that is like what you said yesterday," "that must hurt." These comments do not represent arcane secrets. They are meant to encourage verbal discourse. These statements address the conscious mind. There is one kind of facilitating statement that addresses the unconscious mind. It is an interpretation. This is a statement by a mate to the unconscious of the other mate. People who are married know everything about the other person. They just don't know consciously what they know.
3. Facilitating directions
   Sometimes one mate can direct the other to talk about something that will help that person to get in touch with suppressed or repressed thoughts and feelings.
4. Questions
   This is the major and primary instrument of the listener. Examples are: "What else are you thinking about?" "Can you take it back to your feelings about yourself?" It is more difficult to be a listener than a talker, for two main reasons.
   - The listener has to put his or her feelings aside.
   - The listener is responsible for the process. The listener is never responsible for the other person's feelings. However, through the process, the listener will learn about the talker's soft spots and hopefully love the person and want to be responsive.

If the listener runs out of questions or can't think of any to ask, he or she can appeal to the talker for help in forming them. The talker is the one who is trying to express his or her own feelings.

Feelings and criticisms are not the same thing. Criticism has four steps: an emotion, a person and event, take it back to your inner world connected to the outside person and event, and finally, talk about your insides detached from the outside person and event.

- I am angry
- at you for slamming the door.
- When you do, it causes me to feel unimportant to you.
- I feel unimportant. When I was a child, my father preferred my brother to me.

This is to be compared with a criticism. The first two steps are the same, followed by a judgment and demand.

- I am angry
- at you for slamming the door.
- You are bad for doing it.
- Cut it out.

Initially, only 10 percent of people do this exercise. The reason is that if they do it my way, they can't do it their way. Their way is to argue, and most people would rather fight. They would rather be right than be loved.

In marital therapy we deal with the myths and patterns we have developed based on past psychological issues. One of the basic tasks of marital therapy is to shatter these myths and patterns. The most common myth is that there is a good guy and a bad guy in the relationship. Probably the most important concept in relationships and in marital therapy is that problems in relationships are shared exactly fifty-fifty. We together constructed the problems we share in our marriage and only together can we resolve them.

After the villians in the relationship have been neutralized, the couple can begin working together to understand and resolve the problems in the relationship as well as in themselves. Here we see much less focus on poor communication and much more focus on issues of level three, which express and define the conflicts from childhood that have been projected onto the other person. If all goes well, the two people become able to talk about themselves and what bothers them as two separate, autonomous people with the caring, interest, and respect for each other that we find at level four.

SUMMARY

The main function of marital therapy is to change the oneness of the marriage into a twoness, while still retaining the oneness. This is accomplished by learning how to talk and listen as outlined in the dialogue of intimacy. In relationships there are three rules: communication, communication, and communication. If all of us learn how to talk and listen to each other in a sensitive, caring, empathic, and understanding manner, we can work out anything.

20

Chronic Disconnections: Three Family Contexts

Irene Pierce Stiver

In "Connections, Disconnections, and Violations," Jean Baker Miller (1988) traces the processes by which chronic experiences of disconnection in relationships lead to psychopathology. I would like to use this formulation of how psychological difficulties develop to reframe our understanding of troubled families. I will briefly summarize the major themes in Miller's article that are particularly relevant to the family systems I will be discussing.

The child who grows up in families characterized by chronic and sustained disconnections learns to alter her inner sense of herself to fit with the images imposed on her by others. She also tries to adapt her self image to her understanding of the meanings of the neglect and/or violations she endures from others. More and more of the child's experience is split off, "walled off," leaving her with a very constricted and highly negative image of herself and others. Because of this constriction on self expression and lack of clarity of experience, she cannot fully engage with others in ways that lead to growth and change.

Miller recognizes a significant paradox in these circumstances. Because the child feels more and more isolated, she tries to establish ways of connecting with the only relationships available, but can do this only by *staying out of relationship*. The connections are apt to be static, rigidly programmed, and fixed in place, with little chance of change in all the people involved.

In exploring the ways troubled families impede rather than foster growth-enhancing experiences in their children, we need to attend to the particular conditions or contexts in which relational interactions lead to disconnections in a sustained and relatively chronic fashion. I have chosen three family systems—the alcoholic family, the incest survivor, and the Holocaust survivor family—to explore those conditions that lead to disconnections. There are other family systems and circumstances that illustrate how chronic disconnections develop and get played out, but I have chosen these three primarily because we know a great deal about them. I will also try to identify the variety of ways children growing up in these families maintain some semblance of connection and yet manage to stay out of relationship.

Here are three clinical vignettes that illustrate these different family systems:

> Arthur, a 42-year-old, unmarried, and highly successful businessman, who presents as very warm, charming, and witty, describes a visit home over a weekend. He is sitting in the living room, watching television, reading a book, and eating peanuts. Opposite him is his mother knitting and talking nonstop about the meals she made during the week and what she is planning to cook for him that evening. He is barely aware of the content of her conversation—he is not listening.
>
> He tells me in a therapy session that until recently he was never aware of this dynamic. He had originally entered therapy because he had been in what he believed was a very destructive relationship with a woman; he was also aware that he had had a series of such relationships and wanted to understand this better.

As our work evolved, one of the most significant aspects of his history was that both parents were Holocaust survivors. His mother was the only one in her family who had survived; his father had rescued two of his siblings, but lost everyone else. Arthur was born in Europe and moved at age 7 to the United States, where the family lived in a rather isolated, non-Jewish community. Neither parent ever spoke of that six-year period of the Holocaust.

Although his mother wept often, it was typically in reaction to her husband's criticism of her or his threatening divorce. Arthur's father, on the other hand, rarely showed emotion except when he had rages at those times when his children defied him, and especially when Arthur went out with women who were not Jewish, which was consistently the case.

Over the course of therapy the patient did extricate himself from the relationship that brought him into therapy and he was eventually able to become involved with a warm and engaging woman. When he brought her home she was stunned to see how no one seemed to relate to anyone else; rather there was constant bickering or withdrawal of various family members. It was her perspective, together with his work in therapy, that helped him see and then recount to me that scene in the living room.

He talked then about how he and his parents and sister had all avoided close relationships all their lives because it was too dangerous to try to feel for the other person; it felt like unbearable pain. He saw how much he had been isolated in his life, focusing all his attention on taking care of his parents or stewing about how to get out of a particularly frustrating relationship with the woman he happened to be involved with at that time. He had some male friends but did not discuss personal matters with them. His one area of intense interaction was on the basketball courts, where he was unusually aggressive and intensely involved at the moment; he never saw the other members of the team except at the weekly games.

He began to understand more fully his parents' behaviors and his reactions to them. His mother's constant talk about trivialities reflected her struggle to not talk of anything really important, for fear it might open up such old and painful wounds. His irritation and intolerance of her chatter reflected his deep frustration in trying to connect with her, on the one hand, and being terrified to hear her true story, on the other. His father's rages when Arthur brought home non-Jewish women revealed his deep sense of betrayal by his son, who seemed to him to be joining the outside hostile forces, and he was also clearly terrified that he would lose another family member. Arthur's anger and resistance to his father in turn reflected his attempts to be unburdened by his painful Jewish heritage and to be free to move on in his own life. Arthur could then realize that his parents really did not want him to get married and "go out of the family" and "leave them."

Mary, a 30-year-old woman who had been a very competent sales representative, came to see me about terminating her therapy with a therapist she had been seeing for two years. She felt he was no longer helpful to her. She was recently discharged from a psychiatric hospital, having been admitted for depression and suicidal ideation. In the course of the hospitalization she was diagnosed as a multiple personality.

She had a history of unspeakable sexual abuse from her father, stepfather, and others, and had experienced other great personal tragedies, including her daughter's death in a drowning accident. Her daughter had also been sexually abused by Mary's father. Her presentation completely belied this history. Mary was very attractively dressed, articulate, and apparently very sure of herself, as she outlined all the logical reasons to fire her therapist. She was quite lively and funny, albeit in a rather sardonic fashion, and provocatively challenged me to convince her to stay with her therapist. I knew of some events in her current life that were quite sad and I asked her whether her sadness about these events had anything to do with her decision.

After Mary displayed some convulsive movements, I realized that another personality had emerged. It is extremely difficult to translate into words the power of my emotional reaction to what I saw. I don't think I have ever seen a sadder face. She introduced herself by another name and told me that "she" had never "come out" before; "the others" had kept a tight lid on her lest she upset the host personality, who would surely kill herself if confronted with the new personality's story.

The story was almost unbearable to listen to since it was this personality's profound belief that she had deliberately set the stage for the daughter's death and in the end did not respond to her cries for help. It became clear that the wish to terminate therapy was based on her terror that this awful memory was threatening to break through, which had to be avoided at all costs. After negotiating with her to help her not to have to carry this burden so alone and in such isolation, the host personality returned, still inaccessible in any authentic way, slightly irritable, and anxious to terminate our interview.

This woman had stayed *in* her family in several ways. Until her hospitilization she had never disclosed the secrets of the incest history and even then did so only through one of the multiple personalities. The host personality had only recently begun to realize some of the horrible realities of her past. One might speculate that she had split off, dissociated herself from her inner experience—her terrors and rage—for some time, beginning at age 4 when the incest began. Thus, her anguished belief that she had deliberately caused her daughter's death reflected at the very least her murderous rage directed at herself and her child, on whom she projected her self-hate.

She had no friends; she was well liked by her colleagues at work, but she had only the most superficial contacts with them. She returned to her family almost every weekend, where she continued to be abused verbally and felt obliged to take over major household responsibilities and take care of various sick family members. But she also stayed "at home" within herself; her "community" was self-contained in all the personalities inside of her. The host personality stayed aloof and disconnected from her inner experience while the many other personalities, some of whom represented significant family members, manipulated and contrived various situations that kept her in the dark about her feelings and perceptions and without a sense of agency in making decisions in her life. She had split off crucial aspects of herself and, despite her social demeanor, she remained alone, isolated, in despair, and chronically suicidal.

Lucy, a 40-year-old nurse, came to see me because of intense anxiety, increasing difficulty concentrating at work, and fear that she was becoming addicted to some of the drugs she was self-administering. She was also worried about an increase in her alcohol consumption. Up until then she felt she was highly regarded in her profession, worked longer hours than necessary, and demonstrated great care and concern for her patients; but at the same time she was aware that she was able to stop thinking about them as soon as she left work and did not feel really connected with them.

Recently she found herself feeling more and more burdened in her work. She was thinking about a career change but felt she was "not fit for anything else." Her history was noteworthy in that both her parents had been alcoholic and both died in an alcohol-related automobile accident when she was 15. Her grandmother had lived with the family and she recalled the many nights that she and her grandmother would stay up until they heard her parents arrive home and knew they were safe. While these nighttime vigils were terrifying, since her grandmother would be pacing the floor and sometimes wringing her hands, her grandmother never spoke her fears out loud, and Lucy felt it was her job to help her grandmother feel better. Her parents' alcoholism was never mentioned directly.

As she related her current personal life, it was clear that she was repeatedly replicating this scene. She had a lover who was alcoholic (which she said was an old pattern and that she was always drawn to women who were addicted to drugs and/or alcohol). This woman would spend the evenings going to various bars. When Lucy came home, often late at night after working the evening shift, and found that her lover was not there, she would begin to roam the streets, driving around to the bars, trying to identify her car in order to make sure she did not drive home drunk.

Lucy had tried through drugs and alcohol to numb herself from the pain of feeling disconnected, isolated, and unable to have any impact on her lover, since she was terrified of another major loss. This numbing of herself also kept her out of any danger of getting into a relationship. Through caretaking of others in general and of her lover in particular, she felt less alone, and through pursuing her at night she attempted to control a situation from the past that was so out of her control—all the pacing, staying up at night, and hand wringing had not saved her parents from in effect killing themselves. But she tried over and over to replay the old script and protect her lover from a similar fate.

As a consequence, she also stayed in her family through repeating an old family drama, which kept her connected in a sense with her grandmother, who was with her as she roamed the streets, and with her parents as she continued to worry about someone in the same way she had worried about them. Thus, she stayed stuck in an old dynamic and was not able to see how sad, angry, and alone she truly felt. Through our work she became more aware of the replication of the past, and she was able to better understand the source of her anxiety attacks.

COMMONALITIES

There are significant *commonalities* among these families: (1) secrecy in the family, which is sometimes referred to as a conspiracy of silence; (2) inaccessibility of the parents, so that the children have neither permission nor the opportunity to learn and know about them in terms of inner, affective experiences, as well as information about past life experiences and family history; and (3) parentification of children, whose caretaking of parents and family members is minimally reciprocated. All of these features contribute to significant power imbalances in the family and preclude the development of mutuality in family relationships.

Secrecy

Every family has its share of secrets. However, the pathological effects of secrecy are most apparent in those families that are energetically organized to maintain secrecy about those issues of crucial importance to the family members. The climate of secrecy has enormous ramifications for how one develops a sense of reality, how one understands and trusts one's own experience, and how one establishes relationships with one's parents and siblings.

In the alcoholic family the secrecy is largely in the service of the family denial of the alcoholism. As one member in an Adult Children of Alcoholics group said, "There were two rules in my family: the first was 'there is no alcoholism' and the second 'don't talk about it'" (Brown 1988, p. 34). The alcoholic needs to deny in order to keep drinking; the spouse and the children need to deny, partly to maintain the connection with the alcoholic and also out of shame.

In the incest-survivor family, the conspiracy of silence is essential to the continuation of the incestuous relationship. If the father is the perpetrator, he often threatens, terrorizes, cajoles, and victimizes the child. As in the alcoholic family, other family members maintain the secrecy and denial in order to have some connection with each other. Characteristically, the father exercises extreme control over all family members so that contacts with those outside the family are minimal, and dependency on one another is intensified (Herman and van der Kolk 1987). Research data indicate that at least 31percent of the mothers in these families have a history of sexual abuse themselves, and their need to deny their own pasts is often reflected in their inability to break through the secrecy and acknowledge their daughter's incestuous experience (Goodwin et al. 1981).

Secrecy serves to bond the father and daughter together through terror and compliance, which isolates the child further from other relational possibilities (Lister 1982). The horror of exposure and the enormous guilt and shame engendered contribute to the child's silence and isolation from peers and other adults outside of the family. Many incest survivors continue throughout life to have difficulty speaking about anything personal or speaking "the truth"; one woman entering an incest group with much trepidation said, "I have the sensation that, just as I am ready to talk, a clamp comes over my mouth" (Hays 1987, p. 148).

In the Holocaust survivors' family the conspiracy of silence has a very different meaning, but the consequences on the children are as powerful (Danieli 1980, 1988). The parents have an enormous investment in not remembering and not speaking about the years of the Holocaust. It confronts them with unbearable pain associated with the traumatic experiences and family losses for which there was never an adequate opportunity to "bury the dead" and to mourn and grieve (Krystal 1968). Learning early in their reentry into life that others could not bear to hear their stories served to entrench the conspiracy of their silence. Their children collude in the silence in part to protect themselves from hearing about their parents' suffering and in part to protect their parents from being confronted again with their pain.

Despite the different dynamics around the secrecy that organizes each of these types of troubled families, the consequences are similar, particularly in the ways they interfere with the development of authenticity and relational capabilities. In the presence of secrets parents cannot fully see or acknowledge what they are aware of at some level, and they become deaf to communications that may threaten to stir up affects associated with the family secrets.

Finally, secrecy isolates the child from the world and disempowers her from moving out of the family for support. Even in the family all relationships are so conditional on maintaining a family myth that authentic interactions are often not possible. Again, denial of reality and inner experience and the conspiracy of silence require all family members to collude to maintain some semblance of connection, but all members are keeping out of relationship in the process.

Inaccessibility of Parents

Many of the parents in these families suffer from some degree of posttraumatic stress disorder (PTSD).

What has been called the survivor syndrome in Holocaust survivor families has many of the classic signs of what we now call PTSD. The parents in these families have been described as often demonstrating psychic numbing, anxiety, amnesia, nightmares, flashbacks, and confusion of past and present (Danieli 1985, Krystal and Niederland 1968, Lifton 1968).

As noted earlier, at least 31 percent of mothers of sexually abused children have been sexually abused themselves, and we can assume this is an underreported statistic. Thus, many mothers of incest victims also show symptoms typical of PTSD, with various degrees of dissociation, flashbacks, nightmares, depersonalization, and anxiety (Gelinas 1983, Herman 1981, Herman et al. 1986).

Cermak (1984) and Krystal (1968) present a strong case for classifying the nonalcoholic members in alcoholic families as suffering from

PTSD as well. Cermak argues that they suffer from chronic trauma since for years they have been deeply wounded by the alcoholic's unpredictable, inconsistent, and frightening behaviors.

Thus, many of the parents in these families are to some significant degree apt to be inaccessible emotionally since they are frequently split off from their feelings, and are substantially limited in what feelings they can experience and express. Intense affects may break through in nightmares, in dissociative states, and in alcoholic states; also outbursts of rage or weeping may occur, apparently out of context.

These indications of emotional numbing and restricted affective experience must seriously limit the parents' capacity to be empathic and responsive to their children. In Holocaust survivors' families, the children talk about how much they felt they needed to look cheerful and not express any sadness or distress, lest they upset their parents. The language used to describe the parents in these Holocaust families is consistently focused on how nonemotional they seemed. One woman said, "My father was silent, he never talked or showed emotion." Another said, "My mother seemed to be behind a pane of glass" (Epstein 1979, p. 39). One man said, "You know I don't know my parents. I'm 30 years old and I don't know my parents. They're like strangers to me" (p. 209).

In incest families whatever emotions the abuser does express are apt to be disbelieved or to create terror in the child. These fathers are driven by their impulses more than their feelings. It is safe to assume that they are unable to be genuinely expressive of feelings or emotionally sensitive to their child's experience. One incest survivor said, "My feelings don't matter. . . . That goes back to my grandfather saying how good it felt when it didn't . . . when I was bleeding" (Hays 1987, p. 149). Often the mothers in these families, because of their depression, their own propensity to dissociate, and their need to hold on to the family myths lest they be left alone and abandoned, are unable to express their terror and outrage or see and respond to such feelings in their children (Gelinas 1983).

Mothers of incest victims are reported to be significantly more likely than control mothers to be ill and disabled, to be suffering from alcoholism, psychosis, and depression, and to have been battered and/or sexually abused themselves (Herman and Hirschman 1981).

The alcoholic parent is most inaccessible when drunk. Children growing up in these families talk about their confusion about the apparent presence of their alcoholic parent when he or she was not present at all. Even in the best of circumstances, that is when the alcoholic is neither violent or unpleasant, he or she will often not recall what transpired afterward, will make promises that will be denied later, and will be incapable of consistent affective expression.

In addition to the lack of emotional availability and limited or constricted range of affect tolerance and expression in many of the parents in these troubled families, they are often also strikingly noncommunicative about their histories, about the important people and events in their pasts. As a consequence the children in these families experience considerable difficulty in seeing their parents in context and in empathizing with them and engaging with them.

In Holocaust families in particular, there is a striking silence about the past; since many of the important figures in the past are dead, memories of them are apt to trigger painful feelings as well as enormous guilt in the survivors. A woman whose mother was a Holocaust survivor recalled in therapy how much as a child she had tried to preserve her relationship with her inaccessible mother by trying to understand her; she hoped that her mother could be more responsive to her if only her mother could be less preoccupied with the dead, about whom she rarely spoke (Auerhahn and Prelinger 1983).

The abuser in incest families is particularly difficult to know. The discrepancy between how he presents himself to the outside world and how he appears to the child behind closed doors must be extraordinarily confusing. These fathers often look like model citizens, but the roles they play in the family may be as fluctuating as those of the alcoholic—nurturant one moment, violent and destructive the next (Ganzarain and Buchele 1988).

Parentification

In all three of these family systems the children tend to assume a parenting role prematurely, at least in certain significant areas of family functioning. Parentified behavior is not in itself pathological, since a certain amount of caretaking of parents is part of the reciprocal relationships necessary in a well-functioning family. In learning how to listen and be responsive to their parents' needs, children develop the capacity to empathize and learn relational skills in the process. They can become less self-centered and more responsible for their actions. However, when the caretaking of parents is one-sided and begins long before the child is cognitively and emotionally capable of handling some of the burdens imposed on her, then parentification can be destructive.

In alcoholic families, one of the roles considered to be characteristic of at least one of the children is that of the family hero (Wegscheider-Cruse 1981). This role is often assumed by the eldest child, who learns to feel responsible for the family pain and works hard at making things better. This usually involves achieving and performing at a very high level at home, at school, and in extracurricular activities, thus assuring the family that everything is fine.

Outwardly these children look highly successful, responsible, and self-confident, but underneath they feel very frightened and inadequate; they feel like frauds. They begin very early to feel responsible for the alcoholic; they take on many of the functions that he or she is no longer able to assume, as the alcoholism worsens. One of these adult children described herself as a child as "12 going on 50." Her mother was alcoholic, and she began at a very young age to make breakfast for the family every morning and to get her younger siblings off to school. She felt she could not hang around after school because she needed to go home and check on her mother.

For incest survivors, the beginning of the sexual abuse marks the end of their childhood. The child assumes a pseudoadult sexual life and is encouraged by the father to act as a partner (Ganzarain and Buchele 1988). As noted earlier, in these families the fathers are very controlling of all family members and often undermine the daughter's relationship with her mother as well as with her peers and others (Herman 1988, Schatzow and Herman 1988). The child becomes more and more isolated from outside connections, feels very much alone with her burdens, and is uncertain about how to understand these responsibilities. Typically she grows up thinking these are normal expectations and there must be something wrong with her to feel overwhelmed.

In Holocaust families children also assume parental roles prematurely, but the dynamics are different. The parents in these families are highly overprotective of their children and try to maintain them in their role as children well into their adulthood, yet they also look to their children to assume many parenting roles. As adults, children of Holocaust survivors feel extremely guilty about moving out of the family and into other relationships. They feel they are abandoning their parents, who have sustained so many losses already and have so few people to turn to; they often see them as incompetent to manage their lives. Although these parents may take care of their children, the children tend to experience the care as an attempt to influence and control them rather than as responsive to their feelings and needs.

These various modes of parentifying behaviors are destructive insofar as they preclude true mutuality of caretaking among family members. In addition, these behaviors may lead to precociously developed ego skills at the expense of developing a true sense of mastery through age-appropriate problem-solving behaviors; the result is that these children have low self-esteem and feel a great dissonance between how they are perceived by others and how they experience themselves.

These commonalities in troubled families—secrecy, inaccessibility of parents, and parentification of children—serve to keep children stuck in the family, with little permission or opportunity to seek help and connection with others outside of the family, that is, with peers and other adults.

Yet it is crucial to note that, despite how entrenched these families often appear and how much the parents in these families attempt to keep their children "at home" and discourage and undermine connections with those outside the home, the relational connections within the family are largely based on denial, distancing, and role playing rather than on authentic, mutual interactions.

Growing up in such troubled family settings, children learn how to stay out of relationship while behaving *as if* they are *in* relationship; this is the only mode of survival. For these children and later for them as adults, the dangers of exposing their vulnerabilities through being authentic and empathic in interactions with others will lead them to develop a range of strategies to hide these vulnerabilities and avoid more genuine relational connections.

STRATEGIES USED TO STAY OUT OF RELATIONSHIP

There are many ways not to participate authentically and mutually in relationships. For example, some people manage through withdrawal and avoidance or overinvestment in work to maintain distance from others. And some make strenuous efforts to make connections with others, but remain unable to engage interpersonally in a genuine and empathic fashion.

I suspect that gender differences may be significantly associated with the different ways used to stay out of relationship. Women probably make greater efforts to stay in connection than do men, albeit often through superficial and nonauthentic modes of placating and accommodating others. Men from such families may more often take routes of avoidance, compulsive activity at work or sports, or the like, and make fewer efforts to establish connections.

I have identified three broad categories of strategies of staying out of connection in the three family contexts: (1) emotional disengagement, which includes the extremes of "psychic closing off" (Lifton 1968), dissociative states, and the use of substances that numb affect; (2) role playing, which refers to assuming a persona, a style of performing, that seems adaptive and appropriate, but is not experienced by the person as authentic; and (3) replication of old interactions and family dynamics that are compelling and unrelenting.

Emotional Disengagement

The parents in all three types of families are relatively split off from their feelings, which contributes to how inaccessible they seem to their children. Children growing up in these families in turn develop little tolerance for their own feelings. They learn not to attend to their inner experience and to doubt its validity. With even more serious consequences, they believe emotions are dangerous.

One of the most common consequences of growing up in an alcoholic family is the use of alcohol to deny pain and numb feelings. Alcoholics often report how much alcohol enabled them to adapt to social situations and to look friendly and happy despite their enormous self-doubts and inability to engage authentically with people. The apparent happy conviviality in many barrooms or at parties with a high consumption of alcohol belies the underlying feelings of loneliness and isolation among the participants.

In the incest survivor's family, the young child is overwhelmed by physical and emotional sensations too intense to be assimilated. This is the beginning of her belief that feelings are dangerous and easily get out of control. We know that one of the major techniques these children develop very early is to split off their feelings, and dissociate from their inner experience and what is going on around them. It is the extreme illustration of behaving as if one is present while one is in fact absent, prohibiting any engagement with others.

Some women with a history of incest can identify the moment when they psychologically left the room, the situation, and the relationship, by, for example, focusing on a patch of wallpaper or on a pattern on the ceiling. One incest survivor in talking about finding an object in the room to fixate on when she was molested, poignantly describes how she so often felt "out of relationship": "'I have total recall of the most intimate details of different rooms I've been in. I can't remember who I was talking to or what we were talking about, but I sure can tell you exactly what the windows looked like'" (Bass and Davis 1988, p. 44). Incest survivors also use a range of other techniques to stay out of relationship, including substance abuse to numb their experiences. Compulsive eating is another frequent symptom. The terror of being exploited in relationships and the simultaneous inability to stay away from relationships often result in nonauthentic presentations that are experienced as very dissonant and disingenuous. One woman reported, "'My facial expression didn't match what I said. I was always grinning. I might be down in the dumps, three feet depressed, but I kept smiling so the outside world wouldn't know how much pain I was in, couldn't guess my secret'" (Bass and Davis 1988, p. 197).

Among the Holocaust survivors a very common theme is the need to hide from their parents any sign of their unhappiness and distress; paradoxically, they also experience a deep sense of guilt about not suffering enough. A 40-year-old woman whose parents were both Holocaust survivors recalled that in her adolescent years, when she would come home unhappy and troubled, her mother would look at her face and abruptly turn away from her; she felt erased at those moments, ashamed of her unhappiness and very alone. She also developed a very cheerful, social manner, because she couldn't believe that anyone would want to know or be able to tolerate any expression of her more painful feelings.

Role Playing

Role playing involves a range of behaviors that reflect efforts to please, control, and gain the attention of significant others. Role playing may be pathological to some degree, as a function of how rigidly and how pervasively it is used—how inauthentic, how disengaged, and how nonreciprocal the behaviors are.

When children learn that they must hide their own experience and they feel powerless to have a genuine impact on the other important people in their lives, they soon disbelieve their inner experience and behave according to what they see are the expectations of others. Thus, as they move into adulthood, these children develop a persona that may become so firmly entrenched that it precludes authenticity in relational encounters. Role playing can give the illusion of connection and the presence of a real person when the person is basically absent, since she is not truly in touch with herself and is so intent on behaving according to others' expectations of her.

As noted earlier, one of the major roles these children learn is that of taking care of their parents and the family image. This caretaking role often becomes generalized to other relationships as well. When the child is expected to carry burdens beyond her emotional or cognitive capabilities and when her efforts are not appreciated, the caretaking is not genuinely felt. Instead of feeling increased self-worth, the child feels worse about herself since she cannot connect good feelings with the caretaking behavior.

Descriptions of alcoholic families emphasize the rigidity of the roles played out. Various writers have identified the family hero as the role that most resembles the caretaker; other roles identified are those of the scapegoat, the mascot, and the lost child (Wegscheider-Cruse 1981). Adult children readily identify themselves with one of these roles. What is most relevant is not the particular role played out, but rather the need to keep oneself in a rather constricted range of functioning in order to deal with the unpredictability in the family. In maintaining stereotyped behaviors, a person can have the illusion of knowing what to do in any eventuality and avoid any emotional investments.

Incest survivors can also become adept at assuming caretaking roles, and, even more than the adult child of alcoholics, are under considerable pressure from many directions to become parentified. Perhaps the most dramatic illustration of role playing by the incest survivor is the extent to which different selves exist side by side without integration and often without awareness.

Children of Holocaust survivors also feel considerable pressure to "perform" for their parents, to hide their true feelings. The most significant finding in a study that researched a sample of this population was the disparity between the inner lives of these adult children and their public presentations of themselves (Kolodner 1987).

Replication

This strategy refers to a compelling and unrelenting need to repeat old traumatic interactions. Freud's (1920) understanding of the repetition compulsion was that the need to re-create traumatic experiences maintained the repression of these experiences; he also saw it as an unsuccessful attempt to master the trauma. A more relational understanding of this compulsion is that these repetitions also operate to keep those who grow up in troubled families locked in the relationships of the past and in their families of origin, and locked out of authentic relationships in their current lives. For children growing up in such families, their desperate strivings for connection while at the same time defending against authentic interactions with others contribute to the unrelenting replication of old issues.

In the alcoholic family, there is the propensity for adult children to become alcoholic themselves and/or to marry an alcoholic. Although the genetic etiology of alcoholism may, in part, account for the former, both patterns probably represent replays of the alcoholic family drama (Black 1981).

The dissociated experiences of incest survivors and people with other posttraumatic stress disorders are typically reenactments of the original trauma. Reenactment occurs in nightmares, flashbacks in the waking state, and symbolic expressions in day-to-day behavior (Chu 1987). When a dissociative episode occurs during a therapy hour, the therapist feels the powerful pull of the actual experience since it is experienced by the patient as a contemporary event. As a result, it is often difficult for the therapist and patient to connect as themselves in the here and now.

Many incest survivors repeat their victimizations in their adult lives by putting themselves in dangerous situations and not adequately protecting themselves from continuous exploitation and violation. If such exploitations and sexual assaults have been their most powerful sources of human connection in the past, it is not so surprising that they would seek similar interactions, even when these put them at risk of repeated traumatizations.

Children of Holocaust survivors often attempt to replicate their parents' traumatic experiences. They may have recurrent nightmares, in which they are fleeing Nazis and other dangerous, aggressive figures, looking for a place to hide and feeling helpless about reaching safety. Some of these adult children express puzzlement about the vivid and powerful nature of these nightmares, since they do not recall their parents ever speaking of their terrors or experiences.

A woman whose mother was a Holocaust survivor was told by her mother that when she first arrived in Auschwitz, she saw truckloads of children dumped into a bonfire and consumed alive. The daughter had recurrent dreams of this unspeakable experience, which was her attempt to re-create the emotions that she could not experience with her mother. She felt that if she ceased dreaming this, her mother would be left without anyone. The daughter's dreams represented an attempt to understand, connect with, and help her mother survive. She was not aware of the meanings of her attempts to replicate her mother's history and experienced her mother's alienation, isolation, and depression as her own (Auerhahn and Prelinger 1983).

SUMMARY

Three types of family systems have been described to illustrate significant factors that contribute to powerful disconnections in families. We know that these patterns exist in other kinds of families, too, with various degrees of pathological consequences for the children.

These families vary considerably in degree of constructive and destructive relational possibilities. Some children emerge from these families with great resilience and strength of character. Many, despite all the obstacles to empathic development, become highly sensitive, caring people who in fact work in the helping professions.

These families offer a structure in which we can reframe the ways in which one understands relationships in a family. Our focus was on the relational contexts in which children are relatively helped or hindered in their development of authenticity, and in their capacity to be relatively unafraid to represent themselves more fully and engage more genuinely in their relationships. For it is in these contexts, which foster authentic relational opportunities, that mutual empathy and mutual empowerment can foster growth and enhance the development of all family members. In such families there is no need to separate/individuate. Instead, the children can be empowered by the parents to move out of the family while still remaining deeply connected with family members. When parents are interested in and able to make connections with others outside the family, it gives the children permission and freedom to do so, too.

In healthy families children are encouraged to expand their personal development through their engagement with peers, teachers, and relatives, and they will continue to grow and develop through all the relationships in their lives. For many of the patients we see in our practice who come from the kinds of family settings discussed in this chapter, our major task is to provide another "family context" that will offer new models of connection and growth, in which secrets see the light of day, in which the expression of feelings and needs are encouraged and explored through the mutuality of the therapeutic encounter, and in which the responsibilities of healing are shared by therapist and patient together.

REFERENCES

Auerhahn, N., and Prelinger, E. (1983). Repetition in the concentration camp survivor and her child. *International Journal of Psycho-Analysis* 10:31–46.

Bass E., and Davis, E. (1988). *The Courage to Heal*. New York: Harper & Row.

Black, C. (1981). *It Will Never Happen to Me*. Denver: MAC.

Brown, S. (1988). *Treating Adult Children of Alcoholics*. New York: Wiley.

Cermak, T. (1984). Children of alcoholics and the case for a new diagnostic category of codependency. *Alcohol, Health and Research World* 8:38–42.

Chu, J. (1987). *The repetition compulsion revisited: reliving disassociated trauma*. Paper presented at the International Conference on Multiple Personality/Disassociative States, Chicago, IL, November.

Danieli, Y. (1980). Countertransference in the treatment and study of Nazi Holocaust survivors and their children. *Victimology: An International Journal* 5:355–367.

——— (1985). The treatment and prevention of long term effects and intergenerational transmission of victimization: a lesson from Holocaust survivors and their children. In *Trauma and Its Wake*, ed. C. R. Figley, pp. 278–294. New York: Brunner/Mazel.

——— (1988). Treating survivors and children of the survivors of the Nazi Holocaust. In *Post Traumatic Therapy and Victims of Violence*, ed. F. M. Ochberg, pp. 278–294. New York: Brunner/Mazel.

Epstein, H. (1979). *Children of the Holocaust.* New York: Putnam.

Freud, S. (1922). Beyond the pleasure principle. *Standard Edition* 18:7–64.

Ganzarain, R. C., and Buchele, B. J. (1988). *Fugitives of Incest: A Perspective from Psychoanalysis and Groups*. Madison, CT: International Universities Press.

Gelinas, D. (1983). The persisting negative effects of incest. *Psychiatry* 46: 312–332.

Goodwin, J., McCarthy, T., and DiVasto, P. (1981). Prior incest in mothers of abused children. *Child Abuse and Neglect* 5:87–95.

Hays, K. F. (1987). The conspiracy of silence revisited: group therapy with adult survivors of incest. *Journal of Group Psychotherapy* 39:143–156.

Herman, J. (1981). *Father-Daughter Incest*. Cambridge, England: Cambridge University Press.

——(1988). Father-daughter incest. In *Post Traumatic Therapy and Victims of Violence*, ed. F. M. Ochberg, pp. 175-195. New York: Brunner/Mazel.

Herman, J., and Hirschman, L. (1981). Families at risk for father-daughter incest. *American Journal of Psychiatry* 138(7):967-970.

Herman, J. L., Russell, D. E., and Trocki, K. (1986). Long-term effects of incestuous abuse in childhood. *American Journal of Psychiatry* 143: 1293-1296.

Herman, J., and van der Kolk, B. (1987). Traumatic antecedents of borderline personality disorders. In *Psychological Trauma*, ed. F. M. Ochberg, pp. 175-195. New York: American Psychiatric Press.

Kolodner, A. (1987). *The socialization of children of concentration camp survivors*. Ph.D. dissertation, Boston University.

Krystal, H., ed. (1968). *Massive Psychic Trauma*. New York: International Universities Press.

Krystal, H., and Niederland, W. G. (1968). Clinical observations on the survival syndrome. In *Massive Psychic Trauma*, ed. H. Krystal, pp. 327-348. New York: International Universities Press.

Lifton, R. (1968). Observation of Hiroshima survivors. In *Massive Psychic Trauma*, ed. H. Krystal, pp. 645-652. New York: International Universities Press.

Lister, E. D. (1982). Forced silence: a neglected dimension of trauma. *American Journal of Psychiatry* 139(7):872-876.

Miller, J. B. (1988). Connections, disconnections and violations. In *Work in Progress*. Wellesley, MA: Stone Center for Developmental Studies.

Schatzow, E., and Herman, J. (1988). Breaking secrecy: adult survivors disclose to their families. In *Psychiatric Clinics of North America*, ed. R. Kluft, pp. 337-349. Philadelphia: Saunders.

Wegscheider-Cruse, S. (1981). *Another Chance: Hope and Health for the Alcoholic Family*. Palo Alto, CA: Science and Behavior.

21

A Multigenerational Inquiry into the Relationship between Mothers and Daughters

Barbara Zax
and Stephan Poulter

This chapter explores the formative and fundamental relationships in the lives of the mothers and daughters who have allowed us to accompany them on their sometimes rocky exploration of their relationship. The numerous stories that the daughters shared with us about the pain of significant relationship failures confirmed our belief, and validates those of others who have surveyed family dynamics, that what these women learned about relationships and what they observed in their families as young girls can be the genesis of their present-day struggles in love and work relationships.

Investigating how these women experienced their mothers during early childhood, the elementary school years, adolescence, and young adulthood is the first step in the unfolding of the daughters' journey into adulthood. A thorough examination of the mothers' relationship with their own mothers, the daughters' grandmothers, is the next step on the daughters' road toward the development of autonomy and the capacity for intimacy.

As we watched our patients' sometimes agonizing attempts to fully understand their ongoing and at times problematic relationship with their mothers, we found ourselves amazed at the power of the mother who resides, alive and well, in the minds and hearts of these women. We are convinced that the understanding of how their emotional lives and interactions with others have been affected by the intensity and the power of this primary relationship, is fundamental to the growth, change, and success of the women who have sought our help. It follows that this type of work can be a valuable, eye-opening process for a woman who feels compelled and motivated to examine her part in the multifaceted entity we call family and her role as a woman in society.

As therapists, it has been our experience that the majority of women seeking treatment for the first time display a certain set of characteristics. For the most part, they present symptoms of depression: low self-esteem, feelings of hopelessness and helplessness, low energy, sleep difficulties, appetite changes, and relationship problems. While these women were underfunctioning in most areas of their lives, this underfunctioning was seen most dramatically in their struggle with personal, work-related, and intimate relationships.

Depression, for many of these women, was triggered by a loss, and the most common loss that they experienced was the loss of a significant relationship. As we saw this phenomenon repeated endlessly, we started to ask ourselves: What were these women experiencing internally as a result of these losses? Is their pain a result of a loss in the here and now or is this a repetition of a previous emotional injury?

Many of the women we spoke to experienced relationship loss in a very specific way. They had the expectation (or fantasy) that if they "gave everything I had," if they "became everything my partner wanted me to be," then they would have a perfect relationship and that someone "would love me forever." It is no wonder these women were depressed. They had renounced their own needs in the service of someone else and, in the end, still found themselves painfully alone. Harriet Lerner (1988) eloquently writes in *Women in Therapy* about loss and women's misperception of relationship maintenance: "One particular aspect of loss occurs as women betray or sacrifice the self in order to preserve relationship harmony" (p. 227). Where and how did these women learn to do this?

What was puzzling to us initially in our exploration of this subject was that we seemed to be working with what appeared to be, based on age, very different populations of women. One of us worked primarily with adolescents and women in their early twenties. The other worked with women in their thirties, forties, and fifties. What then proved even more intriguing was that on the surface these groups looked so different, but they also appeared to have much in common. The women were, for the most part, well educated, articulate, and attractive. They had enormous potential, of which they were aware but were not actualizing. This awareness of capacities and possibilities, lost or unmet, contributed to further feelings of depression and frustration. We saw our clients, in all age groups, exhibiting debilitating patterns of self-defeating behavior. Most importantly, every one of these women had a problematic relationship with her mother.

In recent years, we have interviewed many combinations of mothers and daughters. During the course of our interviews, we noticed that certain questions frequently occurred to us as we talked with these women:

- What was happening or happened in this woman's family of origin and particularly in reference to her mother?
- What are the characteristics of each woman's family relationships?
- What degree of fusion was taking place in the family?
- Is or was the daughter required to take care of her mother emotionally?
- If so, how is this caretaking manifested?
- Where and how did the mothers get stuck in their own development so that they had to look to their daughters to meet their emotional needs?
- What role did the unmet dependency needs of the mother play in the problems that her daughter is experiencing in love and work today?
- Can a mother who has not been appropriately mothered herself provide emotional sustenance for her daughter?

These questions became the heart of our research efforts and the foundation for our clinical work with this population.

MOTHERS AND DAUGHTERS—WHAT'S GOING ON?

We wanted to create a more systematic way to work with this population of women. The above questions that we asked ourselves about the family dynamics of our patients seemed to provide an excellent starting point. We believed that by expanding the clinical application of the questions we have just raised, we could activate the potential to build a framework that can be used in working with the mother-and-daughter relationship.

What Are the Characteristics of the Family Relationships?

To answer this question, we first had to take a look at the family's style of relating. Were they enmeshed with one another or disengaged? Enmeshment and disengagement are two opposites on a continuum of family relationships.

In a disengaged family there is little or no emotional contact, intimacy, or communication among the members. If there is communication, it is superficial and void of emotionally intense or volatile issues. Disengaged family members generally have little or no relevant contact with each other.

In this kind of family, for example, it is not uncommon for a parent to be unaware that her daughter has applied to five private universities and has received scholarships. The mother may learn this information from a school counselor or some neutral third party. In this type of home, emotional boundaries are impermeable, and distance is the common denominator for all family interactions. The lack of intimacy and emotional closeness is profound. It always feels "cold" in this household. What is distinctive about this style of relating is the isolation—from one another, from oneself, and from the world. When these people do come together, it is usually over a crisis, death, or emergency. After the crisis has passed, they each go back to their own isolated existence.

The enmeshed family sits at the opposite end of the spectrum. There are no doors or walls; everything is open. The idea of privacy is not accepted or allowed. Actions, thoughts, and feelings are exposed to the entire family for discussion. This lack of boundaries may include extended family members—grandparents, aunts, and uncles—and close family friends.

At the hub of this overinvolved family is the mother, whose presence and influence sets the tone for this style of behavior. Any family member who attempts to move away from the mother or the home runs the risk of being met with resistance, anger, and powerful countermoves to change. This struggle can be intense in its execution for both the mother and the daughter.

> Nancy, after much agonizing and soul searching, told her mother that she needed for her not to come into her home uninvited. Nancy's mother had developed the habit of coming into the house while Nancy was at work, under the guise of checking up on the family pets. While there, she would proceed to go through Nancy's closets, medicine cabinets, desk, and personal papers. She would even listen to the messages on the answering machine. If Nancy received a call from her sister or an aunt, her mother would become angry. She would reproach Nancy because she, the mother, had not received a call from that family member. Her mother's rationale for this behavior was that she was only doing what was best for Nancy. Needless to say, Nancy found this kind of intrusion all too familiar, as it had been part of a life-long saga of relating between the two of them. After many months of asking her mother not to do this, Nancy hired a housekeeper. Feeling displaced and enraged, her mother promptly had a heart attack, which she then blamed on Nancy. Her mother accused Nancy of being cruel and insensitive to her. Nancy's guilt and anxiety were overwhelming. These feelings subsequently turned to rage when the heart attack turned out to be, after three days in the hospital, a bad case of heartburn.

The dynamics of enmeshed and disengaged families are complex and can have far-reaching ramifications. In our experience, the majority of daughters who seek out psychotherapy tend to come from the enmeshed side of the family continuum.

Is or Was the Daughter Required to Take Care of Her Mother Emotionally? If So, How Was This Manifested?

Many of the women that we work with exhibit behavior that can only be described as self-sacrificing. In fact, in childhood, they exhibited symptoms seen in "parentified" (Boszormenyi-Nagy and Ulrich 1981) children, such as the speech and demeanor of someone who appears older, and the ability to accomplish tasks usually performed by adults. Children become parentified when their role in the family is to meet the unmet dependency needs of their parents. Parents who do not get the nurturing and attention they crave from their own parents, will often look to their children to meet these crucial needs. This process frequently takes place without any thought on the part of the parent or protest on the part of the child.

Many of the women we talked to in the course of our research had, as children, become in effect their parents' parents. In looking back at their childhoods, one of the things that was so troubling for these women was that, along with the burdens entailed in being their parents' parents, there were enormous emotional payoffs.

By assuming this role, these parentified children received a great deal of attention from their parents. While the attention they received felt gratifying to a degree, there was an exploitive quality to these interactions. On the one hand, there was the parent's siren song, "Take care of me and I will never leave you." On the other hand, there was the threat, "If you don't take care of my needs, I won't love you." Ultimately, these prematurely burdened children unknowingly sacrificed their childhood and their own needs for emotional nourishment for the sake of their parents.

The nature of the mother–daughter relationship and its effect on the daughter was addressed by Freud (1933) in the essay "Femininity":

> We knew, of course, that there had been a preliminary stage of attachment to the mother, but we did not know that it could be so rich

> in content and so long-lasting, and could leave behind so many opportunities for fixations and dispositions. [p. 583]

Historically, the daughter's process of separation from the mother was recognized as an action that was fraught with pitfalls for both. Although Freud may not have recognized it, this process had been like a family secret. The nature of this particular secret is that everyone knows about it and feels it, but no one dares to talk about it openly.

For both the mother and daughter to look at the process of separating from one another, they each have to acknowledge the consequences of such a step. The effect of this action is confrontation with the painful truth of both their similarities and their differences. The reason differences are so unnerving is that they can lead to a change in the status quo, and that change can be frightening.

A mother can look at a growing daughter and find herself painfully aware of how distinct her daughter is from herself. While this disparity can be a source of pride, it can also be a source of envy, fear, and sadness. Watching her daughter, with the freshness of her youth and her future before her, make her first forays toward autonomy can arouse painful feelings in the mother. For the older woman, fear of aging and memories of her own lost opportunities can create internal conflict that expresses itself as ambivalence toward her daughter's attempts to separate. Therefore, the problematic relationships we have been discussing may result in a daughter who sees the contrasts between herself and her mother and feels afraid—afraid that separation of any degree can lead to abandonment and loss of her mother's love.

There is a common thread in the stories of so many of the women we talked with. In spite of the rules they learned and lived by as children, they do feel different from their mothers. This feeling of being different is tremendously important for the woman who is attempting to define her own life. But what kind of price will she pay for her attempts to create a separate self outside of mother's orbit? How does the mother respond to the daughter who attempts to take full responsibility for herself and to move in her own direction? When this happens, the daughter's first thought may be, "If I'm different from my mother, will my mother feel rejected? Worse yet, will my mother abandon me?" The unspoken thoughts and feelings between the two of them—"Change back," "Don't leave me," "Don't reject me"—so full of fear of loss and longing, may prevent the daughter's necessary and developmentally appropriate moves to grow up and separate from ever happening.

The daughter's moves to separate and differentiate may rekindle feelings in the mother about her own attempts, both successful and unsuccessful, to separate from her mother. We have repeatedly observed this painful phenomenon with the mothers and daughters in our practice. While the elaborate dance of coming together and moving apart illuminates how the process of separating the mother from the daughter and the daughter from the mother can be source of trauma, it also reveals the potential to be an opportunity for growth.

Where and How Did the Mothers Become Developmentally Arrested? Were the Needs of the Mother Not Addressed When She Was Growing Up?

Why, we wondered, would a parent turn to a child to meet one's emotional needs? What would cause this kind of role reversal in a family? While tracing back the family history with our patients, we found a consistent pattern of unmet dependency needs in most of their mothers. These needs appeared as a pervasive feeling of not being needed or wanted and not being valued for being separate. This dynamic seemed to lie at the heart of the mothers' relationships, not only with their daughters but with the world. The daughters we spoke with experienced this deficiency in their mothers profoundly. One of our patients described dealing with her mother's dependency needs as "feeling like a six-inch pipe is being stuck into my side to suck the life juices from me."

If we think of the image of the "life-sucking" mother not as a mother but as an emotionally impoverished child, are we any closer to understanding her? Perhaps. The answer may lie in the stage of emotional development where the mother got stuck. When we think about human development, we think about the stages that we move through in order to reach adulthood. The developmental tasks of toddlers, developing trust in the environment and in their mastery of it, are no less important than those of adolescents, who must try on many hats and behaviors in order to create a sense of their own identity. Whether we look at the stages of development from the point of view of Piaget, Erikson, or Mahler, we can assume that events that interfere with appropriate stages of development may result in a child who becomes emotionally stuck in that particular stage.

For children to accomplish their developmental tasks, they need to have a foundation, a stable base from which they can move out and explore the world. If the mother is not readily available, either physically or emotionally, to soothe and to validate for her children that the world around them is dependable, the children are not going to feel safe.

Can a Mother Who Has Not Been Appropriately Mothered Herself Provide Emotional Sustenance for Her Daughter?

Delving into the nature of the mother's family relationships, we asked ourselves: What could be the root of the neediness displayed by these mothers? We began by looking for significant losses that may have taken place in the lives of the mothers during their formative years. For example, a parent who is chronically ill or who dies is going to cause a crucial disruption in general childhood development. Significant events can occur that will affect not only a child but the emotional well-being of the parents as well: the death of a beloved grandparent, a divorce, a move to a new town that entails the loss of friends and family. The intensity of these losses can provide a fertile breeding ground for the development of depression in the mother. Depression can impair the mother's ability to make the appropriate emotional connections with her child. Without this vital connection, the child will not feel valuable.

What must also be considered about a mother who is unable to nurture appropriately is the emotional availability of her mother, the patient's grandmother. If the grandmother was not able to meet the needs of her children, then the third generation of women in our offices will indeed feel the effects of that deficiency. If grandmother was ill, depressed, distracted, or generally unavailable, where and how was her child, our patient's mother, going to get the emotional supplies she needed to move forward? She could put herself in the role of her mother's caretaker or, as an adult, look to her spouse and to her children to meet her needs.

The importance of the grandmother in the family system encouraged us to expand our quest for data and information beyond the mother–daughter dyad. What we saw on a regular basis was the great impact that the maternal grandmother had/has on the life of her granddaughter. The intensity of this influence, whether it was experienced directly or indirectly through the mother, colored the granddaughter's perceptions and beliefs about herself and her place in the world.

This phenomenon was very aptly called the multigenerational family transmission process by family theorist Murray Bowen (1978). Family members, according to Bowen, tend to repeat certain behaviors, both positive and negative. Recurring issues and events, such as divorce, early marriage, and alcoholism, are seen to stand out as one observes the process through the generation. Bowen discovered that the blueprints of the relationship between family members in previous generations becomes the paradigm for family behavior in the present and future generations. With this in mind, our inquiry into the nature of the relationships between daughters, mothers, and grandmothers has become the foundation for understanding why daughters fail in love and work.

PRACTICAL AND THEORETICAL APPLICATIONS

The multigenerational family transmission process is part of Bowen's theory of the differentiation of self. He defines the process of differentiation as the way one separates him- or herself out of one's family of origin. Bowen conceptualizes that the opposite of differentiation is undifferentiation or fusion and he uses the idea of these polar opposites as a way of describing and distinguishing human functioning along a continuum (Figure 21–1).

We found, not surprisingly, that the majority of the women we worked with had undifferentiated, or fused, relationships with their mothers, and this fusion or feeling of "stuckness" lay at the heart of their difficulties in the creation of an autonomous self.

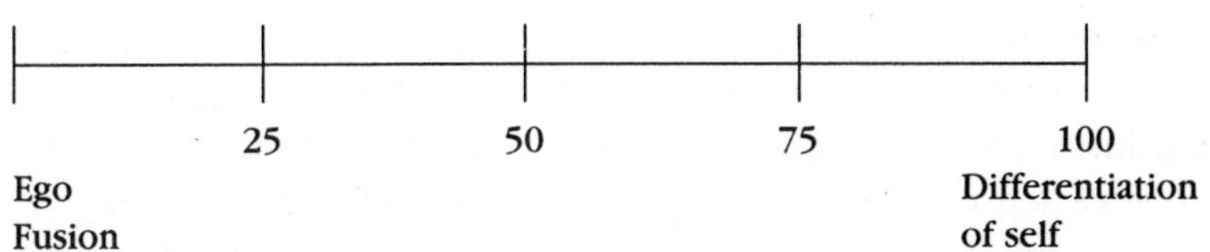

Figure 21–1. The Differentiation of Self Scale.

What are the characteristics of someone who is differentiated? How does that person function differently from someone who is not differentiated? At the heart of the undifferentiated relationship or fused relationship is anxiety. The sources of this anxiety may be old—fear of separation or abandonment—and may have been passed down through previous generations. Nonetheless, change and differences can be threatening, and one of the greatest changes in the family is the separation and individuation process of the child.

In the following case study, we will examine this process in a client. Our purpose is to show how Vicki managed the process of differentiation, and by doing so, created a sense of herself by defining her personal values, beliefs, and priorities.

An example of undifferentiation, or fusion, is a mother who maintains that all of her daughter's thoughts, both conscious and unconscious, should be revealed to her. Despite her daughter's age or level of accomplishment, this mother still insists on defining her daughter's life. The daughter, on the other hand, has a need to share all of her thoughts and activities with her mother. This collusion is not a part of the conscious process of either one of them. It feels as natural to both as the air they breathe. In a relationship like this, there is no room for any degree of independent action.

The goal of the daughter's work is to define a self and move toward differentiation, taking incremental steps toward a separate and autonomous self. When we look at the continuum of our differentiation of self scale, we ask: What does a woman look like at the 25th percentile? This might be a woman who moves out of her parents' home for the first time. She may only move a few blocks away, but she has moved out of her mother's immediate physical orbit. This woman may not have given her mother a spare apartment key. The symbolic nature of that act is the daughter's attempting to take control of her own environment, both physically and emotionally. Taking further steps along the continuum may involve additional life choices that may or may not meet with the mother's approval.

This same woman at the 50th percentile, still wants her mother's approval, but understands that she needs to listen to her own voice. This may mean going against the mother's wishes, while attempting to stay connected to her own beliefs and values. This woman is learning to withstand the subtle or not so subtle pressures to conform to the family value system and norms.

A woman at the 75th percentile, which may take many years to reach, while still desiring her mother's approval, is becoming more and more comfortable not only with her own values and beliefs but also with her feelings about them. In the face of an emotionally charged family issue, she will be able to use her own voice to clearly state her own position. At this place on the continuum, stating her own position is not contingent upon her mother's acceptance or reaction to it. She knows that she runs the risk of her mother's disapproval. Unlike her position at the 25th percentile, she has learned to tolerate the old, fearful feelings that she may be abandoned or not loved. The human reality is not reaching the 100th percentile but having a developing sense of oneself at crucial life junctures.

We also use an instrument called a genogram (McGoldrick and Gerson 1985), which graphically illustrates the nature of our clients' individual family processes and the power of the previous generations to influence their lives. A genogram resembles a family tree. It provides information about generations, about marriages, and about the children of those marriages. The power of the genogram is in its striking portrayal of the repetitive nature of the patterns of relating and dealing with anxiety within a family. This vivid portrait of family interaction allows us, along with our clients, to draw tentative conclusions and make tentative projections about current and future behavior. The following case history uses a genogram; it demonstrates the way we use this information-gathering tool. We anticipate that the genogram will reflect how the client's family's historical patterns of relating can be viewed in the light of her present-day problems.

CASE HISTORY

Vicki is a 38-year-old divorcee. She explained, in great detail, that she was depressed and frustrated. She felt hopeless as a result of a series of unsuccessful and unrewarding relationships with men, a sculpting career that was going nowhere, and ongoing and long-standing conflicts with her family. In spite of being attractive, articulate, and intelligent, she appeared emotionally wounded and highly anxious.

Vicki began her story by saying that she was trained as a sculptor and showed great artistic promise as a child. As an adolescent, she won a full scholarship to a prestigious boarding school for the arts in a neighboring state. Her parents were less than enthusiastic about her artistic and academic achievements. She had a difficult time adjusting to being away from home for the first time. Her anxiety manifested itself as sexual promiscuity. While her core belief is that she is talented, she reports a recurring history of "self-destructive behavior" that has had the effect of damaging career opportunities.

After sixteen years in a loveless, sexless marriage, Vicki divorced her husband, following a passionate love affair. After being divorced for six years, she began a new relationship with a man that she likes and respects. She was adamant that she did not want to sabotage this relationship, and expressed concerned that she would reexperience her painful feelings of dependency, helplessness, and becoming "invisible" in a relationship.

Family History

Vicki was the youngest of four children (Figure 21-2), and the picture that she painted of her childhood was one of chaos. She recalls that her parents were in charge of neither themselves nor of their children. Her parents fought, both verbally and physically, all the time. This hostile atmosphere permeated the household; screaming and yelling were the norm between parents and children. Nothing in her life, she recalls, felt "dependable."

Her maternal grandparents, who lived in a nearby town, had a very antagonistic and conflicted marriage (Figure 21-3). Her grand-

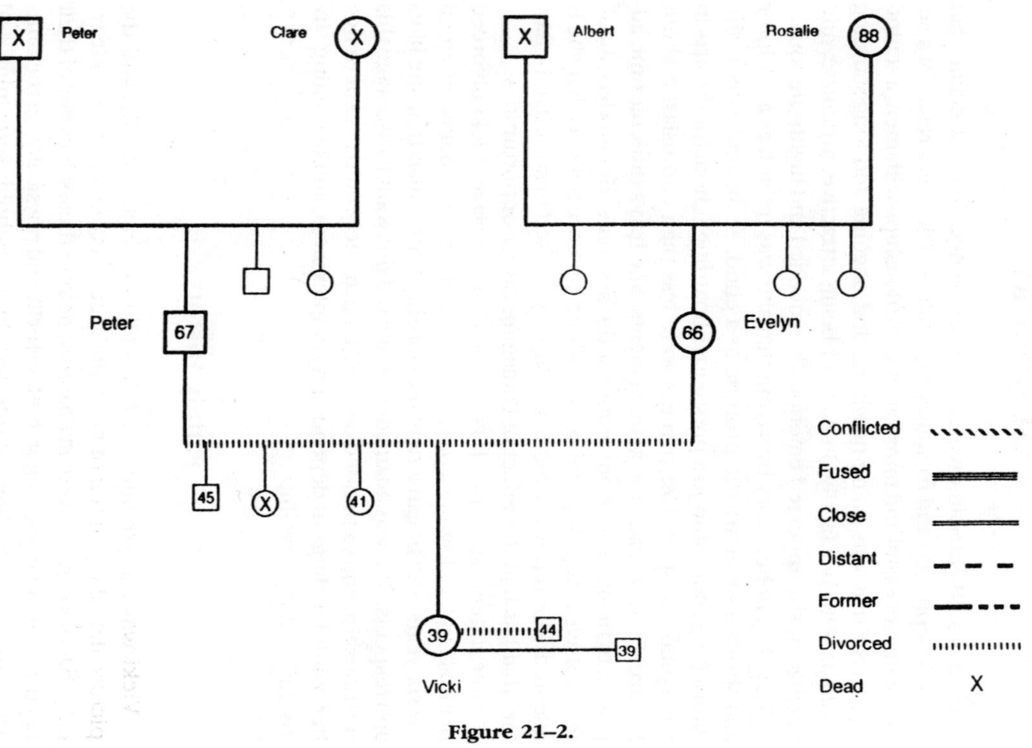

X
Peter
Clare
X
X
Albert
Rosalie
88
Peter
67
66
Evelyn
45
X
41
39
44
39
Vicki
Conflicted
Fused
Close
Distant
Former
Divorced
Dead
X

Figure 21–2.

father Albert was a womanizer and a tyrant, who alternately ignored and verbally abused his wife, Rosalie. Vicki describes Rosalie as being beautiful and intelligent, but very overweight. Ironically, Vicki experienced her as being both controlling, and helpless, and critical of everyone. Her paternal grandfather, Peter Sr., was also a ladies' man, who had to marry his wife when she became pregnant with Vicki's father. Vicki relates with wry amusement that the big family "secret" was that Rosalie had had an affair with Peter Sr., her paternal grandfather.

Evelyn, Vicki's mother, and her three sisters all had very overinvolved and fused relationships with Rosalie (Figure 21-3). In contrast, their interactions with their father, Albert, were filled with anger and hostility. When asked to describe her mother, Vicki paints a picture of her mother as beautiful, intelligent, abused, helpless, and angry at her own mother. Vicki also describes her mother as being "very uptight about sex."

The emotional impoverishment of Rosalie's daughters is reflected in the fact that not one of them had a successful marriage (all four of them divorced and three of them remarried the same man), two joined cults, and one became pathologically obese.

Vicki's father, Peter, was an unsuccessful violinist. He was, according to Vicki, a handsome, narcissistic, and abusive man, who cheated on his wife. Although he was highly talented, he blamed his lack of success on the fact that "the world misunderstood me." Vicki displays a great deal of discomfort when speaking about her father. She remembers him as behaving toward her and saying things that she realized later were sexually inappropriate. Although not physically molested by him, she was aware of feelings of guilt and shame about the things he had said to her.

Vicki and her Mother Evelyn

When speaking about her mother, Vicki expresses a great deal of sadness and anger. She describes a childhood full of attempts to try to please her mother. Despite her efforts, she never felt supported or cared for. In fact, she says that she felt "flawed" and worthless in the presence of her mother (Figure 21-4). Her mother's lack of pride

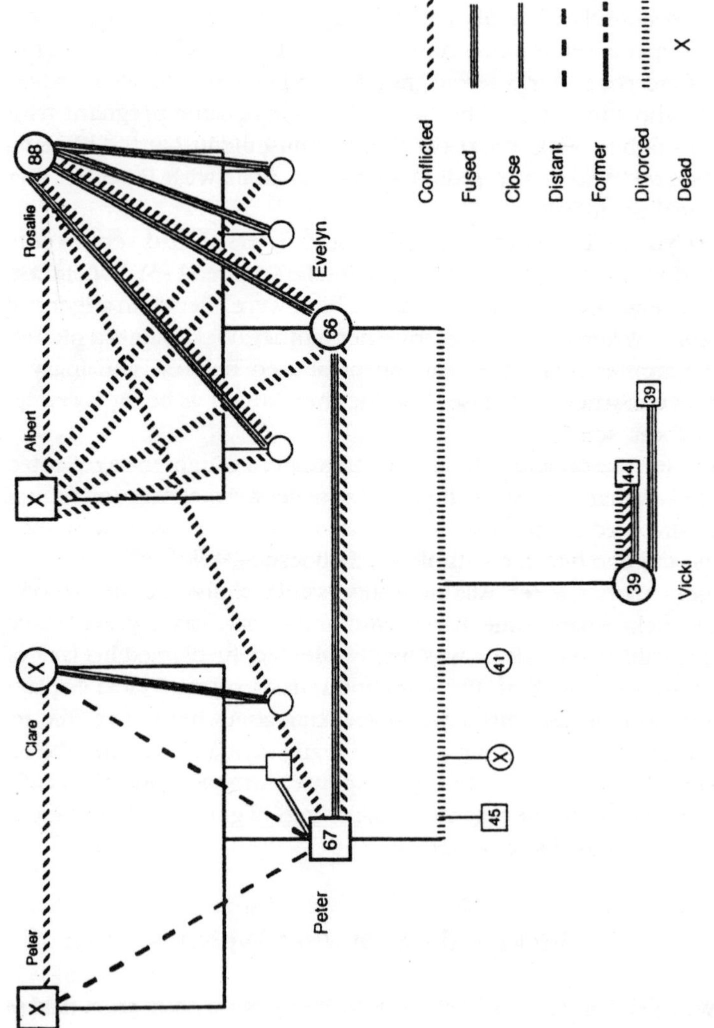

Peter
Clare
Albert
Rosalie
88
Evelyn
66
67
Peter
45
41
39
Vicki
44
39
Conflicted
Fused
Close
Distant
Former
Divorced
Dead
X

Figure 21–3.

and interest in Vicki's accomplishments as a sculptor is a source of ongoing sorrow.

Evelyn and her Mother Rosalie

Vicki reveals that her mother and her grandmother were always at odds (Figure 21-4). According to Vicki, all of Rosalie's frustrations and rage at her philandering husband were directed toward her children. Vicki describes Rosalie as a "know-it-all" who was forever criticizing Evelyn. As a result, Evelyn, who was highly intelligent, took on the persona of a helpless child. The constant stream of abuse from Rosalie resulted in the development of a succession of irrational fears in Evelyn, and an antipathy toward sexuality and sexual behavior.

Vicki and her Grandmother Rosalie

Vicki's relationship with her grandmother was antagonistic (Figure 21-5). Rosalie was highly critical of Vicki's talent and her ambition to become a successful sculptor. According to Vicki, Rosalie's sister had been a artist, and Rosalie constantly compared Vicki with this sister, in terms that were less than flattering to Vicki. Vicki recalls redoubling her efforts in order to attempt to win her grandmother's approval.

Vicki's Parents Peter and Rosalie

Vicki sadly describes her parents as two "talented and beautiful losers." Their angry and disappointment-filled marriage lasted for thirty-five years before they finally divorced (Figure 21-3). Vicki explains that her parents never thought that they deserved anything and as a result they got very little out of life. She recalls that when anything positive happened to either one of them, it would quickly be dismissed as an accident or discounted.

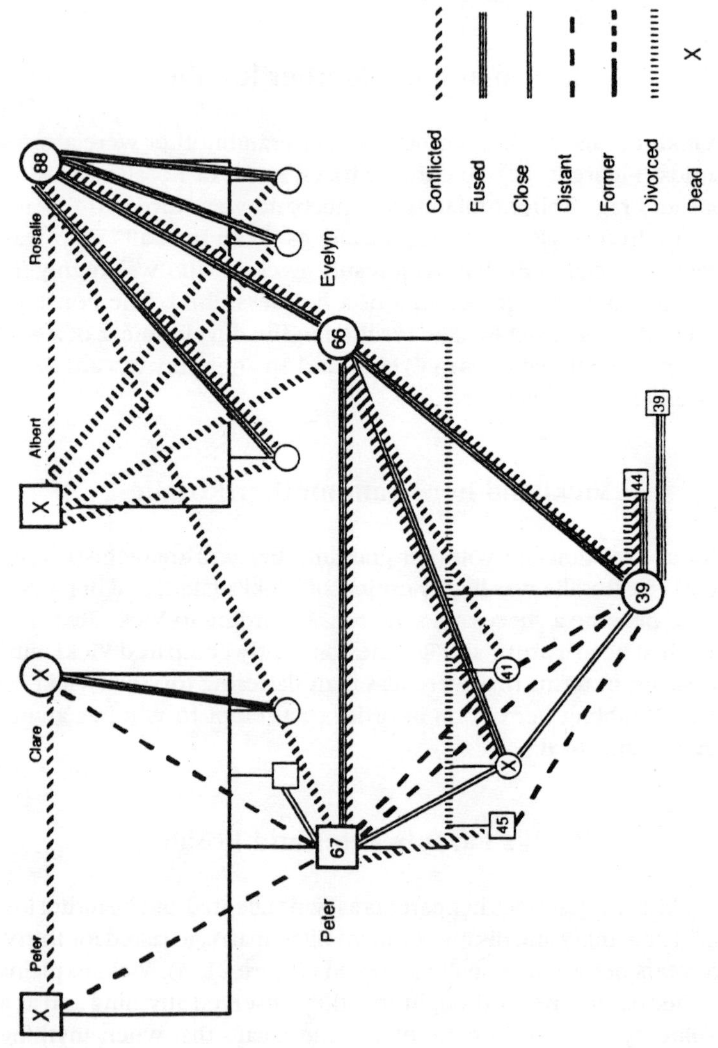

Peter
Clare
Albert
Rosalie
Evelyn
Peter
X
X
X
88
67
66
41
45
39
44
39
Conflicted
Fused
Close
Distant
Former
Divorced
Dead
X

Figure 21–4.

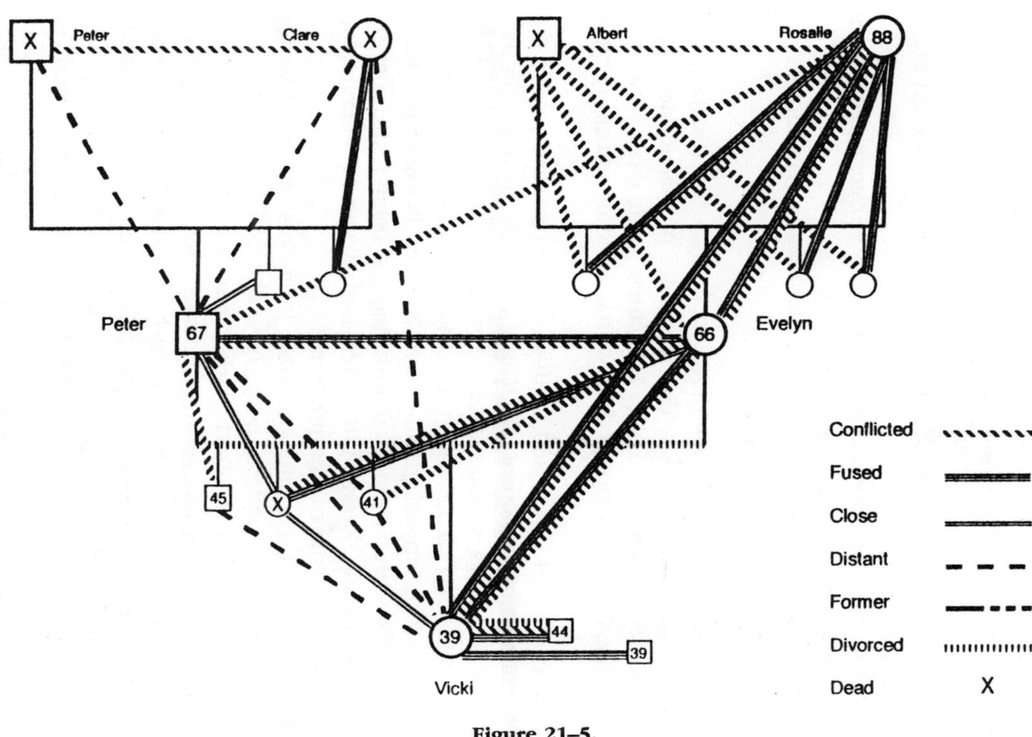
Peter
Clare
Albert
Rosalie
88
Peter
67
66
Evelyn
45
41
39
44
39
Vicki
Conflicted
Fused
Close
Distant
Former
Divorced
Dead

Figure 21–5.

Genogram Analysis

Vicki's genogram, in combination with her family history, introduces the following questions:

- How do we interpret the genogram in the light of Vicki's family history?
- How does the information generated by her genogram illuminate her present-day circumstances?
- How are the interactions of her mother and grandmother impacting Vicki today?

Vicki's genogram is filled with fusion, conflict, and distance, and is a graphic example of how different sides of a family deal with anxiety, depression, and anger. Her father's side dealt with it by distancing. Her mother's side dealt with it by fusing and engaging in conflict.

The pattern of fusion and conflict on the maternal side of the genogram paints a picture of a family where needs were not met because there was no one available to meet those needs. In the light of family history, the needs of the grandmother's (Rosalie) children and the lack of support from her husband kept her from providing her children with the essential nurturing and comfort that they required. As a result, Rosalie's daughters bore the brunt of her frustration and her feelings of victimization.

In his book *Attachment and Loss*, John Bowlby (1969) writes that observing and understanding how children attach to the primary caretaker can clarify the process by which they will form future relationships. As a result of Rosalie's inability to mother her children appropriately, her daughters had to look elsewhere to get their needs met. The logical place to look was to their husbands and their children. The consequence of this action is seen in the development of another generation filled with conflicted and enmeshed relationships between mother and daughters. All of these mothers and daughters seemed starved for connections, and all of them appeared to be fighting over the few scraps of attention and nurturing that were available.

In observing the multigenerational family transmission process in Vicki's family, the issue of adultery appears to stand out in both generations. After observing this on the genogram, Vicki revealed that not only had she had an affair before she divorced, but so had her two sisters. It would appear that in this family system, adultery was another way in which anxiety about their lack of intimacy was dealt with. What is so interesting in observing this kind of pattern is that whether the behavior was talked about or just thought about, it was passed on to the subsequent generation.

In assessing the impact of the interactions of the mother and grandmother on Vicki, one has to return to her feeling of not being able to depend on anything and not being supported. Vicki's talent and goal orientation, in the light of what we have discussed previously about the nature of mother and daughter relationships, appears to have been threatening to her mother. If Vicki became successful in either her work or in a love relationship, then Evelyn would be bereft of one of her main sources of support (her daughter). The message that she sent to Vicki was not at all subtle: "If you leave, if you are more successful than me, I will withdraw the few crumbs of support that I have given you." This message was absorbed by Vicki and acted upon in her various self-destructive relationships and her self-sabotaging behavior in reference to her work.

Fear of success, a huge issue not only for Vicki but for many women, is the result of covert punishment by either one or both parents of the child's attempts at mastery. Any movement toward the world and away from the family is experienced by the parent as threatening. The child, as did Vicki, will many times forgo becoming independently successful in order to prevent the threat of punishment or abandonment by the parent.

The messages that Vicki received, both verbally and nonverbally, from her mother and grandmother were not only "Don't leave me," but also "Don't move beyond me; don't be more successful than me." If a daughter feels that her ability to surpass her mother may cause mother to abandon her, then she finds herself in a classic no-win situation. If she moves out into the world on her own, she runs the risk of losing mother's love. If she, symbolically, remains with mother, she loses herself.

In looking at the genogram, we can see that the relationships between Vicki and her sisters with their mother, Evelyn, are an example of the process described by systems theorist Salvador Minuchin (1974) as enmeshment. In writing about enmeshment, Minuchin talks about interactions between family members that are excessively close and intensely overinvolved. In this type of family atmosphere, closeness has the potential to hinder any attempt by a child to separate. If the child makes some forward progress toward autonomy, this may well be defined by the family as an act of treason.

The dilemma of Vicki's failure to appropriately separate from her family was addressed by Mahler and colleagues (1975) in *The Psychological Birth of the Human Infant:*

> Separation and individuation are conceived of as two complementary developments: separation consists of the child's emergence from a symbiotic fusion with the mother, and individuation consists of those achievements marking the child's assumption of his own individual characteristics. [p. 4]

The authors write that the willingness of the mother to "let go" of her child and to provide him or her with the motivation toward separation is crucial. Whether this separation is physical or emotional, it is the basis of healthy individuation.

In Vicki's case, she and her new boyfriend made the momentous decision to buy a house together. Not long after making this decision, she became overwhelmed with feelings of anxiety. She began acting in a way that could only be termed regressive and childlike. She began to ruminate about all of the things that she could do to "screw it up": picking fights with her boyfriend, acting irresponsibly with money. When she finally began to explore her anxiety and her self-defeating behavior, she remembered that her parents had never owned anything in their lives—not a house, not a car. The idea of acquiring something that would belong to her and taking full responsibility for it was totally unfamiliar. She believed, and her deepest fear was, that she did not deserve a home of her own and that she would be punished in some way for having one.

SUMMARY

All of the women in Vicki's family had a history of unmet dependency needs—pervasive feelings of not being needed or wanted. It is the sense that one cannot or will not be valued for being separate.

In her book, *Too Long a Child: The Mother-Daughter Dyad*, Nini Herman (1989) writes of the developing young woman's need for narcissistic supplies—the need to be loved, to be valued, and to be told she is desirable. To enter into competition with a mother who did not have her own share of these supplies can be both a fruitless and a devastating experience for a daughter. According to Herman and our own investigation, a daughter who doubts her mother's love may become stuck at a stage where she has to please as a way of repressing hostile impulses toward her mother.

We think that the above dynamic provides many of the answers to the four questions that we proposed earlier in this chapter about the nature of the mother-daughter relationship. As one of our clients said to us when she looked at her genogram: "It's hard to give what you don't get."

From our observations, the mothers of the women that we worked with had a particularly difficult time nurturing their daughters appropriately. As we mentioned previously, their own emotional deprivation at the hands of their mothers contributed to an impasse that prevented them from creating a healthy bond with their daughters. This emotional stalemate became the foundation for present and future relationship, career, and self-esteem issues for their daughters.

The repercussions of this impasse is observed in the daughter's need to be different and to do things differently from her mother. Part of our job, at this point in the therapeutic process, is to help the daughter formulate new options that allow her to define herself without losing the relationship with her mother. The challenge, as we have said before, is for the daughter to define herself on the controversial subject of intense emotional issues. These are issues that at one time would have been sidestepped, downplayed, and generally avoided in service of "keeping the peace" with mother.

It is apparent to us that the degree of interdependence between mothers and daughters can be best understood by how the daughter navigates the rough seas of separation, relationships, and career dilemmas. Our job is to help her navigate these difficult waters in such a way that she can create an authentic relationship with herself, her mother, and the world.

REFERENCES

Boszormenyi-Nagy, I., and Ulrich, D. (1981). Contextual family therapy. In *Handbook of Family Therapy*, ed. A. Gurman and D. Kniskern. New York: Brunner/Mazel.

Bowen, M. (1978). *Family Therapy in Clinical Practice*. New York: Jason Aronson.

Bowlby, J. (1969). *Attachment and Loss*. New York: Basic Books.

Freud, S. (1933). Three essays on the theory of sexuality. *Standard Edition* 7:576–599.

Herman, N. (1989). *Too Long a Child: The Mother-Daughter Dyad*. London: Free Association.

Lerner, H. (1988). *Women in Therapy*. Northvale, NJ: Jason Aronson.

Mahler, M., Pine, F., and Bergman, A. (1975). *The Psychological Birth of the Human Infant*. New York: Basic Books.

McGoldrick, M., and Gerson, R. (1985). *Genograms in Family Assessment*. New York: Norton.

Minuchin, S. (1974). *Families and Family Therapy*. Cambridge, MA: Harvard University Press.

22

Perpetually Battling Parents

Carl F. Hoppe

Parents fighting about child custody are distinctly different from other parents. As they ostensibly fight over who is the better parent, they are frequently enacting a specific aspect of character disorder. We have called this "relationship disorder" (Hoppe and Kenney 1994). To avoid specific therapeutic pitfalls while working with divorcing or potentially divorcing parents, therapists must recognize the particular qualities of this special group. This chapter discusses the unique personality and situational characteristics of custody litigants. It also discusses how mental health professionals become involved in custody conflicts in a way that compromises their legitimate role as therapist to the litigant, advisor to the reorganizing family, or expert for the court.

CUSTODY LITIGANTS CONSTITUTE A SPECIAL GROUP WITH SPECIAL NEEDS

During the end of a troubled relationship, the litigant is likely to have a disorder that is characterized by disturbances in self-regulation, odd reasoning, and misperceptions. This is especially true where the estranged spouse or children are concerned. The litigant may think and act very differently in the presence of the estranged spouse than in other situations. He or she may look different in the consulting room alone or with others with whom he or she is neither intimate nor has children. Nevertheless, he or she cannot accurately perceive that the spouse may also perceive the other inaccurately. Two parents once held each other in such intimacy that they created a child or children. But now they mutually embrace a kind of shared delusional disorder. They each believe that the other parent has become (or can only now clearly be seen to be) a clear danger to the child or children. In addition the litigant is subjected to unique social, property settlement, and financial pressures, which increase the wish to fight for custody. There are legal and financial advantages to having the majority of custodial time.

High-conflict custody litigants are a statistically select group. Most marital couples stay married. Of those that divorce, at least half do not have children of an age that presents custody issues for the court. Of the fraction of those who divorce and also have young children, at least 90 percent (Hoppe and Kenney 1994) do not dispute custody issues at court. At a recent conference, one author of a nationally used custody evaluation device exclaimed in exasperation, "Everybody knows good parents don't fight over custody!" (Peek 1995). Less than 2.5 percent of the general population, less than one person in forty, will ever even begin to go to court over custody. Of this small number, many will resolve custody issues before a court hearing occurs. (Among unmarried parents there are also few custody fights.) Thus, those who are involved in custody litigation are a highly select group.

There have been clinical reports for many years that custody litigants as a group have a noticeably different clinical feel from other patients. Curtis (1980) reports that there is a diagnostic entity peculiar to this group. He first called this *relationship disorder*. He theorized that it has its developmental roots in separation and individuation phase-conflicts as described by Mahler and colleagues (1975).

My clinical impression is that, compared with the general population, many custody litigants themselves come from parents with multiple separations. Some have been involved in their own childhood in custody disputes. Many, if not most, have been in psychotherapy or family therapy before initiating the custody suit. Many of the children have been evaluated because of school problems.

Others have noticed this clinical difference, too. Johnston and colleagues (1985) write:

> In clinical assessments of [disputing custody litigants using *DSM-III* criteria] we found the large majority presented with indicators of character pathology. Whereas some fell clearly within well known personality disorder categories, others presented with puzzling new patterns of behavior that clearly evidenced impaired functioning. . . . We were intrigued by the fact that, in a significant number of cases, the disturbed acting-out behavior was almost entirely confined to the sphere of the divorce relationship. In other areas of their lives (in their work, social, and other family relationships), these same people could perform with remarkable decorum and freedom from symptomatology. We suspect that their apparent psychopathology is situational and relational—i.e., that it is limited to certain issues . . . and certain times (pressure of court dates, anniversaries, and holidays) and is confined to the relationship with the ex-spouse and associates. [p. 120]

A variety of stress-related symptoms, both somatic and psychological, are exacerbated during separation and divorce. It is our hypothesis that most custody litigants have the underlying character disorder that has been alluded to by Johnston and colleagues (1985) and specifically a relationship disorder (Curtis 1980).

Psychodiagnostic evaluations done as part of litigation also point to group differences in the test scores of custody litigants and a nonpatient reference group. Statistically based observations from Rorschach studies of litigants provide further reasons to think that custody litigants constitute a special and distinct clinical group. They suggest that most custody litigants have considerable potential for disturbance.

There have been several reports of systematic, statistically significant differences between Rorschach records of custody litigants and nonpatient groups (Hobbs and McCord 1993, Hoppe 1993, Hoppe and Kenney 1994, Hoppe et al. 1995, Kenney 1991). These several studies involve many hundreds of litigants. However, there is a countervailing view. These reports differ from a sample of twenty-five pairs of litigants that Exner (1991) has reported. I do not know how to account for this difference with Exner. Perhaps his sample was not comparable to the others in the importance of the Rorschach evaluation to litigation.

Thus, there are demographic factors, statistical findings, and clinical reports indicating that most custody litigants belong to a distinct clinical group. This is not true of every litigant. Most litigants look like each other on psychological profiles. However, sometimes there are clear psychological differences between the litigants. I would estimate there are clear differences in the general psychological health of litigants in less than one of seven families in litigation. But virtually every litigant believes he or she is the exception.

In addition to characteristically using developmentally primitive psychological defense mechanisms such as denial, splitting, and projection, individuals with relationship disorder defensively distort perceptions of the interactive partner. Rorschach studies indicate that the perceptions of custody litigants are less consensually shared than, and are statistically different from, a nonpatient reference group at the $p < .001$ level of significance (Hoppe 1993, Hoppe and Kenney 1994). Clinically this process of misperception is nowhere as apparent as it is in relationship to the once loved but now lost spouse. Thus, one parent misperceives the other to an extreme degree, and therapists need to be aware of the extent of this distortion.

A recent example of this level of distortion was provided by a divorcing couple appearing before a mediator. The mother said to the father, "When this is done, you'll be a great dad." However, the man insisted that she had cried out, "When I'm done with you, you'd be better off dead." The impression should not be given that this was an instance of the mother having ordinary perception and judgment while the father was nearly delusional. This same mother later caused the filing of unverifiable physical abuse charges based on the most scanty evidence. After the custody decision of the court did not conform to her wish that her small child stay every night in mother's home, the mother complained to a doctor at a public clinic. The doctor, who was new to this case, was obliged by law to file a report of suspected child abuse. A child abuse investigator called on the father at his work, which humiliated and infuriated him. The mother denied that her actions caused the filing. "The doctor insisted on it," she said.

As a group, custody litigants also have significantly more instances of peculiar or primary process reasoning than does a nonpatient reference group. Psychological testing of this group illustrates this faulty reasoning process. There is a Rorschach measure of primary process thinking called the WSUM6 score. This is a weighted sum of six kinds of illogical or inappropriate thinking. The higher the WSUM6 score, the greater the presence of disturbed thinking. The presence of primary process thinking in the sample of litigants as indicated by the WSUM6 score significantly exceeds the primary process thinking in a nonpatient reference sample ($p < .001$) (Hoppe 1993, Hoppe and Kenney 1994). Thus, the justifications of the legal persecution of the bad other parent are likely to be based on strained logic rather than on reality-based considerations. Nevertheless, custody litigants tend to be college educated (84 percent of a sample of 150), middle-aged (mean age 40 for men, 38 for women), socioeconomically advantaged, sophisticated people who individually are quite persuasive (Hoppe et al. 1995).

When misperceptions about one spouse are combined with strained logic, the resulting consensually insupportable conclusions can be made to seem quite reasonable by the other spouse, an individual who is, after all, enacting some antisocial characteristics. What seems clear to the one custody litigant and to the therapist who works just with that one parent may seem to be very out of place to an impartial observer, such as a court. Part of psychotherapy is based on reconstruction of historic events based on the patient's associations. Clinicians sometimes confuse this reconstruction of a personal experience with fact. Well-trained clinicians often look foolish when they enter the custody court with opinions based on careful study of just one of the litigants. In recognition of the high likelihood that any custody litigant is likely to have idiosyncratic perceptions and conclusions, the American Psychological Association (1994) has issued guidelines to its members prohibiting the practice of therapists rendering psychological opinions in custody matters unless they have seen all the individuals involved in the opinion.

Divorcing litigants experience disowned, unresolved dependency conflicts. Again a Rorschach study indicates greater dependency among this group than in a nonpatient reference group ($p < .05$) (Hoppe 1993). They have ambivalent attachments to the other parent that tend to be symbolized only at a concrete level of abstraction and sexualized. The human relationship becomes reduced to sensory experience as a specific variant of their general propensity toward part-object relationships. The sexualization of perceptions and part-object perceptions of sexuality in this group exceeds that of a nonpatient group ($p < .001$). Having many unintegrated aspects of themselves, the litigant group tends to have a vague sense of inadequacy. Associated with this are disturbances to self-esteem and self representation. Again the differences with a nonpatient group are statistically demonstrable (Hoppe 1993).

There is measurably more pathological narcissism in the Rorschachs of this group than in a nonpatient reference group (Hoppe and Kenney 1994). They frequently have difficulty containing and modulating the expression of strong affect. They tend to externalize strong feelings by attempting to project them onto the other instead of containing them. Rorschach data reflect their inability to modulate affect (Hoppe 1993, Hoppe and Kenney 1994, Hoppe et al. 1995, Kenney 1991). This inability to express emotional complexity is associated with the group Rorschach norms for individuals with known character disorders (Erdberg, cited in Meloy 1988).

Averages of Minnesota Multiphasic Personality Inventory (MMPI) and MMPI-2 profiles for large groups of litigants suggest character pathology. The MMPI evidence is less dramatic than the Rorschach evidence because the average of scores is well within normal limits. The Rorschach scores are not. There are reasons for these differences.

The Rorschach is a projective test, while the MMPI and MMPI-2 are written in a true-false format. The intent of asking what an inkblot looks like is much more vague than the intent of the kind of questions asked on true-false tests. Also, the range of possible responses is much greater to an inkblot than to a true-false question. Thus, the task of managing the impression created by responses to the Rorschach blots is a much more complex one than it is for true-false MMPI questions. Most individuals have almost no idea of what qualities of the response the examiner is looking for in deriving a score for a Rorschach response. However, most reasonable individuals who want to manage the impression they create know how to answer true or false to most MMPI questions. The MMPI questions demand a sixth grade reading comprehension level. Nevertheless, these group MMPI data are consistent with the thesis that there is greater character pathology among custody litigants than in a nonpatient reference group of similar age and education (Hoppe and Kenney 1994, Hoppe et al. 1995). We have called this character pathology a "relationship disorder," after Curtis (1980).

CLINICAL QUALITIES OF RELATIONSHIP DISORDER

A relationship disorder is considered to be a transient manifestation of a character disorder in maritally distressed parents. Others in intimate relationships may have similar symptoms, but the particular relationship between one parent, the child(ren), and the other parent intensifies the symptoms. This particular triangular configuration may be necessary for the full expression of the relationship disorder. It is often related to difficulties in the parent's own separation-individuation phase of development. These difficulties are specifically reactivated by tensions between one parent and the other parent concerning the child(ren).

We emphasize the presence of the child for several reasons. The inner vulnerabilities of each parent become confused with the needs of the actual child. Meissner (1978) writes that the arrival of a child marks a decisive turning point in the psychological development of a couple. This occurs as the equilibrium between the father and mother shifts from a dyadic to a triadic configuration. The presence of the helpless child who is the receptacle of the parents' projective identifications (Dicks 1967) also has a particular effect on any witness to the parental struggle, therapists included.

Individuals become vulnerable to the development of relationship disorders when in the course of their own personal development they have persistently denied and split off important characteristics of themselves. An example of this splitting off might be the overcontrolled male who becomes cut off from his feelings by overdeveloping compulsive defenses against expression of a variety of forbidden urges. Another example may be an emotionally effusive and theatrical female who is unaware of her competitive ambitions because of her particular way of denying feelings of inadequacy and envy. These two might meet and become involved with each other as if to achieve between them a sense of wholeness. The effusive one brings back to the constricted other the lost aspects of himself and vice versa. As long as the defensively split-off aspects of the self remain unintegrated, the attachment to the other will be an ambivalent one. The individual's own difficulties become stimulated when the ambivalently held, libidinally idealized other acrimoniously proves himself or herself to be other and separate.

When one parent's reactivated difficulties become projected or otherwise attributed to a child or children, he or she will then try to rescue the child or children from the "bad" influences of the other parent. The other parent is now seen as hopelessly controlling by the effusive one or as recklessly undisciplined by the compulsive one in the example above.

When these unintegrated aspects are perceived by one parent as being in the other parent, he or she will alternatively try to suppress these qualities in the other or to idealize the other as good. He or she sees the other as the carrier of qualities now not even dimly recognized as long lost attributes of the self. However, the other partner, who feels misperceived, uses increasingly desperate means to protect his or her own sense of self. At the same time he or she views the partner through equally distorted lenses. A downward spiral to the relationship results with projections flowing from one parent to the other and then onto the child(ren) and back (Dicks 1967).

The relationship disorder needs an interactive partner for its full expression. Only partners with similar conflicts are prone to this kind of enmeshment and acrimonious mix-up with each other. Thus, the symptoms of one are very likely to be perceived by the other interactive partner through equally distorted lenses and with equally strained logic. These perceptions are distorted by each parent to their maximum strategic advantage in resolving the inner ambivalence toward one of two extremes. One extreme is separation, divorce, and custody litigation. The other is merger with the lost attributes seen in the other. This mix-up involves one parent attributing disowned and ego-dystonic characteristics of the self to the other parent and suppressing those qualities in the other as he or she originally did to the self (Dicks 1967).

As this inner struggle with the ambivalently held, poorly perceived, part-object other parent becomes enacted in a courtroom, the combatants develop a desperate, naive hope. They hope the authorities can convincingly repair their sense of inadequacy and wounded narcissism. They hope their defensive feelings of righteous indignation will be sanctified if not by God then at least by the state. Therapists, friends, and others are enlisted to help resolve inner turmoil by agreeing with selective perceptions of the estranged partner, who was once held close enough to create a child but is now seen as bad. A good measure of vindictiveness helps to distract the parent temporarily from suffering his or her own pain.

Any sense of guilt for what a custody fight might do to children is rationalized by the parents. They do not understand that by fighting they are merely trying to stop their own emotional suffering by converting passively experienced hurts into active infliction of hurt on the other parent. They exaggerate the danger of the other parent to the children. They insist their struggle is only for the best interests of the children. While other adults have some of these characteristics, the relationship disorder is nowhere as apparent as between parents in custody ligation.

And what about the children? Children who are in the middle of two parents who litigate custody with each other have a dilemma. Before early adulthood, they do not have sufficient cognitive development to be capable of simultaneously appreciating multiple points of view (Loevinger 1976). Thus, regardless of the merits of their choices, their cognitive development is such that they will choose sides. When they do, they add to the pain of at least one of their narcissistically injured parents. Often they rapidly alternate stated preferences of parent depending on whom they are with. They are likely to complain to Father that they do not want to be with Mother only a few hours after telling Mother they do not want to be with Father. The children are also trained to make such gratuitous statements by operant conditioning when parents become narcissistically withdrawn. This occurs because nothing gets a custody-litigant parent's full attention so quickly as a valuative statement from the child about the other parent. Because of the turmoil of these divided loyalties, the children may begin to fear the transition from one parent to the other. Sometimes they express this fear to one parent, but often they express it to either parent, depending on which one they have most recently been with. Either parent is likely to interpret such statements to strategic advantage, and to attempt to enlist a mental health expert to do likewise.

THE IMPACT ON THERAPISTS

Therapists or evaluators become involved in litigation in a variety of ways. The clinician can be asked to do an evaluation or therapy for one of the children. A parent in individual therapy may decide to divorce and then be sued for custody. While the therapeutic and evaluative roles may seem to be distinct, there are overt and subtle pulls on the clinician to become simultaneously involved with both roles. Such dual involvement is detrimental to both evaluation and therapy and results in legal headaches for the evaluator and the therapist as well. Understanding each of these roles requires understanding the uniqueness of the situation and personality characteristics of the custody litigant.

Many if not most custody litigants have contact with a mental health professional before initiating a custody suit. Why then are there so many lawsuits about custody? For conscious and unconscious reasons, even well-trained clinicians, who ought to be more cautious, unwittingly slide into the legal fray, or encourage their patients to do so, without personally and impartially evaluating the whole family. Despite professional guidelines prohibiting unilateral opinions (American Psychological Association 1994), they get mixed up about the therapeutic and evaluative roles. If they contribute opinions to a custody suit, they enter a dual role with their client. Making such errors is often aided and abetted by skillful attorneys. They seem only to ask for documentation of what appear to be obvious facts. But those "facts" inevitably appear as interpretations tantamount to biased recommendations when opposing counsel reads them. Opposing counsel may insist on the right of cross-examination. Clinicians are unused to such pressures.

When a patient in ongoing therapy describes marital difficulties, a clinician may become involved in the formation of an "unholy alliance" (Johnston et al. 1985). This unholy alliance consists of doctor, patient, and attorney, together under a sacred banner reading "for the best interests of the child" in a battle soon to be waged in court. This is especially so when the therapeutic work has been aimed at helping the patient to become more autonomous (Johnston et al. 1985).

Involving a clinician in an alliance against the other spouse is not always a conscious ploy on the part of a patient. Well-meaning friends or the patient's attorney may urge the patient to "see what your therapist says about what is best for the child(ren)." The clinician who may have heard many descriptions of the other spouse's drinking or angry tirades may feel it is high time the patient stood up to this. The clinician feels a pull. It seems only reasonable to give some advice about how to protect the children during a separation. A child or some of the children may very well become symptomatic. On learning this, the therapist feels an ethical and human pull to recommend something, perhaps therapy for the child. Slowly the clinician can become involved in the custody evaluation process without realizing that the child therapy recommendation has become in fact a custody evaluation. It has implications for medical child support, property distribution, allocation of amount of time with each parent, and so on. Especially when there is great parental discord any therapeutic recommendation must be addressed to both parents. To do this, however, may compromise the confidentiality of an individual patient.

Becoming involved is not always a conscious decision on the part of the therapist. There are unconscious reasons even seasoned clinicians repeatedly get drawn into making indefensible endorsements of one litigant without adequate assessment of the other parent. Why is this? The specific triangular configuration involving one parent's hostility to the opposite-sex parent over possession of babies pulls on the clinician. It activates rescue fantasies and "re-oedipalizes" the countertransference.

To establish a working therapeutic couple, the therapist and patient must sufficiently work through oedipal features including the therapist's unconscious fantasy of defeating the patient's lover-as-rival. If that had been done, and during treatment the marriage breaks down with an ensuing custody dispute, the litigant-in-treatment's situationally determined distortions and illogical arguments, the drama of the courtroom, the specter of innocent children needing protection, and the allure of being the expert (including the illusion of financial recognition as such) can create an intoxicating hope that the therapist will be better than the patient's mate. This re-triangulates the therapist-as-expert against the "bad parent." Often an added factor is the presence of a skilled legal advocate who seems totally convinced of his or her client's position. With flattery and respect the attorney skillfully extracts just one or two seemingly innocuous "statements of fact" from the therapist.

Furthermore, there seems to be a predisposition for therapists to believe that all important personality characteristics exist trans-situationally. Too many therapists assume that in the consulting room a therapist seeing just one part of the family can comprehend the missing parent by a reconstruction technique. Such reconstructions begin with the patient's perceptions, which are likely to be tainted. Such reconstructions do not take into account the focused distortions a divorcing spouse is capable of (or that the children are capable of) while functioning well elsewhere (Johnston et al. 1985). The following clinical examples illustrate the importance of understanding the relationship disorder as a situation-specific dysfunction.

CASE EXAMPLES

I received a series of phone calls from two well-trained, well-published child therapists with good reputations in the community. They know and respect each other. Each had been treating one of the spouses of a family about to divorce. However, they found themselves vehemently upset with each other because each gave attorneys opposing declarations. They had expected each other to construct the family the same way. But they saw things diametrically differently. How could this be? Neither seemed to know how to avoid giving depositions leading to their eventual appearance in a trial in which they were on opposite sides of the same case. The credibility of the whole profession is damaged when experts oppose each other this way.

As a court-appointed evaluator, I recently learned from a litigant, Ms. A., of a glowing declaration given on her behalf by a well-known professor of psychiatry. This prestigious doctor has university positions. Dr. X. knew Ms. A., a younger colleague, because she worked on research projects with him at the university. He knew her work well and had seen her at work informally for many months. He was aware that she had marital troubles and listened to them sympathetically. Once as Dr. X. attended a party at the university, the husband showed up with Ms. A. They were soon to be estranged. The husband behaved obnoxiously. This party behavior confirmed to Dr. X. Ms. A.'s complaints about the husband's habitual drinking and narcissism. Based on these casual observations and the reports of Ms. A., Dr. X. wrote a definitive declaration stating Ms. A. was the more stable and healthier parent. He explicitly indicated the effect the husband's narcissistic unavailability and other character flaws must have on the young child. He had not met the child. He had only heard Ms. A.'s reports. Dr. X. is an acknowledged authority on development. Therefore, he confidently provided a custody recommendation and submitted it with his 30-page curriculum vitae.

According to the relationship disorder hypothesis, this kind of unilateral endorsement would be seen to be extremely unwise. It is unwise even if the conclusion were somehow correct. The parent best known to the therapist will have systematically filtered her perceptions and built on these faulty perceptions with persuasive but idiosyncratic logic. Her perceptions about other things, such as her work, will be far more accurate. Furthermore, according to the relationship disorder hypothesis, the less well known parent will have been acting out his worst symptoms in this troubled marital situation. He was, after all, being plotted against by his wife and he was at a party with the accessories in her plans against him. In contrast, Dr. X. observed the colleague at work, which is outside the context in which she is most symptomatic. Because of the very great propensity within this population for projection and blame, Dr. X. did not learn about the colleague's provocations and overreactions from her despite his well-known capacity for therapeutic reconstruction.

The husband was known to the court through some computer work he had done in a prestigious legal office. Outside the situation of the troubled intimate relationship he, too, was a model of reliability, responsibility, and sensitivity. The court was baffled by the pronouncements in Dr. X.'s declaration. Therefore, the court was disposed not only in this case but in all future cases to throw out all psychological and psychiatric opinions. The individuals in the case were damaged by having to litigate about the inadequately based recommendations, and Dr. X.'s profession's credibility was also damaged.

Parents exert a poignant pull that even seems sanctioned by professional guidelines. The American Psychological Association's Guidelines for Child Custody Evaluations in Divorce Proceedings (APA 1994) begin with a statement about the best psychological interests of the child. Parents may say, "I just want what is best for my child. Forget the lawyers. Forget us parents. Please simply say what is best for Johnny." (The implicit subtext here is that the one making this appeal already knows what is best. Any competent evaluator will agree, or else.) However, every custody litigant says that he or she wants only what is good for the child. I have yet to meet the litigant who openly says, "I want to injure my ex very badly. I don't care what it does to the children. I want to stop suffering myself even if it costs the child dearly for me to self-righteously blame the other parent." Every custody fight is justified under the rubric "for the best interest of the child."

The clinician faced with this kind of appeal needs to consider how the child is being used as a displacement figure for some aspect of the parent. When litigants demand "Just say what is good for my child," I have found it useful to remember the admonition of Winnicott (1975): "There is no such thing as a baby" (p. 99). The focus on a child must always include that child vis-à-vis both parents. It is useful to say to the potential litigant, "There is no such thing as Johnny without Johnny's other parent." Such a statement will sometimes defuse the projective process.

Therapists are not alone in being drawn into patients' custody fights. Psychological evaluation of a child may also involve a clinician in opinions that have legal implications for custody. This can occur when abuse allegations arrive after the evaluation is well under way. After first having indicated there had been a divorce several years ago from an allegedly alcoholic spouse, a mother expressed concern about the child's school performance. She wanted an assessment of this. At a feedback session after the assessment, the mother asked if the examiner believed a change in visitation could help. Without waiting for an answer, she added that the latency-aged girl complained that the sight of the father's genitals bothers her as they bathe together nude. "Is this mutual naked bathing with Father appropriate for a 9-year-old girl?" she begged. This issue was the hidden agenda of seeking an evaluation. At such times the clinician may feel compelled to give an opinion "for the sake of the child." There is also the issue of filing a mandatory suspected child abuse report to state authorities. Any such opinion or report is likely to be trotted off to the attorney's office, and it will be less than useless if the clinician has not personally seen the father for a significant amount of time and carefully discussed the matter with him.

The remedy to this kind of entrapment is scrupulously to attempt to involve both parents in the evaluation process from its inception. While this is good practice generally, it is particularly important when there is reason to even suspect that a parental divorce or change in custody is imminent.

CONCLUSION

There are special considerations that need to be kept in mind by the clinician doing psychotherapy, evaluation, child counseling, parent guidance, or marital mediation with any parent who may choose divorce. A therapist working with someone who becomes involved in a custody suit will be likely to feel a pull also to get involved. This pull involves conscious pressures as well as unresolved competitive countertransference states. The evaluative and therapeutic functions are best separated. The therapist's role should be to protect the confidentiality of the therapy, and to insist on this confidentiality unless or until a court orders otherwise. The child consultant must refrain from any statement about any family member he or she has not personally seen. This is true even when abuse is alleged.

The theory that the litigant may have a situationally focused character disorder means that it will be extremely difficult for a clinician seeing only one of the litigants to say anything about the other or to be accurate about the interaction between the children and the other parent. This principle is frequently unrecognized by clinicians who believe that the reports of their patients about the relationship can be accurately given. What they learn by seeing either spouse in the context of the troubled marital relationship is not an accurate sampling of that spouse's behavior with the children in other contexts. If forced to testify or to provide depositions by court order, the therapist or evaluator does best by refusing to comment on anyone not personally seen or any behaviors of anyone not personally witnessed, because the patient in litigation is unlikely to represent accurately nuances of behavior of the children or the estranged spouse.

REFERENCES

American Psychological Association (1994). Guidelines for child custody evaluations in divorce proceedings. *American Psychologist* 49(7):677–680.

Curtis, T. A. (1980). *Relationship disorder: a new diagnostic entity seen in custody visitation disputes.* Paper presented at the Joint Convention of the American Academy of Child Psychiatry and the American Academy of Psychiatry and the Law, Chicago, March.

Dicks, H. (1967). *Marital Tensions.* London: Routledge and Kegan.

Exner, J. (1991). *The Rorschach: A Comprehensive System. Vol. 2: Interpretation*, 2nd ed. New York: Wiley.

Hobbs, S., and McCord, T. H. (1993). *The use of the MMPI and Rorschach in custody evaluation: data from forty couples in conflict.* Paper presented at the Society for Personality Assessment Annual Convention, San Francisco, February.

Hoppe, C. F. (1980). *The role of psychological testing in evaluation of families in custody-visitation disputes.* Paper presented at the Joint Convention of the American Academy of Child Psychiatry and the American Academy of Psychiatry and the Law, Chicago, March.

——— (1985). *Towards a psychological profile of the pedophile.* Paper presented at the California Psychological Association Winter Meeting, San Francisco, February.

——— (1991). The role of psychological testing in custody visitation disputes. *Custody Newsletter* 3:4–11.

——— (1993). *Test characteristics of custody-visitation litigants: a data-based description of relationship disorders; a symposium on empirical approaches to child custody determination*. Symposium at the American Psychological Association Annual Convention, Toronto, Canada, August.

Hoppe, C. F., and Kenney, L. (1994). *Characteristics of custody litigants—data from the Southern California group*. Paper presented at the American Psychological Association Annual Convention, Los Angeles, August.

Hoppe, C. F., Kenney L., Gotfried, A., et al. (1995). *MMPI use in child custody evaluations—integrating the data*. Symposium at the Psychological Association Annual Convention, New York, August.

Johnston, J. R., Campbell, L. E. G., and Tall, M. C. (1985). Impasses to the resolution of custody and visitation disputes. *American Journal of Orthopsychiatry* 55(1):112–129.

Kenney, L. M. (1991). *A Rorschach study of child sexual abuse allegations in custody/visitation disputes*. Unpublished dissertation, Pepperdine University, Los Angeles.

Loevinger, J. (1976). *Ego Development Conceptions and Theories*. San Francisco: Jossey-Bass.

Mahler, M. S., Pine, F., and Bergman, A. (1975). *The Psychological Birth of the Human Infant.* New York: Basic Books.

Meissner, W. W. (1978). The conceptualization of marriage and family dynamics from a psychoanalytic perspective. In *Marriage and Marital Therapy*, ed. T. H. Paolino and B. S. McCrady, pp. 25–88. New York: Brunner/Mazel.

Meloy, J. R. (1988). *The Psychopathic Mind*. Northvale, NJ: Jason Aronson.

Peek, L. (1995). *Child custody assessment—a comparison of four empirical approaches: custody quotient*. Symposium at the American Psychological Association Annual Convention, New York, August.

Winnicott, D. W. (1975). *Through Paediatrics to Psycho-Analysis.* New York: Basic Books.

Subject Index

FRANKLIN PIERCE COLLEGE LIBRARY
00118459